OUT OF
THE CRISIS

*Other works by W. Edwards Deming
published by MIT/CAES*

THE NEW ECONOMICS
FOR INDUSTRY, GOVERNMENT, EDUCATION

THE DEMING VIDEOTAPES

OUT OF
THE CRISIS

W. EDWARDS DEMING

The MIT Press
Cambridge, Massachusetts
London, England

First MIT Press edition, 2000

Originally published in 1982 by Massachusetts Institute of Technology, Center for Advanced Educational Services, Cambridge, Massachusetts.

©1982, 1986 The W. Edwards Deming Institute

Printed and bound in the United States of America.

Library of Congress Cataloging-in-Publication Data

Deming, W. Edwards (William Edwards), 1900–1993

   Out of the crisis / W. Edwards Deming.

      p. cm.

   Originally published: Cambridge, Mass. : MIT, Center for Advanced Educational Services, 1986.

   Includes bibliographical references and index.

   ISBN 0-262-54115-7 (pbk. : alk. paper)

      1. Industrial management—United States. 2. Industrial productivity—United States. 3. Quality of products—United States. I. Title.

HD70.U5 D45 2000

658—dc21   00-042729

10 9 8 7 6 5

Contents

About the Author

W. Edwards Deming is the internationally renowned consultant whose work led Japanese industry into new principles of management and revolutionized their quality and productivity. The adoption of Dr. Deming's 14 points for management could help industry in the United States. Dr. Deming has enjoyed a worldwide practice for 40 years.

In recognition of his contribution to the economy of Japan, the Union of Japanese Science and Engineering (JUSE) instituted the annual Deming Prizes for contributions to quality and dependability of product. The emperor of Japan awarded him in 1960 the Second Order Medal of the Sacred Treasure. Dr. Deming has received numerous other awards, including the Shewhart Medal from the American Society for Quality Control in 1956 and the Samuel S. Wilks Award from the American Statistical Association in 1983.

The Metropolitan section of the American Statistical Association established in 1980 the annual Deming Prize for improvement of quality and productivity.

Dr. Deming was elected in 1983 to the National Academy of Engineering, and has been awarded the doctorates LL.D. or Sc.D. *honoris causa* by the University of Wyoming, Rivier College, Ohio State University, University of Maryland, Clarkson College of Technology, and the George Washington University.

Preface

The aim of this book is transformation of the style of American management. Transformation of American style of management is not a job of reconstruction, nor is it revision. It requires a whole new structure, from foundation upward. *Mutation* might be the word, except that *mutation* implies unordered spontaneity. Transformation must take place with directed effort. The aim of this book is to supply the direction. Need for transformation of governmental relations with industry is also necessary, as will be obvious.

Failure of management to plan for the future and to foresee problems has brought about waste of manpower, of materials, and of machine-time, all of which raise the manufacturer's cost and price that the purchaser must pay. The consumer is not always willing to subsidize this waste. The inevitable result is loss of market. Loss of market begets unemployment. Performance of management should be measured by potential to stay in business, to protect investment, to ensure future dividends and jobs through improvement of product and service for the future, not by the quarterly dividend.

It is no longer socially acceptable to dump employees on to the heap of unemployed. Loss of market, and resulting unemployment, are not foreordained. They are not inevitable. They are man-made.

The basic cause of sickness in American industry and resulting unemployment is failure of top management to manage. He that sells not can buy not.

The causes usually cited for failure of a company are costs of start-up, overruns on costs, depreciation of excess inventory, competition—anything but the actual cause, pure and simple bad management.

What must management do? Management obviously have a new job. Where can management learn about the transformation that is necessary?

The fact is that management can not learn by experience alone what they must do to improve quality and productivity and the competitive position of the company.

Everyone doing his best is not the answer. It is first necessary that people know what to do. Drastic changes are required. The first step in the transformation is to learn how to change: that is, to understand and use the 14 points in Ch. 2, and to cure themselves of the diseases in Ch. 3.

Long-term commitment to new learning and new philosophy is required of any management that seeks transformation. The timid and the fainthearted, and people that expect quick results, are doomed to disappointment.

Solving problems, big problems and little problems, will not halt the decline of American industry, nor will expansion in use of computers, gadgets, and robotic machinery. Benefits from massive expansion of new machinery also constitute a vain hope. Massive immediate expansion in the teaching of statistical methods to production workers is not the answer either, nor wholesale flashes of quality control circles (QC-Circles). All these activities make their contribution, but they only prolong the life of the patient; they can not halt the decline. Only transformation of the American style of management, and of governmental relations with industry, can halt the decline and give American industry a chance to lead the world again.

The job of management is inseparable from the welfare of the company. Mobility, here a while and gone, from the management of one company to the management of another, is something that American industry can no longer afford. Management must declare a policy for the future, to stay in business and to provide jobs for their people, and more jobs. Management must understand design of product and of service, procurement of materials, problems of production, process control, and barriers on the job that rob the hourly worker of his birthright, the right to pride of workmanship.

There are conferences almost any day in this country on the subject of productivity, mostly concerned with gadgets and measures of productivity. As William E. Conway said, measurements of productivity are like accident statistics. They tell you that there is a problem, but they don't do anything about accidents. This book is an attempt to improve productivity, not just to measure it.

The book makes no distinction between manufacturing and service industries. The service industries include government service, among which are education and the mail. All industries, manufacturing and service, are subject to the same principles of management.

Anyone in management requires, for transformation, some rudimentary knowledge about science—in particular, something about the nature of variation and about operational definitions. Numerous examples throughout the book illustrate how failure to appreciate the two kinds of variation, special causes of variation and common causes, and to understand operational definitions brings loss and demoralization.

The reader will sense the fact that not only is the style of American management unfitted for this economic age, but that many government regulations and the Justice Department's Antitrust Division are out of step, propelling American industry along the path of decline, contrary to the well-being of the American people. For example, unfriendly takeover and leveraged buyout are a cancer in the American system. Fear of takeover, along with emphasis on the quarterly dividend, defeats constancy of purpose. Without constancy of purpose to stay in business by providing product and service that have a market, there will be further downturn and more unemployment. What is the Securities and Exchange Commission doing about takeover?

When we size up the job ahead, it is obvious that a long thorny road lies ahead—decades.

Dependence on protection by tariffs and laws to "buy American" only encourages incompetence.

It would be incorrect to leave the reader with the impression that no action is taking place. The fact is that management throughout a number of companies are at work on the 14 points and on the diseases that afflict American industry. Substantial results are already recorded. Some schools of business are offering courses in the transformation of the American style of management, based on notes for seminars conducted during the past few years.

Acknowledgments

I am thankful for unusual privileges to work as apprentice to a number of great men, among them Walter A. Shewhart, Harold F. Dodge, George Edwards, all of the Bell Telephone Laboratories, all now deceased. Equally valued is apprenticeship under other esteemed colleagues, such as Morris H. Hansen, Philip M. Hauser, Frederick Franklin Stephan, Samuel Stouffer, General Leslie E. Simon, Eugene L. Grant, Holbrook Working, Franz J. Kallman, P.C. Mahalanobis.

Many kind friends have contributed to my education in the subject attempted here. Among them are Lloyd S. Nelson, William W. Scherkenbach, Myron Tribus, Ronald P. Moen, William A. Golomski, Carolyn A. Emigh, Louis K. Kates, Nancy R. Mann, Brian Joiner, Mervin Muller, Ez Nahouraii, James K. Bakken, Edward M. Baker, Heero Hacquebord. Specific contributions to the text are mentioned by name. Help in clarity has come from Kate McKeown.

I owe to Professor William G. Hunter and some of his students at the University of Wisconsin special debt for help on difficult points, as well as for contributions to the text.

Hundreds of people in my seminars have contributed to the river of knowledge that has swelled deeper and wider year by year.

The careful reader may note use of the word *leadership* where the usual word would be *supervision*. The reason is that for survival, supervision will be replaced by leadership. I owe this observation to my friend James B. Fitzpatrick of General Motors.

This book could never have seen print without the dedicated skill and perseverance of my secretary Cecelia S. Kilian. She has assisted me now 32 years in a lively statistical practice, and has constructed out of scribblings on scribblings written on my lap on aeroplanes one version after another of notes to use as text for my seminars, and finally for this book as the reader finds it.

OUT OF
THE CRISIS

1

Chain Reaction: Quality, Productivity, Lower Costs, Capture the Market

Who is it that darkeneth counsel by words without knowledge?—Job 38:2.

Aim of this chapter. The aim of this chapter is to illustrate a stable system of trouble in a manufacturing plant, and to explain that because the system is stable, improvement of quality is the responsibility of the management. Further examples will appear in later chapters.

Some folklore. Folklore has it in America that quality and production are incompatible: that you can not have both. A plant manager will usually tell you that it is either or. In his experience, if he pushes quality, he falls behind in production. If he pushes production, his quality suffers. This will be his experience when he knows not what quality is nor how to achieve it.[1]

A clear, concise answer came forth in a meeting with 22 production workers, all union representatives, in response to my question: "Why is it that productivity increases as quality improves?"

Less rework.

There is no better answer. Another version often comes forth:

Not so much waste.

Quality to the production worker means that his performance satisfies him, provides to him pride of workmanship.

[1] Taken from the letter from Dr. Tsuda referred to below.

1

Improvement of quality transfers waste of man-hours and of machine-time into the manufacture of good product and better service. The result is a chain reaction—lower costs, better competitive position, happier people on the job, jobs, and more jobs.

A clear statement of the relationship between quality and productivity comes from my friend Dr. Yoshikasu Tsuda of Rikkyo University in Tokyo, who wrote to me from San Francisco as follows, dated 23 March 1980:

> I have just spent a year in the northern hemisphere, in 23 countries, in which I visited many industrial plants, and talked with many industrialists.
>
> In Europe and in America, people are now more interested in cost of quality and in systems of quality-audit. But in Japan, we are keeping very strong interest to improve quality by use of methods which you started. . . . when we improve quality we also improve productivity, just as you told us in 1950 would happen.

Dr. Tsuda is saying that Western industry is satisfied to improve quality to a level where visible figures may shed doubt about the economic benefit of further improvement. As someone enquired, "How low may we go in quality without losing customers?" This question packs a mountain of misunderstanding into a few choice words. It is typical of management's misunderstanding in America. In contrast, the Japanese go right ahead and improve the process without regard to figures. They thus improve productivity, decrease costs, and capture the market.

Awakening in Japan. Management in some companies in Japan observed in 1948 and 1949 that improvement of quality begets naturally and inevitably improvement of productivity. This observation came from the work of a number of Japanese engineers who studied literature on quality control supplied by engineers from the Bell Laboratories then working on General

MacArthur's staff. The literature included Walter A. Shewhart's book *Economic Control of Quality of Manufactured Product* (Van Nostrand, 1931; repr. ed., American Society for Quality Control, 1980). The results were exciting, showing that productivity does indeed improve as variation is reduced, just as prophesied by the methods and logic of Shewhart's book. As a result of a foreign expert's visit in the summer of 1950, the following chain reaction became engraved in Japan as a way of life.[2] This chain reaction was on the blackboard of every meeting with top management in Japan from July 1950 onward; also Fig. 1.

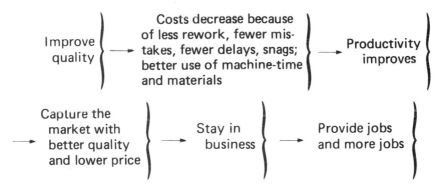

The production worker in Japan, as anywhere else in the world, always knew about this chain reaction; also that defects and faults that get into the hands of the customer lose the market and cost him his job.

Once management in Japan adopted the chain reaction, everyone there from 1950 onward had one common aim, namely, quality.

With no lenders nor stockholders to press for dividends, this effort became an undivided bond between management and

---

2 I am indebted to founding members of JUSE for the early history of their efforts: in particular, Dr. E. E. Nishibori. Work with a number of men in top management in Japan in 1950 and onward provided further help on history. JUSE is the telegraphic code for the Union of Japanese Science and Engineering, Tokyo. See the Appendix.

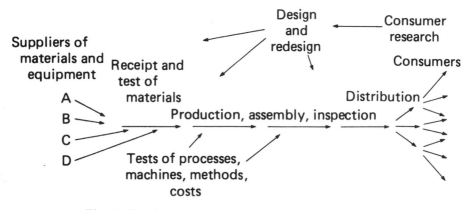

Fig. 1. Production viewed as a system. Improvement of quality envelops the entire production line, from incoming materials to the consumer, and redesign of product and service for the future. This chart was first used in August 1950 at a conference with top management at the Hotel de Yama on Mount Hakone in Japan. In a service organization, the sources A, B, C, etc., could be sources of data, or work from preceding operations, such as charges (as in a department store), calculation of charges, deposits, withdrawals, inventories in and out, transcriptions, shipping orders, and the like.

production workers. An unfriendly takeover or a leveraged buyout does not take place in Japan. Managers are not sensitive to the price:earnings ratio of their stock. The Japanese manager may adopt constancy of purpose (see Point 1 in Ch. 2, p. 23). (The quotations from articles by Tsurumi and Kaus on pp. 99, 100, and 146 are relevant here.)

Flow diagram (Fig. 1). Mere talk about quality accomplishes little. It was necessary to go into action. The flow diagram in Fig. 1 provided a start. Materials and equipment come in at the left. It would be necessary, I explained, to improve incoming materials. Work with your vendor as a partner on a long-term relationship of loyalty and trust to improve the quality of incoming materials and to decrease costs.

The consumer is the most important part of the production line. Quality should be aimed at the needs of the consumer, present and future.

Quality begins with the intent, which is fixed by management. The intent must be translated by engineers and others into plans, specifications, tests, production. The principles explained here, along with the chain reaction displayed on page 3, the flow diagram in Fig. 1, and techniques taught to hundreds of engineers, commenced the transformation of Japanese industry (more in the Appendix). A new economic age had begun.

Management learned about their responsibilities for improvement at every stage. Engineers learned theirs, and learned simple but powerful statistical methods by which to detect the existence of special (assignable) causes of variation, and that continual improvement of processes is essential (Point 5, p. 49). Improvement of quality became at once, with total commitment:

> Companywide—all plants, management, engineers, production workers, suppliers, everybody.
> Nationwide.
> Embracing every activity in production and service— procurement, design and redesign of product and service, instrumentation, production, consumer research.

Need any country be poor? Japan had in fact in 1950 negative net worth. Japan was, as now, devoid of natural resources—oil, coal, iron ore, copper, manganese, even wood. Moreover, Japan had a well-earned reputation for shoddy consumer goods, cheap but worth the price. Japan must export goods in return for food and equipment. This battle could be won only with quality. The consumer will from now on be the most important part of the production line (Fig. 1). This was a difficult challenge for top management in Japan.

If Japan be an example, then it is possible that any country with enough people and with good management, making products suited to their talents and to the market, need not be poor. Abundance of natural resources is not a requirement for prosperity. The wealth of a nation depends on its people, management, and government, more than on its natural resources. The problem is where to find good management. It would be a mistake to export American management to a friendly country.

What is the world's most underdeveloped nation? With the storehouse of skills and knowledge contained in its millions of unemployed, and with the even more appalling underuse, misuse, and abuse of skills and knowledge in the army of employed people in all ranks in all industries, the United States may be today the most underdeveloped nation in the world.

> **References to government service.** In most governmental services, there is no market to capture. In place of capture of the market, a governmental agency should deliver economically the service prescribed by law or regulation. The aim should be distinction in service. Continual improvement in government service would earn appreciation of the American public and would hold jobs in the service, and help industry to create more jobs.

A simple example. Some figures taken from experience will illustrate what happens when we improve quality. A schoolboy can understand them. The superintendent in a plant knew that there were problems with a certain production line. His only explanation was that the work force there (24 people) made a lot of mistakes: that if these people did not make mistakes, there would be none.

The first step was to get data from inspection and to plot the fraction defective day by day over the past six weeks (Fig. 2). This plot (a run chart) showed stable random variation above

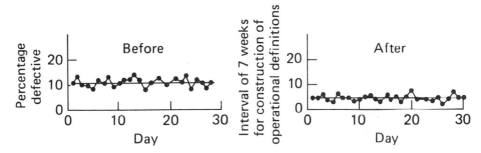

Fig. 2. Proportion defective day by day, before and after attempt to construct operational definitions of what is acceptable work and what is not. The proportion defective was 11 per cent before, 5 per cent after. I express here my indebtedness to David S. Chambers for the privilege to work with him on this example.

and below the average. The level of mistakes, and the variation day to day, were accordingly predictable. What does this mean? It means that here is a stable system for production of defective items (Ch. 11). Any substantial improvement must come from action on the system, the responsibility of management. Wishing and pleading and begging the workers to do better was totally futile.

What could the management do? The consultants made the suggestion, based on experience, that possibly the people on the

Illustration of gain in productivity with improved quality

Item	Before improvement (11% defective)	After improvement (5% defective)
Total cost	100	100
Spent to make good units	89	95
Spent to make defective units	11	5

job, and the inspector also, did not understand well enough what kind of work is acceptable and what is not. The manager and two supervisors eventually accepted this possibility and went to work on the matter. With trial and error they came up in seven weeks with operational definitions, with examples of conforming items and of nonconforming items, posted for everyone to see. A new set of data showed that the proportion defective had dropped to 5 per cent, as shown in the accompanying table and in the right-hand half of Fig. 2.

Gains

Quality up
Production of good product up 6 per cent
Capacity up 6 per cent
Lower cost per unit of good product
Profit improved
Customer happier
Everybody happier

These gains were immediate (seven weeks); cost, zero; same work force, same burden, no investment in new machinery.

This is an example of gain in productivity accomplished by a change in the system, namely, improvement in definitions, effected by the management, to help people to work smarter, not harder.

It could well be that another factor entered, unseen. It could be that the foreman on days when he was pressed for production had accepted poor work to meet his quota, overriding inspection and confusing workers and inspectors concerning what was acceptable work and what was not.

Next step: wipe out the 5 per cent defective. How? First, we note that again the daily points show stable variation about the new average 5 per cent; hence, again, any substantial improvement must come from action on the system. Here are some suggestions to investigate:

Incoming materials difficult to work with.
Some machines not working properly.
There may still be some difficulty in the definitions of what is acceptable work and what is not.

It might be wise to keep a record for two weeks in the form of a chart for fraction defective for each operator. Calculations might show that one or two of them are out of control with respect to the others. If so, make tests to learn whether further training could help them, or whether they should be moved into other jobs (Ch. 8). Look carefully at the incoming materials. Are they causing trouble? How about maintenance of machines?

There were 24 people on the line. The inspector would take a case of items as it went by her, inspect them, and record the results, then intercept another case for inspection. "What do you do with the tickets you fill out?" Answer: "I put them on the pile here, and when the pile gets too high, I discard the bottom half into the trash."

"Could I have the top half?" I asked her. She was delighted.

We took the top half, which gave us the tickets for the most recent six weeks, which gave us the points on the left half of Fig. 2.

Another example: reduction in cost.

Taken from a speech delivered in Rio de Janeiro, March 1981, by William E. Conway, president of the Nashua Corporation:

At Nashua, the first big success took place in March 1980;

improvement of quality and reduction of cost in the manufacture of carbonless paper.

Water-based coating that contains various chemicals is applied to a moving web of paper. If the amount of coating is right, the customer will be pleased with a good consistent mark when he uses the paper some months later. The coating head applied approximately 3.6 pounds of dry coating to 3000 square feet of paper at a speed of approximately 1100 linear feet per minute on a web 6 or 8 feet wide. Technicians took samples of paper and made tests to determine the intensity of the mark. These tests were made on the sample both as it came off the coater and after it was aged in an oven to simulate use by the customer. When tests showed the intensity of the mark to be too low or too high, the operator made adjustments that would increase or decrease the amount of coating material. Frequent stops for new settings were a way of life. These stops were costly.

The engineers knew that the average weight of the coating material was too high, but did not know how to lower it without risk of putting on insufficient coating. A new coating head, to cost $700,000, was under consideration. There would be, besides the cost of $700,000, time lost for installation, and the risk that the new head might not achieve uniformity and economy of coating much better than the equipment in use.

In August 1979, the plant manager asked for help. It was found that the coating head, if left untouched, was actually in pretty good statistical control at an average level of 3.6 dry pounds of coating on the paper, plus or minus 0.4.

Elimination of various causes of variation, highlighted by points outside the control limits, reduced the amount of coating and still maintained good consistent quality. The coater had by April 1980 settled down to an average of 2.8 pounds per 3000 square feet, varying from 2.4 to 3.2, thereby saving 0.8 pound per 3000 square feet (3.6−2.8), or $800,000 per year at present volume and cost levels.

It may be noted that what the people there had been doing was to follow Rule 2 or Rule 3 (p. 329), greatly increasing the variance of the coating, exactly the opposite of what they were trying to do.

Innovation to improve the process. The rest of Mr. Conway's story is still more interesting. Statistical control opened the way to engineering innovation. Without statistical control, the process was in unstable chaos, the noise of which would mask the effect of any attempt to bring improvement. With statistical control achieved, engineers and chemists became innovative, creative. They now had an identifiable process. They modified the chemical content of the material used for the coating and found how to use less and less. Reduction of a tenth of a pound means an annual reduction of $100,000 in the cost of coating.

The engineers also improved the coating head, to achieve greater and greater uniformity of coating. All the while, statistical control of the coating was maintained at ever-decreasing levels of coating, and with less and less variation.

Low quality means high costs. A plant was plagued by a huge amount of defective product. "How many people have you on this line for rework of defects made in previous operations?" I asked the manager. He went to the blackboard and put down three people here, four there, and so on—in total, 21 per cent of the work force on the line.

Defects are not free. Somebody makes them, and gets paid for making them. On the supposition that it costs as much to correct a defect as to make it in the first place, then 42 per cent of his payroll and burden was being spent to make defective items and to repair them.

Once the manager saw the magnitude of the problem, and saw that he was paying out good money to make defects as well as to correct them, he found ways to improve processes and to help the people on the line to understand better the new operation. The cost of rework went down dramatically in a space of two months.

Next step: reduce further the proportion defective in a never-ending program of improvement. The cost of rework is only part of the cost of poor quality. Poor quality begets poor quality and lowers productivity all along the line, and some of the faulty product goes out the door, into the hands of the customer. An unhappy customer tells his friends. The multiplying effect of an unhappy customer is one of those unknown and unknowable figures, and likewise for the multiplying effect of a happy customer, who brings in business (see p. 121).

A. V. Feigenbaum estimated that from 15 to 40 per cent of the manufacturer's costs of almost any American product that you buy today is for waste embedded in it—waste of human effort, waste of machine-time, nonproductive use of accompanying burden.[3] No wonder that many American products are hard to sell at home or abroad.

In some work that I did for a railway, study showed that mechanics in a huge repair shop spent three-quarters of their time waiting in line to get parts.

The reader's own estimate of the cost of common practices in the United States, such as awarding business to the lowest bidder and robbing people of their right to pride of workmanship (Points 4 and 12 in Ch. 2), would add a deplorable amount to Dr. Feigenbaum's estimate.

Handling damage, right in the factory, is in many places appalling, sometimes running from 5 to 8 per cent of the manufacturer's cost. Further loss occurs in transit. Then there is shelf-wear—further loss. Ask any grocer what his losses are from handling damage on his platform, platform to storage shelf, shelf-wear, mauling by curious customers.

New machinery and gadgets are not the answer. We have just seen an example in which important gains in quality and produc-

---

3 A. V. Feigenbaum. "Quality and productivity," *Quality Progress*, November 1977.

tivity were accomplished by learning to use effectively the machinery on hand.

Lag in American productivity has been attributed in editorials and in letters in the newspapers to failure to install new machinery, gadgets, and the latest types of automation such as robots. Such suggestions make interesting reading and still more interesting writing for people that do not understand problems of production. The following paragraph received from a friend in a large manufacturing company will serve as illustration:

> This whole program [design and installation of new machines] has led to some unhappy experiences. All these wonderful machines performed their intended functions, on test, but when they were put into operation in our plants, with our people, they were out of business so much of the time for this and that kind of failure that our overall costs, instead of going down, went up. No one had evaluated the overall probable failure rates and maintenance. As a result, we were continually caught with stoppages and with not enough spare parts, or with none at all; and no provision for alternate production lines.

Gadgets for automation and automatic recording in the office and in the factory are not the answer either. Exhibitions featuring such gadgets are attended by thousands of people seeking an easy way out of the lag in productivity, trusting hopefully to hardware. Some gadgets may increase productivity enough to pay their own expenses, but the combined effect of new machinery, gadgets, and bright ideas is a small packet compared with the gains in productivity that will be accomplished by the management of companies that survive the decline (Chs. 2 and 3).

If I were a banker, I would not lend money for new equipment unless the company that asked for the loan could demonstrate by statistical evidence that they are using their present equipment to reasonably full capacity, and are at work on the 14 points of Chapter 2 and on the deadly diseases and obstacles of Chapter 3.

Service industries. Eventually quality improvement will reach not only the production of goods and food (the birthplace of modern statistical theory was agriculture) but the service industries as well—hotels, restaurants, transportation of freight and passengers, wholesale and retail establishments, hospitals, medical service, care of the aged, perhaps even the U.S. mail.

In fact, one of the most successful examples of improvement of quality and productivity in large operations is in our own Census, not only in the decennial Census, but also in the regular monthly and quarterly surveys of people and of business, an example being the *Monthly Report on the Labor Force.*

Chapter 7 contains a number of examples of improvement of practices in service industries. The section written by William J. Latzko describes methods and results in reduction of errors in a bank. The section written by John F. Hird describes improvements in the purchase, generation, and distribution of electric power to customers, which is one of the most important services of the country. A large power company in the United States, under his guidance, is improving service and cutting costs, with substantial profit, no one working harder, only smarter, from management to linemen and truck drivers (p. 238). (Cf. William G. Hunter, pp. 245ff.)

Some service industries in Japan have been active in improvement of productivity from the start in 1950—for example, the Japanese National Railways, Nippon Telegraph and Telephone Public Corporation, the Tobacco Monopoly of Japan, the Post Office.

Service organizations have won the Deming Prize in Japan; for example, Takenaka Komuten, an architectural and construction firm, won the Deming Prize in 1979. They studied the needs of users (in offices, hospitals, factories, hotels, trains, subways). They reduced by computer the amount and cost of rework in drawings. Research in soils, rocks, movement of earth, machinery, accomplished continual improvement in methods of construction. Kajima Corporation, another architectural and construction firm, won similar recognition in 1982; likewise the Shimizu Construction Company, in 1983. The Kansai Electric Power Company, serving Osaka, Nagoya, and other parts of Central Japan, the biggest power company in the world, won the Deming Prize in 1984.

Measures of productivity do not lead to improvement in productivity. There is in the United States, any day, a conference on productivity, usually more than one. There is in fact a permanent conference on productivity, and there is now the President's Committee on Productivity. The aim of these conferences is to construct measures of productivity. It is important to have measures of productivity for meaningful comparisons of productivity in the United States year by year, and for meaningful comparisons between countries. Unfortunately, however, figures on productivity in the United States do not help to improve productivity in the United States. Measures of productivity are like statistics on accidents: they tell you all about the number of accidents in the home, on the road, and at the work place, but they do not tell you how to reduce the frequency of accidents.

It is unfortunately to be feared that quality assurance means in many places a deluge of figures that tell how many defective items of this type and that type were produced last month, with comparisons month to month and year to year. Figures like this tell the management how things have been going, but they do not point the way to improvement.

One of the lecturers at the meeting of the Bank Administration Institute held in Atlanta in January 1982 advised every bank to establish a productivity office to measure productivity. There are 14,000 banks in the United States. The speaker's plan would thus create 14,000 jobs. Unfortunately, measurement of productivity does not improve productivity.

On the other hand, an orderly study of productivity, to enquire whether any given activity is consistent with the aim of the organization, and what it is costing, can be very helpful to the management. The following paragraphs from Marvin E. Mundel, *Measuring and Enhancing the Productivity of Service and Government Organizations* (Asian Productivity Organization, Aoyama Dai-ichi Mansions, 4–14 Akasaka 8-chome, Minato-ku, Tokyo 107, 1975, pp. 3–4) throw light on this point:

Outputs . . . cannot be considered without considering the goals they are designed to achieve. . . .

In order to provide some background let us analyze a few examples. Thomas A. Edison, the great American inventor, is said to have proposed a voting machine to improve the voting procedure used by the Congress of the United States. He demonstrated his device to the Speaker of the House and the President of the Senate. With his device each Representative and Senator would have had three buttons on the arm of his chair; a red button for *no*, a green button for *yes* and a white button for *abstain*. Edison proposed that, when the signal to vote was given, each Member would push the appropriate button and both a record of how each voted and the totals of the votes would be displayed instantly. Edison proudly assured the Speaker and the President of the Senate that his device would eliminate roll-call errors, reduce the time for a roll-call vote by an enormous percentage, and so forth.

He was utterly astounded when the Speaker of the House and the President of the Senate cut him off brusquely and informed him that such a system was utterly unwanted, undesirable and, rather than improving the operation of the House or the Senate, would completely upset the orderly working of the

Congress of the United States. What was an improvement from Edison's point of view was anything but an improvement from the viewpoint of the Congress. The delays in a roll-call vote were an integral part of the deliberative process with which the Congress had chosen to operate. Mr. Edison's output, a faster vote, was not compatible with the objectives of the Congress.

As an example from the private sector, a large shipbuilding firm sought to improve the performance of the group charged with planning and implementing the shiplaunching ceremony party. Initial efforts were directed at the equipment used to send invitations, and so forth. However, questions were raised concerning possible confusion between the party given (the output) and the purpose of the party (the objective).

The objective of the party planning group was to improve relations with vendors and government officials of the area. When the output (the party) was initiated it had served this purpose. However, when the frequency changed from one-per-year to almost monthly the parties no longer achieved this purpose; they had become a bore and an imposition.

Rather than improve the method of planning and implementing, the format of the party was changed to include only a small, interested group; the owner, his guests and hosts from the company. Twenty employees in the party-giving group were made available for other work. Other additional savings (temporary seat erecting labor; loss of shipway time) were almost as large. Public relations were improved.

2
Principles for Transformation of Western Management

How poor are they that have not patience.—Iago to Roderigo, in Shakespeare's *Othello*, II. iii.

Aim and Preamble

Purpose of this chapter. Western style of management must change to halt the decline of Western industry, and to turn it upward. The purpose of this chapter and of the next one is to explain the elements of the transformation that must take place. There must be an awakening to the crisis, followed by action, management's job.

This chapter and the next also provide criteria by which anyone in the company may measure the performance of management. Everyone in the company will now have a basis by which to answer the question: "How is our management doing?" Union leaders may ask the same question, and judge management by the same criteria.

The transformation can only be accomplished by man, not by hardware (computers, gadgets, automation, new machinery). A company can not buy its way into quality.

Best efforts not sufficient.

By everyone doing his best.   (*Wrong*)

This is the answer that came forth in a meeting of management of a company in response to my question: "And how do you go about it to improve quality and productivity?"

Best efforts are essential. Unfortunately, best efforts, people charging this way and that way without guidance of principles, can do a lot of damage. Think of the chaos that would come if everyone did his best, not knowing what to do.

Need for consistency of effort. Suppose that (1) everybody knew what to do. (2) Everybody did his best. Result: dissipation of knowledge and effort; results, far from optimum. There is no substitute for teamwork and good leaders of teams to bring consistency of effort, along with knowledge.

Theory of management now exists. There is now a theory of management for improvement of quality, productivity, and competitive position. No one can ever again claim that there is nothing in management to teach. Students in a school of business now have a yardstick by which to judge the curriculum that is open to them. Does the school show some attempt to present a curriculum for today's problems, or does it show obsolescence? Obsolescence need not be planned: it can just move in.

Experience alone, without theory, teaches management nothing about what to do to improve quality and competitive position, nor how to do it. If experience alone would be a teacher, then one may well ask why are we in this predicament? Experience will answer a question, and a question comes from theory. The theory in hand need not be elaborate. It may be only a hunch, or a statement of principles. It may turn out to be a wrong hunch.

Management that faces seriously the following questions will perceive the need of an overall integrated plan.[1]

1. Where do you hope to be five years from now?
2. How may you reach this goal? By what method?

What is needed is sustained involvement and participation (William A. Golomski again).

---

1 Contributed by William A. Golomski.

Hopes without a method to achieve them will remain mere hopes (Lloyd S. Nelson, next section). The 14 points of this chapter, and removal of the deadly diseases and obstacles explained in the next chapter, furnish a method.

Guidance from questions and pronouncements of Lloyd S. Nelson. (Dr. Nelson is Director of Statistical Methods for the Nashua Corporation.)

1. The central problem of management in all its aspects, including planning, procurement, manufacturing, research, sales, personnel, accounting, and law, is to understand better the meaning of variation, and to extract the information contained in variation.

2. If you can improve productivity, or sales, or quality, or anything else, by (e.g.) 5 per cent next year without a rational plan for improvement, then why were you not doing it last year?

3. The most important figures needed for management of any organization are unknown and unknowable (see Ch. 3).

4. In the state of statistical control, action initiated on appearance of a defect will be ineffective and will cause more trouble. What is needed is improvement of the process, by reduction of variation, or by change of level, or both. Study of the sources of product, upstream, gives powerful leverage on improvement (p. 355).

The reader of this book will find on nearly every page application of Dr. Nelson's pronouncements.

Short-term profits are no index of ability. Short-term profits are not a reliable indicator of performance of management. Anybody can pay dividends by deferring maintenance, cutting out research, or acquiring another company.

Dividends and paper profits, the yardstick by which managers of money and heads of companies are judged, make no contribution to material living for people anywhere, nor do they improve the competitive position of a company or of American industry. Paper profits do not make bread: improvement of quality and productivity do. They make a contribution to better material living for all people, here and everywhere.

People that depend on dividends to live on should be concerned, not merely with the size of the dividend today, but also with the question of whether there will be dividends three years from now, five years from now, ten years from now. Management has the obligation to protect investment.

Support of top management is not sufficient. It is not enough that top management commit themselves for life to quality and productivity. They must know what it is that they are committed to—that is, what they must do. These obligations can not be delegated. Support is not enough: action is required.

"... and if you can't come, send nobody."

These are the words in a letter that William E. Conway (president and chief executive officer of the Nashua Corporation) wrote to a vice-president in response to the latter's request for an invitation to visit the Nashua Corporation.

In other words, Mr. Conway told him, if you don't have time to do your job, there is not much that I can do for you.

A quality program for a community, launched by ceremonies with a speech by the governor, raising of flags, beating of drums, badges, all with heavy applause, is a delusion and a snare.

Wrong way. It is a common supposition that quality and productivity can be achieved by putting on the screws, and by installing gadgets and new machinery. A new book explains how to "Motivate your people to work at top speed!" Beat horses, and they will run faster—for a while.

A letter went out from a committee of the U.S. Senate to a number of companies to stress the importance of quality and productivity, and to announce a contest. Entrants would be judged on:

Machinery
Automation and robotics
Better information
Profit sharing and other incentives
Training
Job enrichment
QC-Circles
Word processing
Suggestion programs
Zero defects
Management by objective

Truth is stranger than fiction. Haven't we a right to expect something better from a Senate committee? But they were only doing their best.

I have never heard of a word-processor that would generate an idea nor of one that would make a relative pronoun agree in gender and number with its antecedents.

The aim of a new film is to scare the wits out of factory workers, to point out to them what will happen to them if poor quality gets out and into the hands of the purchaser. As is already clear from Chapter 1, the factory worker anywhere has always known what will happen, but is in many places helpless, forced by the system that he works in to turn out poor quality.

MBWA (management by walking around, a term that I learned from Lloyd S. Nelson) is hardly ever effective. The reason is that someone in management, walking around, has little idea about what questions to ask, and usually does not pause long enough at any spot to get the right answer.

Condensation of the 14 Points for Management

Origin of the 14 points. The 14 points are the basis for transformation of American industry. It will not suffice merely to solve problems, big or little. Adoption and action on the 14 points are a signal that the management intend to stay in business and aim to protect investors and jobs. Such a system formed the basis for lessons for top management in Japan in 1950 and in subsequent years (see pp. 1–6 and the Appendix).

The 14 points apply anywhere, to small organizations as well as to large ones, to the service industry as well as to manufacturing. They apply to a division within a company.

1. Create constancy of purpose toward improvement of product and service, with the aim to become competitive and to stay in business, and to provide jobs.

2. Adopt the new philosophy. We are in a new economic age. Western management must awaken to the challenge, must learn their responsibilities, and take on leadership for change.

3. Cease dependence on inspection to achieve quality. Eliminate the need for inspection on a mass basis by building quality into the product in the first place.

4. End the practice of awarding business on the basis of price tag. Instead, minimize total cost. Move toward a single supplier for any one item, on a long-term relationship of loyalty and trust.

5. Improve constantly and forever the system of production and service, to improve quality and productivity, and thus constantly decrease costs.

6. Institute training on the job.

7. Institute leadership (see Point 12 and Ch. 8). The aim of supervision should be to help people and machines and gadgets to do a better job. Supervision of management is in need of overhaul, as well as supervision of production workers.

8. Drive out fear, so that everyone may work effectively for the company (see Ch. 3).

9. Break down barriers between departments. People in research, design, sales, and production must work as a team, to foresee problems of production and in use that may be encountered with the product or service.

10. Eliminate slogans, exhortations, and targets for the work force asking for zero defects and new levels of productivity. Such exhortations only create adversarial relationships, as the bulk of the causes of low quality and low productivity belong to the system and thus lie beyond the power of the work force.

11a. Eliminate work standards (quotas) on the factory floor. Substitute leadership.

b. Eliminate management by objective. Eliminate management by numbers, numerical goals. Substitute leadership.

12a. Remove barriers that rob the hourly worker of his right to pride of workmanship. The responsibility of supervisors must be changed from sheer numbers to quality.

b. Remove barriers that rob people in management and in engineering of their right to pride of workmanship. This means, *inter alia*, abolishment of the annual or merit rating and of management by objective (see Ch. 3).

13. Institute a vigorous program of education and self-improvement.

14. Put everybody in the company to work to accomplish the transformation. The transformation is everybody's job.

Elaboration on the 14 Points

1. Create constancy of purpose for improvement of product and service. There are two problems: (i) problems of today; (ii) problems of tomorrow, for the company that hopes to stay in business. Problems of today encompass maintenance of quality of product put out today, regulation of output so as not to exceed immediate sales by too far, budget, employment, profits, sales, service, public relations, forecasting, and so forth. It is easy to stay bound up in the tangled knot of the problems of today, becoming ever more and more efficient in them, as by (e.g.) acquisition of mechanized equipment for the office.

Problems of the future command first and foremost constancy of purpose and dedication to improvement of competitive position to keep the company alive and to provide jobs for their employees. Are the board of directors and the president dedicated to quick profits, or to the institution of constancy of purpose? The next quarterly dividend is not as important as existence of the company 10, 20, or 30 years from now. Establishment of constancy of purpose means acceptance of obligations like the following:

a. Innovate. Allocate resources for long-term planning. Plans for the future call for consideration of:

New service and new product that may help people to
    live better materially, and that will have a market
New materials that will be required; probable cost
Method of production; possible changes in equipment
    for production
New skills required, and in what number?
Training and retraining of personnel
Training of supervisors
Cost of production
Cost of marketing; plans for service; cost of service
Performance in the hands of the user
Satisfaction of the user

One requirement for innovation is faith that there will be a future. Innovation, the foundation of the future, can not thrive unless the top management have declared unshakable commitment to quality and productivity. Until this policy can be enthroned as an institution, middle management and everyone else in the company will be skeptical about the effectiveness of their best efforts.

b. Put resources into:

Research
Education

c. Constantly improve design of product and service. This obligation never ceases. The consumer is the most important part of the production line.

> It is a mistake to suppose that efficient production of product and service can with certainty keep an organization solvent and ahead of competition. It is possible and in fact fairly easy for an organization to go downhill and out of business making the wrong product or offering the wrong type of service, even though everyone in the organization performs with devotion, employing statistical methods and every other aid that can boost efficiency.

Your customers, your suppliers, your employees need your statement of constancy of purpose—your intention to stay in business by providing product and service that will help man to live better and which will have a market.

Top management should publish a resolution that no one will lose his job for contribution to quality and productivity.

2. Adopt the new philosophy. We are in a new economic age, created by Japan. Deadly diseases afflict the style of American management (see Ch. 3). Obstacles to the competitive position of American industry created by government regulations and antitrust activities must be revised to support the well-being of the American people, and not to depress it. We can no longer tolerate commonly accepted levels of mistakes, defects, material not suited for the job, people on the job that do not know what the job is and are afraid to ask, handling damage, antiquated methods of training on the job, inadequate and ineffective supervision, management not rooted in the company, job hopping in management, buses and trains late or even canceled because a driver failed to show up. Filth and vandalism raise the cost of living and, as any psychologist can aver, lead to slovenly work and to dissatisfaction with life and with the workplace.

American style of management rode along unchallenged between 1950 and 1968, when American-manufactured products held the market. Anyone anywhere in the world was lucky for the privilege to buy an American product. By 1968, forces of competition could no longer be ignored. What had happened in Japan could have happened in America, but did not. The thought still lingers: "We must have been doing something right." This is not an inevitable conclusion.

The cost of living varies inversely with the amount of goods and services that a given amount of money will buy. Delays and mistakes raise costs. Alternative plans in expectation of delays are costly. The economy of a single plan that will work is obvious. As an example, I may cite a proposed itinerary in Japan:

> 1725 h Leave Taku City.
> 1923 h Arrive Hakata.
>   Change trains.
> 1924 h Leave Hakata [for Osaka, at 210 km/hr].

Only one minute to change trains? You don't need a whole minute. You will have 30 seconds left over. No alternate plan was necessary.

My friend Bob King, director of GOAL (Growth Opportunity Alliance of Greater Lawrence, Mass.), while in Japan in November 1983 received these instructions to reach by train a company that he was to visit:

> 0903 h Board the train. Pay no attention to trains at
>   0858, 0901.
> 0957 h Off.

No further instruction was needed.

The following paragraph from a personal letter is illustrative of waste in a service industry. Correction of the error in the bill, and replacement of the defective notebook, must have wiped out the profit on the sale and left the customer with a resolution to try some other stationer on future orders.

> I ordered from a bookstore one case of twenty-four count $1\frac{1}{2}$ inch ring notebooks. Instead, twelve came. On complaint, the bookstore sent the other twelve. I inspected every notebook and found one where the rings were stationary in the open position, useless to me. Twenty-four notebooks qualified me for a discount. The store charged me the full price, with the explanation, when I mentioned this, that the girl that took the order was new.

A manufacturer of beer that I talked to had no problem with cans, he said, because the supplier of cans replaces free any load of cans that are found to be faulty. It had not occurred to him that he is paying for the defective cans, plus the cost of halting production and replacing cans. It had not occurred to him that his customers are footing the bill.

After passing through tight security at the offices and plant of one of America's largest chemical companies, someone observed that (1) the name on the pass that the guard gave to him was wrong and (2) the date was wrong. Otherwise, the pass was in good order.

Transformation is required—adoption of the 14 points, and riddance of the deadly diseases and obstacles described in Chapter 3.

3. Cease dependence on mass inspection. Routine 100 per cent inspection to improve quality is equivalent to planning for defects, acknowledgment that the process has not the capability required for the specifications.

Inspection to improve quality is too late, ineffective, costly.

When product leaves the door of a supplier, it is too late to do anything about its quality. Quality comes not from inspection, but from improvement of the production process. Inspection, scrap, downgrading, and rework are not corrective action on the process.

Rework raises costs. No one likes to do repair work. A pile of items set aside for rework grows and grows, and too often, in desperation downstream for parts, are not repaired at all, but are commandeered and used just as they are.

We must note that there are exceptions, circumstances in which mistakes and duds are inevitable but intolerable. An example is, I believe, manufacture of complicated integrated circuits. Separation of good ones from bad ones is the only way out. Calculations and other paperwork in a bank or in an insurance company is another example. It is important to carry out inspection at the right point for minimum total cost (to be treated in Ch. 15).

a. Inspection does not improve quality, nor guarantee quality. Inspection is too late. The quality, good or bad, is already in the product. As Harold F. Dodge said, "You can not inspect quality into a product."

b. Mass inspection is with rare exceptions of the kind noted unreliable, costly, ineffective. It does not make a clean separation of good items from bad items.

c. Inspectors fail to agree with each other until their work is brought into statistical control. They fail to agree with themselves. Test instruments, cheap or costly, require maintenance and study. (Examples appear in Chs. 8, 11, and 15.) Routine inspection becomes unreliable through boredom and fatigue. A common excuse of anyone on the job, when confronted with data on the number of defectives that he has made, is that the instruments used for the tests are unreliable. Automatic inspection and recording require constant vigil.

d. In contrast, the inspection of small samples of product for control charts to achieve or to maintain statistical control can be a professional job. Inspectors of vendor and customer have time to compare their instruments and tests, to learn to speak the same language.

Put on four more inspectors. This is a commonly accepted reaction to a problem in quality—a sure road to more trouble.

Inspector: A certain critical part here is inspected and signed by five inspectors, or so goes the rule, with five signatures. What do I do? If I am Number One, I inspect the item and sign the record. If I am not Number One, I make the supposition that the first man that signed the record inspected the item, so I just go ahead and sign it.

Incidentally, 200 per cent inspection, as usually carried out, is less reliable than 100 per cent inspection for the simple reason that each inspector depends on the other to do the job. Divided responsibility means that nobody is responsible. (Cf. "Administration of inspection for extra high quality," p. 261.)

My friend David S. Chambers told me about a printing company that proofread everything 11 times. Why do you think the manager called on Mr. Chambers for help? You guessed it: he was plagued with mistakes and complaints from customers. None of the 11 proofreaders had a job: each one depended on the other 10 to do it.

Wrong way. A division in the civil service of a state has the task of preparing titles to automobiles. The foreman of the group described the mistakes that are made: misspelling of name of owner, mistakes in address, mistakes in serial number, in model, and many others—few in number, but costly. She estimates that only one in seven of the mistakes made ever comes back for correction, yet correction of these mistakes costs the state a million dollars per year.

She learned that she could purchase for $10,000 software that would indicate an inconsistency while a title is being typed. Correction could be made at once—in fact would be required. This one-time purchase would eliminate errors and would pay a dividend of a million dollars per year, every year from here onward, she thought.

A better way, in my opinion, would be to improve the forms for clarity and ease; also to introduce training to help the typists to understand what constitutes a mistake and its consequences. When the typists have reached the point where they have no need of the software, then buy it, and constantly improve it. It would then be a wise investment. The output would then be quality to be proud of.

Another example.

Q. Who is responsible for the quality of incoming parts and materials?

A. Our quality control department. It is their job to inspect incoming materials and parts and to make sure that nothing goes out our door that is faulty.

Wrong way.

More details on the evils of routine dependence on inspection will appear in Chapter 3.

> *Remark.* It is a fact, though, that realization of minimum total cost may call for 100 per cent inspection of some items (Ch. 15).
>
> Also in instances of low yield, as of completed integrated circuits, 100 per cent may be a necessary step in the manufacturing process.

4. End the practice of awarding business on the basis of price tag alone. We can no longer leave quality, service, and price to the forces of competition for price alone—not in today's requirements for uniformity and reliability.[2]

Price has no meaning without a measure of the quality being purchased.[3] Without adequate measures of quality, business drifts to the lowest bidder, low quality and high cost being the inevitable result. American industry and the U.S. government, civil and military, are being rooked by rules that award business to the lowest bidder.

The aim in purchase of tools and other equipment should be to minimize the net cost per hour (or year) of life. But this would require long-term thinking, not just cheapest price tag for purchase today. The necessary figures for initial cost, maintenance, and length of life for each important tool are on hand, albeit scattered, and could be assembled. Automatic assembly of such figures for current use is an important project for today.

A buyer's job has been, until today, to be on the alert for lower prices, to find a new vendor that will offer a lower price. The other vendors of the same material must meet it.

The buyer is not at fault. That has been his job for 20 years. Can you blame him for doing his job? The management is at fault for maintaining terms of reference that are outmoded.

The policy of forever trying to drive down the price of anything purchased, with no regard to quality and service, can drive good vendors and good service out of business.

He that has a rule to give his business to the lowest bidder deserves to get rooked.

Municipal transit authorities are an example of legitimate plunder, inviting thievery by their policy of doing business with the lowest bidder. They are forced into this policy, in the United

---

2 Stated in these words by James K. Bakken of the Ford Motor Company on 27 January 1981.

3 Walter A. Shewhart, *Economic Control of Quality of Manufactured Product* (Van Nostrand, 1931; repr. ed., American Society for Quality Control, 1980; reprinted by Ceepress, The George Washington University, 1986).

States, by the Urban Mass Transit Administration, which grants funds only to the lowest bidder.

A few bad experiences in mass transit because of erratic performance of equipment, purchased on the basis of the price tag alone, may have retarded by a generation expansion of mass transit in the United States.

It is my understanding that the government sometimes awards to the lowest bidder contracts for demographic, social, and scientific research and development.

One can find advertisements for the teaching of control charts, at lowest price. Anyone that engages teaching by hacks deserves to be rooked.

The following flagrant example is an actual request, from a government agency, for professional help, to be awarded to the lowest bidder:

> For delivery and evaluation of a course on management for quality control for supervisors. . . . An order will be issued on the basis of price.

Sister Jeanne Perreault, president of Rivier College, repeated to the author the words of her business manager: "We can not afford to purchase equipment and buildings at the lowest price. We have to be careful."

Purchasing managers have a new job. Economists teach the world that competition in the marketplace gives everyone the best deal. This may have been so in days gone by, when the baker had his customers, the tailor his, the cheese-maker his, and so forth. In those days, it was fairly easy to make an intelligent purchase.

It is different today. The price tag is still easy to read, but an understanding of quality requires education.

The purchasing department must change its focus from lowest initial cost of material purchased to lowest total cost. This means education in purchasing. It is also necessary to learn that specifi-cations of incoming materials do not tell the whole story about performance. What problems does the material encounter in production? (Cf. the section "The supposition that it is only necessary to meet specifications," Ch. 3, p. 139.)

Materials and components may all be excellent, each by itself, yet not work well together in production or in the finished pro-duct. It is thus necessary to follow a sample of materials through the whole production process into complex assemblies, and onward, finally, to the customer. There was nothing wrong with the glass in a large building in Boston, nor with the steel. Both met the specifications. Yet somehow they did not work well together in service. Glass windows fell from the steel frames to the ground below.

In one instance, the man in charge of procurement of mate-rials, in attendance at a seminar, declared that he has no prob-lems with procurement, as he accepts only perfect materials. (Chuckled I to myself, "That's the way to do it.") Next day, in one of his plants, a superintendent showed to me two pieces of a certain item from two different suppliers, same item number, both beautifully made; both met the specifications, yet they were sufficiently different for one to be usable, the other usable only with costly rework, a heavy loss to the plant.

The explanation was that one supplier understood what the blocks were to be used for, the other did not—he merely satisfied the specifications.

It seems that difficulties like this lead one to seek solace in one or both of the following remarks:

> This is the kind of problem that we see any day in this business.
>
> *or*
>
> Our competitors are having the same kind of problem.

What would some people do without their competitors?
The manager of a plant that belongs to one of America's finest

corporations lamented to me that he spends most of his time defending good vendors. A typical problem runs like this. A vendor has not for years sent to him a defective item, and his price is right. The corporate purchasing department proposed to award the business to a new and untried vendor because he offers a better price. These parts go into repeaters. The telephone company might incur a cost of several thousand dollars to dig up the pavement and replace a defective repeater. The plant manager, trying to protect the company and the whole system, must spend many hours in argument to hold on to the vendor that knows his business.

Advantages of a single source and long-term relationship. A long-term relationship between purchaser and supplier is necessary for best economy. How can a supplier be innovative and develop economy in his production processes when he can only look forward to short-term business with a purchaser?

There are also operational advantages. Even though two suppliers send excellent materials, there will be differences. Anyone in production knows that change in material from one vendor to material from another causes loss of time. The loss may be only 15 minutes. It may be 8 hours in a stamping mill. It may be weeks. This is so even though both vendors send good material. "Both good but unequal," a factory worker put it. From another factory worker: "The parts from the two different sources were both excellent, but only one was compatible with our needs."

Lot-to-lot variation from any one supplier is usually enough to give fits to manufacturing. It is reasonable to expect that variation between lots from two suppliers will give even more trouble.

Heard on the factory floor. With every new lot of S-T material that comes in (from the same vendor), our troubles with point-defects shoot upward, with a whole new set of problems to conquer. Material from two suppliers would drive us out of our wits.

Moreover, one should not overlook the simplification in the accounting and paperwork from decrease in number of suppliers and fewer shipping points.

A worthy customer should expect his suppliers, if they are wise and looking ahead with constancy of purpose, to compete for selection as the single supplier.

A supplier should himself work toward a single supplier for any one item.

A second source, for protection, in case ill luck puts one vendor out of business temporarily or forever, is a costly policy.

There is lower investment and lower total inventory with a single vendor than with two. (Charles E. Clough, Nashua Corporation.)

Japanese management had a head start in 1950 on the need to improve incoming materials, and on advice to establish with every vendor a long-term working relationship of loyalty and trust.

Uncertainty about date of delivery and quality drives some customers to engage two or three vendors in the hope that one of them will come through. My friend Barbara Kuklewicz, of San Jose, who counsels management, related to me that she asked a vendor if it would not be a good idea to inform the customer that his order will come late. No, he would get mad. Well, what happens when you deliver the order late? He gets mad. Then why didn't you tell him in advance, so that he could prepare? He would get mad twice.

No manufacturer that I know of possesses enough knowledge and manpower to work effectively with more than one vendor for any item.

The purchasing department of one of my clients showed in three years the following record of advancement:

Now, only 1 item in 20 has two or more vendors.
(One in 20 may be close to an irreducible minimum.)
A year ago the proportion was 1 in 16.

Two years ago the proportion was 1 in 12.

Three years ago the proportion was 1 in 2.

Ninety-two per cent of critical parts for three and four years ahead are now in development by teams composed of the chosen supplier, design engineer, purchasing, manufacturing, sales. The price will be settled later, all books open, everybody working toward a common aim, all in conformity with "Today," p. 41.

A company that adopts the recommendations made here will have wide influence. The suppliers that serve one company also serve other companies, and will deliver to all of them better and better quality with better and better economy. Everybody will come out ahead.

It is pleasing to see that this advice is taking wide form and substance (from the *Wall Street Journal*, 6 May 1983, p. 2), adopted from the Pontiac Motor Division of General Motors:

GM Is Said to Seek Long-Term Accords with Steelmakers

By AMAL NAG

Staff Reporter of THE WALL STREET JOURNAL

DETROIT–General Motors Corp., unhappy with its new bidding system for steel purchases, is said to be considering negotiating with individual companies on long-term price and supply contracts.

Last year, in a much-publicized move aimed at cutting costs and improving the efficiency of suppliers, GM required steelmakers to bid

annually for its business. The No. 1
U.S. auto company is the steel industry's largest customer. . . .

By giving fewer suppliers most of its
business, GM hopes to cut their production costs through economies of
scale and other joint efforts, resulting
in lower prices. . . .

In return for steelmakers' cooperation with GM in its cost-cutting objectives, the auto maker is expected to
reward suppliers with multi-year contracts.

In one instance, some people in a company supposed that they were conforming to the recommendation of only one supplier for a given item, because
though they had arrangements with six suppliers, they
ordered the item from only one of them at a time.

Commodities and services. Purchase of commodities and services should also move to the single supplier. The same commodity may be obtainable from several sources at different prices.
However, consideration of inventory and ability to deliver the
goods within a reasonable time, and with certainty of date, are
important to the customer. Important also are the right freight
car or type of trailer for haul of a commodity in or out, and its
condition in respect to cleanliness and state of repair. In instances of materials that are difficult to handle, a good wholesaler may send a man to assist with the unloading and storage of
goods purchased. Thus, choice of a single vendor for a given
commodity may accordingly be a wise procedure. Likewise,
choice of a single carrier for outbound shipments from a specific
location may also be wise.

A purchasing manager told me that this course

(single shipper) lifted off her shoulders the burden of shopping around for cheaper transportation, with the hazards of poor service and irresponsibility. She uses to advantage the time saved. As she anticipated, however, some of her customers complained that they knew how to get lower prices for the carriage. The fact is that anyone can find something at a lower price for almost anything. Anybody could have bought tires at a cheaper price than the ones that came on his automobile. What would he get for his money? Inferior quality. One must take into account the time spent in dickering for lower prices at every turn. In the long run, one comes out ahead by working with the single supplier, provided that he upholds his responsibility for continual improvement.

One vendor, multiple shipping points. I am indebted to James K. Bakken of the Ford Motor Company for the observation that two shipping points from the same vendor give the same problems as material from two vendors. The following question and answer were recorded in a visit to a plant. "What about two shipping points from the same vendor?" I asked a plant manager. "Just as bad as two suppliers," was his answer.

A supplier with two shipping points may serve a customer with two plants by specifying one shipping point for one plant, the other shipping point for the other, no substitution or mixing.

How does a supplier qualify? Almost every company has a manual by which to "qualify" vendors. Military Standard 9858A is an example. Teams of unqualified examiners visit suppliers to rate them.

A better plan would be to discard these manuals and teams and let suppliers compete to be the chosen one, not on price tag, but at the right stage, on the basis of qualifications that have meaning. Let suppliers present evidence of active involvement of their management with the 14 points, especially Point 5, never-ending improvement of processes, along with abolishment of the diseases to be learned in Chapter 3. The same criteria that would be good for rating a division of a corporation apply equally to choice of supplier (p. 121).

One may also include, as a basis for choice of supplier:

1. Budgeted expense for research and development.
2. Past record for development of product.

(Contributed by Norbert Keller, General Motors.)

Beware of conference-room promises. (Ronald Moen.)

Heard in a seminar. We as a supplier must be qualified for services that our customer requires—extra parts for 15 years, tests of our product, delivery. We must be able to participate in tests of our product in the assembly that our customer turns out.

Single purchase contrasted with continuing delivery of material. It is important that buyers know the difference between a single-time purchase and continuing delivery. An example of a single-time purchase could be the grand piano, the furniture and fittings for the office force, furniture and fittings to go into a hotel, two hundred small motors for two hundred refrigerators of a special kind. The selection of the grand piano or of two hundred small motors—examples of a one-time purchase—will be based on the manufacturer's reputation, along with previous experience with him.

Necessity for mutual confidence and aid between purchaser and vendor. What one company buys from another is not just material: it buys something far more important, namely, engineering and capability. These requirements of a supplier must be established long before he produces any material. The customer that waits for delivery of material to learn what he has bought will take what he gets.

Components, small and large, change rapidly in some industries, for example, in communication, switching, and transmission of voice and of data. The component gives problems, or it does well, only to be succeeded by something else in six months.

The big problem is engineering design of subassemblies and assemblies. Engineering changes are costly, and are in some cases impossible. This is true for any product.

Some individual parts may nevertheless be nearly the same over a long stretch of time. They may come in by the thousand. Constant improvement of their incoming quality is possible, along with reduction in price, if vendor and purchaser work together.

Once again, the quality of parts is built in before they leave the vendor's door.

> Traditional: Engineers formulate the design of a part or subassembly.
>
> Purchasing people let contracts for the parts.
>
> Some of the contracts went to the company's own allies, other contracts went to outside vendors. Difficulties in manufacture and faults in assemblies led to many engineering changes. Engineering changes led to increases in cost, and have been, by tradition, a way of life.
>
> Today: *Example 1*
>
> Teams composed of experts from the supplier chosen for this material (part or component); plus your own design engineer, process engineer,

> manufacturing, sales, or any other knowledge that is needed
>
> Long lead time, enough to do the job right
>
> Result: Better and better quality as time goes on, with lower and lower costs
>
> *Example 2.* A team for development of paper for facsimile printing
>
> The chosen manufacturer of the paper
>> His chemist
>>
>> His buyer of raw materials (wood pulp, chalk, aluminum oxide, titanium oxide, other)
>>
>> His manager of production
>
> Customer
>> His senior scientist, in charge of research and development
>>
>> His chemist
>>
>> His manager of production
>>
>> His manager of marketing

The following paragraphs may indicate that in Japan a steady dependable source, responsive to needs, on a long-term arrangement, is more important than price.

A final point made by American firms is that the large markups generated by Japan's multilayered distribution system often eliminate whatever price advantages imports have at dockside.

The Japanese respond that problems can be better understood as an extension of the long-standing customer–supplier relationship in Japan. Buyers expect suppliers to be a reliable source of merchandise, to understand their needs and respond quickly to them, and to offer reliable after-sales service. The relationship depends heavily on these factors, to the exclusion of such economic considerations as lowest cost in the quality range required. Thus, although a firm customer–supplier relationship is not intended to shut out competitive foreign firms, working within the system can be frustrating. (Japan Economic Institute, *Japan's Import Barriers: Analysis of Divergent Bilateral Views*, Washington, 1982.)

Japanese management learned in 1950, with the flow diagram of Fig. 1 (p. 4) on the blackboard, that the best solution to improvement of incoming materials is to make a partner of every vendor, and to work together with him on a long-term relationship of loyalty and trust.

Dialogue between customer and producer. (Robert Brown, Nashua Corporation, 1985.)

This is what I can do for you.
Here is what you might do for me.

American companies find it difficult to understand that price is of little consideration in an attempt to open up negotiations with Japanese firms. More important than price in the Japanese way of doing business is continual improvement of quality, which can be achieved only on a long-term relationship of loyalty and trust, foreign to the American way of doing business.

A supplier has a duty to himself and to his customer to insist that he be the sole supplier. The sole supplier needs the whole attention of his customer, not divided attention (Mary Ann Gould, President of Janbridge, Inc., Philadelphia).

Cost-plus. There is a bear trap in the purchase of goods and services on the basis of price tag that people don't talk about. To run the game of cost-plus in industry, a supplier offers a bid so low that he is almost sure to get the business. He gets it. The customer discovers that an engineering change is vital. The supplier is extremely obliging, but "regrets," he discovers, that this change will double the cost of the items. It is too late for the customer to try to make other arrangements. Production is under way and must be continued without interruption. The vendor comes out ahead.

Excerpts from a Report[4]
Japanese Automotive Stamping
Written by a Team, December 1981

A. FACILITIES

1. *Plant and equipment.* . . . . Stamping presses are conventional in design. They are densely spaced, served by more complete transfer and handling systems (often mechanized), and exhibit few special features, except capability for quick change of die.

2. *Extraordinary housekeeping.* The extreme cleanliness in every area of the plants was a striking feature. Clear aisles, clean equipment, spotless painted concrete floors, employees in clean white or pastel shop uniforms and caps were the rule. Floors were absolutely free of spilled lubricant, rags, hand tools, scrap, slugs, butts and other debris—*everywhere.*

The Japanese strongly believe that an atmosphere of cleanliness adds to quality.

B. PRODUCTION OPERATIONS
⋮

2. *Minimum inventory and storage.* The widely publicized just-in-time delivery system (known as the Kanban plan at Toyota, and by other names elsewhere) was observed universally. Shipments of stampings, subassemblies and assemblies are made directly to the auto assembly line several times a day. Side-loading

---

4 I am indebted to Mr. Ralph E. Stinson, president of the Bettcher Manufacturing Corporation, for a copy of this report.

trucks drive into the assembly plant and containers of parts are dropped off at the appropriate work-station on the line without incoming inspection and counting. Parts are assembled into the automobiles, as received. The virtual absence of inventory results in an estimated space saving of 30 per cent as compared with comparable U.S. auto operations.

The same low-inventory philosophy is followed at the contract stamping plants. Coil and strip stock is received several times a week from steel suppliers. Relatively little plant area is devoted to storage, and inventory is typically turned over in less than a week.

3. *Quick changes of dies.* Dies are typically changed three to five times a shift in even the largest presses. Dedication to quick change reaches almost unbelievable proportions. Extraordinarily rapid die changes are made possible by use of standardized die sets, standardized bolster plates and adaptor plates, standardized press shut heights, frequent use of rolling bolsters, and mechanical handling equipment.

⋮

During changes of die even the largest presses are rarely out of service for more than 12–15 minutes. As an example, a line of 5 presses, including one 500-ton press, was converted to produce a completely different part in the remarkable time of just $2\frac{1}{2}$ minutes.

4. *High utilization of equipment.* Relatively high rates of utilization—estimated at 90 to 95 per cent—are the rule. Observations covering nearly 1,000 presses revealed very few idle or standby presses, no presses disassembled for repair, and no die repairing in the press. There was strong evidence of effective preventive maintenance.

5. *No wasteful lubrication.* Stock is lubricated only to the absolute minimum extent necessary for successful production. Spot

lubrication is widely practiced, and use of pre-lubricated material (wax or oil base) is common. Resultingly, little lubricant is wasted, part cleaning requirements are reduced, and lubricant is not splattered on equipment, employees or the floor.

6. *Health and safety.* Rules for eye protection were strictly observed and hard hats were common. Other protective clothing included heavy aprons in spot welding and die making areas.

In general, machine guarding involved relatively few barrier guards, but use of presence sensing devices was widespread. No pull-back devices were seen. It was noted that die setting practices commonly require little inching or jogging of the press. No ram props were seen.

7. *Hours of operation.* Typically the plants operated two 8-hour shifts, with the shifts separated by 4-hour intervals during which preventive maintenance, housekeeping and major die repairs were accomplished. During periods of increased production the workday consists of two 10-hour shifts separated by intervals of 2 hours.

8. *Production and quality control.* Stamping equipment is operated at normal rates of speed, but because press downtime is held to remarkably low levels, the output per man-hour is much higher than in the U.S. Emphasis on mechanization and widespread use of simple transfer devices further contribute to productivity.

Quality control is an obsession. Equipment operators share direct responsibility for the quality of their production. Scrap rates and rejects are regularly held to near 1 per cent, and are often lower.

C.   WORK FORCE

1. *Training.* In general, plant employees were clearly better trained, more widely skilled, and more flexible in their job assignments than their U.S. counterparts. Machine operators regularly

make minor repairs, perform maintenance work, record machine performance data, and check parts for quality.

Companies obviously regard their employees as their most significant competitive asset and provide good general orientation as well as training in specific skills which far exceed normal practice in the U.S.

2. *Employee involvement.* Production workers regularly participate in operating decisions, including planning, goal setting, and monitoring of performance. They are encouraged to make suggestions and take a relatively high degree of responsibility for overall performance.

The well-known "Quality Circle" concept, involving small teams of 5–15 employees, was widely observed. A positive team spirit, along with intense loyalty and high motivation, are further enhanced by effective management communication. Visual communications in the plant—posters, signs, graphs—were extremely numerous.

Company unions are the rule, instead of industry-wide unions, and it is clearly understood that the interests of the union are tied to the success of the company. Work practices, therefore, seem less restrictive and appear to enhance personal productivity.

D. CUSTOMER RELATIONSHIPS

1. *Make or buy?* According to our hosts, the Japanese auto manufacturer buys 70–80 per cent, by dollar volume, of his stamping requirements from contract metal stampers, and makes 20–30 per cent of his requirements. The reverse is true in the U.S.

Japanese auto makers apparently assume that quality, delivery, inventories, and related costs can be better governed by the purchasing department in a buy situation, than by making it yourself.

2. *"Arms around" relationship.* Auto makers and their vendors

have an extremely close "arms around" rather than "arm's length" relationship in which control by the customer is the key concept. In some cases the auto maker insists that the contract stamper supply him exclusively. This tends to concentrate production in relatively few, long-term suppliers, and builds a type of captive relationship in which the favored suppliers become so-called "business associates."

This close-knit, dependent relationship between customer and supplier presumably provides the supplier with ample rewards for achievement. The penalty for failure, however, is devastating.

Production contracts are usually long-term (as long as six years), and may include requirements for product design and testing. They invariably contain demanding expectations. The expectations include: (1) exceptional quality requirements; (2) reliable just-in-time delivery; (3) exact quantities—no over- or under-runs; and (4) continuously improving productivity resulting in long-term cost reductions.

Steel prices are generally firm for an entire year.

E. IMPLICATIONS

It was repeatedly observed that the positive working relationships between steel suppliers, contract stampers, unions, and auto manufacturers reinforce productivity rather than interfere with it, as is often the case in the more adversarial relationship existing between these groups in the U.S. There is a common, unified dedication to competitive excellence throughout the Japanese industrial structure which is largely absent here.

This dedication extends from the top executive of the largest company to the lowest employees of the smallest company and directs all their efforts toward a common goal. Thus they are driven to minimize waste in every form: (1) human, physical and financial resources; and (2) time.

They capitalize on their principal competitive resource—

people—and train, motivate, and manage them with particular effectiveness.

5. Improve constantly and forever the system of production and service. A theme that appears over and over in this book is that quality must be built in at the design stage. It may be too late, once plans are on their way. Every product should be regarded as one of a kind; there is only one chance for optimum success. Teamwork in design, as illustrated on page 41, is fundamental. There must be continual improvement in test methods (p. 142), and ever better understanding of the customer's needs and of the way he uses and misuses a product.

We repeat here from page 5 that the quality desired starts with the intent, which is fixed by management. The intent must be translated into plans, specifications, tests, in an attempt to deliver to the customer the quality intended, all of which are management's responsibility.

Downstream, there will be continual reduction of waste and continual improvement of quality in every activity of procurement, transportation, engineering, methods, maintenance, locations of activities, sales, methods of distribution, supervision, retraining, accounting, payroll, service to customers. With continual improvement, the distributions of the chief quality-characteristics of parts, materials, and service become so narrow that specifications are lost beyond the horizon.

> We in America have worried about specifications: meet the specifications. In contrast, the Japanese have worried about uniformity, working for less and less variation about the nominal value—e.g., diameter 1 cm. (Contributed by John Betti, Ford Motor Company.)

This statement is in accord with a formal model introduced by

G. Taguchi years ago, which leads to lower and lower costs as quality is improved.[5] (Continued on p. 139.)

Mere allocation of huge sums of money for quality will not bring quality. There is no substitute for knowledge. But the prospect of use of knowledge brings fear (Point 8, p. 59).

The management of a company, seized with determination to change, will continue to try to master the meaning of the 14 points and to understand and eradicate the deadly diseases and obstacles of Chapter 3. (Continued in Point 14, p. 86.)

Everyone might well ask himself every day what he has done this day to advance his learning and skill on this job, and how he has advanced his education for greater satisfaction in life.

Is every job in a job shop done better than the one before? Is there continual improvement in methods to understand better each new customer's needs? Is there continual improvement of materials, of selection of new employees, of the skills of people at work on the job, and of repeated operations?

> *Overheard with Dr. Nelson.*
>
> *Manager of a job shop.* We make only about twenty-five at a time. How can we use quality control?
>
> *Dr. Nelson.* You are thinking the wrong way. You are thinking about measuring waste and productivity at the end. It is better to work on the processes, and on equipment and on materials and components that go into your product, and on your procedures for testing these components before they go into the final product. Also—most important—your tests of the final

---

5 See G. Taguchi and Yu-In Wu, *Off-Line Quality Control* (Central Japan, 4-10–27 Meieki Nakamura-ku, Nagoya, 1979); G. Taguchi, *On-Line Quality Control during Production* (Japanese Standards Association, 1-24 Akasaka 4-chome, Minato-ku, Tokyo, 1981). See also Peter T. Jessup (Ford Motor Company), "The value of improved performance," paper delivered at a meeting of the Automotive Division, American Society for Quality Control, Detroit, 4 November 1983.

product: Are these tests in statistical control? If not, they will mislead you.

Every hotel just completed (building and furnishings) should be better than the last one just completed, better than one completed a year ago, and better than one completed two years ago. Is it? Why not? Why repeat over and over the same mistakes? Why are old hotels preferred to new ones?

Does a company engaged in construction, as of hotels, hospitals, office buildings, apartment houses, show continual improvement in planning and in operation? (Continued on pp. 95 and 96 and in Ch. 7.)

Do rate clerks in a trucking company or in a railway improve year by year? (More on p. 195.)

Never-ending improvement in manufacturing means continual work with vendors and eventual reduction to one vendor and one shipping point for any one item (Point 4).

Improvement of the process includes better allocation of human effort. It includes selection of people, their placement, their training, to give everyone, including production workers, a chance to advance their learning and to contribute the best of their talents. It means removal of barriers to pride of workmanship both for production workers and for management and engineers (Point 12).

Putting out fires is not improvement of the process. Neither is discovery and removal of a special cause detected by a point out of control. This only puts the process back to where it should have been in the first place (an insight of Dr. Joseph M. Juran, years ago).

Improvement of a process may require study of records to learn more about the effects of changes in temperature, pressure, speed, change of material. Engineers and chemists, aiming to improve the process, may introduce changes and observe the effects.

The cause of a fault that appears periodically or seems to be associated with some recurring event is usually easy to trace. Periodic appearance of any characteristic should be traced.

Adjustment of a process that is in statistical control, initiated on appearance of a faulty item or a mistake, as if it arose from an obvious immediate cause, will only create more trouble, not less (a theorem due to Lloyd S. Nelson; see p. 20; also p. 110). Specifications limits are not action limits (see Ch. 11).

The great advantage of the Kanban system (delivery just in time) is the discipline behind it—processes in control; quality, quantity, and regularity predictable.

6. Institute training. Training must be totally reconstructed. Management needs training to learn about the company, all the way from incoming material to customer. A central problem is need for appreciation of variation.

Management must understand and act on the problems that rob the production worker of the possibility of carrying out his work with satisfaction (Point 12a).

Japanese management has by nature important advantages over management in America. A man in Japanese management starts his career with a long internship (4 to 12 years) on the factory floor and in other duties in the company. He knows the problems of production. He works in procurement, accounting, distribution, sales.

People learn in different ways. Some have difficulty to learn by written instructions (dyslexia). Others have difficulty to learn by the spoken word (dysphasia). Some people learn best by pictures; others by imitation; some by a combination of methods.

> How many men have been cashiered out of the army in disgrace for alleged disobedience of (verbal) instruction, when they could not understand the spoken word?

Production worker (recorded): They give you no instruction.

What they do is to set you down at a machine and tell you to go to work.

There is nobody to teach you?

My colleagues help me, but they have their own work to do.

Don't you have a foreman?

He knows nothing.

Isn't his job to help you to learn yours?

If you need help, you don't go to somebody that looks dumber than you are, do you? He wears a necktie, but he doesn't know anything.

But the necktie helps, doesn't it?

No.

A big problem in training and in leadership in the United States arises from a flexible standard of what is acceptable work and what is not. The standard is too often dependent on whether the foreman is in difficulty to meet his daily quota in terms of numbers.

The greatest waste in America is failure to use the abilities of people. One need only listen to a tape of a meeting with production workers to learn about their frustrations and about the contribution that they are eager to make (pp. 79–81). Anyone would be impressed to observe how articulate most production workers are, in spite of criticisms of our schools.

Money and time spent for training will be ineffective unless inhibitors to good work are removed (Point 12). Training for a job must teach the customer's needs; see Point 14, page 86. (Contributed by William W. Scherkenbach.)

It should be noted further in connexion with Points 6 and 13 that money spent on training, retraining, and education does not show on the balance sheet; it does not increase the tangible net worth of a company. In contrast, money spent for equipment is on the balance sheet, and increases the present net worth of the company. (Contributed by Brian L. Joiner.)

Note. There is an important distinction between

Points 6 and 13. Point 6 refers to the foundations of training for the management and for new employees. Point 13 refers to continual education and improvement of everyone on the job—self-improvement.

7. Adopt and institute leadership. The job of management is not supervision, but leadership. Management must work on sources of improvement, the intent of quality of product and of service, and on the translation of the intent into design and actual product. The required transformation of Western style of management requires that managers be leaders. Focus on outcome (management by numbers, MBO, work standards, meet specifications, zero defects, appraisal of performance) must be abolished, leadership put in place. Some suggestions follow.

a. Remove barriers that make it impossible for the hourly worker to do his job with pride of workmanship (Point 12).

b. Leaders must know the work that they supervise. They must be empowered and directed to inform upper management concerning conditions that need correction (inherited defects, machines not maintained, poor tools, fuzzy definitions of acceptable workmanship, emphasis on numbers and not on quality). Management must act on the corrections proposed. In most organizations, this idea is only an idle dream, as the supervisor knows nothing about the job.

c. A further common fallacy of leadership may be illustrated here, an example related to me by my friend David S. Chambers. A supervisor held out for examination and discussion the defective items that her seven people made during the day. She would spend the last half-hour of the day with her seven people for examination and scrutiny, with great patience and compassion, of every defective item produced that day. Her seven people thought that she was a great supervisor, and so did everyone else.

The fact is that the system was stable.

What was wrong? The seven people did not make the mistakes; the system did. They were treating every fault and every blemish as a special cause, not working on improvement of the system. They were applying Rule 2 or Rule 3 with the funnel (p. 328), making things worse, not better, and guaranteeing forever this elevated level of trouble. We shall see more examples of this same fault—people only doing their best. How could they know? Clarification will come in Chapters 8 and 11.

d. The manager of a plant assembles every morning his 30 supervisors to recount with German thoroughness all that went wrong the day before. He was making the same mistake, treating every fault and every blemish as a special cause, to be tracked down and removed. As it turned out, most of his systems were stable. He was thus making things worse, and guaranteeing forever this elevated level of trouble. How could he know?

e. There was a time, years ago, when a foreman selected his people, trained them, helped them, worked with them. He knew the job. Today, 19 foremen out of 20 were never on the job that they supervise. They have no part in the selection of their people. They can not train them nor help them, as the job is as new to the foreman as it is to his people. He can count. Hence, his job gravitates to numbers, quotas, get out so many pieces today, so many for the month. At the end of the month, everything counts, ship it no matter what. Some foremen try to learn something about their work, and this effort helps to soften the adversarial relationship between production worker and supervisor. Most do not gain the confidence of the people that they supervise because they can only be concerned about numbers, unable to help the production worker improve his work. (Contributed by James K. Bakken, Ford Motor Company.)

f. Supervision on the factory floor is, I fear, in many companies, an entry position for college boys and girls to learn about the company, six months here, six months there. They are smart enough, and some of them do indeed try to learn the work, but how can anyone learn it in six months? It is easy to understand an hourly worker who stated that if he goes to his foreman with a problem, he (the foreman) just smiles and walks away. He does not understand the problem, and could get nothing done about it if he did.

g. Much supervision could be described as supervision by ordinal numerics and percentages. Examples of fallacies:

> Anybody whose production is below average is causing loss.
> Anybody whose average proportion defective is above average is causing loss.
> Everyone should come up to the average.

Some leaders forget an important mathematical theorem that if 20 people are engaged on a job, 2 will fall at the bottom 10 per cent, no matter what. It is difficult to overthrow the law of gravitation and laws of nature. The important problem is not the bottom 10 per cent, but who is statistically out of line and in need of help (Ch. 3).

Examples from everyday life. Half of our presidents have been above average (from the *San Diego Union*, 21 February 1983, p. C-2):

Historians Rate America's
Leaders Past and Present
By Bob Dvorchak

"In general, we have been blessed with above-average leadership," said Robert K. Murray, who is tabulating the responses of 970 historians questioned in the survey.

"We've been remarkably lucky, considering the relatively haphazard way we select a president. Historians have determined that almost one out of every four has been great or near great, and over half are above average," said the professor of history at Pennsylvania State University.

Note. Greatness is achieved by a place in the top 25 per cent.

One may ponder over the meaning of a report ascribed to the Nuclear Regulatory Commission (*Wall Street Journal*, 14 September 1981; brought to my attention by Robert E. Lewis, writing in the *New York Statistician*, May–June 1982):

NRC Study Rates 15 Nuclear Plants 'Below Average'
By a WALL STREET JOURNAL STAFF REPORTER

WASHINGTON—Nuclear reactors at 15 of the nation's 50 power plant sites have failed on a Nuclear Regulatory Commission "report card" and will get closer attention from federal inspectors.

The NRC staff, based on studies concluded at the end of last year, found the 15 power plants "below average" in overall performance, including maintenance, radiation and fire protection and management control.

An NRC spokesman said, " . . . the
purpose of the study was to make sure
we focus our inspections on plants
showing below-average performance."

"Below average" in the report of the Nuclear Regulatory Commission[6] apparently means unsatisfactory, the definition of which is not clear. Apparently the NRC had not the benefit of the methods set forth in Chapters 3 and 11 for decision on which installations are out of line. Nor did they propose constant improvement of all installations.

The aim of a system of supervision of nuclear power plants or of anything else should be to improve all plants. No matter how successful this supervision, there will always be plants below average. Specific remedial action would be indicated only for a plant that turned out, by statistical tests, to be an outlier.

Another example (reported to the author by a manager of marketing). An automotive company has three dealers in Dayton. One of them is below the average of the three (no fooling). His performance is obviously inferior. Something must be done. Perhaps we ought to urge him to sell his business so that we may get a replacement.

Examples of suggestions for ways to improve leadership appear throughout the book.

Still another. (From the *Wisconsin State Journal*, 11 March 1983, contributed by Brian L. Joiner.)

Half still under median
Despite the increase, union officials
said, more than half the league's

6 U.S. Nuclear Regulatory Commission, *Systematic Assessment of Licensee Performance*, NUREG-0834, Washington, 20 October 1981.

players earned less than the league-
wide median of $75,000 a year.

Next step, bring the lower half up to the median. Or at least reduce to half the proportion below the median.

And another. My friend Heero Hacquebord of Pretoria told
me that the teacher at the school that his little girl entered gave
two examinations and called father to report that his little girl
was below average in both of them. He told the teacher that
failure of eight consecutive examinations would be cause for concern, but hardly two. One must nevertheless appreciate the good
intentions of the teacher.

The educational system in a country that I recently worked in
puts children of age 15 through examinations, and by design
passes 50 per cent of them. Advertisements for help specify
"School certificate required." The system of grading thus brands
as failures for life half of the children.

Guests in some hotels are informed that the maid is responsible for all the towels and sheets in the room. In other words, the
maid is held liable for what somebody else may elect to carry
away. Is this a good way for the management to build up loyalty
and trust with the employees?

8. Drive out fear.[7] No one can put in his best performance unless he feels secure. *Se* comes from the Latin, meaning without,
cure means fear or care. *Secure* means without fear, not afraid to
express ideas, not afraid to ask questions. Fear takes on many
faces. A common denominator of fear in any form, anywhere, is
loss from impaired performance and padded figures (p. 264).

There is widespread resistance of knowledge. Advances of the

---

7 I am indebted to William J. Latzko for pointing out to me long ago the
prevalence of fear and the economic losses therefrom.

kind needed in Western industry require knowledge, yet people are afraid of knowledge. Pride may play a part in resistance to knowledge. New knowledge brought into the company might disclose some of our failings. A better outlook is of course to embrace new knowledge because it might help us to do a better job.

Some people may wonder whether at this stage of life they can learn something new. If there were a change, where would I be?

New knowledge would cost money. Would we get our money back? When?

New business, for export or for the domestic market, comes from fundamental research, followed by development of new levels of quality and of new product. Fundamental research, to be effective, requires infusion of knowledge. It is interesting to note that 83 per cent of funds for fundamental research in the United States come from government sources, the rest from private industry. The percentages are the reverse in Japan.

Some actual expressions of fear follow.

I am afraid that I may lose my job because the company will go out of business.

I have a feeling that Dave (higher up) may move to another company. If he does, what will happen to me?

I could do my job better if I understood what happens next.

I am afraid to put forth an idea. I'd be guilty of treason if I did.

I am afraid that my next annual rating may not recommend me for a raise.

If I did what is best for the company, long term, I'd have to shut down production for a while for repairs and overhaul. My daily report on production would take a nosedive, and I'd be out of a job.

I am afraid that I may not always have an answer when my boss asks something.

I am afraid to contribute my best efforts to a partner or to a team, because someone else, because of my contribution, may get a higher rating than I get.

I am afraid to admit a mistake.

My boss believes in fear. How can he manage his people if they don't hold him in awe? Management is punitive.

The system that I work in will not permit me to expand my ability.

I'd like to understand better the reasons for some of the company's procedures, but I don't dare to ask about them.

We mistrust the management. We can't believe their answers when we ask why we do it this way. The management have a reason, but tell us something else.

I may not make my quota today (hourly worker or plant manager).

I do not have time to take a careful look at my work. I must turn this job out, and start on another one (engineer).

More on fear. Another loss from fear is inability to serve the best interests of the company through necessity to satisfy specified rules, or the necessity to satisfy, at all costs, a quota of production.

An example appears in Chapter 8 (p. 268), where the foreman dared not halt production for repairs. He knew what was best for the company, but he could only push ahead on his quota of castings for the day, at the risk of breakdown. Sure enough, the bearing froze. He not only failed to put out his quota; worse, the whole line went down for four days for repairs. Other examples appear in Chapter 8.

A department had failed miserably for months to produce enough items for the market. The general manager appointed a task force (one man) to discover what was wrong. What he found was inspectors overpowered with fear. They had taken the idea into their heads that if the customer found an item to be faulty, the inspector that passed the item would lose his job. As a consequence, the inspectors held up almost the total output. They were incorrect about the consequences of passing a faulty item, but it is rumor that runs an organization. (Contributed by J. J. Keating of Richland, Washington.)

Some managers say that a certain amount of fear is necessary to get the work done.

The production workers did not wish a mistake of a continuing nature to be discovered. They were hiding it, afraid that management would find it out.

Fear amongst salaried workers may be attributed in large part to the annual rating of performance (see Ch. 3).

Wrong way to manage. A manager looks at a report of complaints by category. His eye falls on the highest figure on the paper; takes the telephone to wade in on the poor devil that is responsible for that category. This is another form of management by fear, and of management by numbers. Management's first step should be to discover by calculation, not by judgment, whether this category is out of control with respect to the others. If yes, then this category requires his special attention and help. He must also work on the system to reduce all complaints. (Contributed by William W. Scherkenbach.)

9. Break down barriers between staff areas. People in research, design, purchase of materials, sales, and receipt of incoming materials must learn about the problems encountered with various materials and specifications in production and assembly. Otherwise, there will be losses in production from necessity for rework caused by attempts to use materials unsuited to the purpose. Everyone in engineering design, purchase of materials, testing materials, and testing performance of a product has a customer, namely, the man (e.g., a plant manager) that must try to make, with the material purchased, the thing that was designed. Why not get acquainted with the customer? Why not spend time in the factory, see the problems, and hear about them?

A new president came in, talked with the heads of sales, design, manufacturing, consumer research, and so forth. Everybody was doing a superb job, and had been doing so for years.

Nobody had any problems. Yet somehow or other the company was going down the tube. Why? The answer was simple. Each staff area was suboptimizing its own work, but not working as a team for the company. It was the new president's job to coordinate the talents of these men for the good of the company.

Servicemen learn from customers a great deal about their products. There may unfortunately be in some companies no routine procedure for use of this information. In one instance, the service department, in response to frantic calls from customers, had routinely cut off a tube that conveys abrasive material to a downward outlet, and reversed the auger beyond the outlet. The problem was that the auger jammed the material into the end of the tube. The manufacturing department kept right on making the auger as always before, while the service department, on a call from a customer, routinely made the correction. The management were unaware of the lack of teamwork between manufacturing and service, and of the loss. (Contributed by Kate McKeown.)

People in design worked with people in sales and with engineers to design a new style. Salesmen, showing prototypes to wholesalers, piled up orders. The outlook was bright until the bad news came—the factory could not make the item economically. Small changes in style and specifications turned out to be necessary for economic production. These changes caused delay in the factory. Moreover, the salesman had to explain the changes to the wholesalers that had signed up for the product. The result was loss of time and loss of sales in a changing market. Teamwork with the manufacturing people at the start would have avoided these losses.

Management often complicate the work of the people in design by making last-minute changes in style and engineering, after the plans are submitted and production is ready, leaving to the design and production engineers only a few weeks to do a year's work.

Engineers get blamed perennially for engineering changes. I

Fig. 3. Man running upstairs.

"Do it right the first time." A lofty ring it has. But how could a man make it right the first time when the incoming material is off-gauge, off-color, or otherwise defective, or if his machine is not in good order, or the measuring instruments not trustworthy? This is just another meaningless slogan, a cousin of zero defects.

"Getting better together." Production workers have told me that this slogan makes them furious. Together! What is that when no one will listen to our problems and suggestions? Another useless poster, a cruel joke:

> Be a quality worker.
> Take pride in your work.

What is wrong with posters and exhortations? They are directed at the wrong people. They arise from management's supposition that the production workers could, by putting their backs into the job, accomplish zero defects, improve quality, improve productivity, and all else that is desirable. The charts and posters take no account of the fact that most of the trouble comes from the system. Calculations that indicate what proportion of defects and mistakes and high costs comes from the system (responsibility of management) and how much from the people on the job should be one of the chief tools of management, and certainly of leadership, as explained in Chapter 11.

Exhortations and posters generate frustration and resentment. They advertise to the production worker that the management are unaware of the barriers to pride of workmanship. The quotation on page 397 from Goethe may have wider application than he thought.

The immediate effect of a campaign of posters, exhortations, and pledges may well be some fleeting improvement of quality and productivity, the effect of elimination of some obvious special causes. In time, improvement ceases or even reverses. The campaign is eventually recognized as a hoax. The management needs to learn that the main responsibility is theirs from now on to improve the system, and, of course, to remove any special causes detected by statistical methods. (See p. 322 and Fig. 33 in Ch. 11.)

Stable system of defective items. I saw in the cafeteria of a company the charts in Fig. 4. Great idea. Set goals. Give people something to work toward. These are typical. What do they accomplish? Nothing? *Wrong:* their accomplishment is negative.

This poster exhibits a stable system of output and a stable system of production of defective items (Ch. 11). The management naturally wishes to see higher production and fewer defective items. Their method was to entreat the production workers.

The poster talks to the wrong people. The production workers may not have studied this book, but as they see it, the management are asking them (production workers) to do what they are unable to do. The effect is fear and mistrust of the management.

The improvement in production at the 20th week, perhaps obvious from the chart, arose from installation of two new machines. This increase in production led to a new goal. The new goal will create questions and resentment among production

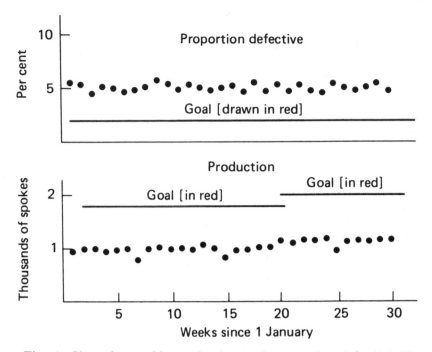

Fig. 4. Chart for weekly production and proportion defective. The goals, set by industrial engineering, are demoralizing and ineffective. The points indicate stability, which means that the responsibility for improvement rests with the management (in this case, the industrial engineers).

workers. Their first thought is that the management is never satisfied. Whatever we do, they ask for more. Here are the fruits of exhortations:

1. Failure to accomplish the goal
2. Increase in variability
3. Increase in proportion defective
4. Increase in costs
5. Demoralization of the work force
6. Disrespect for the management

Posters that explain to everyone on the job what the management is doing month by month to (for example) purchase better quality of incoming materials from fewer suppliers, better maintenance, or to provide better training, or statistical aids and better supervision to improve quality and productivity, not by working harder but by working smarter, would be a totally different story: they would boost morale. People would then understand that the management is taking some responsibility for hangups and defects and is trying to remove obstacles. I have not yet seen any such posters.

An individual will of course have his own goals. A man may set his heart on a college education. He may resolve to study harder to pass a course or an examination. I resolve to finish this chapter before morning: I give myself a deadline. Goals are necessary for you and for me, but numerical goals set for other people, without a road map to reach the goal, have effects opposite to the effects sought.

The company will of course have goals—for example, constancy of purpose and never-ending improvement.

Exhortations may be found in daily bulletins issued by companies. An example follows, from a Navy yard:

> I want to reemphasize that improved quality of work is critical to every one of our jobs. True productivity should translate into increased production of an acceptable professional product. Shoddy work does not improve productivity no matter how quickly [sic] or in what quantity it is completed. We would only discredit ourselves and disserve the public by turning out poor quality work.
>
> The importance of the concept of accountability of individuals, and the power of a pervasive human knowledge among the workers, supervisors, managers and that each individual will be held accountable for his work products can not be overstressed. Audit trails must be maintained that document completed work

and the supervisors responsible for such work. People generally want to do the right thing, but in a large organization they frequently don't really understand what is the right thing. Management must make crystal clear what is expected from each employee and that personal performance is essential to holding a job or to being promoted. When instructions and expectations are made absolutely clear, and follow-up action is taken swiftly where failures occur, compliance will result. Proper managerial conduct will result in a loyal, highly motivated and very capable work force with tremendous surge capability. The managerial ability to pull all of this together in a manner that supports human development is a vital ingredient in our shipyards. We should intensively and analytically evaluate how to handle compliance (holding workmen, supervisors, and managers accountable) and to deal with failure in a manner that will have the highest payoff in improving quality and productivity.

Words like these sound persuasive. Hold people accountable! For what? What is meant by "crystal clear"? What is failure? Whose failure—the employee's failure or the system's failure?

We shall learn in Chapter 9 that the only communicable meaning of any word, specification, instruction, proclamation, or regulation is not what the writer thereof had in mind, but is instead, the result of application. How does the instruction work in practice? What happens?

11a. Eliminate numerical quotas for the work force. Numerical quotas for hourly workers are sometimes known as measured day work; also as rates, or as work standards. Naturally, the comptroller (or accountant) needs to have in hand prediction of costs. Industrial engineers try to estimate this cost. This cost then becomes a standard cost, a work standard, a rate, a quota.

Rates for production are often set to accommodate the average worker. Naturally, half of them are above average, and half below. What happens is that peer pressure holds the upper half to the rate, no more. The people below the average can not make the rate. The result is loss, chaos, dissatisfaction, and turnover. Some rates are set for the achiever, which is even worse.

A quota is a fortress against improvement of quality and productivity. I have yet to see a quota that includes any trace of a system by which to help anyone to do a better job. A quota is totally incompatible with never-ending improvement. There are better ways.

The intent of application of a work standard is noble: predict costs; establish a ceiling on costs. The actual effect is to double the cost of the operation and to stifle pride of workmanship. There are more engineers engaged in construction of work standards, and people counting production, than there are people engaged in actual production.

One will see any day in hundreds of factories, men and women standing around the last hour or two of the day, waiting for the whistle to blow. They have completed their quotas for the day; they may do no more work, and they can not go home. Is this good for the competitive position of American industry? These people are unhappy doing nothing. They would rather work.

A bank that I worked with had just engaged a consulting firm to set work standards. The consulting firm came up with figures on the number of customers that a teller ought to handle in an hour, the number of computations of interest and penalty that someone ought to compute in an hour, and a figure for every other activity, but not a word about quality of workmanship, and not a suggestion for improvement.

One of my students told the class that he worked in a bank in which everybody made note of every action—a telephone call, a calculation, use of a computer, waiting on a customer, etc. There was a standard time for every act, and everybody was rated every day. Some days this man would make a score of 50, next day 260, etc. Everybody was ranked on his score, the lower the score, the higher the rank. Morale was understandably low.

"My rate is 155 pieces per day. I can't come near this figure—and we all have the problem—without turning out a lot of defective items." She must bury her pride of workmanship to make her quota, or lose pay and maybe also her job. It could well be that with intelligent supervision and help, and with no inherited defects, this operator could produce in a day and with less effort many more good items than her stated rate.

Some people in management claim that they have a better plan: dock her for a defective item. This sounds great. Make it clear that this is not the place for mistakes and defective items. Actually, this may be cruel supervision. Who declares an item to be defective? Is it clear to the worker and to the inspector—both of them—what constitutes a defective item? Would it have been declared defective yesterday? Who made the defective item? The worker, or the system? Where is the evidence? (Cf. Ch. 11.)

Piece work is more devastating than work standards. Incentive pay is piece work. The hourly worker on piece work soon learns that she gets paid for making defective items and scrap—the more defectives she turns out, the higher her pay for the day. Where is her pride of workmanship?

There is no piece work in factories in Japan.

Work standards, rates, incentive pay, and piece work are manifestations of inability to understand and provide appropriate supervision. The loss must be appalling. Bonus for extra achievement backfires and burns out.

Management that is interested in raising dividends will take immediate, decisive steps to eliminate work standards, rates, and piece work, to put in their place intelligent supervision, following principles and examples in this book. They will remove the barriers that stand between the production worker and his pride of workmanship (Point 12).

A woman in my class at the Graduate School of Business Administration of New York University described her job with an airline, which was to answer the telephone, to make reservations, and to give information. She must make 25 calls per hour. She must be courteous, don't rush callers. She is continually plagued by obstacles: (a) the computer is slow in delivery of information that she asks for; (b) it sometimes reports no information, whereupon she is forced to use directories and guides. Christine, what is your job? Is it:

To make 25 calls per hour?

or

To give callers courteous satisfaction; no brushoff?

It can not be both. How can she take pride in her work when she does not know what her job is? Yet the accountant must have in advance a figure for his budget.

Here are suggestions on the outline of a possible plan by which to improve economy and service. Pride of workmanship would follow naturally, as everyone would have a part in the improvement.

These suggestions are only preliminary. A statistician on the job will of course modify and revise them to suit his own inclinations and local conditions.

1. Give to the accountant a figure for his budget, to be revised.

2. Make it clear to every one of the 500 people on this job that the aim is to give satisfaction to the customer, to take pride in her work.

3. Everybody will keep a record of calls made. The record would show the time of day when a call comes, and the time finished; also for each call the delay in seconds for any display of information requested, and the number of seconds spent on manual methods to acquire information. A dozen code-keys could record the type of enquiry. Most of this record can be automatic.

4. Each worker will turn over to the supervisor a customer

that has a special problem, out of the ordinary, not a regular part of the job. For example, a customer wishes to travel to Buffalo (no problem), but then wishes, after a few days, to go on to London from Toronto via Canadian Pacific Air. The customer needs information on departure and fares from Toronto to London; also on departures from Buffalo to Toronto.

5. At the end of a week, draw a sample of 100 stations. Plot the distribution. There may be information in a run chart plotted point by point against age of incumbent, or length of service, or by some other characteristic.

6. Repeat Steps 2, 3, 4, 5 for several more weeks, a new sample each week.

7. Study the results. Compare weeks. Compare people. What patterns emerge?

8. Establish a continuing study following the above steps, but on a reduced basis.

There will be a distribution of performance. Half the operators will be above average, half below. Study of the results would provide continuing improvement of quality and service. The record would provide data for charts and calculations that would indicate which people if any are outside the system with respect to (e.g.) number of calls referred to the supervisor, number of calls completed per hour on any code, hence in need of special help or attention of the leader (Chs. 3, 8, 11).

In the end, the accountant will have year by year a reasonable figure for prediction of costs (the budget). Every operator will know that her job is to give service, not to meet a quota, yet she will know that she is rendering service at minimum reasonable cost. Everyone will have a part in improvement of service and reduction of cost. This is the best kind of quality of work life.

The above suggestions can be modified and applied in any activity, in any kind of industry, governmental included.

For example, an official of the postal service was continually annoyed because the people that sort mail make so many mistakes. How do you pay them? I asked. "Sort 15,000 pieces of mail per day. That is his job." The source of his problem is obvious. With this method of payment, there will never be improvement in sorting mail, nor will costs of sorting mail decrease. Suggestions parallel to those just made for the airline would continually reduce mistakes in sorting mail, would improve productivity, and give to the sorters some basis for pride of workmanship.

The job of management is to replace work standards by knowledgeable and intelligent leadership. Leaders must have some understanding of the job, and of the principles expounded in Chapters 8 and 11. Wherever work standards have been thrown out and replaced by leadership, quality and productivity have gone up substantially, and people are happier on the job.

11b. Eliminate numerical goals for people in management. Internal goals set in the management of a company, without a method, are a burlesque. Examples: (1) Decrease costs of warranty by 10 per cent next year; (2) Increase sales by 10 per cent; (3) Improve productivity by 3 per cent next year. A natural fluctuation in the right direction (usually plotted from inaccurate data) is interpreted as success. A fluctuation in the opposite direction sends everyone scurrying for explanations and into bold forays whose only achievements are more frustration and more problems.

For example, the manager of a purchasing department declared that his people are going to increase productivity 3 per cent next year, by which they meant to increase by 3 per cent the average number of purchase orders accomplished per man-year. When I enquired about methods, they admitted that they had no plan. As Lloyd S. Nelson said (p. 20): "If they can do it next year with no plan, why didn't they do it last year?" They must have been goofing off. And if one can accomplish improvement of 3 per cent with no plan, why not 6 per cent? Moreover, it was numbers only; no plan for all-out effort to minimize total cost.

A man in the Postal Service told me that his organization intends to improve productivity 3 per cent next year. Enquiry about the plan or method for this accomplishment brought forth the usual answer: no plan—they were simply going to improve.

If you have a stable system, then there is no use to specify a goal. You will get whatever the system will deliver. A goal beyond the capability of the system will not be reached.

If you have not a stable system, then there is again no point in setting a goal. There is no way to know what the system will produce: it has no capability. Study of Chapter 11 will help here. (Contributed by Edward M. Baker, Ford Motor Company.)

To manage, one must lead. To lead, one must understand the work that he and his people are responsible for. Who is the customer (the next stage), and how can we serve better the customer? An incoming manager, to lead, and to manage at the source of improvement, must learn. He must learn from his people what they are doing and must learn a lot of new subject matter. It is easier for an incoming manager to short-circuit his need for learning and his responsibilities, and instead to focus on the far end, to manage the outcome—get reports on quality, on failures, proportion defective, inventory, sales, people. Focus on outcome is not an effective way to improve a process or an activity.

As we have already remarked, management by numerical goal is an attempt to manage without knowledge of what to do, and in fact is usually management by fear.

Anyone may now understand the fallacy of "management by the numbers."

The only number that is permissible for a manager to dangle in front of his people is a plain statement of fact with respect to survival. Examples: (1) Unless our sales improve 10 per cent next year, we shall be out of business. (2) The average level of carbon monoxide in an area, over an 8-hour period, must not exceed 8 parts per million. Reason: 9 or more parts per million has been declared injurious to health.

12. Remove barriers that rob people of pride of workmanship.

These barriers must be removed from two groups of people. One group is management or people on salary. The barrier is the annual rating of performance, or merit rating, to be treated in Chapter 3. The other group is hourly workers, which we proceed into herewith.

The production worker in America is under handicaps that are taking a terrific toll in quality, productivity, and competitive position. Barriers and handicaps rob the hourly worker of his birthright, the right to be proud of his work, the right to do a good job. These barriers exist in almost every plant, factory, company, department store, government office in the United States today.

How can anyone on the factory floor take pride in his work when he is not sure what is acceptable workmanship, and what is not, and can not find out? Right yesterday; wrong today. What is my job?

People whether in management or on the factory floor have become, to management, a commodity. I met with 40 skilled tradesmen in a company that is doing well. Their main complaint was that they do not know till Thursday of any week whether they will work the next week. "We are a commodity," one of them said. That is the word that I had been seeking—commodity. The management may hire them at the price posted, or may not, depending on need. If not needed next week, they go back on the market.

People in management are accustomed to long hours, faced with declining sales, declining quarterly dividends, increases in costs of almost everything. They have plenty to worry about. They can face these problems, but are helpless to face the problems of people. They shrug off problems of people with crab walk and wishful thinking, hoping that the problems will go away. They establish employee involvement, employee participation, quality of work-life, all as smoke screens. All these hopes wither away in a few months where the management is not ready to take action on suggestions.

A production worker told me that instructions for every job where she works are printed and visible, but that nobody ever read them more than halfway through. Anyone by the time she is halfway through is already so confused that she is afraid to go on; she could only be more confused.

How can a production worker take pride in his work when there are problems with inspection—inspectors not sure what is right, instruments and gauges out of order, and the foreman pushed from above to meet a daily quota of numbers, not quality?

How can he, when he must spend time trying to correct or hide defective workmanship or off-gauge material in a previous operation or handling damage?

How can he, when his job is to produce X number of items as a day's work (work standard), good, defective, and scrap, all combined willy-nilly?

How can he, when the machine is out of order, and no one listens to his plea for adjustment?

How can he, when, after stopping his machine to adjust it because it was making only defective product, the foreman comes along and orders him in two words, "Run it." In other words, "Make defective product."

The man (production worker) that told me about this incident described it as failure of communication:

> "Failure of communication?" I asked. "You understood what the foreman said, didn't you?" Reply: "He ordered me to make defectives. Where is my pride of workmanship?"

How can a production worker take pride in her work when she

must spend a substantial fraction of her time changing tools—"soft, low-quality," she explained.

"But the company saves money by buying cheap tools," I remarked. "Yes," she said, "and loses ten times what they save because the tools wear out and use up our time."

"But you get paid for your time; what is the problem?"

"I could turn out much more work were it not for those poor tools."

Some more examples of actual conversations:

Hourly production worker (recorded): The superintendent is afraid to make a decision. If he does nothing, he has nothing to explain to his superiors. No explanation is required of a man in management for doing nothing. How can anything improve if he passes the buck?

What about productivity?

We can't get productivity when the conveyor is not working right, and we have to handle most of the stuff by hand. The stuff is hot and raises blisters if we handle it by hand as fast as it comes out. We have to slow down. We can't get any action from the management.

How long has this been going on?

Seven years.

Another production worker (recorded): A supervisor comes in and is gone in five weeks. Another one comes in. He likewise knows nothing about this job, and has no intention to learn much about it, as he too will move on any day.

Another production worker (recorded): We [sic] had for years a contract for one-and-a-half million linear feet of our product. Our management decided to cut costs, improve profits. They gave us poorer and poorer materials to work with. We lost that business. That loss made a deep cut in our profit margin. We can't produce quality with inferior materials.

Production workers told me about the machine that they were trying to use, bought new two years ago, still a disappointment. Other hourly workers showed me machines badly maintained. The maintenance man had for years cannibalized discarded machines instead of using new parts. Penny wise, pound foolish.

Production worker (recorded): Hoses come in too long, and we have to cut them off.

All the hoses?

All of them for a while, then a batch comes in all right; then too long again.

What difference does it make? You get paid the same.

We get paid the same but we [*sic*] lose money.

Production worker (recorded): You can't build quality by inspection, but when the quality is not there, inspection may be the only answer.

Production worker (recorded): Our work is difficult because so many people are absent. We have to try to do their work, and ours too. We have a hard time to keep up, and the quality suffers.

Why are people absent?

They don't like the work.

Why not?

We can't do good work.

Why can't you do good work?

Too much rush. Anything goes. The foreman must meet his quota. We don't like it that way, so some people stay home.

> *Comment.* Absenteeism is largely a function of supervision. If people feel important to a job, they will come to work.

Production worker (recorded): My machine, programmable logic, is down a lot of the time, and I can't do my work when it is down.

But you get paid for your time, whether you work or not, so what is the problem?

I can't work when the machine is down.

Can't you repair it?

Hardly ever. I repair it when I know how. I send for the technician when I don't. He is a long time coming.

But you get paid for your time. What is the problem?

Money can not pay me for the stress that I endure, waiting for that man to come.

Production worker (recorded): Our foremen are college boys that have studied human relations. They know nothing about the job here. They can not help us.

Production worker (recorded): What good comes of making a suggestion to your foreman? He just smiles and walks away.

> *Comment:* What else could he do? He does not understand the problem, and could get nothing done if he did. A job of foreman is an entry position for college boys and girls.

Production worker (recorded): Our machines run till they burn up; then we lose time. There is insufficient preventive maintenance.

Foreman (recorded): I fill out a report when anything goes wrong. Someone from management, I was told, would come and take a look at the problem. No one has ever come.

Another example. This one occurred in a factory that makes electrical equipment. The most visible and absorbing activity seemed to be inspection. "What proportion of your capital equipment is invested in gauges, instruments, and computers?" I asked.

"About eighty per cent," was the answer, "including printing of reports."

"What proportion of your payroll goes for inspection?"

"Between fifty-five and sixty per cent. We have to be sure of our quality. We have a reputation to maintain."

A memory chip on each finished piece of apparatus held information that could print out the serial number of every one of the 1100 parts in the piece of apparatus, with indication of whether this item was accepted on first test or was a replacement for items that had failed.

"Because of so much inspection," the engineer in charge explained to me, "we don't need quality control."

Later, in a meeting with union representatives, two of the women present enquired thus: "Why do we have to spend so much of our time straightening out these plastic plates before we can work on them? A third of them come in warped."

"Why do they come in warped?" I asked.

"Handling damage, we think."

"What difference does it make to you? You get paid by the hour."

"Yes, but we could turn out more work if we didn't have to spend our time straightening out those warped plates," they said—and couldn't I do something about it?

"How long have you had this problem?" I asked.

"I have been screaming about it for three years, but nothing has happened."

One may wonder what she and her people thought of the management, taking no heed of her cries for help to eliminate this cause of waste.

Later on with the top management, I put to them this question: why is it that with 80 per cent of your capital equipment in gauges, instruments, and computers printing piles of machine sheets, and with 55 per cent of your man-hours going for inspection, no one except the production workers knew about the warped plates?

You are concerned because one of your best customers is looking around for a supplier for lower prices and better quality. You may lose a good customer. You can't blame him. Your prices are high because of waste of human effort (rework, inspection) and because of huge expense in equipment for inspection and storage of useless information.

Another. A pilot sat beside me on an aeroplane from Minneapolis. He complained that he was being paid for this ride, but doing nobody any good. He could just as well be driving an aeroplane earning money for the company, he said. (His management had apparently not explained to pilots that some deadhead travel is inevitable.)

More on problems of the production worker appear here and there in the book.

Barriers against realization of pride of workmanship may in fact be one of the most important obstacles to reduction of cost and improvement of quality in the United States.

There are other losses from incompetent leadership, as if poor quality and low productivity were not by themselves enough cause of loss. For example, it is fairly well known that the average number of days off with pay for accidents on the job goes sky-high under poor supervision.

Turnover goes up as the proportion of defective items goes up, and turnover goes down when it becomes obvious to employees that the management is trying to improve the process.

He that feels important to a job will make every effort to be on the job. He will feel important to the job if he can take pride in his work and may have a part in improvement of the system. Absenteeism and mobility of the work force are largely the result of poor supervision and poor management.

(Contributed by Heero Hacquebord, consultant, Pretoria:)

I spoke with 45 production workers about the inhibitors that stand in their way to improvement of quality and productivity.

> Inadequate training in technology: "I do not understand what my job is."
> Delays and shortages of components.
> Inadequate documentation on how to do the job.
> Rush jobs (bad planning).
> Outdated drawings.
> Inadequate design (drawings changed after job completed, leading to rework and repair).
> Foremen do not have sufficient knowledge to give leadership.
> Inadequate and wrong tools and instruments.
> No lines of communication between them and management.
> Poor working environment (cold in winter, hot in summer, inadequate extraction of gasses).
> "I do not know how my performance is measured. The merit rating is a farce."
> "Defective items come in from the suppliers and hold up my job."
> Struggle to get technical help from engineers.

I discussed these problems with the manager, and he promised to do something about them. He may do so, as he attended your seminar in Pretoria.

Another example. Salaried employees took over production

during a strike of hourly employees. The manager of a department reported that he found machines out of order, some sadly so, some badly in need of maintenance, one a candidate for outright replacement. Production doubled when he tuned up the machines. Were it not for the strike, he should never have known about the sad state of the machines, and production would have continued at half the capability of the process. "Well, Hal," I said, "you know whose fault it was, don't you?" Yes, he knows. It won't happen again. From now on, there will be a system by which employees may report trouble with machines or with materials and by which these reports will receive attention.

What happens? In my experience, people can face almost any problem except the problems of people. They can work long hours, face declining business, face loss of jobs, but not the problems of people. Faced with problems of people (management included), management, in my experience, go into a state of paralysis, taking refuge in formation of QC-Circles and groups for EI, EP, and QWL (Employee Involvement, Employee Participation, and Quality of Work Life). These groups predictably disintegrate within a few months from frustration, finding themselves unwilling parties to a cruel hoax, unable to accomplish anything, for the simple reason that no one in management will take action on suggestions for improvement. These are devastatingly cruel devices to get rid of the problems of people. There are of course pleasing exceptions, where the management understands their responsibilities, where the management participates with advice and action on suggestions for removal of barriers to pride of workmanship.

The possibility of pride of workmanship means more to the production worker than gymnasiums, tennis courts, and recreation areas.

Give the work force a chance to work with pride, and the 3 per cent that apparently don't care will erode itself by peer pressure.

13. Encourage education and self-improvement for everyone. What an organization needs is not just good people; it needs people that are improving with education.

In respect to self-improvement, it is wise for anyone to bear in mind that there is no shortage of good people. Shortage exists at the high levels of knowledge, and this is true in every field. One should not wait for promise of reimbursement for a course of study. Moreover, study that is directed toward immediate need may not be the wisest course.

There is widespread fear of knowledge, as we saw in Point 8, but advances in competitive position will have their roots in knowledge.

We have already seen that everybody has responsibilities in the reconstruction of Western industry, and needs new education. Management must go through new learning.

People require in their careers, more than money, ever-broadening opportunities to add something to society, materially and otherwise.

PLAN FOR ACTION

14. Take action to accomplish the transformation.[8]

1. Management in authority will struggle over every one of the above 13 points, the deadly diseases, the obstacles (Ch. 3). They will agree on their meaning and on the direction to take. They will agree to carry out the new philosophy.

2. Management in authority will take pride in their adoption of the new philosophy and in their new responsibilities. They will have courage to break with tradition, even to the point of exile among their peers.

3. Management in authority will explain by seminars and other means to a critical mass of people in the company why change is necessary, and that the change will involve everybody.

---

8 I thank Dr. Phyllis Sobo of Philadelphia for help on this plan of action.

Enough people in the company must understand the 14 points, the deadly diseases, and the obstacles of Chapter 3. Management is helpless otherwise.

> This whole movement may be instituted and carried out by middle management, speaking with one voice.

4. Every activity, every job is a part of a process. A flow diagram of any process will divide the work into stages. The stages as a whole form a process. The stages are not individual entities, each running at maximum profit. A flow diagram, simple or complex, is an example of a theory—an idea.

$$\longrightarrow \text{Stage 1} \longrightarrow \text{Stage 2} \longrightarrow \text{Stage 3} \longrightarrow$$

Work comes into any stage, changes state, and moves on into the next stage. Any stage has a customer, the next stage. The final stage will send product or service to the ultimate customer, he that buys the product or the service. At every stage there will be:

> Production—change of state, input changes to output. Something happens to material or papers that come into any stage. They go out in a different state.
> Continual improvement of methods and procedures, aimed at better satisfaction of the customer (user) at the next stage.

Each stage works with the next stage and with the preceding stage toward optimum accommodation, all stages working together toward quality that the ultimate customer will boast about. We recall these words from page 43:

> This is what I can do for you.
> Here is what you might do for me.

> I could do a much better job (fewer mistakes) if I knew what the program is to be used for. The

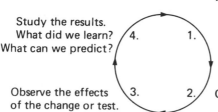

Study the results.
What did we learn?
What can we predict?

Observe the effects
of the change or test.

What could be the most important
accomplishments of this team?
What changes might be desirable?
What data are available? Are new
observations needed? If yes, plan
a change or test. Decide how to
use the observations.

Carry out the change or test decided
upon, preferably on a small scale.

Step 5.   Repeat Step 1, with knowledge accumulated.
Step 6.   Repeat Step 2, and onward.

Fig. 5. The Shewhart cycle.

specifications don't tell me what I need to know (programmer).

5. Start as soon as possible to construct with deliberate speed
an organization to guide continual improvement of quality, as
recommended in Chapter 16.

The Shewhart cycle[9] (Fig. 5) will be helpful as a procedure to
follow for improvement of any stage; also as a procedure for
finding a special cause detected by statistical signal (Ch. 11).

The reason to study the results of a change is to try to learn
how to improve tomorrow's product, or next year's crop. Planning requires prediction. The results of a change or test may
enhance our degree of belief for prediction, for planning.

Step 4 of the Shewhart cycle (study the results; what did we
learn from the change?) will lead (a) to improvement of any

9 The perception of the cycle shown in Fig. 5 came from Walter A. Shewhart,
Statistical Method from the Viewpoint of Quality Control (Graduate School,
Department of Agriculture, Washington, 1939; Dover, 1986), p. 45. I called
it in Japan in 1950 and onward the Shewhart cycle. It went into immediate
use in Japan under the name of the Deming cycle, and so it has been called
there ever since.

stage, and (b) to better satisfaction of the customer for that stage. The results may of course indicate no change at all, at least for now.

If the results of the change or test are favorable, we may decide to go through the cycle again, preferably under different environmental conditions, to learn whether the favorable results of the first cycle were spurious or are valid over a range of environmental conditions.

Any step in the Shewhart cycle may need guidance of statistical methodology for economy, speed, and protection from faulty conclusions from failure to test and measure the effects of interactions.

The effect of a change that is suggested may sometimes be studied by calculation on paper, or by simulation, or by change of an engineering drawing, avoiding actual experimentation. Examples appear in Chapter 15, where simple arithmetic combined with simple theory of probability indicates whether and where to carry out inspection in order to minimize total cost.

Another simple example of a change was suggested by Dr. Ivor S. Francis at a seminar at the W. Edwards Deming Institute of New Zealand in August 1985: lengthen the coffee break from 15 minutes to 30 minutes. Result: time saved; commotion avoided. Explanation: 15 minutes is not enough time for 350 people to get their coffee and return. Given 30 minutes, they have time and are ready.

A loop may now be thrown around three or more stages, to improve everything by study of interaction of changes in one or more stages, again by the Shewhart cycle.

6. Everyone can take part in a team. The aim of a team is to improve the input and the output of any stage. A team may well

be composed of people from different staff areas. A team has a customer.

Everyone on a team has a chance to contribute ideas, plans, and figures; but anyone may expect to find some of his best ideas submerged by consensus of the team. He may have a chance on the later time around the cycle. A good team has a social memory.

At successive sessions, people may tear up what they did in the previous session and make a fresh start with clearer ideas. This is a sign of advancement.

7. Embark on construction of organization for quality as described by Fig. 61 on page 467, and in the accompanying text. This step will require participation of knowledgeable statisticians.

A group, a team, should have an aim, a job, a goal. A statement thereof must not be specific in detail, else it stifle initiative.

By working in this way, everyone will see what he can do and what only top management can do. The following questions for this purpose were contributed by Edward M. Baker of the Ford Motor Company.

Questions to help a team to start

Your organization:

    a. Where in the total organizational structure does your department fit?

    b. What products and services does it provide?

    c. How does it provide these products and services; i.e., what processes are used?

    d. What would be the effect if your organization (unit, section, department) stopped producing its products and services?

You:

    a. Where do you fit in your department? What is your job?
    b. What do you create or produce; i.e., what are the results of your work?
    c. How do you do this? (E.g., give a general description of what you do.)
    d. How do you know if you produce good results or poor results; i.e., are there standards or criteria of good performance?
    e. How were these standards established?

Concerning your customers:

    a. Immediate customers
      i. Who receives directly the products or services that you produce? (He is your customer.)
     ii. How does your customer use what you produce?
    iii. What would happen if you did not do your job right?
    iv. How do your errors affect them?
     v. How do you find out if you are not meeting the needs or requirements of your customers (e.g., from customer, boss, reports)?
    b. Intermediate and ultimate customer
      i. How far beyond your immediate customer can you trace the effect of what you do?

Concerning your suppliers:

    a. How is your work initiated (e.g., assignment from boss, request of customer, self-initiated)?
    b. Who supplies you with material, information, services, and other information that you need to do

your job (e.g., boss, customer, co-worker—same group; people in other areas)?

c. What would happen to you if your suppliers did not do their job?

d. Do they have performance standards?

e. How do their errors affect you?

f. How do they find out if they are not meeting your needs or requirements? Are you working with them? Are you fulfilling your obligation to them?

Things are happening. The clock is moving rapidly toward better quality and into conditions by which everyone may take pride in quality. The time is near when the whole world of people here will work in harmony with each other.... We see new employees, and old ones rehired, skeptical, unable to believe that quality is top priority, here to stay. (Contributed by Juanita Lopez, in the Fiero plant of the Pontiac Motor Division.)

Types of gaps in information about the performance of incoming materials. Any batch of material sent to a plant falls into one of four categories.

1. Used in production with no problem.

2. Used in desperation, being unsuited to the requirements of manufacture and finished product, invariably with waste of material or cost of rework, or both. Example: a block, dished out at the top. Should be flat for cement. Requires rework before use. Another example is a panel (veneer or hide) of nonuniform color. Some of the material must be discarded, with loss of time and material, or risk that the finished product will be condemned.

In another example, there was only one vendor capable of supplying the right material, but to meet a large contract the company ordered the same material from other vendors, which, as it turned out, were not able to produce the grade desired. This material was used, nevertheless, in desperation, with the consequences of rework and waste.

3. Totally unusable, in the judgment of the plant manager. A way to decide what to do on this problem is to call a meeting attended by the plant manager and the buyer, possibly also by an expert from the laboratory. These men may decide:

> That the plant manager was justified in his complaint, the material is unfit for use; return it to the vendor.

> *or*

> That he did not understand the requirements of the finished product, that he may find it possible to use the material.

> *or*

> That the trouble lies in specifications that did not make sense for the use intended. Hold the material for other uses, or try to sell it; possibly sell it back to the vendor (usually at a loss). Procure the right material for the purpose.

4. Material in inventory. This consists of the following: (i) Material bought, held for use. Unfortunately, material in inventory, held for use, comes in many instances from sources unknown. Some of it turns out to be defective. With origin unknown, the only safe course is 100 per cent inspection. A better way is to avoid inventory except for protection against a rise in price or against an imminent strike. (ii) Material bought for use, not to be used. Examples: (a) Product discontinued. (b) Customer canceled the order before work started. (c) Customer contracted for 2000 items; there is enough material for only 1000; he can not use 1000, and can not wait for attempts to procure more material, so he cancels the order. (d) The product

would reach the customer too late; the season will be over; customer cancels the order. There are several possible solutions to this class of item. One is to sell it back to the vendor. Another is to put it into inventory, hoping to find use for it later. Still another is to call up your competitor: he may be looking for precisely this material.

The accounting department of the company will have exact figures on Categories 3 and 4, but few companies have any clear idea about the magnitude of Categories 1 and 2.

In my experience, Category 3 (totally unusable) is very small, less than 1 per cent of the dollar value of materials bought. The dollar value of Category 2 (used in desperation), large as it may be, must be far less than the waste of effort spent in trying to use it.

One of a Kind[10]

Everything is one of a kind. There are more products characterized as one of a kind than one might suppose. As a matter of fact, nearly everything that is made is one of a kind, as we saw in Point 5. We commonly think of a home as one of a kind, and so it is; likewise the rug on the floor of this office, and the grand piano in your home. A job shop is a producer of one of a kind, although the shop may make one or it may make two hundred of the same thing. A certain model of automobile is one of a kind: once in production, little can be done about resistance to purchase, any more than one can remodel a battleship once built. A company may build 6 aeroplanes of specified design, or 37 of them. They are one of a kind. A building, once under construction, is pretty well fixed. Changes are costly.

Machinery, once bought, becomes a fixture. So it is with a home, a grand piano, a building, an automobile, an aeroplane.

---

10 I owe to my friend William A. Golomski the perception that a large portion of products and of service as well are one of a kind. I am indebted to him also for some of the examples in this section.

How do you test a battleship?

Remark. The reader may recall the notes on a job shop on page 50.

Example 1. The engines of the aeroplane started. We shall soon be off the ground, Nashville to Washington. All was in readiness except for nine people standing in the aisle looking for their seats. The flight attendant begged them to sit down, anywhere. Why were they standing? They were trying to find their seats. The numbers that designate the aisles were too small for easy visibility, and obscured by bright lights alongside the numbers. Who could make an aeroplane at a cost of several million dollars, yet give no attention to the passenger? Somebody did. Who would buy it? Somebody did.

Example 2. Ask anyone knowledgeable in the airline business about the difficulty to transfer luggage from one airline to another in most of our airports. A passenger makes a connexion; the luggage does not. The luggage follows, sometimes at huge cost to the airline and at great inconvenience to the passenger. Who would design an airport without reference to the problem of transferring luggage from one airline to another? This is what happens when the authority of the airport pushes for reduction in cost, without regard to total cost, including use.

Fig. 6. Lights in the corridor of a hotel obscure keyholes.

Example 3. Here is a hotel (Fig. 6), almost new, the lights placed so that the keyholes for the doors are in darkness. Customers complained, but the manager was helpless. He inherited the problem. He can not rebuild the hotel. Customers conquered the problem by sense of touch. No one, so far as I could learn, spent the night in the corridor, failing to gain access to his room. What architect would be so completely oblivious to the customer? One was. What purchaser of the building would have the same failing? One did. (More in Ch. 7.)

Example 4. A conveyor belt, two feet off the floor, carries glass jars of food. Jars fall off, break, and spill messy contents on to the floor. Some of the mess runs under the conveyor. To clean it up, a man must be under two feet in height or else crawl on his knees over broken glass to reach under the conveyor. What architect or engineer would suppose that there would never be need to clean house? One did.

Example 5. What company would build an aeroplane with no individual reading lights for passengers? The aeroplane costs millions of dollars, and is well designed (I hope) with respect to engineering and aerodynamics, but it seems that the airline traded dollars for comfort of passengers. What airlines would buy several of these aeroplanes without thought of the needs of the passenger? One did.

3

Diseases and Obstacles

My people are destroyed for lack of knowledge.—Hosea 4:6.

Aim of this chapter. The 14 points of Chapter 2 constitute a theory of management. Their application will transform Western style of management. Unfortunately, deadly diseases stand in the way of transformation. We try here to understand their deadly effects. Alas, cure of some of the diseases requires complete shakeup of Western style of management (fear of takeover, for example, and short-term profit).

There are diseases and there are obstacles. The distinction is intended to be partly in terms of difficulty of eradication and partly in terms of severity of the injury inflicted.

A. The Deadly Diseases

Deadly diseases afflict most companies in the Western world. An esteemed economist (Carolyn A. Emigh) remarked that cure of the deadly diseases will require total reconstruction of Western management.

Enumeration of the deadly diseases.

1. Lack of constancy of purpose to plan product and service that will have a market and keep the company in business, and provide jobs.
2. Emphasis on short-term profits: short-term thinking (just the opposite from constancy of purpose to stay in business), fed

by fear of unfriendly takeover, and by push from bankers and owners for dividends.

3. Evaluation of performance, merit rating, or annual review.

4. Mobility of management; job hopping.

5. Management by use only of visible figures, with little or no consideration of figures that are unknown or unknowable.

> Peculiar to industry in the U.S., and beyond
> the scope of this book.

6. Excessive medical costs.

As William E. Hoglund, manager of the Pontiac Motor Division, put it to me one day, "Blue Cross is our second largest supplier." The direct cost of medical care is $400 per automobile ("Sick call," *Forbes*, 24 October 1983, p. 116). Six months later he told me that Blue Cross had overtaken steel. This is not all. Additional medical costs are embedded in the steel that goes into an automobile. There are also direct costs of health and care, as from beneficial days (payment of wages and salaries to people under treatment for injury on the job); also for counseling of people depressed from low rating on annual performance, plus counsel and treatment of employees whose performance is impaired by alcohol or drugs.

7. Excessive costs of liability, swelled by lawyers that work on contingency fees.[1]

We are ready now for elaboration of the deadly diseases.

1. The crippling disease: lack of constancy of purpose. Much of American industry is run on the quarterly dividend. It is better to protect investment by working continually toward improvement of processes and of product and service that will bring the customer back again (Points 1 and 5 in Ch. 2).

---

1 Eugene L. Grant, interview in the journal *Quality* (Chicago), March 1984.

2. Emphasis on short-term profits. Pursuit of the quarterly dividend and short-term profit defeat constancy of purpose. Whence cometh the scramble for the quarterly dividend? What is the driving force that leads to the last-minute rush into a good showing on the quarterly dividend? Anyone can boost the dividend at the end of the quarter. Ship everything on hand, regardless of quality: mark it shipped, and show it all as accounts receivable. Defer till next quarter, so far as possible, orders for material and equipment. Cut down on research, education, training.

A stockholder that needs dividends to live on is more interested in future dividends than simply in the size of the dividend today. To him, it is important that there be dividends three years from now, five years from now, eight years from now. Emphasis on short-term profit defeats constancy of purpose and long-term growth. The following paragraph from an article by Dr. Yoshi Tsurumi in the Op-Ed page of the *New York Times* for 1 May 1983, p. F-3, is eloquent:

> Part of America's industrial problems is the aim of its corporate managers. Most American executives think they are in the business to make money, rather than products and service. . . . The Japanese corporate credo, on the other hand, is that a company should become the world's most efficient provider of whatever product and service it offers. Once it becomes the world leader and continues to offer good products, profits follow.

An annual report to stockholders is usually a feat of color coating in English, combined with creative accounting. An annual report that claims value added, as benefit to a community or to a society, is rare. An attempt to rescue ruins is a feat of management.

Management at all levels was strengthened during

1983 through the recruitment of seasoned executives for key positions. The company also implemented a number of major cost control programs, including further manpower reductions, consolidation of facilities and improved accounts receivable and inventory management. The purpose of these and other measures under consideration is to improve operating margins.

An eloquent explanation of how the Japanese system is better adapted to greater productivity and to world trade than the American system is explained in the following paragraph from Robert M. Kaus, "The trouble with unions," *Harper's*, June 1983, pp. 23–35, p. 32 in particular.

Japanese enterprises do not appear to be organizations that maximize profits for the benefit of stockholders. Capital is obtained through bank loans, with fixed rates of return. With no shareholders to please, Japanese firms are free to operate on behalf of another constituency—their workers. "Large businesses are run primarily for the employees who, in traditional legal terms, are the 'beneficial owners,'" Peter Drucker has observed. Since the workers are the beneficiaries of what would otherwise be profits, labor-management trust comes naturally.[2]

Fear of unfriendly takeover. A publicly held company whose stock falls for any reason—even for long-range planning—may be in fear of takeover, and one that does too well is in the same danger. Fear of unfriendly takeover may be the single most important obstacle to constancy of purpose. There is also, besides the unfriendly takeover, the equally devastating leveraged buyout. Either way, the conqueror demands dividends, with vicious consequences on the vanquished.

Must American management be forever subject to such plunder?

Paper entrepreneurialism is both cause and consequence of America's faltering economy. Paper profits are the only ones easily available to professional managers who sit isolated atop organizations designed for a form of production that is no longer appropriate to America's place in the world economy. At the same time, the relentless drive for paper profits has diverted attention and resources away from the difficult job of transforming the productive base. It has retarded the transition that must occur, and made change more difficult in the future. Paper entreprencurialism thus has a self-perpetuating quality that, if left unchecked, will drive the nation into further decline. (From Robert B. Reich, "The next American frontier," *Atlantic*, March 1983, pp. 43–57.)

Banks could help long-range planning, and thus protect funds entrusted to them. In contrast, here is an actual example in America. (Banker:) "Jim, this is not the time to talk about quality and the future. This is the time to cut expenses, close plants, cut your payroll."

It is of course possible that a takeover may, in the long run, by combining operations in two companies, improve overall efficiency of industry in a country, and eventually be of benefit to the welfare of the people therein. It is rough, however, on people that suddenly find themselves out of a job. Japanese companies that merge somehow take care of their people, albeit perhaps some of them in management at reduced pay.

3. Evaluation of performance, merit rating, or annual review.
Many companies in America have systems by which everyone in management or in research receives from his superiors a rating every year. Some government agencies have a similar system.

Management by objective leads to the same evil. Management by the numbers likewise. Management by fear would be a better name, someone in Germany suggested. The effect is devastating:

> It nourishes short-term performance, annihilates long-term planning, builds fear, demolishes teamwork, nourishes rivalry and politics.

> It leaves people bitter, crushed, bruised, battered, desolate, despondent, dejected, feeling inferior, some even depressed, unfit for work for weeks after receipt of rating, unable to comprehend why they are inferior. It is unfair, as it ascribes to the people in a group differences that may be caused totally by the system that they work in.

Basically, what is wrong is that the performance appraisal or merit rating focuses on the end product, at the end of the stream, not on leadership to help people. This is a way to avoid the problems of people. A manager becomes, in effect, manager of defects.

The idea of a merit rating is alluring. The sound of the words captivates the imagination: pay for what you get; get what you pay for; motivate people to do their best, for their own good.

The effect is exactly the opposite of what the words promise. Everyone propels himself forward, or tries to, for his own good, on his own life preserver. The organization is the loser.

Merit rating rewards people that do well in the system. It does not reward attempts to improve the system. Don't rock the boat.

If anyone in top management asks a plant manager what he hopes to accomplish next year, the answer will be an echo of the policy (numerical goal) of the company. (James K. Bakken, Ford Motor Company.)

Moreover, a merit rating is meaningless as a predictor of performance, except for someone that falls outside the limits of differences attributable to the system that the people work in (cf. later pages).

Traditional appraisal systems increase the variability of performance of people. The trouble lies in the implied preciseness of rating schemes. What happens is this. Somebody is rated below average, takes a look at people that are rated above average; naturally wonders why the difference exists. He tries to emulate people above average. The result is impairment of performance.[3]

President Reagan came through in the spring of 1983 with a wonderful idea: promotion in the Civil Service must hereafter depend on performance. The problem lies in the difficulty to define a meaningful measure of performance. The only verifiable measure is a short-term count of some kind. He repeated a few months later the same fallacy (*Washington Post*, 22 May 1983, pp. 1, 6).

Merit Pay System Suggested as a Way to Improve Schools
By JUAN WILLIAMS
Washington Post Staff Writer

SOUTH ORANGE, N.J., May 21— President Reagan took on the nation's major teachers' organizations here today, saying public schools are failing and that one way to improve them without more federal funds is to start paying teachers according to merit rather than seniority.

That is anathema to most teachers' groups, who say there is no accurate way to measure teacher quality and that such traditional signs as pupil test scores are misleading.

3   Contributed by William W. Scherkenbach of the Ford Motor Company.

Where were our President's economic advisors? He was only doing his best.

Dangerous precedent. From the *Virginia Weekly, Washington Post*, 12 April 1984, p. 1.

Officers' Evaluations
Are Based in Part
on Their Ticket Totals

By MICHAEL MARTINEZ

Washington Post Staff Writer

Police officials say that the evaluation programs do not establish quotas, but instead guide officers on how to perform their jobs and work efficiently while they are patrolling the streets. A few officers, however, protest that the pressure to meet standards forces them to write up motorists they would ordinarily let go with a warning and interferes with more important police activities.

In Alexandria, 32 police officers in one patrol division are rated as "outstanding," "exceeds requirement," "meets requirement," "below requirement," or "unsatisfactory," according to the number of parking and traffic tickets issued in one month. An officer earns an outstanding rating if he issues 25 or more traffic tickets and 21 or more parking tickets in a month.

Alexandria Lt. William Banks said the performance standards were agreed upon by officers and their supervisors last September as part of a new citywide evaluation system. All officers will eventually be subject to similar standards, Banks said.

Falls Church Lt. Paul Lucas said the department works to meet a number of goals listed in its annual budget, including a projected number of traffic tickets. For fiscal year 1984, the department will try to issue 551 drunk driving tickets, 2592 speeding tickets and 3476 other traffic tickets, Lucas said.

"It's not a quota," he said. "It's a department goal. It's not an individual goal."

Degeneration to counting. One of the main effects of evaluation of performance is nourishment of short-term thinking and short-time performance. A man must have something to show. His superior is forced into numerics. It is easy to count. Counts relieve management of the necessity to contrive a measure with meaning.

Unfortunately, people that are measured by counting are deprived of pride of workmanship. Number of designs that an engineer turns out in a period of time would be an example of an index that provides no chance for pride of workmanship. He dare not take time to study and amend the design just completed. To do so would decrease his output.

Likewise, people in research and development are rated on the number of new products that they develop. They tell me that they dare not stay with a project long enough to see a product into manufacturing; that their rating would suffer if they did.

Even if his superior appreciates effort and ability to make

lasting contributions to the methods and structure of the organization, he must defend with tangible evidence (viz., counts) his recommendations for promotions.

A federal mediator told me that he is rated on the number of meetings that he attends during the year. He improves his rating by stretching out to three meetings negotiations between (e.g.) Ford and the UAW, when he could have settled all the problems in one meeting.

Number of meetings attended is offset partially by credit for number of settlements accomplished. A settlement is a settlement, whether it puts a company out of business or defrauds the work force, or is of lasting benefit to the American people.

A buyer in the U.S. Postal Service told me that she is rated on the number of contracts that she negotiates during the year, and every contract must be at lowest cost. A long-term contract would require time, and would reduce her output for the year.

Such indexes are ridiculous, but they are typical throughout American industry and government.

So long as people in the purchasing department are rated on number of contracts accomplished, they will have little incentive to take time to learn about the problems in production and the losses that their purchases cause.

A good rating for work on new product and new service that may generate new business five or eight years hence, and provide better material living, requires enlightened management. He that engages in such work would study changes in education, changes in style of living, migration in and out of urban areas. He would attend meetings of the American Sociological Society, the Business Section of the American Statistical Association, the American Marketing Association. He would write professional papers to deliver at such meetings, all of which are necessary for the planning of product and service of the future. He would not for years have anything to show for his labors. Meanwhile, in the absence of enlightened management, other people getting good ratings on short-run projects would leave him behind.

Stifling teamwork. Evaluation of performance explains, I believe, why it is difficult for staff areas to work together for the good of the company. They work instead as prima donnas, to the defeat of the company. Good performance on a team helps the company but leads to less tangible results to count for the individual. The problem on a team is: who did what?

How could the people in the purchasing department, under the present system of evaluation, take an interest in improvement of quality of materials for production, service, tools, and other materials for nonproductive purposes? This would require cooperation with manufacturing. It would impede productivity in the purchasing department, which is often measured by the number of contracts negotiated per man-year, without regard to performance of materials or services purchased. If there be an accomplishment to boast about the people in manufacturing might get the credit, not the people in purchasing. Or, it could be the other way around. Thus, teamwork, so highly desirable, can not thrive under the annual rating. Fear grips everyone. Be careful; don't take a risk; go along.

> *Heard in a seminar.* One gets a good rating for fighting a fire. The result is visible; can be quantified. If you do it right the first time, you are invisible. You satisfied the requirements. That is your job. Mess it up, and correct it later, you become a hero.

Two chemists work together on a project, and write up their work as a scientific paper. The paper is accepted for a meeting in Hamburg. However, in these times, only one of the pair may go to Hamburg to deliver the paper—viz., the one with the higher rating. The one with the lower rating vows never again to work close with anyone else.

Result: every man for himself.

The chemists in the company can well understand that there are times when the number of people that attend a meeting must be limited. A good plan would be to let the men decide who will go to any one meeting. They will rotate themselves in an equitable manner.

Management in America gives high awards for new technology, thus discouraging people to work on other aspects of the system. When a design is completed, rewards are offered for suggestions for improvement. A committee studies suggestions. A suggestion may be turned down because, though good, it is too costly to introduce at this point. Upstream, it would have had a chance for consideration. The proper place for improvement is in early stages of development. The rating system thus runs the risk of losing out on some good ideas that would raise quality and reduce costs. In America, the man that brings in a suggestion is not present, and the committee may well fail to understand the meaning and possibilities of a suggestion.

In Japan, suggestions are considered by the group, and the man that makes the suggestion is present. The decision does not fall on one person, but on the group. The group comes to a conclusion for the good of the company. Once the decision is unanimous, everyone works together to deliver his best for the group. Any dissenter, or anyone that does not deliver his best, will find his way into another group or into other work.

Evaluation of performance nourishes fear. People are afraid to ask questions that might indicate any possible doubt about the boss's ideas and decisions, or about his logic. The game becomes one of politics. Keep on the good side of the boss. Anyone that presents another point of view or asks questions runs the risk of being called disloyal, not a team player, trying to push himself ahead. Be a yes man.

Top levels of salaries and bonuses are in many American companies sky-high. It is human nature for a young man to aspire eventually to arrive in one of these positions. The only chance to reach a high level is by consistent, unfailing promotion, year after year. The aspiring man's quest is not how to serve the company with whatever knowledge he has, but how to get a good rating. Miss one raise, you won't make it: someone else will.

A man dare not take a risk. Don't change a procedure. Change might not work well. What would happen to him that changed it? He must guard his own security. It is safer to stay in line. The manager, under the review system, like the people that he manages, works as an individual for his own advancement, not for the company. He must make a good showing for himself.

> *Manager* (to his people): Don't work with those people [in another group]. Your time belongs to our project.

A sigh of relief would go up from everyone on elimination of the annual rating.

Questions to ponder over. (1) How would you rate yourself? By what method or criteria? For what purpose? (2) What are you trying to measure when you rate someone? How would your rating of someone aid prediction of his performance in the future: (a) on this job; (b) on some higher job (more responsibility)?

Another Irving Langmuir? Can American history, under handicap of the annual rating, produce another Irving Langmuir, a Nobel Prize winner, or another W. D. Coolidge? Both these men were with the General Electric Company. Could the Siemens Company produce another Ernst Werner von Siemens?

It is worthy of note that the 80 American Nobel prize winners all had tenure, security. They were answerable only to themselves.

Fair rating is impossible. A common fallacy is the supposition that it is possible to rate people; to put them in rank order of performance for next year, based on performance last year.

The performance of anybody is the result of a combination of many forces—the person himself, the people that he works with, the job, the material that he works on, his equipment, his customer, his management, his supervision, environmental conditions (noise, confusion, poor food in the company's cafeteria).

These forces will produce unbelievably large differences between people. In fact, as we shall see, apparent differences between people arise almost entirely from action of the system that they work in, not from the people themselves. A man not promoted is unable to understand why his performance is lower than someone else's. No wonder; his rating was the result of a lottery. Unfortunately, he takes his rating seriously.

The following numerical examples will illustrate the unbelievable differences between people that must be attributed to action of the system, not to the people. Outstanding performance may be attributed only to someone that by appropriate calculations falls beyond the limits of variation of the system, or creates a pattern (p. 115).

It must be emphasized that any actual system will create even greater differences between people than those observed here, where we are able to simulate pretty well a constant cause system.

Example 1. For an illustration, let six people take part in a simple experiment. Each person will stir a mixture of red and white beads (4000), 20 per cent red, draw blindfolded his sample of 50 beads, then return to the mixture for the next person. The aim is to produce white beads: our customer will not accept red beads. Actual results follow.

Name	Number of red beads produced
Mike	9
Peter	5
Terry	15
Jack	4
Louise	10
Gary	8
Total	51

It would be difficult to construct physical circumstances so nearly equal for six people, yet to the eye, the people vary greatly in performance.

But let us think with the aid of statistical theory. We calculate the limits between employees that could be attributable to chance variation from the system. This calculation is based on average performance and on the supposition that the people and their production of red beads are all independent.

The reader that is unfamiliar with calculations that follow may wish to turn to Chapter 11, or find a teacher, or turn to one of the books listed at the end of Chapter 11.

$$\bar{x} = \frac{51}{6} = 8.5 \qquad \text{(average number of red beads per worker)}$$

$$\bar{p} = \frac{51}{6 \times 50} = 0.17 \quad \text{(average proportion red)}$$

Calculation of limits of variation attributable to the system:

$$\left.\begin{array}{l}\text{Upper limit}\\ \text{Lower limit}\end{array}\right\} = \bar{x} \pm 3\sqrt{\bar{x}(1-\bar{p})}$$

$$= 8.5 \pm 3\sqrt{8.5 \times 0.83}$$

$$= \begin{cases} 16 \\ 1 \end{cases}$$

The six employees obviously all fall within the calculated limits of variation that could arise from the system that they work in. There is no evidence in these data that Jack will in the future be a better performer than Terry. Everyone should accordingly receive the same raise. Anyone with seniority over another will of course be at a higher level of pay.

It would obviously be a waste of time to try to find out why Terry made 15 red beads, or why Jack made only 4. What is worse, anybody that would seek a cause would come up with an answer, action on which could only make things worse henceforth.

The problem for management, meanwhile, is to improve the system to make it possible for all the people to make more white beads, fewer red ones. (More in Ch. 11.)

Example 2. (Contributed by William W. Scherkenbach, Ford Motor Company.) You are a manager with nine employees reporting directly to you. They have essentially the same responsibilities and in the past year they have recorded the following number of mistakes. Each employee had about the same chance as another to make a mistake.

Name	Number of mistakes
Janet	10
Andrew	15
Bill	11
Frank	4
Dick	17
Charlie	23
Alicia	11
Tom	12
Joanne	10
Total	113

The mistakes counted here could be errors in book-keeping, mistakes on engineering drawing, errors in calculation, errors of assembly workers, or anything else.

It is now time for evaluations and recommendations for merit raises. Whom do you reward? Whom do you penalize? First, what allowance should we make for effects of the system that the people work in? The calculations follow.

$$\bar{x} = \frac{113}{9} = 12.55$$

Calculation of limits of variation attributable to the system:

$$\left.\begin{array}{l}\text{Upper limit} \\ \text{Lower limit}\end{array}\right\} - 12.55 \pm 3 \sqrt{12.55}$$

$$= \begin{cases} 23.2 \\ 1.9 \end{cases}$$

Thus, no one of the nine people falls outside the calculated limits. The apparent differences between the nine people could all be ascribed to action of the rest of the system. All nine people should accordingly be subject to the company's formula for raises in pay (page 118).

Note that the figures in both examples could as well be derived from a composite index.

Example 3. (Contributed by Ronald Moen, General Motors.) The process is design of a part, a "request." Stages:

1. Origin of the request (allotted to a product engineer).
2. The engineer draws up a design.
3. He presents his design to a release engineer. The release engineer may accept the design, or request another try at it, in which case the product engineer repeats Steps 1, 2, 3.
4. The release engineer accepts the design.

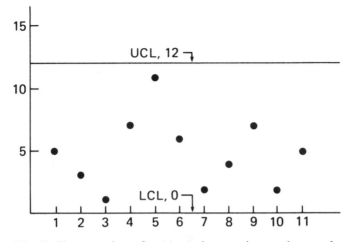

Fig. 7. Chart to show for 11 product engineers the number of engineering changes made for each one, over the course of a year. (The order on the horizontal is merely alphabetical.) No one of them fell outside the control limits. They thus all belong to a system. (Ronald Moen.)

Records of the number of changes for each of the 11 product engineers in a division over the course of development of a project are plotted in Fig. 7. Control limits, based only on independence of changes, are calculated as follows. The total number of changes for all 11 engineers was 53; average 4.8.

$$\begin{matrix} \text{UCL} \\ \text{LCL} \end{matrix} = 4.8 \pm 3\sqrt{4.8}$$

$$= \begin{cases} 11.4 & \text{(round to 12)} \\ 0 \end{cases}$$

No one of the 11 engineers falls outside the limits. They thus form a system. No one of them, on this evidence, will do better than another next year. They should all receive the same raise in pay. Every one of the 11 engineers gave identical reasons for changes:

Difficult request; special; new product; there never was anything like it.

Tough release engineer.

More on leadership. Anybody whose point falls outside the calculated limits of differences to be ascribed to the system is outside the system. Good leadership requires investigation into possible causes. If he is outside the limit of variation of the system on the good side, there is rational basis to predict that he will perform well in the future: he deserves recognition. The cause of a point outside the limit of variation of the system on the bad side may be permanent; it may be ephemeral. Someone that can not learn the job would provide an example of a permanent circumstance. The company hired him for this job; hence has a moral obligation to put him into the right job. Likewise, someone who is worried about his health, or about someone in the family, may show poor performance. Counseling will in some cases restore confidence and performance. A system that sends to some worker extra difficult material to work on might throw him outside limits on the bad side. This circumstance might continue unnoted, and the man, afraid to complain, says nothing about it. The same could be true of someone whose equipment is out of order. If no one knows what the trouble is, or if no one does anything about it, the man's points may well show up out of limits on the bad side year after year.

Need of spectacles would be an example of an ephemeral circumstance which might easily be altered by sending the man to the oculist. (The reader is referred to the 11 welders, p. 256.)

What about repetition of a pattern? What we are saying is that apparent differences—even huge differences—could be caused entirely by a constant cause system. We note again that any actual system will cause even greater differences between people.

A person may earn his place as high man or low man with respect to the others, with persistent performance, maintaining the same relative position through at least seven successive time periods (which may be seven years). If a man persists in holding a superior relative position over seven periods, we may safely conclude that he is indeed superior in whatever be the index of performance, whether it makes sense or not. After 20 years, star performers may definitely emerge, provided that the index of performance makes sense. Number of designs that an engineer turns out in a period of time would be an example of an index that gives the man no chance for pride of workmanship.

A useful criterion for recognition of outstanding performance is unquestionable demonstration of improvement year by year over a period of seven or more years, in skill, knowledge, leadership. The opposite criterion, namely, persistent deterioration over a period of seven years, may indicate people that are in need of help.

All this may be mere dreamland, because no group of people will all stay in the same jobs so long a time. In some applications, however, the period of time may be compressed, which it naturally will be with production workers. For them, there may be data by the week on number of items produced. Seven or more successive weeks may give trustworthy indication of relative performance.

"It can't be all bad." Abolishment of the annual rating of performance is delayed by the top management in some quarters by refuge in the obvious corollary that "It can't be all bad. It put me into this position." This is a trap that is easy to fall into. Every man that I work with is in a high position and is great, worth working with and arguing with. He reached this position by coming out on top in every annual rating, at the ruination of the lives of a score of other men. There is a better way.

Modern principles of leadership. Modern principles of leadership, explained and abundantly illustrated in this book, will replace the annual performance review. The first step in a company will be to provide education in leadership. The annual performance review may then be abolished. Leadership will take its place. This is what Western management should have been doing all along.

The annual performance review sneaked in and became popular because it does not require anyone to face the problems of people. It is easier to rate them; focus on the outcome. What Western industry needs is methods that will improve the outcome. Suggestions follow.

1. Institute education in leadership; obligations, principles, and methods.

2. More careful selection of the people in the first place.

3. Better training and education after selection.

4. A leader, instead of being a judge, will be a colleague, counseling and leading his people on a day-to-day basis, learning from them and with them. Everybody must be on a team to work for improvement of quality in the four steps of the Shewhart cycle shown in Fig. 5 on page 88.

5. A leader will discover who if any of his people is (a) outside the system on the good side, (b) outside on the poor side, (c) belonging to the system. The calculations required (illustrated on p. 114, Ch. 11, and elsewhere) are fairly simple if numbers are used for measures of performance. Ranking of people (outstanding down to unsatisfactory) that belong to the system violates scientific logic and is ruinous as a policy, as may be clear from the text and from Chapter 11.

In the absence of numerical data, a leader must make subjective judgment. A leader will spend hours with every one of his people. They will know what kind of help they need. There will sometimes be incontrovertible evidence of excellent performance, such as patents, publication of papers, invitations to give lectures.

People that are on the poor side of the system will require individual help. We have seen examples and shall see more.

Monetary reward for outstanding performance outside the system, without other, more satisfactory recognition, may be counterproductive.

6. The people of a group that form a system will all be subject to the company's formula for raises in pay. This formula may involve (e.g.) seniority. It will not depend on rank within the group, as the people within the system will not be ranked No. 1, No. 2, No. last. (In bad times, there may be no raise for anybody).

7. Hold a long interview with every employee, three or four hours, at least once a year, not for criticism, but for help and better understanding on the part of everybody.

8. Figures on performance should be used not to rank the people in a group that fall within the system, but to assist the leader to accomplish improvement of the system. These figures may also point out to him some of his own weaknesses (Michael Dolan, Columbia University, March 1986).

Improvement of the system will help everybody, and will decrease the spread between the figures for the performances of people.

The day is here when anyone deprived of a raise or of any privilege through misuse of figures for performance (as by ranking the people in a group) may with justice file a grievance.

The reader may wish to turn at this point to page 274.

The lone worker. There are abundant examples of people that can not work well in a team, but who demonstrate unquestionable achievement in the form of respect of colleagues and of peers, through inventions and publications in scientific journals. Such a man may make fabulous contributions to the company as well as to knowledge. The company must recognize the contributions of such people, and provide assistance to them.

Leadership instead of the annual rating at Ford. The foregoing principles became clear a few years ago to Donald E. Petersen, now Chief Executive Officer of the Ford Motor Company. Ford's changes will be a powerful signal to all Western industry that at least one big company is vitally concerned about the company's most important resource, viz., the people that work there. The main reason to make the change is to remove an important inhibitor to the company's program of continual improvement of quality and productivity.[4]

Problems in governmental service. (Contributed by Georgianna M. Bishop.) There is increasing concern within the professional civil service that the ability to attain constancy of purpose is becoming a lost cause. Having worked in the personnel field through four rapidly changing administrations with significantly divergent philosophies, we now see upheaval and total change in management every four years throughout the civil service system. Loss of continuity, efficiency, and job satisfaction are a natural consequence. The American public loses more and more with each attempt to improve (change) the career civil service system. The method for change has always been political, requiring approval of Congress, but we are now seeing major regulatory changes that enhance the potential for upheaval with each change of administration. Our political system, which elects the senior management for our federal service, must understand above all else the importance of constancy of purpose and the importance of knowledge. Politically appointed managers must comprehend the 14 points and the deadly diseases and the obstacles. Only then may they place themselves in roles of leadership.

From a federal worker:
 Average tenure of the Secretary of the Treasury, 18
  months: some tenures shorter, some longer.
 Average tenure of the Deputy, also 18 months: again,
  some tenures shorter, some longer.

---

4 William W. Scherkenbach, "Quality in the driver's seat," *Quality Progress*, April 1985, pp. 40–46.

The political process encourages short-term performance. The minute someone is elected, he is campaigning for the next election.

The perspective of the people that we report to has a span of two weeks.

The following paragraph from the book by Marvin E. Mundel cited earlier (p. 16), may also be helpful with respect to government service:

> ... Government today, within the developed countries, is such an enormously complex affair that it is doubtful whether the relationship between a given society and its government is really understood by any large segment of the society. Further, there appears some doubt that modern government responds fully to any coherently stated objectives of the society it serves; indeed there is reason to doubt that these objectives are ever stated fully in a feasible, comprehensible form. In many ways such government is of a habit-formed nature *and just is*. This hardly seems tolerable. Also, it should be obvious that within such a framework one cannot talk meaningfully about improvement, as the term is used in this book. To discuss bringing into a more desirable state an organization whose objectives, and the necessary and appropriate limitations and constraints, are really not stated is to take on an impossible task.

4. Mobility of management. A company whose top management are committed to quality and productivity, with roots, does not suffer from uncertainty and bewilderment. But how can anyone be committed to any policy when his tenure is only a few years, in and out?

J. Noguchi, managing director of the Union of Japanese Scientists and Engineers, made the remark in conversation with a client of mine that "America can not make it because of the mobility of American management."

The job of management is inseparable from the welfare of the company. Mobility from one company to another creates prima donnas for quick results. Mobility annihilates teamwork, so vital for continued existence. A new manager comes in. Everyone wonders what will happen. Unrest becomes rampant when the board of directors go outside the company to bring someone in for a rescue operation. Everyone takes to his life preserver.

Failure to make a good grade in the annual rating leads a man to look around for better opportunities elsewhere. It is not unusual for the strongest competitor to be someone that split off on failure to receive a promotion.

Mobility of labor in America. Mobility of labor in America is another problem, almost equal to the mobility of management. A strong contributing factor is dissatisfaction with the job, inability to take pride in the work. People stay home or look around for another job when they can not take pride in their work. Absenteeism and mobility are largely creations of poor supervision and poor management (see p. 80).

5. Running a company on visible figures alone (counting the money). One can not be successful on visible figures alone. Now of course, visible figures are important. There is payroll to meet, vendors to pay, taxes to pay; amortization, pension funds, and contingency funds to meet. But he that would run his company on visible figures alone will in time have neither company nor figures.

Actually, the most important figures that one needs for management are unknown or unknowable (Lloyd S. Nelson, p. 20), but successful management must nevertheless take account of them. Examples:

1. The multiplying effect on sales that comes from a happy customer, and the opposite effect from an unhappy customer.

The happy customer that comes back for more is worth 10 prospects. He comes without advertising or persuasion, and he may even bring in a friend.

It pays to keep the customers satisfied: if a car owner likes his car, he's apt to buy four more cars of the same make over the following twelve years, says Technical Assistance Research Program, a Washington consulting firm that specializes in consumer behavior. The customer is also likely to spread the good news to eight other people. But woe to the car company that delivers a shoddy product. An angry car buyer will tell his troubles to an average of sixteen people. (*Car and Driver*. August 1983, p. 33.)

2. The boost in quality and productivity all along the line that comes from success in improvement of quality at any station upstream.

3. Improvement of quality and productivity where the management makes it clear that the policy of the company will henceforth be to stay in business suited to the market: that this policy is unshakable, regardless of who comes and goes.

4. Improvement of quality and productivity from continual improvement of processes (Point 5 of the 14 points in Ch. 2); also from elimination of work standards, and from better training or better supervision (Points 6, 7, 11).

5. Improvement of quality and productivity from a team composed of the chosen supplier, the buyer, engineering design, sales, customer, working on a new component or redesign of an existing component (p. 41).

6. Improvement of quality and productivity from teamwork between engineers, production, sales, and the customer.

7. Loss from the annual rating on performance.

8. Loss from inhibitors to pride of workmanship of employees.

9. In transportation of motor freight, for example, where are

figures for the cost of free astrays? for delays from poor maintenance?

He that expects to quantify in dollars the gains that will accrue to a company year by year for a program for improvement of quality by principles expounded in this book will suffer delusion. He should know before he starts that he will be able to quantify only a trivial part of the gain.

Visible figures showed that the credit department of a company had succeeded in retaining mostly only customers that pay promptly. The credit department had performed well on the job allotted to them. They deserve a good rating. Figures not so visible, it came to light, showed that the credit department had driven to the competition some of their best customers. Top management looked too late at the total cost.

Costs of warranty are plainly visible, but do not tell the story about quality. Anybody can reduce cost of warranty by refusal or delayed action on complaints.

Another note on management by figures. As the outlook for a company grows bleaker and bleaker, management falls heavier and heavier on the comptroller for management by figures. In the absence of knowledge about the problems of production, the comptroller can only watch the bottom line, squeeze down on costs of materials purchased, including the costs of tools, machinery, maintenance, supplies. Neglect of the more important invisible figures unknown and unknowable, on the total costs of these moves, causes further shrinkage of profit from whatever business remains.

The management of a company that is run on visible figures alone may well move into gardens in the country or to Honolulu, or to any desired spot in the world, receive figures by any of the various channels of communication, and try to use them in the usual way. The following paragraphs from *Business Week*, 25 April 1983, p. 68, tell how easy it is today to collect and assemble visible figures.

The advent of desk-top computers and other information tools, linked together by advanced telecommunications networks that provide access to widely
diverse sources of data, heralds a huge surge in productivity for the approximately 10 million managers in
the U.S. Some of the new wizardry is already in place:

Individual managers now make decisions by combining information developed within their companies
with outside data bases, including economic and industry statistics. Such data allow them to put together
studies of their businesses, markets, competition, pric-
ing, and forecasts in a few hours—studies that once
took months of work.

New systems can turn reams of numbers into charts
and colorful graphs that are easy for managers to
understand. Printouts can thus be more quickly
digested for faster action.

Electronic mail allows reports, memos, and drafts
to be transmitted simultaneously to a number of
people within the company. Such systems greatly
speed in-house communications.

A company may appear to be doing well, on the basis of
visible figures, yet going down the tube for failure of the management to take heed of figures unknown and unknowable.

How about corporate ratings of divisions? Like the annual rating of performance of individual people, the corporate rating of
divisions—all that I have seen—create short-term thinking, and
deflect effort away from long-term improvement. For example,
the procedure in one corporation is to select "at random" 20
specifications from the thousands of specifications of the thousands of parts that a division manufactures; then select "at random" 20 parts subject to each specification; then determine what
proportion of parts made last week met the specifications.

The joke of it is that a division could month after month attain top rating, and win trophies, along with increases and bonuses for the management of the division, and go down the tube all at the same time.

It is easy to see what is wrong. Just meet the specifications: that will do it. At the same time, the division could be losing its shirt on (1) time lost on the factory floor from attempts to use materials not suited to the job; (2) poor maintenance; (3) rework; (4) poor leadership; (5) cheap tools; (6) failure to act on complaints of customers; (7) inept design of product; (8) failure to improve processes; etc.

No one can blame the head of a division for being deeply interested in the corporate rating of his division. His salary and bonus depend on the rating!

This type of rating is management downstream, managing the outcome, too late, so much easier than to provide leadership on improvement. A better way would be to enquire into advancement during the past year on:

1. Removal of barriers to pride of workmanship for hourly workers.
2. Reduction in number of suppliers.
3. Number of parts made today by one supplier compared with the number a year ago.
4. Accomplishments toward teamwork with the chosen supplier (p. 41). Number of teams thus at work on critical parts.
5. Tightening of distributions of a selected number of parts or assemblies made by this division during the past year.
6. Other evidence of improvement of processes.
7. Better training of people that come into the company.
8. Education for employees.

One could go on and on. But all this or any part of it would require innovation in the corporate office, and change.

The same criteria for rating a division are adaptable to choice of a supplier for a given item, treated on page 40.

B.   Obstacles

There are, besides the deadly diseases, a whole parade of obstacles. Some obstacles are in fact candidates for front rank in effectiveness, along with the deadly diseases, though most of them are easier to cure than the deadly diseases. Some of them appeared in Chapter 2 and need no further illumination. Others are new here.

Hope for instant pudding.[5] An important obstacle is the supposition that improvement of quality and productivity is accomplished suddenly by affirmation of faith. Letters and telephone calls received by this author disclose prevalence of the supposition that one or two consultations with a competent statistician will set the company on the road to quality and productivity—instant pudding. "Come, spend a day with us, and do for us what you did for Japan; we too wish to be saved." And they hang up in sorrow. It is not so simple: it will be necessary to study and to go to work. One man actually wrote to me for my formula, and the bill therefor.

A magazine, much read by American people, published in 1981 in its section on business and economics an article on Japan. The author of the article spoiled his otherwise splendid piece of writing by saying in effect, "Dr. Deming went to Japan in 1950 and gave a lecture, and just look what happened." A million readers, I surmise, must have been misled into the supposition that it is all very simple for American industry to copy the Japanese.

An example of expectation of quick results without effort and without sufficient education to the job is exemplified in a letter

5 A term aptly used by James K. Bakken of the Ford Motor Company.

received by Dr. Lloyd S. Nelson, statistician with the Nashua Corporation, which reads as follows:

> The President of my company has appointed me to the same position that you hold in your company. He has given me full authority to proceed, and he wishes me to carry on my new job without bothering him. What ought I to do? How do I go about my new job?

Appointment of someone to the same job that Dr. Nelson has will not create another Dr. Nelson. It would be difficult to convey in four lines so much misunderstanding. The president's supposition that he can resign from his obligation to lead improvement of quality is a glaring fallacy. And who would accept such a mandate from the head of an organization? Only someone that is a complete novice on quality and improvement of quality.

The supposition that solving problems, automation, gadgets, and new machinery will transform industry. No one should sneer at savings of $800,000 per year, or even $1000 per year. A group of workers took pride in changes that saved $500 a year. Every net contribution to efficiency is important, however small.

The big gain is not the $500 per year that the men saved. What is important is that these men could now take pride in the improvement. They felt important to the job and to the company. The quality of their output improved along with outturn. Moreover, this improvement brought forth better quality, productivity, and morale all along the line. This improvement can not be quantified. It remains as one of the invisible figures, so important for management (p. 118).

Incidentally, computation of savings from use of a gadget (automation or robotic machinery) ought to take account of total cost, as an economist would define it. In my experience, people are seldom able to come through with figures on total cost.

Search for examples. Improvement of quality is a method, transferable to different problems and circumstances. It does not consist of cookbook procedures on file ready for specific application to this or that kind of product.

It is not unusual for a consultant to receive an enquiry for examples of success in a similar product line. One man enquired if the methods of this book had ever been used in the manufacture of wheelchairs. Another enquired about compressors for air conditioners: did I know of any application? Another man enquired about the management of a hospital: would the 14 points apply? Another wondered about application in a large accounting firm. Another man wondered if the principles taught in this book had ever been used in the manufacture of automobiles, as if he had never heard of Japan's automobiles. A banker wondered about application in banks. (See Ch. 8.)

> A man just called on the telephone from Johannesburg with the proposal that he come to this country and visit with me six companies that are doing well. He needed examples, he said.

My answer to such enquiries is that no number of examples of success or of failure in the improvement of quality and productivity would indicate to the enquirer what success his company would have. His success would depend totally on his knowledge of the 14 points and of the diseases and obstacles, and the efforts that he himself puts forth.

Too often this is the story. The management of a company, seized with a desire to improve quality and productivity, knowing not how to go about it, having not guidance from principles, seeking enlightenment, embark on excursions to other companies that are ostensibly doing well. They are received with open arms, and the exchange of ideas commences. They (visitors) learn what the host is doing, some of which may by accident be in accordance with the 14 points. Devoid of guiding principles, they are both adrift. Neither company knows whether or why any procedure is right, nor whether or why another is wrong. The question is not whether a business is successful, but why? and why was it not more successful? One can only hope that the visitors enjoy the ride. They are more to be pitied than censured.

It is a hazard to copy. It is necessary to understand the theory of what one wishes to do or to make. Americans are great copiers (QC-Circles, *Kanban* or just in time, for example). The fact is that the Japanese learn the theory of what they wish to make, then improve on it.

QC-Circles contribute vitally to industry in Japan. American management, without understanding management's role in a QC-Circle, try to copy QC-Circles, only to find some time later that they have a dud. QC-Circles that enjoy cooperation and action by management will do well anywhere. We return to QC-Circles on page 136.

It was related to me during a seminar (source unfortunately unrecorded) that the management of a company that makes furniture, doing well, took it into their heads to expand their line into pianos. Why not make pianos? They bought a Steinway piano, took it apart, made or bought parts, and put a piano together exactly like the Steinway, only to discover that they could only get thuds out of their product. So they put the Steinway piano back together with the intention to get their money back on it, only to discover that it too would now only make thuds.

"Our problems are different." A common disease that afflicts management and government administration the world over is the impression that "Our problems are different." They are different, to be sure, but the principles that will help to improve quality of product and of service are universal in nature.

Obsolescence in schools. People often enquire if planned obsolescence is not one of the many causes of decline in the position of U.S. industry. Obsolescence need not be planned.

As profits declined, generally, from 1970 onward, many American companies attempted to bolster their earnings by acquisition and paper profits. The people in finance and law became the important people in the company. Quality and competitive position were submerged. Schools of business responded to popular demand for finance and creative accounting. The results are decline. (Private communication from Robert B. Reich.)

Students in schools of business in America are taught that there is a profession of management; that they are ready to step into top jobs. This is a cruel hoax. Most students have had no experience in production or in sales. To work on the factory floor with pay equal to half what he hoped to get upon receipt of the M.B.A., just to get experience, is a horrible thought to an M.B.A., not the American way of life. As a consequence, he struggles on, unaware of his limitations, or unable to face the need to fill in the gaps. The results are obvious.

A student in a school of business in the U.S. today might well ask himself and his teachers which courses that the school offers would provide anybody with knowledge that could be directed toward improvement of our balance of trade. Mathematics, economics, psychology, statistical theory, theory of law, yes, but most studies of accounting, marketing, and finance are skills, not education; most use of computers for paperwork, likewise.

The best way for a student to learn a skill is to go to work in some good company, under masters, and get paid while he learns. Faults in education were stated well by Edward A. Reynolds in *Standardization News* (Philadelphia), April 1983, p. 7:

> There are many reasons why U.S. quality/productivity (they go hand in hand) have not kept ahead. A few of the major ones are: the educational system that turns out math ignoramuses and emphasizes the MBA (which teaches managers how to take over companies, but not how to run them); the short-term goals of corporate heads (this year's profit for bonus or a better job elsewhere); the practice of moving about the country, and finally out of it, for cheaper labor (despite the fact that direct labor is a small minority of costs); the change from honest leadership and work ethic to "get yours" and "everyone does it" at all levels.
>
> Practically all of our major corporations were started by technical men—inventors, mechanics, engineers, and chemists, who had a sincere interest in quality of products. Now these companies are largely run by men interested in profit, not product. Their pride is in the P & L statement or stock report.

Poor teaching of statistical methods in industry. Awakening to the need for quality, and with no idea what quality means nor how to achieve it, American management have resorted to mass assemblies for crash courses in statistical methods, employing hacks for teachers, being unable to discriminate between competence and ignorance. The result is that hundreds of people are learning what is wrong.

No one should teach the theory and use of control charts without knowledge of statistical theory through at least the master's level, supplemented by experience under a master. I make this statement on the basis of experience, seeing every day the devastating effects of incompetent teaching and faulty application.

The teaching of pure statistical theory in universities, including the theory of probability and related subjects, is almost everywhere excellent. Application to enumerative studies is mostly correct, but application to analytic problems—planning for improvement of tomorrow's run, next year's crop—is unfortunately, however, in many textbooks deceptive and misleading.[6]

Analysis of variance, t-test, confidence intervals, and other statistical techniques taught in the books, however interesting, are inappropriate because they provide no basis for prediction and because they bury the information contained in the order of production. Most if not all computer packages for analysis of data, as they are called, provide flagrant examples of inefficiency.

A confidence interval has operational meaning and is very useful for summarization of results of an enumerative study. I use confidence intervals in legal evidence in enumerative studies. But a confidence interval has no operational meaning for prediction, hence provides no degree of belief for planning.

A repeated and repeatable pattern (Method 2 performs better than Method 1), without unexplained failure over a range of environmental conditions, leads to a degree of belief for purposes of planning. Degree of belief can not be quantified as 0.8, 0.9, 0.95, 0.99. So-called probability levels of significance between Method 1 and Method 2 do not provide any measure of degree of belief for planning—i.e., for prediction.

For example, certain polymers mixed 60 minutes in Köln work better in succeeding manufacturing processes than the same polymers mixed 30 minutes (at the same temperature, of course). One might suppose, for purposes of planning, that the comparison would be about the same in Dayton.

This leap of faith would be taken by knowledge of chemistry, not by statistical theory. One must never forget the importance of subject matter.

---

6 W. Edwards Deming, *Some Theory of Sampling* (Wiley, 1950; Dover, 1984), Ch. 7; *Sample Design in Business Research* (Wiley, 1960), p. 356.

No matter how strong be our degree of belief, we must always bear in mind that empirical evidence is never complete.[7]

People with master's degrees in statistical theory accept jobs in industry and government to work with computers. It is a vicious cycle. Statisticians do not know what statistical work is, and are satisfied to work with computers. People that hire statisticians likewise have no knowledge about statistical work, and somehow suppose that computers are the answer. Statisticians and management thus misguide each other and keep the vicious cycle rolling. (From a conversation with R. Clifton Bailey, 7 July 1984.)

Use of Military Standard 105D and other tables for acceptance. Many thousands of dollars worth of product changes hands hourly, lots subjected to acceptance or rejection, depending on tests of samples, drawn from the lots. Examples of such plans are Military Standard 105D, and Dodge–Romig AOQL (average outgoing quality limit) or Dodge–Romig LTPD (lot tolerance percentage defective). Such plans can only increase costs, as will be clear from Chapter 16. If used for quality audit of final product as it goes out the door, they guarantee that some customers will get defective product. The day of such plans is finished. American industry can not afford the losses that they cause. (More in Ch. 15.)

Incredibly, courses and books in statistical methods still devote time and pages to acceptance sampling.

"Our quality control department takes care of all our problems of quality." Every company has a quality control department. Unfortunately, quality control departments have taken the job of quality away from the people that can contribute most to quality—management, supervisors, managers of purchasing,

---

7 Clarence Irving Lewis, *Mind and the World-Order* (Scribner's, 1929; Dover, 1956), Chs. 6–9.

and production workers. They have failed to explain to management the importance of good management, including the evils of (e.g.) purchase of materials on the basis of price tag, evils of multiple vendors, of work standards, awkward and costly arrangements of plant. Management, mystified by control charts and statistical thinking, are glad to leave quality to people that mystify them.

Unfortunately, the function of quality assurance in many companies is too often to provide hindsight, to keep the management informed about the amount of defective product produced week by week, or comparisons month by month on levels of quality, costs of warranty, etc.

What management needs are charts to show whether the system has reached a stable state (in which case management must take on the chief role for improvement), or it is still infested with special causes (Ch. 11).

In my experience, some quality control departments apparently work on the supposition that the more charts the better. Quality control departments plot points and file the charts. This is what happened in America in the years 1942 to 1948. By 1949, all charts had disappeared. Why? Management then, as now, did not understand their jobs and the contributions that only they could make.

"Our troubles lie entirely in the work force." The supposition is prevalent the world over that there would be no problems in production or in service if only our production workers would do their jobs in the way that they were taught. Pleasant dreams. The workers are handicapped by the system, and the system belongs to management.

It was Dr. Joseph M. Juran who pointed out long ago that most of the possibilities for improvement lie in action on the system, and that contributions of production workers are severely limited.

> There is here [in Czechoslovakia] the same widespread unsupported assumption that the bulk of de-

fects are operator-controllable, and that if the operators would only put their backs into it, the plant's quality-problems would shrink materially. (Joseph M. Juran, *Industrial Quality Control* 22, May 1966: p. 624.)

Only recently, the entire management of a large manufacturing concern supposed, by their own declaration, that if all 2700 operations in the plant were carried off without blemish, there would be no problems. I listened for three hours to their exciting achievements with statistical methods on the shop floor. Their engineers, I found, were treating every problem as a special cause—find it and remove it—not working on the system itself (Ch. 11). At the same time, costs of warranty were soaring upward, and business was on the decline. The management seemed to be totally unaware of the need for better design of their main product, and more attention to incoming materials. Why did they put so much faith in statistical methods on the shop floor? Answer: What else is there? Quality is for other people, not for us.

A huge bank in Chicago ran adrift on to rocky shores. This trouble would still have occurred even if every calculation and every piece of paper handled by the bank had been free of error.

A grocery store barely pays its way or goes out of business from failure of the manager to adjust his wares to the needs and income level of the community, even though there be no mistakes at the counter, and no item ever out of stock.

It is thus not sufficient to improve processes. There must also be constant improvement of design of product and service, along with introduction of new product and service and new technology. All this is management's responsibility.

False starts. False starts are deceptive. They give satisfaction, something to show for effort, but they lead to frustration, despair, disappointment, and delay.

One kind of false start arises from the supposition that wholesale teaching of statistical methods to enough people in production will turn things around. The fallacy of this supposition has been amply demonstrated.

Understanding of variation, special causes and common causes, and the necessity to reduce constantly the variation from common causes, is vital. It is a fact, though, with a clean record, that a company whose management abrogates their responsibility for quality and depends wholly on statistical methods on the shop floor, and forces those methods on to suppliers, will within three years toss these methods out, along with the people engaged on them.

A friend, a consultant far abler than I am, spent six weeks in the spring and summer of 1983 in a division of one of America's best-known companies. Here is what he found:

1. The plant shipped on 30 June (the last day of a quarter) 30 per cent of the items that had been produced there during the month. Policy: at the end of the quarter, ship it. Defer purchases and payment till the new quarter begins.

2. One hundred fifty-four control charts were kept in the plant, but only five were calculated and used correctly.

3. Annual rating of performance was carried to an unbelievable extreme: the ratings handed out to any group of people, even of five people, must range from outstanding high to redundant.

4. Five levels of management above the plant manager. No wonder the plant manager could not get any action from his superiors.

5. A new plant manager taking office in one of the plants ordered every man in management to wear a necktie. Result: chaos, mutiny. (Not that it is sinful to wear a necktie, but that the men could not understand the connexion between necktie and performance.)

Another false start is QC-Circles. The idea has appeal. The production worker can tell us a lot about what is wrong and how improvements can be made: why not tap this source of information and help? Effectiveness of QC-Circles is in most American companies years off, as Dr. Tsurumi points out at the end of this chapter. A QC-Circle can thrive only if the management will take action on the recommendation of the Circle. Many QC-Circles are, I fear, management's hope for a lazy way out.

Experts whose business it is to start and monitor QC-circles are careful to work first with the manager, to lay a foundation that has a chance of success.

Taken from a speech by Dr. Akira Ishikawa at the
Newark Museum, 16 November 1983

In the U.S., a QC-Circle is normally organized as a formal staff organization, whereas a QC-Circle in Japan is an informal group of workers. A manager in Japan serves as an advisor or a consultant. In the U.S., a manager of production, to get rid of the job, appoints facilitators for Quality of Work Life, Employee Involvement, Employee Participation, QC-Circles, all of which disintegrate.

The second contrast is in the selection of a theme for a meeting and the way in which the meeting is guided. In the U.S., the selection of a theme or project and how to proceed on it are proposed by a manager. In contrast, in Japan, these things are decided by the initiative of the member-workers.

The third feature is the difference in hours for a meeting. A meeting in the U.S. is held within working hours. A meeting in Japan may be held during working hours, during the lunch period, or after working hours.

In the U.S., monetary reward for a suggestion goes to the individual. In Japan, the benefit is distributed to all employees. Recognition of group achievement supersedes monetary benefit to the individual.

A good place to start a QC-Circle in America is with the management. For example, managers of purchasing need to follow through the production lines the materials that they purchase. This would call for a QC-Circle consisting of purchasing, production, research, engineering design, and sales. Many companies already have a QC-Circle in management but never thought of them as QC-Circles. QC-Circles composed of supervisors and inspectors are excellent, and will be spontaneous with a little encouragement. The letter that follows has been helpful to the author.

> In the seminars, many participants asked about QC-Circles (QC-C). Besides, I have heard that many plants in the world are now starting QC-Cs. Many executives and managers might be possessed with serious illusion that, if they succeed in establishing QC-Cs they could solve major problems in their plants. Then, they would not begin any management improvement activities for quality by themselves. There is no doubt that QC-Circles are a very powerful force to solve problems in quality and productivity at the operational level, but it should be well understood that a QC-Circle is not a cure-all. Defects are caused not only by faulty operation of workers, but also usually more seriously and frequently by poor design, poor specifications, poor education and training, poor arrangement and maintenance of machines, and so on. These are all problems of management, which a QC-Circle can not solve. (Letter from my friend Dr. Noriaki Kano of the University of Electro-Communications, Tokyo.)

"We installed quality control." No. You can install a new desk, or a new carpet, or a new dean, but not quality control. Anyone that proposes to "install quality control" unfortunately has little knowledge about quality control.

Improvement of quality and productivity, to be successful in any company, must be a learning process, year by year, top management leading the whole company.

The unmanned computer. A computer can be a blessing. It can also be a curse. Some people make good use of computers. Few people are aware, however, of the negative input of computers. Time and time again, in my experience, when I ask for data on inspection, to learn whether they indicate that the process is in control, or out of control, and at what time of day it went out, and why, or ask about differences between inspectors and between production workers, or between production workers and inspectors, in an attempt to find sources of trouble and to improve efficiency, the answer is, "The data are in the computer." And there they sit.

People are intimidated by the computer. They can not tell it what data or charts they need: instead, they take whatever the computer turns out, which is reams of figures.

An advertisement of a computer sets forth this accomplishment—instant figures at the press of a button on sales as of yesterday, or of accounts receivable.

This is of course a great accomplishment, electronically. But for purposes of management, it may be only another bear trap. A single figure (as of yesterday, for example) by itself conveys little information. It is a candidate for misuse. Figures will vary day to day, unless they are held constant by fear. What management needs is understanding of variation. Figures of yesterday plotted on a chart, and interpreted with some understanding of variation, will indicate existence of a special cause of variation that should be investigated at once, if one exists, or that the variation should be attributable to the system.

The supposition that it is only necessary to meet specifications. Specifications can not tell the whole story. The supplier must know what the material is to be used for. For example, a specification for sheet steel of a certain composition and thickness is not sufficient for the inside door panel of an automobile. The inside panel must undergo a considerable amount of stretching and warping. If the supplier knows that the steel will be used for the inside panel, he may be able to supply steel that will do the job. Steel that merely meets the specifications can cause a lot of trouble.

A programmer has a similar problem. She learns, after she finishes the job, that she programmed very well the specifications as delivered to her, but that they were deficient. If she had only known the purpose of the program, she could have done it right for the purpose, even though the specifications were deficient.

A vice-president in charge of manufacturing told me that half his problems arise from materials that met the specifications.

The problem is not merely to find good vendors for good parts. Two vendors may both be able to meet your requirements for statistical evidence of quality, and both make superb product. There may nevertheless be a problem in changeover from the cylinder heads made in the United States to cylinder heads made in Italy. Both are of excellent quality, but five hours are required to change from one to the other.

A still more serious problem exists in the manufacture of complex apparatus, such as a fiberglass cable to run from one city to another. The system requires more than a good cable. It requires repeaters and loading coils, carrier equipment and filters, and a myriad of other essential items of equipment. These items are not bricks and mortar to be put together by a skilled workman. They must be designed together, tested over and over in small subassemblies, modified as required, then in a multitude of bigger subassemblies, and so on.

Anyone who has bought his computer equipment from several sources can testify to problems. Whatever happens, any trouble is always laid to some other part of the equipment, made by someone else.

My friend Robert Piketty of Paris put it this way: listen to the

Royal Philharmonic Orchestra of London play Beethoven's Fifth Symphony. Now listen to some amateur orchestra play it. Of course, you like both performances: you enjoy home-grown talent. Both orchestras met the specifications: not a mistake. But listen to the difference. Just listen to the difference!

The ultimate customer (e.g., owner of an automobile) does not care about the specifications of the eight hundred parts in the transmission. He only cares whether the transmission works, and if it is quiet.

The fallacy of zero defects.[8] There is obviously something wrong when a measured characteristic barely inside a specification is declared to be conforming; outside it is declared to be nonconforming. The supposition that everything is all right inside the specifications and all wrong outside does not correspond to this world.

A better description of the world is the Taguchi loss function in which there is minimum loss at the nominal value, and an ever-increasing loss with departure either way from the nominal value. (See the footnote on p. 50.)

It will not suffice to have customers that are merely satisfied. An unhappy customer will switch. Unfortunately, a satisfied customer may also switch, on the theory that he could not lose much, and might gain. Profit in business comes from repeat customers, customers that boast about your product and service, and that bring friends with them. Fully allocated costs may well show that the profit in a transaction with a customer that comes back voluntarily may be 10 times the profit realized from a customer that responds to advertising and other persuasion.

Gadgets and servomechanisms that by mechanical or electronic circuits guarantee zero defects will destroy the advantage

8 I am indebted to William W. Scherkenbach of the Ford Motor Company for the content of this section.

of a beautiful narrow distribution of dimensions. They slide the distribution back and forth inside the specification limits, achieving zero defects and at the same time driving losses and costs to the maximum. They apply Rule 2, 3, or Rule 4, with the funnel, page 328, creating trouble. Better off than on.

Inadequate testing of prototypes. A common practice among engineers is to put together a prototype of an assembly with every part very close to the nominal or intended measured characteristic. The test may go off well. The problem is that when the assembly goes into production, all characteristics will vary. In the most ideal state, they will vary on a distribution about the nominal or intended value. In practice, there may be no predictable distribution of many of the parts, the state of statistical control being still far in the future. The fact is that volume production may turn out only one part in 100,000 that will perform like the prototype.

Anyone engaged in testing should ask himself the following questions:

1. What will the results refer to?

2. Will they refer to tomorrow's run or to next year's crop?

3. Under what conditions will these results predict results of tomorrow's run or of next year's crop?

4. Will they add to my degree of belief for some prediction that I need for planning?

5. In what way will they help me to plan a change?

6. What is an operational meaning of the verb "To learn," in studies of a process, with the aim to improve it?

Monte Carlo methods can be of help in testing, especially in the stage of computer-assisted design, by varying dimensions, pressure, temperature, torque, over reasonable and unreasonable ranges. The same methods are equally helpful in tests of actual hardware, although the number of combinations of departures from nominal values must be drastically reduced.

Failure to understand variation in tests delayed some years the science of genetics. Ratios of (e.g.) tall and dwarf peas varied wildly below and above nature's average value 1:4. This variation bothered everyone, including the monk Gregor Mendel, discoverer of the simple dominant gene.[9]

"Anyone that comes to try to help us must understand all about our business." All evidence points to the fallacy of this supposition. Competent men in every position, if they are doing their best, know all that there is to know about their work except how to improve it. Help toward improvement can come only from some other kind of knowledge. Help may come from outside the company, combined with knowledge already possessed by people within the company but not being utilized.

Heard and Seen

1. The customer's specifications are often far tighter than he needs. It would be interesting to ask a customer how he arrives at his specifications, and why he needs the tolerances that he specifies.

2. We rejected a load of material and returned it to the vendor. He sent it back to us, and this time our inspection passed the lot. He learned in a hurry what to do. In fact, our two drivers met each other over coffee on the road, one returning a load, the other returning a rejected load to see if it would pass on second trial.

3. Figures on the amount of rework do not provide a signpost on how to reduce it. They do provide, however, a basis for understanding the magnitude of the problem. Anyone can see what rework is costing us, and that we would be justified in spending a lot of money to learn how to reduce it.

4. Our budget allows us six per cent for rework. Just think

9 O. Kempthorne, *An Introduction to Genetic Statistics* (Wiley, 1957).

how profits of the company would soar if we had no rework! The allowance of six per cent provides no incentive to do better. It becomes a work standard: meet it, but don't beat it.

5. A complicated machine requires a special oil, expensive. The plant manager had orders to cut expenses. He did. He bought oil locally from a dealer at a big saving. Result: repairs, $7500.

6. Machine out of order, but running, turning out product, every piece wrong, yet usable. Final product, blemished. The operator had reported three times that this machine was out of order, but nothing had yet happened.

7. There are eleven hundred parts on each circuit board. By terms laid down by the government, every piece must be inspected by four people, and signed, the fourth one being the government's inspector. This means forty-four hundred signatures for one circuit board. We have more trouble with the signatures than with the circuit boards. For example, all four men failed to inspect a part. We have to bring all four men back here to inspect the part and sign the record. All four men inspected a part, but one of them failed to sign for it. Where is he?

8. *Foreman* (to production worker in response to question): Just do your job.

9. A woman on the job was held up by a wrong count. She was making a batch of 24 items. A box of a certain part turned up 1 short. Result: 35 minutes lost for search for a part of the right size.

10. Samples of shoes sent out; orders are coming in. Production is ready to start, but for one hitch: the purchasing department can not find material to match well enough the color and texture of the samples. No one had foreseen this difficulty.

11. A company shipped to a customer a machine. The salesman looked at it on the customer's premises before he started it up and observed that it would leak abrasive. The salesman did not wish to tell the customer that it was defective, so he called at once the service department to come and make the changes that

would be required. The service manager said that he knew that it would leak, but that he could do nothing about it, because the people in engineering design would not believe him until it failed in operation. It failed, and brought down upon the customer a delay of five weeks. The customer withheld $10,000 for loss in production. (Related to me by Kate McKeown.)

12. *Operator* (running four lathes simultaneously): Before I had the control chart, I could not tell what I was doing. I could only learn later: too late. We were making one defective item out of ten. Now I can see what I am doing before it is too late. The three of us on the three shifts use the same chart. We do not need to make adjustments when we come on the job. We can see where we are at. We are now making no defectives. I am happier. *Consultant:* Why are you happier? *Operator:* Because I am not making any defects now.

13. A housing authority put up a hundred dwelling units in an area for low-cost housing. The government engaged three inspectors to report on the construction once it was finished. When winter came, occupants of dwelling units found bills for heat in the neighborhood of $300 per month, not fitting to the bank accounts of occupants of low-cost housing. Why was the cost of heating so high? "No insulation in the attic" was the answer. All three inspectors declared that they were aware of the failure of the builder to put insulation in the attic, but each one decided not to make note of the failure, as he was sure that the other two inspectors would not observe it, and he wished not to discredit his colleagues.

14. We have been making brake lining all these years, and we never understood what we were doing, nor what brake lining the customer wished to have. We had many arguments; in fact, nothing but, though he did take our brake lining, such as it was. Perhaps he had no other source to depend on. We decided a few years ago to work together, to develop operational definitions of what he wished to have, and what we could make. Of course, this was a big job, because brake lining is measured by many charac-

teristics. We now furnish to the customer $\bar{x}$- and R-charts for the chief characteristics of the brake lining that he buys from us, and we have no problems.

15. We tried QC-Circles among the hourly workers, without first educating the management into their responsibilities to remove obstacles reported. We learned our lesson the hard way: our QC-Circles disintegrated.

16. We have for twenty-five years been working on problems, and not on the processes that caused the problems.

17. We don't need control charts here nor design of experiments. We have computers to take care of all of our problems of quality. (Quoted from a manufacturer of intricate electronic equipment, in reply to a customer that wished to talk about problems with this manufacturer's product, and about the possibility to work together for better quality by use of control charts and improvement of processes and procedures.)

18. I saw this company carrying out 100 per cent inspection on brake discs, when the control chart told them that no inspection was required, except, of course, samples for the control chart. (Quoting Heero Hacquebord, Pretoria.)

American Management Has Missed the Point—the Point Is Management Itself[10]

By YOSHI TSURUMI

American managers have been impressed, especially after touring Japanese businesses. Over the past year hundreds of businesses in this country have experimented with quality control circles. Yet very few of the fifty large Japanese manufacturing firms here have extensively used quality control circles. Most Japanese managers know that the establishment of them is not the first but the last step in building a corporate culture that will

10 Condensed from Dr. Tsurumi's article in *The Dial*, September 1981. I am deeply indebted to Dr. Tsurumi and to the publishers of *The Dial*.

support a company's total commitment to product quality and high productivity.

No concept has been more misunderstood by American managers, academics, and workers than productivity. For workers in America a call for increased productivity carries with it the threat of layoffs. Managers understand productivity to be an economic trade-off between efficiency and product quality. Business-school courses on management are often watered down to numerical games of inventory control and production flow in which financial budgeting and tight control are oversold as effective management tools. On production floors and in corporate offices, sociological verbiage has replaced a basic understanding of human behavior.

Attempts to cope with the human side of labor have often been superficial. American managers have come up with solutions both to soothe emotions and to boost lagging production. Workers now greet these management fads with skepticism, having seen too many of them come and go. Background music and suggestion boxes and psychological counseling were tried and abandoned. These efforts are just naive attempts, workers say, to get them to work harder. Are quality control circles any different? they ask, especially after one electronics firm that had acted on the idea abruptly laid off workers so it could meet its budgeted profit.

In Japan, when a company has to absorb a sudden economic hardship such as a 25 per cent decline in sales, the sacrificial pecking order is firmly set. First the corporate dividends are cut. Then the salaries and the bonuses of top management are reduced. Next, management salaries are trimmed from the top to the middle of the hierarchy. Lastly, the rank and file are asked to accept pay cuts or a reduction in the work force through attrition or voluntary discharge. In the United States, a typical firm would probably do the opposite under similar circumstances.

Quality control circles can never replace management's fundamental responsibility to redefine its role and rebuild the corporate culture. As long as management is quick to take credit for a firm's successes but equally swift to blame its workers for its failures, no surefire remedy for low productivity can be expected in American manufacturing and service industries.

Big Japanese corporations treat human resources as their most renewable resources. The hiring, the training, and the promotion of employees and managers are the responsibility of the corporation as a whole. Even a chief executive officer does not dangle the threat, implied or otherwise, of firing a subordinate. Instead, it is management's job to encourage working toward the shared goals of the firm by helping to satisfy the human needs of job satisfaction and self-fulfillment.

One Japanese plant manager who turned an unproductive U.S. factory into a profitable venture in less than three months told me: "It is simple. You treat American workers as human beings with ordinary human needs and values. They react like human beings." Once the superficial, adversarial relationship between managers and workers is eliminated, they are more likely to pull together during difficult times and to defend their common interest in the firm's health.

Without a cultural revolution in management, quality control circles will not produce the desired effects in America. Nor can anyone guarantee that job security for the rank and file would be enough to produce high productivity and product quality. However, without a management commitment to the personal welfare of its workers, it will be impossible to inspire employees' interest in company productivity and product quality. With guaranteed job security, management's job becomes far more difficult and challenging.

For the first time in its history, the United States faces the job of managing economic growth with an increasing scarcity of capital, raw materials, energy sources, managerial skill, and market opportunities. There are strained business–government relations and antagonistic management–employee relations. It is not going to be easy for the United States to learn Japan's secret.

4

When? How Long?

Whoso removeth stones shall be hurt therewith; and
he that cleaveth wood shall be endangered thereby.—
Ecclesiastes 10:9.

Catch up? People enquire how long it will take America to
catch up with the Japanese. This is a fuzzy question, sincere, but
born of lack of understanding. Does anyone suppose that the
Japanese are going to sit still and wait for someone to catch up?
How can you catch up with someone that is all the time gaining
speed? We know now that it will not suffice to meet the competition; that he that hopes only to meet the competition is already
licked. We must do better with end runs, and we can. Decades
will be required.

Rehearsal of some of the problems. We live in a society dedicated to dividends, organization, decision, orders from top to
bottom, confrontation (every idea put forth must win or lose),
and all-out war to destroy a competitor be he at home or abroad.
Take no prisoners. There must be winners, and there must be
losers. This may not be the road to better material living.

We live in an era in which everyone expects to see an ever-
rising standard of living. A little arithmetic sometimes helps to
clarify thinking. Whence cometh the ever-increasing supply of
worldly goods that build up an ever-increasing supply of food,
clothing, housing, transportation, and other services? It is

difficult to understand how any economic upturn of importance can take place in the United States till our products become competitive at home and abroad.

How can one purchase other people's goods if he can not sell his own product and service? The only possible answer lies in better design, better quality, and greater productivity.

Only better management can bring the needed improvement. The big question is, how long will it be until top management become active in their responsibilities? And then how much longer will it take? Where is American industry headed toward? Restoration? Not restoration, but transformation. Solving problems and installation of gadgets are not the answer.

The big problem for management may be difficulty to make any kind of change. This difficulty may in fact amount to paralysis.

The pay and privilege of the captains of industry are now so closely linked to the quarterly dividend that they may find it personally unrewarding to do what is right for the company. The most important step that could be taken in any company would be for the board of directors to declare their interest in the long-range prospects for the company. To protect them in this resolve, it may be necessary to pass laws forbidding takeover bids and leveraged buyouts.

Retardation to transformation. How rapidly will American management remove the obstacles that block the road to restoration of American leadership? Chapters 2 and 3 have described a parade of deadly diseases and an additional host of destructive ones. These are all products of American management. Only American management can eradicate them.

There are other alleged impediments which, whether real or not, conveniently deflect the public's attention from the failure of management. Some of them could be artificial rates of exchange of currencies, nontariff and hidden barriers to trade, government interference. All of these alleged impediments rolled up together would make a small bundle compared with the obstacles that American management has created for themselves.

For example, can the management of a company adopt constancy of purpose for product and service in the future as the prime reason for existence of the company, and hold on to their jobs long enough to get started on this road?

Constancy of purpose to stay in business, to provide jobs for our people, by planning now for product and service that will have a market in the future, is vital, as early pages have explained. However, it is not easy to adopt this policy. Anyone that sets off on this course runs the risk of being dismissed for using funds that could otherwise be put into dividends. An example was recorded in *Business Week* for 15 March 1982. A man who had been engaged by a large company to lead plans for the future was dismissed because dividends for the fourth quarter of 1981 took a dip.

Management has led stockholders to believe that dividends are a measure of management's performance. Some schools of business teach their students how to maximize profits on a short-term basis. It may well be that stockholders are smarter than management. That is, stockholders, including managers of pension funds invested in industry, may be far more interested in growth and in future dividends than in today's dividends. When will management learn that they have a moral obligation to protect investment?

How long? How long will it take to change the climate? An advertising agency changed in a decade an entire nation with respect to one commodity.[1] Could an advertising agency change a nation's views on quick profits, to give to management a new outlook and a chance to adopt constancy of purpose? If yes, how long would it take? A decade? Two? More like three.

---

1 Edward Jay Epstein, "Have you ever tried to sell a diamond?" *Atlantic*, February 1982, pp. 23–34.

How many years will pass before economists learn the new economics, and teach it? A decade? Two?

What about inhibiting forces from government? How many years will pass before government regulatory agencies learn that the forces of competition for price do not solve the problems of quality and of service: that competition that destroys service may not be a desirable aim of regulation? Two decades? Three?

Regulatory agencies, victims of mandates that are not clear, or are outdated, not knowing how to take into account the interest of the public, may meanwhile continue to make it difficult for industry to improve productivity. The Justice Department's Antitrust Division has already wrecked our systems of telephone communication and transportation, under the tenet that competition for price is better for the dear public. Hard lessons lie ahead.

It is wasteful and ridiculous, for example, that men in Ford and Pontiac and Chrysler can not work together to reduce from 15 to perhaps 5 the number of gauges of steel for the left front fender of automobiles. How can American industry compete with Japanese industry on costs when Americans are victims of government regulations?

Will bankers, owners, government agencies with administrative power accept the challenge to serve American industry? Or will they continue the ceremony of traditional worship?

> The history of recent years is replete with examples of government regulations that were born of good intentions, but which wound up far deadlier than the disease that they were supposed to cure. (Editorial, *Business Week*, 3 July 1978, p. 112.)

> But the problems of antitrust extend beyond that of a changing environment. Enforcement often loses sight of what should be the predominant question. How do we make America more productive? . . . We

still need further improvements in the ratio of intelligence to body weight in antitrust matters. (Lester C.
Thurow, *Newsweek*, 18 January 1982, p. 63.)

An additional factor [that inhibits productivity] is
government regulation, which requires business to
spend huge sums and man hours in complying with af-
firmative action, safety, and other programs. The cost
of regulation to American business in 1976 alone was
estimated at approximately $30 billion.

We all know about the miles and miles of red tape
that banking has had to deal with. The Truth in Lend-
ing Act is a classic example. We have also had to hire
huge legal staffs to cope with the red tape. (Leland S.
Prussia, chairman of the board of the Bank of America, at the meeting of the Bank Administration Institute in Atlanta, 25 January 1982.)

Let us reflect further. Even when the management of a company embarks in earnest on the 14 points for quality, productivity, and competitive position, advancement will at the best
appear to be sluggish. One must allow five years for the purchasing department to learn their new job and to put it into effect,
namely, to shift from (a) search for lower prices and award of
business to the lowest bidder to (b) purchase based on evidence
of quality as well as on price. Concurrently, a company may
embark on other improvements, such as to cease dependence on
mass inspection and reduction of the number of vendors to those
that deliver their product along with statistical evidence of
quality.

Companies with good management will require five years to
remove the barriers that make it impossible for the hourly
worker to take pride in his work. Many companies will require
ten years.

Other points of the 14 will also require time; likewise cure of the diseases in Chapter 3, even in companies where the management have removed obstacles to constancy of purpose.

When? It may be obvious to anyone, on reflection on the obstacles that we have seen, that a long, thorny road lies ahead in American industry—10 to 30 years—before we can settle down to an acknowledged competitive position. This position along with the associated standard of living that lies ahead may be second place, may be fourth.

By that time, products that have been the backbone of export may dwindle or vanish, while new products swell forth from companies that are putting faith and resources into their own future.

The question may not be when, but whether.

Agricultural products have been helpful the past few years in our balance of payment: without them the deficit would be much larger than it is. Will soil and water hold out? Are we to become an agrarian society?

It might be of interest to note that the business of agriculture has become ever more and more efficient to the point where today in the United States one person raises food to feed himself and another 77, surplus and all. People in agriculture have never lost a chance to adopt immediately any possible practice or product that might improve efficiency. Incidentally, innovation in agricultural practice comes largely from experimental stations the world over, all of which use statistical methods for efficiency and reliability of tests.

Unfortunately, the business of agriculture has concentrated on production, relying on cowardly tariffs, quotas, and government subsidies for protection. The same effort and brains devoted to new uses and to marketing of our agricultural products worldwide, instead of letting the government manage development and sales, might bring to American agriculture new levels of profit and awakening to a new frontier.

Agriculture might become even more productive if governmental support of prices were removed.

Survival of the fittest. Who will survive? Companies that adopt constancy of purpose for quality, productivity, and service, and go about it with intelligence and perseverance, have a chance to survive. They must, of course, offer products and services that have a market. Charles Darwin's law of survival of the fittest, and that the unfit do not survive, holds in free enterprise as well as in natural selection. It is a cruel law, unrelenting.

Actually, the problem will solve itself. The only survivors will be companies with constancy of purpose for quality, productivity, and service.

5

Questions to Help Managers

I held my tongue and spake nothing. I kept silence, yea, even from good words, but it was pain and grief to me.—Psalms 39:3.

Purpose of this chapter. This chapter consists of questions that may provide to management some basis to assist their understanding of their responsibilities.

THE QUESTIONS

1a. Has your company established constancy of purpose?

b. If yes, what is the purpose? If no, what are the obstacles?

c. Will this stated purpose stay fixed, or will it change as presidents come and go?

d. Do all employees of your company know about this stated constancy of purpose (raison d'être), if you have formulated one?

e. How many believe it to the extent that it affects their work?

f. Whom does your president answer to? Whom do your board of directors answer to?

2a. Where would you wish your business to be five years from now?

b. How do you think you will accomplish these aims? By what method? (Repeated from William A. Golomski, p. 19.)

3a. How may you learn whether, with respect to some

quality-characteristic, you have a stable process or stable system?

b. If stable, where lies the main responsibility for further improvement? Why is it in this circumstance futile to plead with the plant manager, superintendents, division chiefs, and the work force, for better quality?

c. If not stable, what is different? What would be different about your attempt to accomplish improvement?

4a. Have you established teams to work on each of the 14 points in Chapter 2, and on the deadly diseases and obstacles of Chapter 3?

b. How are you doing on Point 14?

c. What are you doing to create teamwork between purchasing and production?

5a. Is absenteeism in your company a stable process?

b. How about fires?

c. How about accidents?

d. If yes, where lies the responsibility for improvement? (Answer: with the management.)

6a. Why is transformation of management necessary for survival?

b. Are you creating a critical mass of people to help you to change?

c. Why is this critical mass necessary?

d. Do all levels of your management take part in the new philosophy?

e. Can any of them initiate proposals for consideration? Do they?

7. If you run a service organization:

a. What proportion of the people in your company know that you have a product, that this product is service?

b. Does every employee know that he has a customer?

c. How do you define quality? How do you measure it?

d. Is your service better than it was a year ago? Why? How do you know?

    e. (If yes.) Why is this?

    f. Do you have more than one vendor for any item that you purchase repeatedly?

    g. (If yes.) Why is this?

    h. If you have one vendor for an item, do you have a long-term loyal relationship with him?

    i. Is absenteeism at a stable rate?

8. If you run a construction company:

    a. Is your service to your customers better than it was two years ago?

    b. In what way?

    c. What have you done to try to improve it?

9. What are you doing to create teamwork between:

    a. design and production of product (or service)?

    b. design and sales of product (or service)?

    c. design and purchasing of product (or service)?

10. What are you doing to close the gap between design of product and service, and actual production and delivery? In other words, what are you doing to improve test of your product and your service before you go into production and delivery?

11. What steps are you taking to improve quality of:

    a. incoming materials for production?

    b. tools, machinery, and nonproductive items?

    c. internal communications (delivery of mail, papers, telephone, telegraph)?

12a. Does your purchasing department stick to the lowest bidder? If yes, why? And what is this policy costing you?

    b. Does cost of use come into consideration? How?

13a. What is your program for reduction in number of suppliers?

    b. For four important items that you use on a regular basis, including commodities and transportation.

    c. For each of these items, how many suppliers have you?
        Now?
        How many a year ago?

How many two years ago?

How many three years ago?

d. What is your program for developing long-term relationships of loyalty and trust with your suppliers (including commodities and transportation)?

14. Do your people in management receive an annual performance rating? If yes, what are you doing to supplant this system with a better plan?

15. Does your management know about the costs of engineering changes? What is the underlying cause of engineering changes? Do your engineers have time to do their work right in the first place? How are they rated? Do you see any problems with your system for rating your engineers? If yes, what are you planning to do about it?

16. Does training and retraining in any operation in your company teach the requirements of the next operation?

17. What proportion of your workers have a chance to understand the requirements of the next operation? Why does not everybody have an understanding of the next operation?

18. How would you calculate the loss from failure of everyone to have a chance to understand the requirements of the next operation? (This is one of those unknown and unknowable figures—deadly disease No. 5 in Ch. 3.)

19. What is your program for elimination of work-standards (numbers, measured day work on the factory floor), replacing them by competent knowledge and leadership? (Reference: Ch. 2.)

20a. Do you manage by objective? If yes, how much is this mode of management costing you? Do you understand what is wrong with this practice? What are you doing to replace it with better management? (Reference: Chs. 2 and 3.)

b. Do you manage by numbers (require a man to improve productivity or sales by a specified amount, or to reduce scrap or payroll or expenses by some specified amount, such as 6 per cent)? (Reference: Chs. 2 and 3.)

c. Show that a figure that is forced (e.g., a requirement that the plant turns out 1200 items every day, or that a salesman is expected to take orders for $7200 per day) is not an example of a stable system. It is either meshed like gears, or the figures are adjusted through fear to meet the requirement but nothing more.

21. Are you changing supervision to leadership, at least in some areas of your organization?

22a. How do you select foremen? In other words, how do your foremen come to be foremen?

b. What do your foremen know about the job?

c. Do they know how to calculate who if anybody is in need of individual help, not part of the system?

d. Do they know how to calculate who is outstanding, not part of the system?

23. What are your plans for elimination of:

a. piece work?

b. incentive pay?

24a. Would any good accrue to the morale of the people involved if the management sent a letter every month to dealers that did more than the average amount of business that month?

b. How may you know which ones should receive commendation?

c. How may you know which ones are in need of special help or special direction of some kind?

d. What about letters to people that fall below the average?

25. What is your plan and what are you doing about it for removal of barriers that rob the hourly worker of his pride of workmanship?

26. Do you plaster your walls with goals and exhortations? If yes, what are you doing to supplant them with news about activity of your management to reduce the barriers that rob the hourly worker of his pride of workmanship?

27. What steps are you taking to reduce paperwork?

28a. What steps are you taking to reduce to one the number

of signatures required for travel vouchers, payment to vendors, etc.?

    b. What steps are you taking to reimburse straightaway the traveler for expenses incurred?

    29. How much did you lose in the past year for mistakes in paperwork?

    30a. What is your program for development of new product and new service for the future?

    b. How do you plan to test your new designs or ideas?

    31a. What do you know about the problems of your customers in the use of your products? What tests do you make of your products in service?

    b. How do your customers see your product in relation to competitive products? How do you know? What data have you?

    c. Why do they buy yours? How do you know? What data have you?

    d. What problems or dissatisfaction do customers see in your product? How do you know? What data have you?

    e. What problems or dissatisfaction do customers see in your competitors' products? How do you know? What data have you?

    32. Will your customers of today be your customers a year hence? Two years hence?

    33a. Do your customers think that your product lives up to their expectations? What did your advertising and your salesmen lead your customers to expect? More than you can deliver? How do you know?

    b. (If applicable.) Are your customers satisfied with the service that you or your dealers provide? If yes, what is satisfactory about it? The quality of workmanship? The lag between your call and appearance of the serviceman? How do you know?

    34a. How do you distinguish between your quality as your customer perceives it and quality as your plant manager and work force perceive it?

b. How does the quality of your product, as your customer sees it, agree with the quality that you intended to give him?

35a. Do you depend on complaints from customers to learn what is wrong with your product or service?

b. Do you depend on costs of warranty?

36a. Why is it that customers switch?

b. Where lies your main chance for profit? (Repeat customers.)

c. What must you do to hold on to a customer?

37a. Who makes the decisions about whether to buy your product?

b. What new design would serve better four years from now?

38. What inspection or verification are you carrying out:

a. on incoming materials?

b. in process?

c. of final product?

(Do not try to answer this question for every one of your products. Answer it for only three or four important products, or for three or four production lines.)

39a. How reliable is your inspection at each of these points? How do you know?

b. What data have you to show whether your inspectors are in line with each other?

c. What about your test instruments, or rather, your use of them? Can you present evidence of statistical control of the system of measurement or classification? Visually? Or by instrument?

40a. Where is inspection being carried out where no inspection would minimize total cost? (See Ch. 15.)

b. At which points are you carrying out no inspection where you ought to carry out 100 per cent inspection to minimize cost? (See Ch. 15.)

41a. What records do you keep of these inspections? In what

form? In the form of control charts or run charts? If not, why not?

b. What other use do you make of the records that you keep?

c. If you keep no records, why don't you?

d. If you keep no records at some point, why don't you cut the inspection there?

42a. How much material that goes into the production line is used in desperation by the production manager (invariably with waste of material or rework or both)? (Try to answer the above question for two or three important production lines.) How often do you encounter examples like the following?

—Material that met the specifications but was not suited to the process or to the finished product.

—Inspection of incoming material was considered to be necessary, but inspection was hurried or skipped, owing to high vacuum on the production side.

b. How much incoming material turns out to be totally unusable in the judgment of the production managers? (Again, answer this question only for two or three important production lines.)

c. What system have you for report and correction of these problems?

43a. What arrangements have you with your suppliers for receipt from them of evidence of statistical control, so that you may safely decrease inspection?

b. What cooperative work are you carrying on with your suppliers to make sure that you are both talking about the same kind of centimeter, and the same kind of test?

44a. What are you doing to make quality (and productivity) everybody's job, including management?

b. Do you know the loss that ensues from a defective item or product or from a mistake at any point along the line?

45. Are you still using Military Standard 105D or Dodge–

Romig plans for sale or for purchase of materials? Why? (See Ch. 15.)

46. What proportion of your costs are chargeable to defects inherited from previous operations?

47. What proportion of the troubles that you have with quality and productivity are the fault of (i) the production workers? (ii) the system (management's responsibility)? How do you know? (Answer this question for three or four main items only.)

48. How much loss do you attribute to handling damage (i) along the production line? (ii) in packing, transportation, installation? What data have you on these problems? What are you doing about them?

49. What are you doing to improve the training of new employees? What about retraining to keep up with new product and new procedures and new equipment?

50a. Why is it that every endeavor to put out a product or service is one of a kind? (Once the plans are part way under action, subsequent changes are costly in time and money.) There is accordingly little chance for improvement, once the original plans go into action.

b. Why is it that lessons for training for a job, or lessons for retraining for a new job, or lessons on the piano or on the violin, are one of a kind? (A pupil once taught can not be reconstructed.)

51. If you run a job shop:

a. Are your customers better satisfied now, one by one, than they were two years ago? Why?

b. How about materials and equipment? How many suppliers have you for any one type?

c. If more than one, why? What steps are you taking toward reduction?

d. How about maintenance of equipment: improving?

e. How about performance on the job?

f. How about your turnover rate?

g. What about repeated operations that do not change with the product: do you keep a running record and a control chart on some of them?

h. Are some of your problems stable? If yes, where lies the responsibility for improvement? (With the management.)

52a. Do your people that are engaged in training understand when an employee is trained and when he is not yet trained?

b. Do they know that they have only one chance? That an employee once trained can not be helped by further training in the same procedures?

53. Are you guilty of setting numerical goals on the factory floor for production?

54. If you have a competent statistician in your company, are you making maximum use of his knowledge and ability? Is he teaching statistical thinking to your management, engineers, chemists, physicists, production workers, foremen, supervisors, purchasing agents, in your department of commercial research and design of future product? Do you send him to statistical meetings? Is he working throughout your company to find problems and to find causes and results of corrective action? Is he working on all your problems of design, quality, procurement, specifications, testing of instruments? Does he have authority and responsibility to look anywhere in the company for problems, and to work on them? If not, why not? (Ch. 16.)

55a. Are you trying to set up your statistical work in conformity with the best interests of the company? (See Ch. 16.)

b. If you have no competent statistician, what efforts are you putting forth to find one to help you with your problems of quality, productivity, procurements, redesign of product?

56. Do you encourage self-improvement of your people? How? In what way?

57. Do you have an educational program within the company?

58. Do you provide information to your employees about courses in local schools?

59a. Do you run your company on visible figures alone?

   b. If yes, why?

   c. What steps are your management taking to learn the importance of figures unknown and unknowable?

60. Does your company participate in committees of standardizing bodies?

61. What is your company doing for the community?

62. Do you rid yourself of problems with people on the factory floor by establishing EI groups (Employee Involvement Groups), EPG (Employee Participation Groups), QC-Circles, QWL (Quality of Work Life), and then leave them stranded with no participation of management?

63a. Are all activities in the company taking part in improvement? Are some lying dormant?

   b. What steps are you taking to discover dormant areas, and to help them?

64a. What is your understanding of a stable system?

   b. Has some annoying problem of quality or of low productivity stabilized? How do you know? Why were efforts to bring improvement so effective and encouraging at first? Why did quality level off toward a stable system (Ch. 11)?

   c. If a process has stabilized, whose responsibility is it to invent and apply methods and changes for improvement? (Answer: yours.)

65. Are you depending on EI (Employee Involvement), EPG (Employee Participation Groups), QWL (Quality of Work Life), QC-Circles, posters, exhortations, for quality, instead of doing your job?

66. What are you doing about quality that you hope to provide to your customers four years from now?

> The list of questions for the Deming Application Prize, page 188 in the book, Kaoru Ishikawa, *What Is Total Quality Control?* (Prentice-Hall, 1985), may be a helpful extension here.

6

Quality and the Consumer

Most of the early problems with this unit [to show sound film] were due to an inadequate instruction book, translated from the German into English by someone illiterate in both languages.—*Bulletin of the Washington Society of Cinematographers*, November 1967.

The industry is in continuous development, and so are the tempers of consumers. Both demand more and better quality.—Spokesman for the Egyptian Cotton Exporting Companies, quoted in the *New York Times*, 15 January 1971.

Aim of this chapter. The aim here is to raise questions about quality, what it is, who defines it, who cares, who makes the decision on whether to buy your product? We shall learn that impressions of quality are not static. They change. Moreover, the customer is not in a good position to prescribe product or service that will help him in the future. The producer is in far better position than the consumer to invent new design and new service. Would anyone that owned an automobile in 1905 express a desire for pneumatic tires, had you asked him what he needed? Would I, carrying a precise pocket-watch, have suggested a tiny calculator and quartz time-piece?

Several faces of quality.

1. Management's decision on specifications for the quality-characteristics of parts, final product, performance, what service to offer now. The plant manager and all the people in production

are concerned about the specifications of today. They have to know what their job is, now.

2. Management's decision on whether to plan ahead for product or service of the future (see Ch. 2).

3. The consumer's judgment of your product or service.

For many kinds of product and service, the consumer's judgment may require a year or even several years for formation. The purchaser of a new automobile can give you in a year from the date of purchase a more useful evaluation of the quality of the automobile than he could when it was new.

A man shows off with enthusiasm in the spring his new lawn mower, just purchased, but his influence on future sales will depend on how much of his enthusiasm remains at the end of the summer.

What is quality? Quality can be defined only in terms of the agent. Who is the judge of quality?

In the mind of the production worker, he produces quality if he can take pride in his work. Poor quality, to him, means loss of business, and perhaps of his job. Good quality, he thinks, will keep the company in business. All this is as true in the service industries as it is in manufacturing.

Quality to the plant manager means to get the numbers out and to meet specifications. His job is also, whether he knows it or not, continual improvement of processes and continual improvement of leadership.

Concerning advertising, a clever observation by my friend Irwin Bross in his book *Design for Decision* (Macmillan, 1953), p. 95:

> The purpose of studies in consumer preference is to adjust the product to the public, rather than, as in advertising, to adjust the public to the product.

The problems inherent in attempts to define the quality of a product, almost any product, were stated by the master, Walter

A. Shewhart.[1] The difficulty in defining quality is to translate future needs of the user into measurable characteristics, so that a product can be designed and turned out to give satisfaction at a price that the user will pay. This is not easy, and as soon as one feels fairly successful in the endeavour, he finds that the needs of the consumer have changed, competitors have moved in, there are new materials to work with, some better than the old ones, some worse; some cheaper than the old ones, some dearer.[2]

What is quality? What would someone mean by the quality of a shoe? Let us suppose that it is a man's shoe that he is asking about. Does he mean by good quality that it wears a long time? Or that it takes a shine well? That it feels comfortable? That it is waterproof? That the price is right in consideration of whatever he considers quality? Put another way, what quality-characteristics are important to the customer? What would one mean by the quality of a woman's shoe? What is a major defect in a shoe? A tack in the insole? A heel that came off straightaway? Smudges? What qualities create dissatisfaction in the customer's mind? How do you know?

The quality of any product or service has many scales. A product may get a high mark, in the judgment of the consumer, on one scale, and a low mark on another. This paper that I am writing on has a number of qualities.

1. It is a sulfate paper, 16 pounds.
2. It is not slick. It takes pencil well; ink likewise.
3. Writing on the back does not show through.
4. It is standard size: it fits into my three-ring notebook.

1 Walter A. Shewhart, *Economic Control of Quality of Manufactured Product* (Van Nostrand, 1931; American Society for Quality Control, 1980; reprinted by Ceepress, The George Washington University, 1986), Ch. 4.
2 The reader will at this point enjoy the book by Eugene H. Mac Niece, *Industrial Specifications* (Wiley, 1953), esp. pp. 32, 33 and Ch. 5.

5. Replacement is for sale at any stationery store.
6. The price is right.

The paper under examination rates well on all six counts. I need also letterheads, but letterheads must be on rag content. I therefore place an order for 10 reams of the sulfate scratch paper, and investigate other paper with rag content for letterheads.

Product put on the market today must do more than attract customers and sales: it must stand up in service. Satisfaction of the customer that buys today's output can unfortunately only be assessed some time in the future—too late. Everything is one of a kind—one chance (pp. 49, 94).

What is the quality of a textbook, or of any book that its authors intended to carry a message of some kind? To the printer, quality is determined by style of type, legibility, size, paper, freedom from typographical error. To the author, and to readers, quality requires clarity and importance of message. To the publisher, sales are important in order that he may stay in business and publish another book. The reader requires, in addition, some spark of learning, or of entertainment. The quality could be high in the eyes of the printer and high in the eyes of the author, yet low for readers and for the publisher.

What is the quality of educational videotapes? Is it the photography that customers appreciate, or content? To the maker of slides for a lecture, quality means lots of color, orange printing on red background. That the printing is illegible is not his affair. To the audience, quality in a slide means legibility. (The content of the slide is of course a totally different matter, the responsibility of the man that gives the lecture.)

Moving stairs and farecard machines in Washington's Metro are a constant source of irritation. They worked very well when unveiled for dress rehearsal, but when put into service, problems of design and maintenance painted a new image. The management of the Washington Metropolitan Transit Authority had a goal of 5.7 per cent out of order. Where do you suppose the management's goal of 5.7 per cent came from? Why not continual improvement with aid of appropriate methods? What is the meaning of quality to the transit authorities?

Quality of medical care. A suitable definition for quality of medical care is a perennial problem among administrators of medical care and people doing research in the subject. It seems simple to anyone that has not tried it. Quality of medical care has been defined in many ways. Each way serves some special type of problem:

1. Comfort of patients under medical care. (How would you measure comfort?)
2. Proportion of people under medical care, male and female, by age in each group.
3. (Applicable to a day care centre for the aged.) The number of people kept out of the hospital or nursing home because of good care at the day care centre.
4. Facilities for tests, such as laboratories, X-ray scan.
5. Public health.
6. Mean life of people discharged from institutions, by age of discharge.
7. Amount of money spent by an institution, per patient.

It is obvious that some of these definitions are antithetical. For example, the number of patients under care, if large, might indicate good medical service—serving many people. On the other hand, it could indicate the opposite. It might be large because of poor measures of public health, or it could be large because day care centres are not doing the job. The rate of patients discharged from nursing homes, if high, could mean that the care that they receive is excellent: patients stay in the institution only a short while, and are soon rehabilitated sufficiently to live at home. It could also mean that the policy of the management is to discharge a patient when he reaches a stage of acute care and would be a burden in a nursing home. The amount of money spent by an institution is almost no indication of the care offered. Facilities available is one thing; how to use them effectively is another.

I listened to papers on medical care delivered in an international meeting on medical care. One physician measured medical care in terms of physical equipment for medical tests. Another one measured medical care in terms of education of physicians and nurses. Another measure of medical care turned up as men met me on arrival in a city in Europe. They were from the medical service of the country and had a problem. In spite of the fact that their country has superb medical facilities and physicians that have studied in the best medical schools in the world, the general population was not using these facilities. A disease left unattended can become serious, as everyone knows, and this was happening. The men had in mind a survey of the general population to learn why people do not make better use of their medical facilities, and how to persuade them to come in for service and for examination. The quality of medical care was thus excellent from the standpoint of facilities, physical and professional, but not good, in the judgment of the heads of the service, from the standpoint of service rendered.

This example merely illustrates the difficulty of definition of the quality of medical service.

A further illustration may display more difficulties (taken from David Owen, "The secret lives of dentists," *Harper's*, March 1983, p. 49):

> More to the point, how many dentists, compulsive or otherwise, do magnificent work?
>
> The question is impossible to answer, for the simple reason that there has never been a definitive study of quality in the dental profession; nor is there likely to be one. Partly because they tend to work alone, dentists resist the idea of being evaluated, or even

observed, by others. And because inferior dental work may not be discovered until years after it is performed, patients are seldom in a position to make informed judgments.

Remark on quality of teaching. How do you define quality of teaching? How do you define a good teacher? I offer comment only in respect to higher education. The first requisite for a good teacher is that he have something to teach. His aim should be to give inspiration and direction to students for further study. To do this, a teacher must possess knowledge of the subject. The only operational definition of knowledge requisite for teaching is research. Research need not be earthshaking. It may only be a new derivation of knowledge or principles already established. Publication of original research in reputable journals is an index of achievement. This is an imperfect measure, but none better has been found.

In my experience, I have seen a teacher hold a hundred fifty students spellbound, teaching what is wrong. His students rated him as a great teacher. In contrast, two of my own greatest teachers in universities would be rated poor teachers on every count. Then why did people come from all over the world to study with them, including me? For the simple reason that these men had something to teach. They inspired their students to carry on further research. They were leaders of thought—by name, Sir Ronald Fisher in statistics at University College, and Sir Ernest Brown in lunar theory at Yale. Their works will remain classic for centuries. Their students had a chance to observe what these great men were thinking about, and how they built roads into new knowledge.

Example: Another publishing house was preparing a new edition of its widely used series (elementary readers). One of us, asked to consult, objected in detail to the blandness of the stories proposed. The

company's vice-president in charge of textbooks con-
fessed that he, too, thought that the stories would bore
young readers, but he was obliged to keep in mind that
neither children nor teachers buy textbooks: school
boards and superintendents do.[3]

Latent recognition (too late). William R. Dill, when he was
dean of the Graduate School of Business Administration of New
York University, invited me about 1972 to work with him on a
study of students with known addresses that had graduated five
or more years before: how are they doing? and what might be
characteristics of background for success? One question was
this:

> Did any teacher here affect your life?
> If so, what was his name?

Responses showed that every student that had taken a course
with any one of six teachers answered yes. Moreover, every one
that answered yes remembered the name of the teacher. Almost
no one was mentioned aside from the six.

Unfortunately, this recognition came too late. No special
effort was made by authorities of the school to hold on to these
six men—the kind that make an institution famous—and none
of them received from the student body the award "Great
Teacher of the Year."

The consumer, the most important part of the production line.
The customer is the most important part of the production line.
Without someone to purchase our product, we might as well shut

3 Bruno Bettelheim and Karen Zelan, "Why children don't like to read,"
Atlantic, November 1981, p. 27.

down the whole plant. But what does the customer need? How can we be useful to him? What does he think he needs? Can he pay for it? No one has all the answers. Fortunately, it is not necessary to have all the answers for good management.

Necessity to study the needs of the consumer, and to provide service to product, was one of the main doctrines of quality taught to Japanese management in 1950 and onward.

Foremost is the principle that the purpose of consumer research is to understand the consumer's needs and wishes, and thus to design product and service that will provide better living for him in the future.

A second principle is that no one can guess the future loss of business from a dissatisfied customer. The cost to replace a defective item on the production line is fairly easy to estimate, but the cost of a defective item that goes out to a customer defies measure.

It was Oliver Beckwith who remarked in 1947, in a meeting of Committee E-11 of the American Society for Testing and Materials, that a dissatisfied customer does not complain: he just switches. Or, as my friend Robert W. Peach put it for Sears, Roebuck & Co.:

The goods come back, but not the customer.

Who is the consumer? One might suppose that the man that pays the bill is the customer, the one to be satisfied, or that the man or company that will use the product is the one to be satisfied. There are curious exceptions. Three examples will suffice here. They will call to the reader's mind other examples. The customer for a selenium drum for a copying machine is the technician, the man that answers a call for repair, or who carries on regular maintenance of the copying machine. He is the one that will decide whether a selenium drum is of good quality. A mere scratch or dent at the end of the drum would not affect its performance in any way, yet the technician may reject the drum, or decide to install some other brand. Neither the people that use the copying machine nor the man that pays the bills for use and maintenance takes part in this decision.

Who decides on the quality of the label that is affixed to a packet of beef in the retail market? Not the person that buys the meat. He cares nothing about the label, provided the price is legible. To the manager of the store, however, a label that is impervious to air will cause slight darkening of the beef in the package just under the label. The purchaser of the package would never see this dark spot, and would not be concerned anyhow, as it disappears in a while after the wrapper comes off.

Thus, the maker of selenium drums must satisfy technicians, and the maker of labels for beef must satisfy the managers of retail markets.

The optician that ground the lenses in the spectacles that you are wearing never saw you. His customer is the optical fitter that you took your prescription to. We just saw another example on page 173.

Triangle of interaction. Neither the building of a product nor tests thereof in the laboratory and on the proving ground are sufficient to describe its quality and how it will perform or be accepted. Quality must be measured by the interaction between three participants, as shown in Fig. 8: (1) the product itself; (2) the user and how he uses the product, how he installs it, how he takes care of it (example: customer permitted dirt to fall into roller bearing), what he was led (as by advertising) to expect; (3) instructions for use, training of customer and training of repairman, service provided for repairs, availability of parts. The top vertex of the triangle does not by itself determine quality. I am reminded of an old Japanese poem:[4]

4   Quoted in Edward W. Barankin, "Probability and the East," *Annals of the Institute of Statistical Mathematics* (Tokyo), vol. 16 (1964), p. 216.

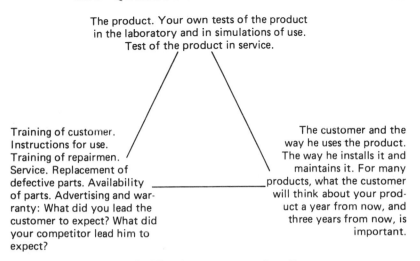

The product. Your own tests of the product in the laboratory and in simulations of use. Test of the product in service.

Training of customer. Instructions for use. Training of repairmen. Service. Replacement of defective parts. Availability of parts. Advertising and warranty: What did you lead the customer to expect? What did your competitor lead him to expect?

The customer and the way he uses the product. The way he installs it and maintains it. For many products, what the customer will think about your product a year from now, and three years from now, is important.

Fig. 8. The three corners of quality.

Kane ga naru ka ya
Shumoku ga naru ka
Kane to shumoku no ai ga naru

Is it the bell that rings,
Is it the hammer that rings,
Or is it the meeting of the two that rings?

Learning from the consumer. The main use of consumer research should be to feed consumer reactions back into the design of the product, so that management can anticipate changing demands and requirements and set economical production levels. Consumer research takes the pulse of the consumer's reactions and demands, and seeks explanations for the findings.

Consumer research is a process of communication between the manufacturer and users and potential users of his product, like this:

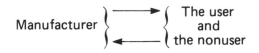

This process of communication may be carried out reliably and economically today by sampling procedures and tests designed in conformity with appropriate statistical procedures. Through this process of communication the manufacturer discovers how his product performs in service, what people think of his product, why some people will buy it, why others will not, or will not buy it again, and he is able to redesign his product, to make it better as measured by the quality and uniformity that are best suited to the end users of the product and to the price that the consumer can pay.

Quality of service. A fair question is: what do you mean by quality of service (laundry and dry cleaning, banking, the mail, service on your automobile)?

We shall see in the next chapter (p. 186) that some characteristics of quality of service are as easy to quantify and to measure as the characteristics of quality of manufactured product. As with a manufactured product, there are also forces and interactions not well understood that determine satisfaction.

One could sketch for any service a triangle of forces and interactions that lead to satisfaction and dissatisfaction of the customer similar to those in the triangle in Fig. 8. We pursue further in the next chapter these remarks and principles.

Complaints come in too late. We learned in Chapter 3 (p. 141) that it will not suffice to have customers that are merely satisfied. Customers that are unhappy and some that are merely satisfied switch. Profit comes from repeat customers—those that boast about the product or service.

Quality is already built in before a customer complains. Study of complaints is certainly necessary but it gives a biased picture of performance of a product or of a service. Study of costs of warranty have of course the same deficiency. These principles apply equally well to service and to manufactured product.

The old way and the new way. In the olden days, before the industrial era, the tailor, the carpenter, the shoemaker, the milkman, the blacksmith knew his customers by name.[5] He knew whether they were satisfied, and what he should do to improve appreciation for his product. I quote:

> A grocer used to be very fussy about his cheese. Cheddar was made and sold by hundreds of little factories. Representatives of the factories had particular customers, and cheese was prepared by hand to suit the grocers, who knew precisely what their patrons wanted in rat cheese, pie cheese, American and other cheeses. Some liked them sharper; some liked them yellower; some liked anise seeds in cheese, or caraway. (Philip Wylie, "Science has spoiled my supper," *Atlantic*, April 1954.)

With the expansion of industry, this personal touch is easy to lose. The wholesaler, the jobber, and the retailer have now stepped in, and in effect have set up a barrier between the manufacturer and the ultimate consumer. But sampling, a new science, steps in and pierces that barrier.

---

5 This section is taken largely from Walter A. Shewhart, *Statistical Method from the Viewpoint of Quality Control* (Graduate School, Department of Agriculture, Washington, 1939; Dover, 1986), p. 45.

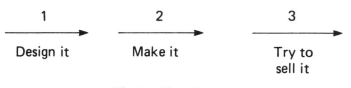

Fig. 9a. The old way.

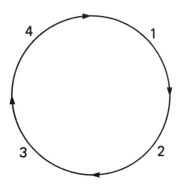

Fig. 9b. The new way. Introduce a fourth step: test the product in service.

Manufacturers used to think of manufacturing in three steps, as shown in Fig. 9a. Success depended on guess-work—guessing what type and design of product would sell, how much of it to make. In the old way, the three steps of Fig. 9a are independent.

In the new way, management introduces, usually with aid of consumer research, a fourth step (see Fig. 9b):

1. Design the product.
2. Make it; test it in the production line and in the laboratory.
3. Put it on the market.
4. Test it in service; find out what the user thinks of it, and why the nonuser has not bought it.

Continuation of the four steps leads to a helix of continual im-

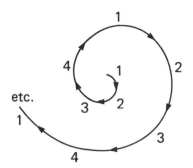

Fig. 10. The helix. Continue the cycle, over and over, with never-ending improvement of quality, at lower and lower cost.

provement of satisfaction of the consumer, at a lower and lower cost (Fig. 10).

Manufacturers have always been interested in discovering needs and reactions of users and potential users, but until the advent of modern statistical methods, they had no economical or reliable way to investigate them.

It is not to be supposed that the first three steps are the same in the old and new ways. Consider, for example, design—Step 1 of Fig. 9 or Fig. 10. Proper design today means not only attention to color, shape, size, hardness, strength, and finish, but attention also to a suitable degree of uniformity. Paradoxically, through improvement of quality, guided by consumer research, the ultimate result is not only better quality but also lower cost and improvement of competitive position.

Communication between the manufacturer and the user and the potential user gives the public a voice in the design of product and in the delivery of service. It gives to him product and service better suited to his needs, at less cost. Democracy in industry, one might say.

A word about consumer research. I interject the warning that any attempt to cut costs by accepting shoddy design of a study, or shoddy workmanship, will lead to incalculable losses from wrong information, or from information whose errors and limitations are not appreciated. Unfortunately, many courses in marketing research fail to make the distinction between (a) research for discovery of problems, such as reasons for dissatisfaction; and (b) research for quantitative estimates of numbers and proportions of households or of other users that have these problems—share of market by type of user; and (c) research to obtain information on which to base prediction of the consumer's reaction to a change in the product, which might be only a change in size or color of package. Problems (a) and (c) are analytic; problem (b) is enumerative (cf. p. 131).

New product and new service. A consumer can seldom say today what new product or new service would be desirable and useful to him three years from now, or a decade from now. New product and new types of service are generated, not by asking the consumer, but by knowledge, imagination, innovation, risk, trial and error on the part of the producer, backed by enough capital to develop the product or service and to stay in business during the lean months of introduction.

Innovation to invent new product and new service has been accomplished in every case in my experience by application of innovation and knowledge.

7

Quality and Productivity in Service Organizations

No English minister to the United States has ever been so popular: and the mediocrity of his talents has been one of the principal causes of his success.—Diary of John Quincy Adams: On the departure of the Right Honourable Sir Charles Bagot, minister from England to the United States, 1819.

Aim of this chapter. All that we learned about the 14 points and the diseases of management applies to service organizations, as well as to manufacturing. In this chapter we focus on service organizations.

Remarks on Service Industries

Who needs improvement? A system of quality improvement is helpful to anyone that turns out a product or is engaged in service, or in research, and wishes to improve the quality of his work, and at the same time to increase his output, all with less labor and at reduced cost. Service needs improvement along with manufacturing. Anyone that ever registered at a hotel in the United States will endorse this statement, I am sure. Inefficiency in a service organization, just as in manufacturing, raises prices to the consumer and lowers his standard of living. The principles and methods for improvement are the same for service as for manufacturing. The actual application differs, of course, from one product to another, and from one type of service to another, just as all manufacturing concerns differ from one to another.

Economic importance of employment in service. What is a service organization? Here are some examples, with no attempt at completeness:

Restaurants
Hotels
Banks
Providers of health care, including hospitals and nursing homes
Day care centres for children and for old people
All government service, including the mail and services supplied by the municipality
Education—government, parochial, private
Wholesale and retail establishments
Transportation of goods and of passengers, by any mode
Insurance companies
Accounting services
Painters (houses, buildings, furniture)
Printing
News service
Software
The sacred ministry
Communication (telephone, telegraph, transmission of voice and of data)
Real estate
Maintenance of buildings
Plumbers, electrical repair and alteration
Security
Sale and delivery of electric power
Construction
Laundry and dry cleaning

Figures published by the Census show that 75 people out of 100 are employed in service organizations. If we add to this figure the people in the manufacturing industries that are engaged in service, we find that 86 people in 100 are engaged in service, leaving only 14 out of 100 to make items that we can drive, use, misuse, drop, or break, and this 14 includes agriculture—food, fruit, cotton, tobacco.[1]

In spite of the relatively few people that are engaged in manufacturing and in agriculture, it is they that are almost wholly responsible for our balance of trade.

It is obvious from the above figures that because there are so many people engaged in service in the United States, improvement in our standard of living is highly dependent on better quality and productivity in the service sector. The cost of living, if it is high, is high because we pay more than necessary for what we get. This is pure inflation.

Quality of service (continuation from p. 178). Satisfaction of customers with respect to any given service or manufactured item, by whatever criterion, if they have any opinions to offer, will show a distribution that ranges all the way from extreme dissatisfaction to highly pleased, elated.

A man may scream bitterly to the dealer that sold him a lemon, yet not give a thought to the quality of work done by his laundry or dry cleaner, nor (in the U.S.) about the deteriorating quality of the mail—deliveries slow and infrequent compared with what they were fifty years ago.

Many people are satisfied with any kind of copy that comes off a copying machine. A copy is a copy. My friend Elbert T. Magruder whom I worked with in the Chesapeake and Potomac Telephone Company in Washington observed from visits to a sample of subscribers that none of them with a frayed cord, or with a broken handset, or with a crooked dial, or with a cracked frame, were aware that anything was wrong. If a conversation

---

1 A. C. Rosander, "A general approach to quality control in the service industries," *Proceedings of the American Society for Quality Control* (Costa Mesa, Calif.), 2 October 1976. The figure 86:14 came from my friend Dr. Marvin E. Mundel.

could be held, the apparatus was in good order. On the other end of the distribution were customers that asked for a replacement at the slightest scratch.

Many customers of carriers of freight care little about the time of transit, or about the number of hours that elapse before an empty car comes ready to load, or about the number of hours that elapse from the time the car is loaded until a switch engine comes to pull the loaded car away and off. On the other end of the distribution, some people count every hour (p. 211, p. 219).

Some characteristics of quality of service are as easy to quantify and to measure as the characteristics of quality of manufactured product. Accuracy of paperwork, speed, dependability of time of delivery, care in handling, care in transit, are important characteristics of service, and are easy to measure. The laundry washes out all the dirt, or does not. The shirt is fit to wear, or it is not, and the same for a suit that comes back from the cleaner.

The customer's reaction to what he calls good service or poor service is usually immediate, whereas reaction to the quality of manufactured product may be retarded. How a customer will rate a product or service a year hence or two years hence can not be ascertained today. Judgment of the consumer may shift with respect to service as well as with manufactured product. His needs may change. Alternate choices of service may appear on the market, as with manufactured product. Moreover, service may deteriorate. Manufactured product may be subject to latent defects.

Problems of salesmen. Meetings with salesmen indicate that their problems are all about the same, regardless of type of product or of service:

> Poor quality of the product or service that they are
>   trying to sell
> Wrong count

Mistakes in orders
Slow delivery

It is hard for them to sell quality that does not come up to the customer's requirements nor to the salesman's pride. Salesmen promise time of delivery that is impossible, in order to meet the needs of the customer and promises made by the competition.

Some services contribute to our balance of trade. We must look primarily to the manufacturing industries and to agricultural and other commodities (coal, lumber, wheat, cotton) for export to pay for imported goods. Some service industries, if well managed, could reduce costs of manufactured product and commodities, and thereby improve the competitive position of American products, here and abroad.

A hotel may not generate new goods for the market, but by improving its service and lowering costs, it could decrease costs of doing business, and thus make a contribution to the competitive position of American industry. In some countries (e.g., Switzerland, Yugoslavia), hotels and other facilities attract tourists and hard currency.

Improvement of quality of transportation, and consequent reduction in freight rates, could decrease the cost of the manufacture of finished product, and could thus also improve the market for American products. Banks, by focusing on long-term capital gain, seeking loans to companies that have adopted the 14 points of Chapter 2, instead of focusing on short-term results, could help American industry, as banks in Japan help Japanese industry.

Storage and transmission of data, of voice, and of copy, at remarkably low cost, with clarity that was only a dream a few years ago, is a service that contributes to lower costs of manufacture and thus helps our balance of trade. One may dial a telephone number in almost any part of the world, and hear it ring in a few seconds. The clarity of transmission was only another dream a few years ago.

The mail, domestic and international, contributes to our balance of trade. Better service, with higher prices, could contribute more. Messenger services between parts of a city, between cities in the U.S., and to and from cities in other countries, make their contribution. Research carried out and published by our National Bureau of Standards and by the National Institutes of Health are examples of contributions to industry, and in the long run, to our balance of trade.

Some differences and similarities between service and manufacturing. An important difference is that a production worker in manufacturing not only has a job: he is aware that he is doing his part to make something that somebody will see, feel, and use in some way. In spite of the problems illustrated in Chapter 2, he has some idea about what his job is, and some idea about the quality of the final product. He visualizes the final customer, satisfied or unhappy with the product of his organization. In contrast, in many service organizations, the people that work there only have a job. They are not aware that they have a product, and that this product is service; that good service and happy customers keep his company in business and provide jobs; that an unhappy customer may bring loss of business and of his job. (Contributed by Carolyn A. Emigh.)

Another difference between a service establishment and a manufacturing establishment is that most service establishments have a captive market. Service organizations rarely have to compete head to head with a foreign firm. Our choice of restaurants, laundries, transportation, and mail is narrow.

Still another difference between service and manufacturing is that a service organization does not generate new material for the world market. A freight carrier, for example, can only haul what someone else produces. He can not generate material to haul. To him, the only way to get ahead, when industry is in decline, is to take business away from a competitor, with the hazard of starting a cutthroat war. A better plan for freight carriers would be to improve service and thus to decrease costs. These cost savings, passed on to manufacturers and to other service industries, would help American industry to improve the market for American products, and would in time bring new business to carriers of freight.

In most service industries one finds:

1. Direct transactions with masses of people: customer, householder, depositor, insured, taxpayer, borrower, consumer, shipper, consignee, passenger, claimant, another bank.

2. Large volume of transactions, as in the main business in sales, loans, premiums, deposits, taxes, charges, interest.

3. Large volumes of paper involved in the main business: sales slips, bills, cheques, credit cards, charge accounts, claims, tax returns, mail.

4. Large amount of processing—for example, transcription, coding, calculation of freight charges, calculation of division of revenue, calculation of interest to pay, punching, tabulation, construction of tables.

5. Many transactions with small amounts of money. However, some transactions involve huge amounts (as a transfer from one bank to another, or a huge deposit). A telephone company that I worked with received one day when I was there a bill for $800,000 which should have gone to another company.

6. An extremely large number of ways to make errors.

7. Handling and rehandling of huge numbers of small items—for example, in communications, mail, federal, state, and city governments, your own payroll department, your own purchasing department.

A denominator common to manufacturing and any service organization is that mistakes and defects are costly. The further a mistake goes without correction, the greater the cost to correct it. The cost of a defect that reaches the consumer or recipient may be the costliest of all, but (to repeat from other chapters) no one knows what this cost is (an invisible figure, Ch. 3).

Ask anyone in an airline that knows the figures how much it costs to find and deliver or hold a piece of luggage that failed to come along with the passenger. The main cause of failure of luggage to arrive with the passenger is not sluggish performance of employees, but delays in connexion. Features built into a large airport on the West Coast, newly erected at a cost of many millions of dollars, impede transfer of luggage from international arrivals to domestic flights, with great inconvenience to passengers and huge costs to the airlines—another problem of one of a kind (Ch. 2).

Ask anyone that knows how much it costs to correct a mistake in the customer's bill sent out by a department store, or the cost of sending the wrong goods. The direct costs are staggering. The unmeasurable cost of loss of future business may be much greater.

Many companies have a rule to disregard a difference under $150, as the cost to both parties to investigate the difference would exceed this amount. A repeated pattern of difference should of course be investigated.

A remittance sent by a bank to the wrong bank or firm will eventually be straightened out. One of the costs, piled on top of the cost to try to find out what happened, is for interest that the bank pays on a wrong remittance till the mistake is cleared up.

A bank that embarrasses a customer by reporting incorrectly that funds in the customer's account are insufficient to cover a cheque incurs substantial cost to set the matter straight, and runs the risk of losing business.

It is amazing how many cheques on payrolls are incorrect, and how many go to the wrong man. The total amount paid out may nevertheless be virtually correct. The cost to clear up these mistakes is not small, and the cost is even greater to explain how it happened.

An official in the Department of Justice where the State guarantees title to property transferred, in attendance at a seminar, told me that 40 per cent of applications for deeds are afflicted with errors in the paperwork serious enough to require rework (not for substance of the deed, but in the paperwork that supports the deed). This rework raises costs to everybody concerned, and retards completion of the deed.

Many mistakes are never discovered. We saw an example on page 30 where only one mistake in seven titles was ever discovered.

One finds in service organizations, as in manufacturing, absence of definite procedures. There is an unstated assumption in most service organizations that the procedures are fully defined and followed. This appears to be so obvious that authors avoid it. Yet in practice this condition is often not met. Few organizations have up-to-date procedures. Consider a manufacturer who has full specifications for making a product, but whose sales department does not have guidelines of how to enter an order. A control on errors on placing orders would require procedures for the sales department. I have seen numerous service-oriented operations functioning without them. (Contributed by William J. Latzko.)

It is not always easy to describe procedures. A defect in manufactured product may be difficult to define operationally. The same kind of problem afflicts some service organizations. The correct code and a mistake in coding are in many studies as difficult to define operationally as a defect in the production line in the manufacture of shoes. Courses of study to the extent of several months are required of people employed for occupational coding and industrial coding in the Census and in other government bureaus. There are nevertheless disagreements now and then about what code to ascribe on some situations. Disagreement between the verifier and the original coder may be only honest difference of educated opinion.[2] Different interpretations of the code for commodity sometimes lead to honest differences between two rate clerks on the calculation of division of revenue between two railways on an interline haul.

Contact with the customer. It is only the salesman and the serviceman of manufactured product—apparatus, machinery, utensils, automobiles, trucks, railway cars, locomotives, and the like—that see the customer. These men do not make the items that they sell, repair, and maintain. They are in a service organization, independent or owned by the manufacturer.

Many people work in a bank. The officers and tellers see customers; the rest do not. Some people in a department store, restaurant, hotel, railway, trucking company, or bus company see customers; others do not.

Everyone, whether he sees the customer or not, has a chance to build quality into the product or into the service offered. The people that see customers have a role that is not usually appreciated by supervisors and other management. Many customers form their opinions about the product or about the service solely by their contacts with the people that they see—contact men, I will call them.

It is customers that keep a company in business, both in manufacturing industries and in service industries.

Ability to please the customer should be, for good management, top priority for hiring and training of employees. My impression is that many people that serve customers in restaurants, hotels, elevators, banks, and hospitals would enjoy the job much more were it not that customers come in and interrupt

2 Dr. Philip M. Hauser, personal communication regarding the Census of 1940.

their conversations. A bus driver in Washington was obviously expert at driving the bus, and knew his route. Customers boarded and descended. His job would have been so much more enjoyable to him were it not for those pesky passengers that boarded and descended or needed directions and help—such a bother they were.

Actually, the job might be enjoyable to him were he to understand that a sizable proportion of the people that ask questions for directions and guidance are a potential source of future revenue for the company, and that he can help to build up business to ensure his job in the future. Likewise in hotels, stores, restaurants, banks, trains, and a multitude of other types of shops and services, the people that see the customers are the marketing department. Do they know it? Does the management teach drivers that they are not only drivers, but a potential influence to increase patronage? How about screening applicants for their adaptability to this role?

The woman that runs the elevator in a department store plays an important role in the customer's opinion of the quality of everything for sale in the store. The Japanese know this. The woman that runs the elevator in a department store in Japan receives training over a period of two months on how to direct people, how to answer questions, and how to handle them in a crowded elevator—this in spite of the gracious manners in a Japanese home.

Service in motor freight. A driver, as he descends the stairs to take charge of his truck in the Baltimore terminal of Roadway Express, sees himself in a full-length mirror with this caption:

YOU ARE LOOKING AT THE ONLY PERSON IN YOUR
COMPANY THAT OUR CUSTOMERS EVER SEE.

This caption is not a useless exhortation (Point 10, pp. 65–70). It reminds the driver that he may lose business by giving snarly service, or by looking like a vagabond. He may practice on his customers some of the rudiments of courtesy. He can help to hold business, though he can not change the system that he works in (delays from poor maintenance, mistakes on the platform, for example).

A splendid example of management comes from Reimer Express Lines of Winnipeg, with my thanks to Messrs. Donald S. Reimer and John W. Perry. In the interest of improving their performance as managers, they passed out a small form one day to each of their 35 city drivers in one of their terminals with the simple question on it, "How in one sentence would you explain the business that we are in?" The 35 drivers came through with 32 different answers, none of which went deep enough to explain the business that the management thought that they were in. Here are two of the answers, along with Reimer's comments:

> The truck business. (This could mean that we are in the business of buying and selling trucks. No indication of requirements or standards that apply to our business, which is service.)
>
> Transport business. (This could mean that we transport people by train, bus, or air, or that we sell buses.)

The letter from Reimer Express continues:

> When we started to dig deeper, in a question-and-answer session with the men, I began to describe service as a process. To complete a service we must also complete various segments of our activities to ensure that the process is successful. For example, to suggest that we are in the freight business without any exposure to the services that we can provide between Eastern Canada and Western Canada is really missing the point.
>
> It is up to the management to help the employees to understand that they are an important part of the

overall business activity, the activity being service. So we worked for a few weeks with our drivers in Eastern Canada in reference to linking their pick-ups to our line-haul operations and to delivery in cities 1500 or 4000 miles to the west.

We have found that frustrations over various problems of drivers have disappeared as we improve the process, in contrast with acceptance of frustrations from trying to solve effects and not to get rid of causes. I should like to give you one small example.

Recently in Vancouver our terminal manager travelled with a different driver each day. He called me up one day excited about one driver, who, for a number of months, both he and the despatcher had deemed to be hopeless in productivity. Travelling with this driver, the manager noted that the radio was not working well. Vancouver is very hilly, and this driver served a number of our customers in the valleys, in which the reception was poor or non-existent. When the manager looked into it, he discovered that the driver had complained a few times to our local supervisors about radio reception, but we had not listened. The driver often had to drive miles out of his route to get out of the shadows of the hills, to seek audible reception in order to report a problem in collection or delivery, and to keep in touch with the despatcher.

How to increase costs of billing in motor freight. A carrier issues to the shipper a freight bill for any shipment. The charges on the freight bill are determined by rate clerks on the basis of a description of the goods hauled, weight, origin, and destination, as shown on the shipping order, and by consulting volumes of published tariffs and more volumes of published discounts or increases that apply to the published tariffs.

Rate clerks make mistakes. These mistakes lead some shippers to send their freight bills to an auditing company, which works on a commission basis on overcharges discovered. The carrier is obligated to refund any overcharge discovered and confirmed. The carrier can only lose on this audit.

Concurrently or otherwise, a carrier may send copies of these freight bills to his own auditor for discovery of undercharges, also on a commission basis. The carrier may send to a shipper a bill for undercharge. More likely, he does not. The shipper in receipt of such a bill may pay it; he may not.

For the carrier it is heads, you win; tails, I lose.

The only way out of this loss is for a carrier to reduce by principles and procedures described in this book the frequency of mistakes in freight bills to the point where the yield to the auditing companies is unattractive. In other words, put them out of business.

The customer can help. We shall see on page 376 suggestions by which customers of motor freight may help the carrier to reduce mistakes.

A letter sent out by Commonwealth Industries of Detroit under date of 10 January 1984 to their customers explained faults of Commonwealth Industries and ways in which customers could help Commonwealth Industries to serve them better. Commonwealth Industries does heat-treating of fasteners. The suggestions in the letter are based on a study of 35,000 lots from customers. The following list is much abbreviated from the original letter but will serve for illustration here.

Faults found in performance of Commonwealth Industries

Faulty control of temperature
Wrong selection of temperature for the job required
Faulty scheduling, owing to rush jobs requested by customers
Overloading
Breakdown of equipment

Problems caused by customers

Specification of range of hardness too narrow—beyond the capability of the process
Mixed heats of steel
Mixed steels
High variability in content of manganese within the heat
Wrong identification of steel, or no identification at all
Wrong application of steel for a given part or specification
Low side chemistry of steel to be treated

Administrative Applications in the Ford Motor Company

By WILLIAM W. SCHERKENBACH

Organization	Application
Central laboratory	Time to process request of customer
	Errors in laboratory (based on audits)
Power train and chassis engineering	Time for supplier to notify company of failure
	Number of failures per month
Ford parts and service division	Errors in filling orders for dealer
Accounting	Time to process travel expense
Ford tractor operations engineering	Time to process engineering changes
Manufacturing staff, manufacturing engineering and systems	Time to review report on productivity sent from various Ford locations
Computer graphics	Variation in time of usage of discs
Product engineering office	Number of computer sign-on calls that gave busy signal
	Number of times that files (cabinets) were used for information

Organization	Application
Product development, comptroller's office	Run chart on number of revisions in word processing Wasted man-hours due to late start of meetings
Comptroller's office	Errors in accounts payable, resulting in late payment of invoices to suppliers
Saline plant	Costs from errors in scheduling
Purchasing staff, transportation, and traffic office	Transit time by rail from manufacture of part to assembly plants
Transmission and chassis division	Errors in shipments of components to assembly plants (quantity, wrong parts)

Anecdote on construction. A driver backed his truck through the gate and into the area where a building was under construction. Where to unload his cargo, was his question. He must keep moving: no motion, no profit. No one had any good idea, but two men helped the driver to unload his cargo. Anywhere would do.

Next day, a foreman discovered that the cargo was on the spot where his gang must work. He and his gang moved the cargo. This scenario was repeated three more times before the cargo reached its appointed resting place. Results: costs increased. (Contributed by Margaret Miller.)

Government service is to be judged on equity as well as on efficiency. I quote here from an interview with Oscar A. Ornati.

A deeply embedded laissez-faire ideology has mistaught this country the importance of productivity from a very narrow, very mechanistic definition. We have forgotten that the function of government is more equity oriented than efficiency oriented. The notion that we must be "efficient" in the same way in both sectors is fallacious. For government, efficiency must be subsumed to equity. If we do not keep equity in the forefront of the public sector, we will destroy our society. It is unfortunate that we tend to lavish so much praise on management specialists who laud the techniques of private sector management in the public sector. Many such techniques are good, but there is a danger in the privatization of public management techniques if we forget about the required orientation to equity and the reality of different accountability processes. Actually, we need both. The public sector must search for and apply the appropriate private management techniques to improve its analyses and evaluations of outcomes. On the other hand, some private sector policies such as moving to the suburbs, may produce short-run benefits for the company, but are counterproductive in the long run for society and the company.[3]

Adaptation of the 14 points to medical service. The 14 points of Chapter 2 apply to a service organization with little modification. For example, my friends Dr. Paul B. Batalden and Dr. Loren Vorlicky of the Health Services Research Center, Minneapolis, have written the 14 points for medical service:

1. Establish constancy of purpose toward service.

 a. Define in operational terms what you mean by service to patients.

 b. Specify standards of service for a year hence and for five years hence.

 c. Define the patients whom you are seeking to serve—those here, those that you seek, those that have been here only once.

3 Interview with Oscar A. Ornati, *Public Productivity Review*, vol. vi, nos. 1 and 2 (March and June 1982), p. 48.

d. Constancy of purpose brings innovation.

e. Innovate for better service for a given cost; planning for the future will require the addition of new skills, training, and retraining of personnel, satisfaction of patients, new treatments, new methods.

f. Put resources into maintenance of equipment, furniture, and fixtures; new aids to production in the office.

g. Decide whom the administrator and the chairman of the board are responsible to and the means by which they will be held responsible for working for constancy of purpose.

h. Translate this constancy of purpose to service into patients and to the community.

i. The board of directors must hold on to the purpose.

2. Adopt the new philosophy. We are in a new economic age. We can no longer live with commonly accepted levels of mistakes, materials not suited to the job, people on the job that do not know what the job is and are afraid to ask, failure of management to understand their job, antiquated methods of training on the job, inadequate and ineffective supervision. The board must put resources into this new philosophy, with commitment to in-service training.

3a. Require statistical evidence of quality of incoming materials, such as pharmaceuticals, serums, and equipment. Inspection is not the answer. Inspection is too late and is unreliable. Inspection does not produce quality. The quality is already built in and paid for.

b. Require corrective action, where needed, for all tasks that are performed in the hospital or other facility, ranging all the way from bills that are produced to processes of registration. Institute a rigid program of feedback from patients in regard to their satisfaction with services.

c. Look for evidence of rework or defects and the cost that may accrue as a result—an incorrect bill, an incorrect or incomplete registration.

4. Deal with vendors that can furnish statistical evidence of

control. This will require us to examine generic lowest-price buying; it will cause us to ask more penetrating questions about prospective colleagues regarding their interactions and the track record of their interactions with patients and with colleagues.

We must take a clear stand that price of services has no meaning without adequate measure of quality. Without such a stand for rigorous measures of quality, business drifts to the lowest bidder, low quality and high cost being the inevitable result. We see this throughout the United States industry and government by rules that award business to the lowest bidder.

Requirement of suitable measures of quality will, in all likelihood, require us to reduce the number of vendors. The problem is to find one vendor that can furnish statistical evidence of quality. We must work with vendors so that we understand the procedures that they use to achieve reduced numbers of defects.

5. Improve constantly and forever the system of production and service.

6. Restructure training.

    a. Develop the concept of tutors.

    b. Develop increased in-service education.

    c. Teach employees methods of statistical control on the job.

    d. Provide operational definitions of all jobs.

    e. Provide training until the learner's work reaches the state of statistical control, and focus the training to assist the learner to achieve the state of statistical control.

7. Improve supervision. Supervision belongs to the system and is the responsibility of the management.

    a. Supervisors need time to help people on the job.

    b. Supervisors need to find ways to translate the constancy of purpose to the individual employee.

    c. Supervisors must be trained in simple statistical methods for aid to employees, with the aim to detect and eliminate special causes of mistakes and rework. Supervisors should find causes of trouble and not just chase anecdotes. They need information that shows when to take action, not just figures that describe the level of production and the level of mistakes in the past.

d. Focus supervisory time on people that are out of statistical control and not those that are low performers. If the members of a group are in fact in statistical control, there will be some that are low performers and some that are high performers.

e. Teach supervisors how to use the results of surveys of patients.

8. Drive out fear. We must break down the class distinctions between types of workers within the organization—physicians, nonphysicians, clinical providers versus nonclinical providers, physician to physician. Discontinue gossip. Cease to blame employees for problems of the system. Management should be held responsible for faults of the system. People need to feel secure to make suggestions. Management must follow through on suggestions. People on the job can not work effectively if they dare not enquire into the purpose of the work that they do, and dare not offer suggestions for simplification and improvement of the system.

9. Break down barriers between departments. Learn about the problems in the various departments. One way would be to encourage switches of personnel in related departments.

10. Eliminate numerical goals, slogans, and posters imploring people to do better. Instead, display accomplishments of the management in respect to assistance to employees to improve their performance. People need information about what the management is doing on these 14 points.

11. Eliminate work standards that set quotas, commonly called also measured day work. Work standards must produce quality, not mere quantity. It is better to take aim at rework, error, and defects, and to focus on help to people to do a better job. It is necessary for people to understand the purpose of the organization and how their jobs relate to the purpose of the organization.

12. Institute a massive training program in statistical techniques. Bring statistical techniques down to the level of the individual employee's job, and help him to gather information in a systematic way about the nature of his job. This kind of in-service training must be married to the management function rather than to the personnel function within the organization.

13. Institute a vigorous program for retraining people in new skills. People must be secure about their jobs in the future, and must know that acquisition of new skills will facilitate security.

14. Create a structure in top management that will push every day on the above 13 points. Top management may organize a task force with the authority and obligation to act. This task force will require guidance from an experienced consultant, but the consultant can not take on obligations that only the management can carry out.

Suggestions on study of performance in a hospital.

A run chart, or in some instances a distribution, on any of the following characteristics of performance will show management where retraining and special help are needed, and will indicate whether changes in the system have been successful.[4]

Delays in posting laboratory results to charts of patients
Incorrect dosages of drugs to patients
Wrong drug given
Improper administration of drug
Inadequate monitoring of patients during drug therapy
Number of toxic reactions observed to drugs given
Number of laboratory tests ordered but not performed

4 This list was contributed by Paul T. Hertz and Miss Debra Levine.

Number of incomplete medical records

Number of unnecessary surgical procedures performed

Total number of surgical procedures performed

Number of surgical complications

Death rate, total

Mortality rate during surgery

Mortality rate in emergency room

Number of surgical procedures by type

Number of transfusions

Number of transfusion reactions (caused by such factors as illegible writing on blood bag, given to wrong patient)

Preoperative–postoperative discrepancies (e.g., diagnosis made by internist or surgeon doesn't agree with tissue findings from pathologist)

Fires, chemical spillage, and other accidents in laboratory

Experimental drug usage

Complaints from patients

Average length of stay in hospital

Number of patients in isolation, weekly average

Number of X-rays ordered

Number of laboratory tests ordered

Number of radiation procedures

Number of EEG and EKG examinations

Number of illegible requests and illegible reports on patients

Errors in laboratory

Percentage of rework in laboratory

Time between collection of specimen and receipt at the laboratory

Number of unacceptable specimens due to:
    Improper container
    Quantity not sufficient (QNS)

Name of patient missing or illegible
Name on requisition disagrees with name on container
Container broken or leaking
Specimen sat around too long
Shortage, by item
Overstock, by item
Computer downtime, distribution by length of time out
Number of expired reagents or media
Record of overtime; number of personnel out sick or otherwise absent
    Regular
    Volunteer

Suggestions on study of performance of an airline.

Records kept in some rational form, as by flight, or by location, by week, will yield run charts and distributions that will detect existence of special causes, and will measure the effects of attempts to improve the system. A list of characteristics of the airline industry follows:

Number of standbys taken per flight
Number of passengers bumped per flight
Load factors
Distribution of time of delay and time of arrival
Number of near-misses
Distribution of time that passengers spend at counter to:
    Purchase tickets
    Check baggage
Distribution of time for delivery of baggage
Number of lost pieces astray or delayed

Suggestions on study of performance in a hotel.

> Average time to pick up empty trays after delivery by
>   room service
> Costs of energy
> Costs of laundry
> Theft
> Litigation costs
> Errors in reservations
> Frequency of overbooking
> Turnover of managers
> Turnover of other people

Examples and Suggestions

Application in the Bureau of the Census. One of the earliest and most successful full-scale efforts in a large organization toward improvement of quality and productivity in all its phases originated around 1937 in the Bureau of the Census under the leadership of Morris H. Hansen. Myriads of operations take place in the production line between (a) Census enumerators in the field, or between mailed responses, and (b) the final published tables.

Monthly and quarterly surveys carried out by the Census on unemployment, starts of housing units, movements of wholesale goods, morbidity, and other characteristics of people and of business, are of prime importance for business purposes and for governmental planning. The precision of such surveys, to be maximally useful, must never be in question.

Speed is necessary, before the figures become obsolete, but not at the cost of accuracy. Improvement in both speed and accuracy has been accomplished by new methods of training and supervision, with the help of statistical methods.

Important papers and books appeared under the authorship of Morris H. Hansen and colleagues for improvement of sampling and reduction of nonsampling errors; also for an economic balance between sampling and nonsampling errors. A compendium of papers and books that had their origin in the Census between 1939 and 1955 can not be attempted here. It will suffice to mention the book *Sampling Survey Methods and Theory* by Hansen, Hurwitz, and Madow, Vols. 1 and 2 (Wiley, 1953).

The contributions to quality and productivity from our Census could not have taken place without the leadership and support of the top management and advisors in the Census. In fact, the story is one of joint authorship with Philip M. Hauser, J. C. Capt, Calvert L. Dedrick, Frederick F. Stephan, Samuel A. Stouffer, and others.

Census people the world over are a fraternal group, continually learning from each other. Our own Census thus played an important role in improvement of quality and productivity all over the world.

It is worthy of note that Censuses are service organizations, and governmental.

Quality and productivity in the Bureau of Customs. The U.S. Bureau of Customs weighs a shipload of incoming bales of wool, or tobacco, or rayon, by weighing only a small sample of the bales and computing the total weight on board by means of the sample, making use of ratio-estimates and other statistical techniques. The Bureau of Customs computes also, in the case of wool, by tests of a sample of cores bored from the sample of bales, the clean content of the wool in order to compute the duty to be paid. Weighing by means of samples of bales reduces greatly the cost of weighing and puts ships out on to the water days before they would be out if every bale were weighed, as was the procedure prior to adoption of statistical methods. The benefit is not only reduction in time and savings of cost to the Bureau of Customs, as well as savings of thousands of dollars for berthing charges to the shipping companies, but also improved accuracy of the weights and of the clean content of the incoming wool.

The Bureau of Customs, in spite of advances in management and contributions to techniques of measurement, still hands out to each person to fill out on entry to the United States a form that asks for

Last name   First name   Middle initial

in spite of the fact that a third of people in the Anglo–Saxon world go by first initial and middle name. Examples: H. Herbert Hoover, C. Calvin Coolidge, J. Edgar Hoover.

Problems in a payroll department. A company had trouble with mistakes on payroll cards. There were nine hundred people on the payroll, making fifteen hundred mistakes every day (not a bad production record). The payroll department, because of so many mistakes, succeeded only with great effort to get cheques to the employees four days after the close of the week. Could the burden be lightened? The time card is shown in Fig. 11. Note that two signatures were required, the employee's and the foreman's.

Why have two people signed the card? Who is responsible for the accuracy of the card? The requirement of two signatures means that nobody is responsible: trouble guaranteed. Suggestions:

1. Require only the signature of the employee. Make him responsible for the card.

2. Do not ask an employee to record nor compute the total for the day. Do this arithmetic in the payroll department.

My prediction was that the problems would evaporate in three weeks. Actually, they evaporated in one week.

Clerical problems in purchase. In another instance, the purchasing department complained that 3 out of 4 purchase orders came to them incomplete or incorrect in some way, such as wrong item number, obsolete number, no such vendor, vendor name misspelled, no signature of the buyer, and a host of other nuisances. My suggestion was to send the form back immediately

Date _____ _____ _____
Day   Month   Year

Identification
number ————————   ————————————
Signature

Clock		Elapsed	Job	Pay	Amount
In	Out	time	code	code	earned
Total earned this day					

————————————————————

Foreman

Fig. 11. Payroll time card. Too many signatures. Too much arithmetic for the employee.

to the buyer if anything was amiss. My prediction was that the problem would evaporate in three weeks. Actually, irregularities dropped to 3 in 100 in two weeks. Most of the remaining problems can be eliminated with care in supervision—for example, provide buyers with information that is up to date.

Travel vouchers. Management in the Department of Education in Washington found that several signatures were required on every claim for reimbursement for travel.[5] Every person that signed a claim tried to clean it up before it moved onward for the next review and signature.

A simple change in procedure eliminated most of the problems and hastened reimbursement: (1) revise the instructions, for better clarity; (2) do not supply data for figures obviously omitted by the traveler. Instead, send the voucher back to the traveler for correction, with an explanation that his omission may cause delay in reimbursement. The problem all but disappeared in a short while. Rumors travel fast.

Many companies are equally guilty of piling paperwork on paperwork. My suggestion is to pay at sight every claim for travel and for petty cash, and to investigate thoroughly a sample of claims, such as 1 in 50. The sample would include also 100 per cent of any transactions suspected of being shady. Investigation of the sample will tell how the system is working. Some mistakes there will be, but their net effect will be trivial compared with the economy of transfer to useful work of layers of reviewers.

Accounting procedures: present worth of physical plant and inventory. Accounting procedures now require that the auditor's report contain an evaluation of the physical plant, rolling stock, and inventory. For a large company, this evaluation can be carried out with accuracy by statistical methods of sampling, to esti-

5 I am indebted to Robert Caccia and to Emmett Fleming and Joseph Teresa
   for the privilege to work with them on this illustration.

mate (a) the physical condition of each category of plant, and (b) the reproduction cost new of each category; then by multiplication to estimate the present worth. The actual fieldwork requires inspection of only a relatively small number of items, in total only four thousand for a plant like that of the Illinois Bell Telephone Company, whose total reproduction-cost-new minus depreciation exceeds $2,000,000,000. The work can be done by skilled inspectors in the space of a few weeks. Use of judgment-samples could only end up in crude guess-work.

Along with the information obtained to evaluate reproduction-cost-new minus depreciation comes free of charge information by which to forecast the cost of repairs and replacement during the next five years for each type of plant. This forecast is far more objective than the reports of division managers, all of whom know that he who screams loudest gets the most money for repairs and replacement. Estimates of the proportion of underground duct space not in use, by size of duct, constitute an example of another bonus.

Reduction of inventory through study of time of transit. Parts for automobiles in the United States are made in various cities in the United States and Canada, and are shipped by rail and by motor freight to the customer.[6] Study of time of transit of parts from the factory to the customer shows in some corridors of traffic pretty good statistical control except for special causes in the nature of delays for repairs of cars that break down en route. An upper limit of regular time of transit is then a simple calculation.

In an example, the corridor was Buffalo to Kansas City. Inventory en route plus inventory in Kansas City constitute investment. The requirement on inventory in Kansas City had been fixed as 5 days. The upper limit, once the time of transit was observed to be in statistical control (except for breakdowns), was

6 I am indebted to Messrs. Richard Haupt and Charles Richards and to Edward Baker of the Ford Motor Company for the privilege to work with them on this problem.

calculated as 4.2 days. The difference, 0.8 day, translates into savings of $500,000 per year for the parts involved in this calculation.

This and similar calculations for scores of other routes added up to $25 million, interest on which is easily $100,000 per day at present rates.

Time for major repair of a railway car is hardly ever less than 24 hours. Inventory sufficient to cover shortage that arises from breakdowns en route is costly. There is another way to work on this problem. The whereabouts of every railway car en route is known at all times at headquarters by telegraphic communication with the railway. Quick action in the form of rapid despatch by truck from the car that broke down, or from another plant, of enough parts to fill in the gap created by a breakdown is a workable solution.

A hotel. As was emphasized in Chapter 2, nearly everything is one of a kind. Once the plans are part way in place, it is too late to build quality into a product. A hotel is a perfect example. A hotel consists of a building, along with heat, the air conditioning, lifts. Then the furniture comes in. Many hotels (in the U.S., at least) were monstrosities before construction commenced. The only place for the bed in many hotels is directly in the blast of air that blows in for heating or for cooling. The furniture in a hotel may cost a million dollars, without a semblance of a desk in any room. In a new hotel where I held a seminar, the lifts are about half the number required to handle the traffic, and are unbelievably slow. Small wonder that the maker of the lifts did not attach his identification.

Guests are requested to turn off lights when they leave the room. To carry out this request, somebody must go to every light that is on, search for the switch, then try to discover which way is off. Every light is a puzzle. Architects of two hotels in this world used their heads (perhaps after staying in a hotel). There is a master switch at the door in the Constellation Hotel in Toronto. On and off are automatic at the door in the Mandarin Hotel in Singapore.

Are hotels improving, each new one better in some way than one completed a year ago? (See p. 51.) The manager of a hotel is helpless, an inheritor of a blunder. What would happen to the manager of a hotel if he would suggest to the owners that he offer the furniture at auction, and use the proceeds to buy functional furniture? He would be out of a job tomorrow. The same fate would await him if he were to suggest that the management put in new ducts for air conditioning, or rewire the rooms, or add a lift. Helpless, he can only try to help guests to forget the rooms, and to admit that the bar, the service, and the music are superb.

It would be simple, and much appreciated by guests, for a hotel to provide honest coat hangers in the rooms. Some hotels do. Examples: the Broadway Inn in Columbia, Missouri; Loews Paradise Inn, near Phoenix; Travelodges in New Zealand; the Drury Lane Hotel in London; the Imperial Hotel in Tokyo.

Observations on a statistically planned basis could keep management informed on characteristics of performance such as these:

> The proportion of rooms that are put into satisfactory order before registration of new arrivals.
>
> The distribution of the time required for putting vacated rooms into order for new arrivals. Do these periods of time form a statistical distribution, or are there outliers?
>
> If there are outliers, what is the cause? Would it be economical to remove the cause?
>
> The proportion of guests that needed a desk where none was provided.
>
> The proportion of rooms without adequate light on the desk.
>
> The proportion of rooms without adequate supplies of stationery.

The proportion of rooms in which the telephone is not
working properly.
The proportion of guests that complain that the air
conditioning is noisy.

Any reader can add other problems found in hotels.[7]

A stable system, indicated by a chart, would indicate that the
responsibility for improvement rests wholly with the management (Chs. 1 and 11).

The Postal Service. One may wonder why the first-class mail
service in the United States is about the worst in the industria-
lized world. It may be, at the same time, the most efficient in the
world. Losses to business from poor mail service in the United
States are huge and deplorable. Better service would of course require higher postal rates.

Messenger service, men carrying envelopes or machine-sheets
from one business to another, within the same city or between
(e.g) New York and Philadelphia has of late become a growth industry in the United States, owing to delinquency of the U.S.
mail.

The problem lies, of course, in the management of the Postal
Service, which has never had the privilege to decide what should
be the function of first-class mail. Should it be slow, infrequent,
and cheap, or speedy with more deliveries at higher cost? Both
alternatives would be possible with a priority system of postage.

Overbooking. Any airline that practices overbooking needs
statistical guidance to optimize the gains and to minimize the
losses that may arise from several sources, including penalties.
There are two losses to consider: (1) seats vacant, representing

---

7 The book by Philip B. Crosby, *Quality Is Free* (McGraw-Hill, 1979), tells on
pp. 59–63 how to lose money and fold up in the hotel business.

loss of revenue; (2) seats oversold, with a possible penalty to pay every passenger left behind. The penalty may be a free ride on some other airline, plus a sum of money. (Overbooking in a hotel may not be as serious: The manager can often find a room across the street in another hotel.)

The statistical problem is to minimize the net loss from the two possible mistakes (penalty for more passengers than seats, and loss from more seats than passengers). One needs no statistical theory to achieve a clean record on a resolve (a) never to overbook and (b) never to pay a penalty.

In good management, one has a rational plan dictated by statistical theory to minimize the net loss from both eventualities, including penalty for failure to have a seat for a passenger as booked.

The first step is a historical record of demand for each trip, with a study of weekly and other cycles, on which to base a rational prediction of demand a few days ahead, with confidence limits attached thereto. One can then compute the optimum number of seats to book beyond capacity for greatest profit.

Copying machines. Appropriate analysis of records of service of copying machines, as well as for installations of other apparatus and machinery, showing the time elapsed between (a) the customer's request for service and (b) the serviceman's call, would provide statistical signals that indicate special causes of delay, and would describe in meaningful terms the performance of the service department. By appropriate design, the service company could learn the proportion of trouble that lies in:

The machine as a whole; also for any specified compo-
nent thereof
The customer
The repairman

Which repairmen need further training or should be shifted to other work? In the case of copying machines, some customers are satisfied with wretched copies. Others are very particular, and call the serviceman at the least blemish. The records kept by servicemen would disclose which category a customer belongs to, and they would indicate where improvements in design might be desirable. They would also indicate whether customers need education on what to expect of a machine, and need of better instruction on how to use it and how to take care of it. Some customers may need a more expensive machine, or one less expensive.[8]

A restaurant. I have often wondered in a restaurant, seated and helpless waiting for the next course, or equally helpless wondering how to get the bill in order to square up and vacate one seat, seeing a line of people waiting to be seated, how much lost capacity the restaurant suffers from failure of supervision. If people could be served with despatch (not with haste), and the bill delivered when they are ready for it, to give up their places to incoming patrons, productivity, capacity, and profits would all increase substantially, and customers would be better satisfied.

How many patrons, of those seated, are trying in vain to signal a waiter? How many waiters are at this very time standing by, gazing into the heavens? How much food has been ready 10 minutes for waiters to deliver to the table, fit to eat 10 minutes ago, now ready for rejection? What kinds of food are only half-consumed? Snap-counts, at random times by Tippett's methods, would provide answers at low cost.[9]

8 Two excellent references are these: Nancy R. Mann, Raymond Schafer, and Nozer D. Singpurwalla, *Methods for Statistical Analysis of Reliability and Life Data* (Wiley, 1974), and Richard E. Barlow and Frank Proschan, *Statistical Theory of Reliability* (Holt, Rinehart and Winston, 1975).

9 See Marvin E. Mundel, *Motion and Time Studies* (Prentice-Hall, 1950; rev. ed., 1970), p. 128; L. H. C. Tippett, "Ratio-delay study," *Journal of Textile Institute Transactions* 36, no. 2 (February 1935); R. L. Morrow, *Time Study and Motion Economy* (Ronald Press, 1946), pp. 176–199; C. L. Brisley, "How you can put work sampling to work," *Factory* 110, no. 7 (July 1952): 84–89; J. S. Pairo, "Using ratio-delay studies to set allowance," *Factory* 106, no. 10 (October 1943): 94.

What foods listed on the card outsell others? Which of them hardly ever sell? Which ones cause loss? Could they be eliminated without severe loss of patronage? Which ones could be offered once a week at a profit instead of daily at low profit or downright loss? Of the various costs, which ones are heaviest? How could they be reduced? Alterations of food and service could be made in anticipation of a heat wave or a blizzard predicted by the National Weather Service.

A city's transit system. Observations, carried out by appropriate statistical design, would show where there is business, and at what time of day, to meet needs of the public. Timetables posted at stops, and rigid adherence thereto, would generate new business. One need only visit any city in Europe to discover what can be done to improve service in the United States.

Transit systems in the United States are hampered by the requirement to give business to the lowest bidder (as remarked in Ch. 2).

More examples in motor freight. Samples of freight bills issued by carriers of general freight in the United States and Canada, selected and processed by procedures that are based on the theory of probability (to get the maximum amount of information per unit cost), furnish information for the following:

> For hearings before the Interstate Commerce Commission, on requests of the carriers for increases or restructuring of rates for hauls of various weights and mileages. The same data furnish also a basis for negotiation with shippers in respect to rates for shipments of various weights and mileages.
>
> For business purposes. The carriers may observe, from the results of the continuing studies, what routes, weights, and mileages, and what classes and

commodities, lead to unprofitable business, and which ones to profitable business.

No other industry has information in such detail, accuracy, and timeliness for use for business purposes or as a rational basis for rates.

These continuing studies of traffic are done by the carriers themselves (not by any government agency), under statistical procedures designed and monitored by this author.

Other types of studies lead to reduction of mistakes in loading, in pickup and delivery, reduction in damage and claims for damage, errors in billing.

Another study shows whether and how effective are various steps aimed at reduction of fuel—heavier loading, idling fans, regular tuning (or irregular, whichever is more cost-effective), enforcing economical speed on intercity routes.

A railway. Studies of data obtained by appropriate statistical design could provide information by which to:

1. Reduce errors in interline settlements, and in local billing as well.
2. Decrease idle time of cars, which would in turn decrease the rent paid out for use of cars. Customers would receive with less delay their requests for empty cars to load.
3. Learn whether delays in transit form a statistical system. If there are outliers, what are the causes of the outliers? Why not eliminate these causes (if outliers are found)?

What can be done to shrink the ranges of the distribution of time of transit? Shrinkage of the distribution would mean better service to the customer and savings to the railway through more dependable and uniform performance. An example appeared on p. 211.

Does the railway construct and use the distribution of time spent by cars in shops for repair, by different types of repair? The railway pays rent for every hour for a car in a shop, no matter who owns the car. They have the records of repairs, or can get them.

Where, for any important terminal, is the distribution of hours that elapse between the time a customer informs the railway that he is ready to load a car or several cars and the time an empty car or cars are delivered to him? How many of the cars delivered were the right type of car? How many were dirty? Where is the distribution of hours elapsed between the time the car is ready and the time when it was pulled away?

It would be possible by methods based on probability sampling to make periodic tests of samples of rolling equipment, signaling equipment, equipment in warehouses and on docks and on trucks, to determine the proportion and number of items that are depleted and in need of repair or immediate replacement, and to estimate the costs to be incurred next year for maintenance and replacement. Examination of tracks, roadbed, and grading at points selected by statistical methods would furnish information for repairs needed. The methods of probability sampling for such studies are a powerful tool of administration.

Do customers care about the service rendered? Even if they don't, improvement in performance would realize more profit from existing equipment and tracks, or even permit sale of some existing equipment, and improve service to customers.

In a survey that I conducted for a railway, it turned out that mechanics spent three-quarters of their time waiting in line for parts.

Studies in the operation of a telephone company.
1. By appropriate statistical design, estimate the usage of

circuits and carrier equipment: What proportions of the time are circuits and carrier equipment used for voice, for the press, for transmission of data, private telegrams, public telegrams, etc.?[10] The results are used as a basis for fixing rates for the various services.

2. By appropriate statistical design, estimate the ratio of usage of switches and other central office equipment for local service to toll service. The results are used as a basis for division of revenues between local telephone service and toll service, and ultimately for rates.

3. By appropriate statistical design, estimate the physical depreciation of the various kinds of equipment—switches, relays, private branch exchanges, underground exchange cable, underground toll cable, community dial offices, ducts, loading coils, poles, aerial cable, terminals on poles and in buildings, telephone apparatus, signaling devices.

4. Achieve reduction of errors in billing, accomplished at reduced cost.

5. Perform tests of records of physical plant. Are the records satisfactory? What kinds of mistakes need correction and for what areas?

6. Reconcile joint usage of property, such as poles. The telephone company may own a pole, or the electric company may own it, or they may own it jointly 50:50 or otherwise. They pay rent to each other for use of poles. Is one company paying the other too much? Studies by appropriate statistical design provide answers of demonstrable precision. Continuing studies keep the payments in balance. (A complete reconciliation would be

---

10 I am indebted to friends in telephone companies for help in this section, in particular, Dr. Robert J. Brousseau of AT&T, James N. Kennedy of the Illinois Bell Telephone Company, and Dr. J. Franklin Sharp, author of "Managing statistics and operations research for management," paper delivered at a meeting of the American Statistical Association, Boston, August 1976. Last, I am grateful for the privilege to work with a number of telephone companies, from 1949 onward, on numerous types of studies.

impossible because of the sheer size of the job, and if attempted, would introduce a whole new set of errors, and the last state would be worse than at the beginning.)

7. Study the effectiveness of advertising to boost revenue from long-distance calls.

8. Conduct a simulation of a telephone office. Certain types of additional involvement of operators were proposed by corporate psychologists with the goal of enrichment of job. As the proposed changes might have drastic effects on productivity, the research group set up a simulated model to study a number of possible changes.

9. Conduct studies to decrease the time for telephone operators by working smarter, not harder, to handle various types of calls. Mechanization of the analysis, with a carefully designed sampling procedure for carrying out radio-delay studies, provides results on a continuing basis.

10. Study optimal routes for messenger service between telephone company locations within a metropolitan area. A telephone company may have one or more central despatch systems for intracompany mail and numerous mail routes for pickup and delivery of company mail in a large number of locations. The Bell Laboratories developed an integer programming algorithm to help to determine the optimal number of routes and the stops to be made on each route.

11. Determine the optimal location of new equipment. Savings in operating costs can be achieved by replacing electromechanical switching equipment by electronic equipment, or by installing electronic equipment rather than additional electromechanical equipment. Bell Laboratories has developed a nonlinear programming algorithm to help determine where and when electronic equipment should be installed. Other research men in telephone companies have developed some user-oriented software and incorporated some additional procedures for financial analysis.

12. Perform continuing studies of expenses and usage of

common equipment, following statistical procedures designed by Dr. Robert J. Brousseau of the American Telephone and Telegraph Company, in a joint effort with other telephone companies, forming the underlying base for interline settlements of revenue and charges for use of joint equipment, mainly toll circuits.

13. Study inventory and reconciliation of engineering records and accounting records of underground cable and repeaters, aerial cable, and other equipment; the same for telephone equipment, including wiring and installation (station equipment), on the premises of customers.

14. Estimate unit costs of material and labor in station connexions.

15. Develop aids for training operators.

16. Estimate the cost of dental care for employees.

17. Conduct studies by which to reduce the risk of failure of the company to collect the amount due for telephone service rendered to people that move away without settling their bills for telephone service (loss of several million dollars in one year for Illinois Bell alone).

18. Estimate usage of the Yellow Pages, and how to make them more useful.

19. Study problems that customers have to decipher their telephone bills, the aim being to improve the format of bills.

A department store. Observations by departments on the length of time that customers wait for service, and the number of people that walk away unable to get service, would provide a basis for use of a loss function that would help the management to decide whether, where, and when additional service might pay a dividend.

> There is one big gap in the use of a loss function for such purposes: no one knows the loss that accrues to the store from ill will of people that give up and walk away. One unhappy customer can influence a lot of other people; so can a happy customer.

Observations are required at snap times on:

Attitude of clerk toward customer
Attitude of customer toward clerk

Automobiles and the customer. We pause here for only a brief remark that is easy to expand to wide application. A large manufacturer of automobiles, in recognition of the need to learn about the problems of the purchaser of an automobile, sends out to every purchaser, after a year from date of purchase, a questionnaire to learn about his problems and experience. Half the questionnaires come back; half do not. Now every statistician knows the perils of drawing conclusions from incomplete returns, even if 90 per cent of them come back. Refuge in the argument that the hazards that lurk in incomplete returns may be small if the conclusions are confined to trends is only an expression of hope, with little foundation.

A simple modification, well known,[11] would be to send out questionnaires to only a sample of a thousand purchasers, appropriately selected; then to follow up by personal interview with the nonrespondents. This modification would greatly reduce the cost of the study, and would yield results that could be used with an ascertainable degree of confidence.

The same procedure could be applied to any other product for which a list of purchasers exists. In fact, this suggestion is regular practice with some companies, as anyone engaged in consumer research knows.

Reduction of Mistakes in a Bank

By WILLIAM J. LATZKO

A bank. Friends in the banking business acknowledge that the management of banks know less about their customers than the

---

11 See any textbook on sampling or survey procedures.

management in any other business. Starts are being made by pulling together the accounts of any one customer—his chequing account, savings accounts, fiduciary accounts, trust accounts, loans. This coordination is greatly simplified by modern data-processing machinery. But this is far short of knowing the needs of customers, and to what extent the bank fails to meet these needs. Why does a customer of the bank get a loan elsewhere for the purchase of an automobile or to buy a home, or to remodel his present home? Neither the fact nor the reasons are on the record. Some consumer research might answer this and a host of other questions about customers.

The big mistake. There is, in a bank, as in other businesses, the perennial problem of reduction of mistakes. There are two purposes of inspection in a bank. One is to discover errors before they go out to a customer, the other is to forestall dishonesty. The search for quality in banking is by no means new; it dates back to the time of the pharaohs. Traditionally, the banker's only check for quality has been the reviewer or signer, with layer upon layer of inspection into the system, under the supposition that the only costly error is the one that leaves the bank to annoy the customer. All work, time, and money spent in forestalling such a disaster has been simply a cost of doing business, absorbed in operational costs and only rarely visible to the management. There are four kinds of cost:

1. Costs of appraisal, verification, and inspection of work. This is the traditional inspection system—the army of people in every bank that are engaged in verifying and verifying again.
2. Cost of internal failure, probably the real villain in banking's story. Mistakes that are caught are reworked at great expense.
3. Cost of external failure. These are the errors that get out to the customer and lead to expensive investigations, adjustments, penalties, and lost accounts.

4. Cost of prevention, the analysis and systematic control of quality. The theory is simple. Detection and correction of trouble at the earliest stage decrease costs all down the line and improve quality and reduce costs.

There are two types of quality in any system, whether it be banking or manufacturing. The first is quality of design. These are the specific programs and procedures that promise to produce a saleable service or product: in other words, what the customer requires. The second type is quality of production, achievement of results with the quality promised.

Quality control works both with the product and with the design of the product. And it is at this point that quality control begins to differ from the traditional system. To find the mistake is not enough. It is necessary to find the cause behind the mistake, and to build a system that minimizes future mistakes.

Improvement of performance. The quality improvement program operates at the level of first-line supervisor. It has brought the results shown in Fig. 12 and has improved morale, as employees are now confident that they will not be blamed for errors that are not under their governance.

A record, charted on a regular basis by computer, provides the process capability of each individual. The performance of the individual can then be compared with the performance of the group. Help can be given to people that fall outside the tolerances for the group.

Morale of employees. Previously, when rejection rates went up, computer operators began blaming each other. Shift would react against shift and department against department. In the end, everyone would blame "the machine." The results were discord, disharmony, and low morale. With statistical methods, the reason for an abnormal rejection rate can be automatically

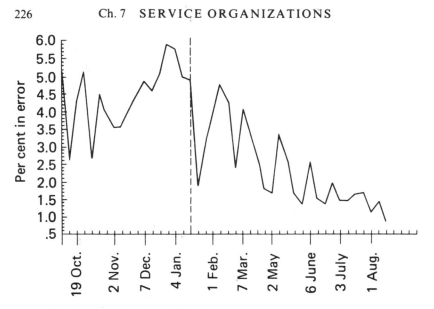

Fig. 12. Results of quality improvement program. It refers specifically to typing in the telegram department. Problems are now detected long before they become critical.

traced to the department, to the shift, to the machine, to the operator, and finally to the important thing, the problem. For, as stated before, statistical methods require identification of the problem, not the individual. With such a philosophy, everyone works together to point his finger at the real culprit, the problem.

Some experts on banking declare that between 40 and 60 per cent of any bank's staff is involved in verifying the work of other staff members. Statistical methods help to reduce the frequency of mistakes. They have a far-reaching and dramatic impact on the future of banking. With concentration of inspection on critical items, such as those of high dollar value, and sample verification of other items, greater accuracy can be obtained with decrease in the amount of inspection.

Programs of improvement can be instituted at any bank, regardless of size, for they can be tailored to meet specific needs and designed to grow with the bank, expanding as new areas of application become apparent.

Each unit being studied, whether it be a human operator, a machine or a system, is monitored over a period of time to determine its process capability: what it can predictably do under current conditions (see Ch. 11). The process capability of an operation can usually be determined in about three months.

Should management decide that the process capability is not within the acceptable limits, then management must do something about the process or system. Quality can not exceed the capability of the system. Quality can not be inspected into a product or service; it must be built into it (Harold F. Dodge; see Ch. 3).

Suggestions for Additional Continual Studies in a Bank[12]

Aim: continual improvement of economy and reduction of mistakes.

Techniques: run charts, control charts, Tippett's techniques.

Rejection rate of cheques processed through high-speed MICR sorters

Maintenance and downtime of MICR machines

Vendor performance measures—periodic review of cheques from outside printers for errors, i.e., number of poorly encoded symbols and numbers on cheques or number of missing symbols and numbers

Cost of handling exceptions

Time elapsed between receipt of request from customer and action taken

Number of customers waiting in line

Distribution of time for transaction by tellers

---

12 The existence of this list was called to my attention by Paul T. Hertz and Miss Debra Levine.

Turnover rate of tellers

Error rates of tellers

Percentage of default on loans per grade category (a measure of the quality of the grading system on loans, which provides early warning of difficulties)

Error rate associated with cheques processed from lock-box plan

Average time to process items via lock-box plan

Error rates reported by customers, rather than those picked up by in-house means

Number of cheques or commercial notes returned because of errors in completion

Downtime of computers

Error rate associated with money transfer

Number of past-due accounts

Average and variation in age of outstanding loans (Monitoring of the two preceding areas may permit reduction of costs associated with policing past-due loans.)

Time to correct errors, by important types of error

Dollar volume generated

Total number of accounts

Average loan yield: net yield per loan (The three preceding measurements reflect profitability of the banking institution.)

Number of new accounts opened

Number of calls made to solicit new accounts

Number of classified loans and charge-offs

Profitability of Accounts

1. Errors on DDA analysis statements
2. Errors on compensating balance statements
3. Errors on service charges
4. Ledger and float adjustments required

Adjustments

1. Difference-tickets generated
2. Customer enquiries received
3. Backlog of unresolved differences
4. Backlog of unresolved customer enquiries
5. Breakdown of errors by type and area creating error
6. Timeliness of error resolution
7. Differences charged off

Building

1. Tenant complaints regarding temperature, humidity, cleanliness, elevator service, etc.

Bonds

1. Errors on trades received (monitor and report to originator)
2. Equipment downtime
3. Dollar impact of securities deadlines missed
4. Keypunch/processing errors on trades
5. Balancing errors in safekeeping
6. Fed Fund processing errors
7. Number and impact of backdated trades and Fed Fund activity
8. Overdrafts due to Bond entries
9. Adjustments to DDA balances required due to late Bond entries

Commercial Loans

1. Collateral documents missing on loans booked
2. Rejects on entering loans to system
3. Backdates required
4. Returned corporate statements
5. Corrections required on loan transactions

Computer Services

1. Timeliness of courier deliveries
2. Timeliness of reports from Computer Centre to the bank
3. Timeliness of computer input from the bank to the Computer Centre
4. Amount of time the on-line system is down
5. Amount of time the on-line system is not current
6. Evaluation by users of services provided by the Computer Centre

Processing of Consumer Accounts

1. Missing cheques/statements at statement preparation
2. DDA and savings application rejects
3. Forgeries paid
4. Stop payments missed
5. Errors in preparation of statement
6. Problems with equipment for preparation of statements

Consumer Banking

1. New DDA and savings deposits rejected because new account information not processed in time
2. CRT input errors
3. Walkouts
4. Customer perception of quality
5. Resolution time of complaints from customers
6. Attrition of accounts
7. Errors in orders for cheques

Information to Customers

1. Incoming customer calls that are blocked (busy signal) or abandoned (put on hold and customer hangs up)
2. CIF rejects

3. Errors on name and address changes
4. Timeliness of processing CIF and name and address forms
5. Customer complaints/problem enquiries
6. Telephone transfer errors
7. On-line applications not on CIF
8. DDA and savings statements returned (wrong address)

Corporate Accounting (General Ledger)
1. FIS items posted inaccurately
2. FIS items not posted
3. Timeliness of processing bills

Corporate Account Processing
1. Missing cheques and statements
2. Attrition of accounts
3. Rejects on sequencing (handsorting)
4. Payable through/ARP tape problems
5. Forgeries paid
6. Stop payments missed

Corporate Customer Information
1. Incoming customer calls that are blocked or abandoned
2. CIF rejects
3. Input errors on CIF entries
4. Input errors on name and address changes
5. Telephone transfer errors
6. Returned DDA statements (wrong address)
7. Customer complaints/problem enquiries
8. On-line applications not on CIF

Consumer Credit
1. Dollar value and number of overdrafts
2. Dollar value and number of charge-offs
3. Overdraft charges reversed

4. Accounts closed for unsatisfactory handling
5. Cheques missing that should be returned
6. Customer complaints
7. Number of warning letters sent
8. Status change errors
9. Occurrences of ready reserve and general ledger being out of balance

Customer Reference

1. Address charge—CIF errors
2. CIF maintenance rejects
3. Timeliness in verifying name and address forms
4. Number of notifications of change of address
5. Missing and illegible signatures on fiche
6. On-line applications not on CIF
7. Returned DDA and savings statements (wrong address)
8. Complaints of customers

Federal Reserve Bank

1. High-speed and low-speed rejects
2. Missing information on Fed advices
3. Missing/missent advices
4. Problems with Series E bonds
5. Occurrences of late inclearings activity
6. Occurrences of missing/extra/missent clearings
7. Number and dollar amount of cash letter discrepancies

Graphic Services

1. Timeliness of processing new/revised form requests
2. Downtime of equipment
3. Volume of poor-quality copies on copiers
4. User perception of service provided by Graphic Services

5. Timeliness of duplication, addressograph, and other reproduction requests
6. Rework/reruns
7. Number of user requests that cannot be filled

Instant Cash/Electronic Operations
1. Rejected Instant Cash card and request
2. Defective transmittal letters received
3. ATM transactions not completed
4. ATM downtime
5. Customer complaints

International Accounting
1. Rejects and ticket errors
2. Bookings/loan sheet errors
3. Errors on contracts
4. Holdover on interbank transfers

International Control
1. Missing documentation on new acceptances and loans
2. Rejects of tickets on loans, ALC's, letters of credit
3. Input errors on FX contracts booked
4. Holdover—interbank transfers
5. Timeliness of reports
6. Timeliness of foreign due from reconciling

International Finance
1. Errors on acceptances and loan booking sheets
2. Missing documentation on new loans and acceptances

International Letters of Credit
1. Errors on acceptance booking sheets
2. Timeliness of processing import/export documents
3. Computer ticket errors/rejects
4. Holdover

International Paying and Receiving

1. Processing errors and incoming and outgoing payment orders
2. Incorrect tests on outgoing Telexes
3. Errors on outgoing messages
4. Holdover
5. Incorrect wires

Item Processing

1. Volume of missing/extra items
2. Out-of-balance entries
3. Prime pass rejects (by type of work)
4. Dollar value of float lost
5. End-of-day balancing errors
6. Missent cash letters
7. Reconciling errors
8. Keying errors
9. Downtime of equipment
10. Off-line rejects
11. Missorts

Mail Distribution

1. Misdirected mail, internal and external
2. Timeliness of mail deliveries
3. Unidentifiable incoming customer mail
4. Customer complaints regarding mail
5. Returned mail (wrong address)

MICR Q.C. Coordinator/Pretesting Function

1. Prequalified banks with a reject rate greater than 2%
2. Orders for new forms and cheques that fail to pass the testing criteria

Money Transfer

1. Errors on Fed transfers and bank wires
2. Late wire transfers—TWX

3. Dollar value and number of items outstanding
4. Equipment downtime
5. Downtime of Fed communications program and incoming line (monitoring to report back to Fed)
6. Service messages requested regarding verification of information on wires

Noncash Items

1. Errors on City, Country, and Cash Draft items
2. Coupon processing errors (Bond)
3. Float dollars incurred in the collection process when immediate credit is given for coupons
4. Average number of days to collect for coupons
5. Customer complaints— service
6. Outstanding items (Fed)

Productivity and Quality Analysis

1. Timeliness of studies conducted
2. Management acceptance of recommendations
3. Timeliness of productivity analysis and quality analysis reports
4. Quality level of total bank
5. Deviation from projected productivity and quality improvements (dollar value)

Proof

1. Rejects on work encoded by Proof
2. Proof differences/errors
3. Out-of-balance conditions (deposits)
4. Deadlines missed at end-of-day closeout
5. End-of-day extra items
6. Errors on input to Proof (reported to source areas)

Purchasing

1. Equipment downtime (all areas of bank)
2. Timeliness of filling orders from the stockroom

Records Services
1. Unable to locate documents requested
2. Records destroyed past destruction date
3. Records improperly prepared for storage
4. Backlog of records to be prepared for storage
5. User evaluation of service provided

Return Items
1. Errors on processing of returned items
2. Timeliness on processing of returned items
3. Customer complaints

Special Services (Corporate)
1. Errors on lockbox and concentration accounts
2. Data transmission deadlines missed
3. Rejects on work processed by Special Services
4. Timeliness of error resolution

Special Services (Consumer)
1. Errors on Bank by Mail
2. Deposits not credited
3. Timeliness in posting deposits

Tellers
1. Differences between tellers
2. Downtime of equipment
3. Customer perception of service/quality
4. Times cash limits are exceeded
5. Inadequate staffing of windows
6. Charge-offs
7. General cash/suspense tickets outstanding
8. Errors on cash in and out tickets, universal tickets, and other internal tickets
9. Missing and illegible entries

Telecommunications
1. Improperly directed calls to switchboard
2. Customer complaints (excessive transferring)

Trust Accounting

1. Timeliness in generating customer accountings
2. Customer complaints
3. Processing errors

Trust Institutional Support Services

1. Signed pension cheques that are stopped or cancelled
2. Timeliness of processing accountings and cheques
3. Accounting that requires retyping of pages
4. Processing errors
5. Reruns required

Trust Receivables Control

1. Omissions on vault control list
2. Errors on bond interest credited to customers
3. Errors on due-bill cheques

Trust Records and Control

1. Keyboard errors
2. Rejected tickets
3. Timeliness of report distribution
4. Unpostable tickets

Trust Securities

1. Open items (purchases, withdrawals, deposits, re-registrations)
2. Ticket errors
3. Unpostable tickets

Vault Operations

1. Vault/teller differences
2. Series E bonds spoiled/cancelled
3. Microfiche camera downtime
4. Holdover
5. Timeliness of processing Series E bonds

6. Series E bond balancing problems
7. Unprocessed currency
8. Errors—food stamps
9. Customer perception of quality
10. Timeliness of service unit deliveries

Word Processing

1. Errors on documents typed
2. Equipment downtime
3. Turnaround time of documents typed
4. User perception of service/quality

An Electric Utility

By JOHN FRANCIS HIRD

Some points about generation and distribution of electric power.
One of the leading electric utilities in the New England area has
embarked on a program of improvement of quality and profit by
use of well-known technology. Every transaction with its customers must be processed through the system.

The generation, transmission, and distribution of electrical
energy is a continuous process. Needs of customers must be
satisfied every minute of every day. The industrial and residential
communities depend upon electric power. Livelihood, life,
health, safety, and welfare depend on it.

Every failure, delay, and error can cause dissatisfaction of customers, and increases the cost of electric energy.

An Ishikawa chart helps us to find our way through the maze
of activities that are required in the day-to-day operations of a
typical electric utility (reference on p. 368).

The charge for services is scrutinized by consumers and by the
local public utilities commission. Fig. 13 displays the costs of service. A few explanations may help:

> *Fuel*: An electric utility buys coal, oil, gas, and nuclear
> fuel. These are expenses.

Plant and equipment: Machinery wears out or becomes obsolete. The electric utility must earn enough to make replacements.

Cost of money: This is payment made for the investors (lenders) for the money that they advance to the utility.

Labor and administration: The people that work for the utility must be paid.

Taxes: Local, state, and federal taxes imposed to operate government.

Other operating expenses: Supplies, materials, and outside services purchased or engaged.

Some of the elements defined above are fixed by outside forces, and are therefore excluded from this discussion.

There are many other elements of the business that are influenced by the people in the various departments that make up the operating structure of the company, and which can be monitored and improved.

Customer services. One of these activities is known as Customer Services. This department is responsible for reading metres, billing, receiving payment, telephone operations, and centres for enquiry and requests of customers. It provides the latest technological development in communications and computer systems. During wide or prolonged failure of power, the company suspends normal services to customers and handles emergency calls only. The Customer Service Centre then becomes a clearing house for exchange of information between the customer and the team that is sent out for the restoration of power.

Each working group uses Pareto charts to discover the main problems, Ishikawa charts, and statistical control charts for its meetings.

There are many factors to govern in order that a generating plant may deliver the maximum number of watt-hours for the

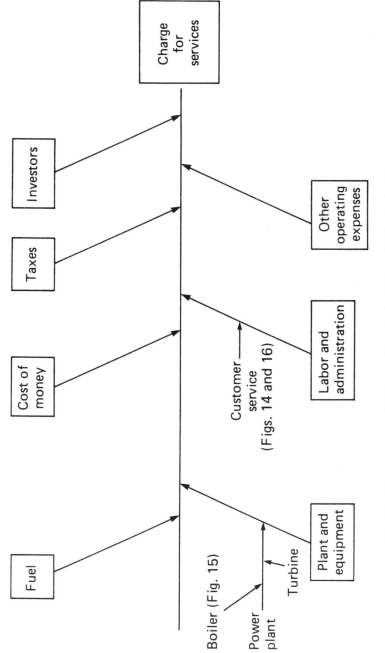

Fig. 13. Components of all costs for a typical (hypothetical) electric company.

minimum number of British thermal units (Btus.) expended. This requires study of many interacting systems within the generating plant. Fig. 14 is an Ishikawa diagram that shows components of cost of service to customers. Figs. 15 and 16 show control charts used for the boiler room and for service to customers.

Reduction of failures in underground transmission. Another example is underground transmission. This electric utility was confronted with an alarming increase in the frequency of failures in a 115,000-volt underground transmission line, 33 years old. Repair of failures of cable as they occur was expensive, and an annoyance to customers. Replacement of the existing cable with a new cable by the same route or by another route was also expensive.

Members of the engineering and underground departments formed a QC-Circle and developed an alternative approach to correction of the problem at greatly reduced expense. They developed a system for prediction of failure at the joints of the cable, well ahead of failure. Analysis of data indicated that flexing in the joints caused by surges of power produces chemical changes in the oil that circulates around the cable to cool and insulate it. One of the chemical changes, increase in the amount of carbon monoxide in the oil, was a leading indicator, and showed good correlation with the degree of mechanical movement in the cable racks in the underground holding chambers.

This information is used to plan a program of replacement each year of the 10 cable joints with the highest probability of failure, until all cable joints were considered safe, thus spreading the cost and reducing the effort required to maintain the cable network.

The QC-Circle, consisting of two engineers, eight cable splicers, six testers, in turn developed new and faster methods for replacement of joints in manholes, working in a vastly superior and safer environment. This work included redesign of the truck and associated equipment that is used to do the job.

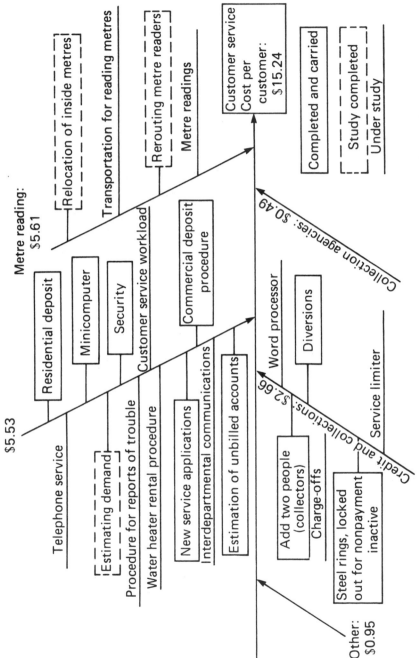

Fig. 14. Components of cost of service to customers for a typical (hypothetical) electric company.

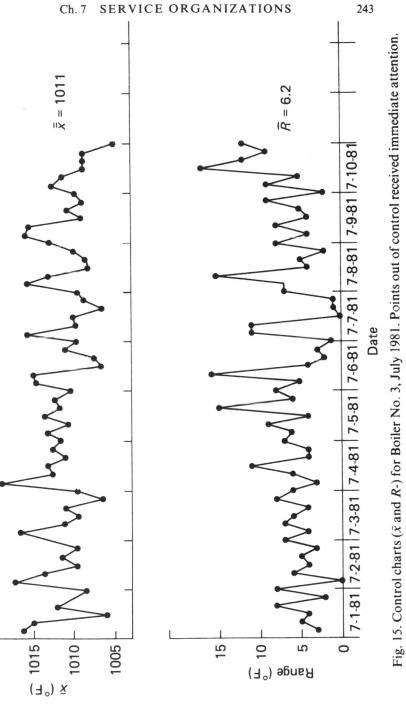

Fig. 15. Control charts ($\bar{x}$ and R-) for Boiler No. 3, July 1981. Points out of control received immediate attention.

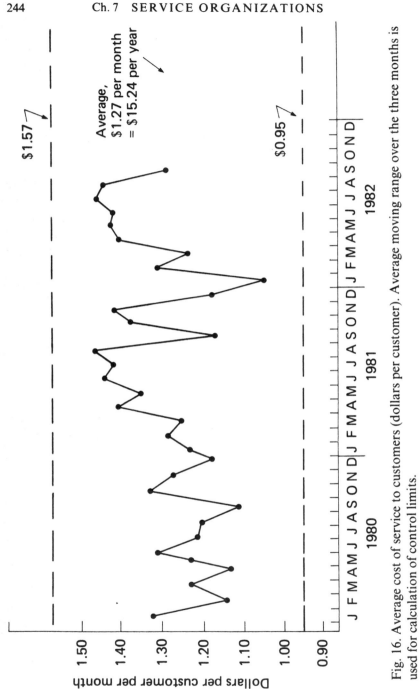

Fig. 16. Average cost of service to customers (dollars per customer). Average moving range over the three months is used for calculation of control limits.

Samples of oil are now chemically analyzed annually on a statistical basis to diminish failures of cable joints. There has been only one failure in three years. The replacement program of joints saved the electric utility several hundred thousand dollars and has reduced to nil interruptions in service. This venture into improvement of quality and productivity is not a program with a beginning and an end, but a philosophy that directs efforts at all levels of responsibility towards the more effective use of the resources available to meet the needs of customers.

Improvement of a Municipal Service

By WILLIAM G. HUNTER

The Motor Equipment Division of the City of Madison maintains garbage trucks, police cars, and other city vehicles. In 1984 there were many complaints about quality of service. The morale of the mechanics was low. Mayor Joseph Sensenbrenner decided to transform the management of the division. Improvement of quality would require the Motor Equipment Division to meet the needs of their customers and their expectations (and if possible, to exceed them). The mechanics accordingly first gathered information on specific complaints and suggestions from their customers—the Streets Division, the Police Department, and others that rely on their service. They did this by talking with representatives from those groups and by sending out questionnaires.

A major complaint was excessive downtime of vehicles. The mechanics accordingly drew a flow diagram of the process for repair of vehicles. They collected data to determine how much time was required to complete each step. The mechanics studied these results and started to make changes to reduce downtime.

They prepared a comparison of the cost of some actual repair jobs and the cost to prevent the problem in the first place. For example, the cost to rebuild a certain jeep was $4200. It had been used to haul salt in the winter. The salt caused corrosion. Simple maintenance procedures (estimated cost $164) would have saved the vehicle from corrosion from salt.

The main conclusion that the mechanics reached, by analysis of the information that they had collected, was to institute a comprehensive maintenance program. The mechanics presented this recommendation to the Mayor and some other members of city government on 14 September 1984, with supporting analysis. The mechanics conducted a tour to show examples of work in progress. The Mayor was then presented with a memento of the occasion—a paperweight. It was a large broken aluminum piston, with a head of a steel exhaust valve jammed into it at an oblique angle. After it was accepted with thanks, the Mayor was told that it had cost $3200, the cost to remove the broken piston from a disabled truck and to make the necessary repairs. He was then shown a spring that cost $1.50, and was told, "If we had had a good preventive maintenance program, we would have replaced sixteen of these springs on that engine, and you wouldn't have that paperweight."

The Mayor was convinced by the mechanics of the need for a comprehensive preventive maintenance program. "You know how to find problems, you know how to solve them, and you wish to solve them. We should get out of your way and let you do it. I am very impressed with what you have shown us here today, and we are going to extend these methods to other departments in the city. I see no reason why they should not also be used in state and federal government."

Postscript. The mechanics, who are union members, were invited to attend a seminar on statistical control of quality at the University of Wisconsin. They came, on their own time. They did other work on their own time. When they were offered payment for some of their overtime work, they said, "No, thanks. We are doing this stuff on the Deming Way because we are really interested. It is important to us. We are not doing it to get paid."

Note. The same principles for improvement wrought by Dr. Hunter, with the help of Peter Scholtes and the men of the Motor Equipment Division of the City of Madison, apply to any fleet of automobiles and trucks, whether run by a municipality, department store, railway, trucking company, or any other company.

8

Some New Principles of Training and Leadership

Understanding is a wellspring of life unto him that hath it; but the instruction of fools is folly.—Proverbs 16:22.

Your views, so far as they have any merit, have already been fully considered and rejected.—Secretary of State Dean Rusk to Ambassador to India John Kenneth Galbraith, as reported in *Harper's*, November 1967.

Aim of leadership. The aim of leadership should be to improve the performance of man and machine, to improve quality, to increase output, and simultaneously to bring pride of workmanship to people. Put in a negative way, the aim of leadership is not merely to find and record failures of men, but to remove the causes of failure: to help people to do a better job with less effort. Actually, most of this book is involved with leadership. Nearly every page heretofore and hereafter states a principle of good leadership of man and machine or shows an example of good or bad leadership. This chapter summarizes some of the principles already learned and adds a few more examples.

Specifically, a leader must learn by calculation wherever meaningful figures are at hand, or by judgment otherwise, who if any of his people lie outside the system on one side or the other, and hence are in need either of individual help or deserve recognition in some form. We saw examples on pages 111–115. See also pages 258ff.

The leader also has responsibility to improve the system—i.e., to make it possible, on a continuing basis, for everybody to do a better job with greater satisfaction.

A third responsibility is to accomplish ever greater and greater consistency of performance within the system, so that apparent differences between people continually diminish. All this is parallel to principles learned in Chapter 3, page 115.

Tell a worker about a mistake? Why not? How can a man improve his work if we fail to point out to him a defective item that he has made, so that he can see where he went wrong? We wish it to be understood that defectives and mistakes will not be tolerated here. These are the usual responses to the question posed. The answers are in fact spontaneous, as if the answers must be obvious.

Importance of training. Anyone, when he has brought his work to a state of statistical control, whether he was trained well or badly, is in a rut. He has completed his learning of that particular job. It is not economical to try to provide further training of the same kind. He may nevertheless, with good training, learn very well some other kind of job.

It is obviously of the utmost importance to train new people, when they come on to a job, to do the job well. Once the learning curve levels off, a control chart will indicate whether and when a person has reached the state of statistical control (see Ch. 11). When he reaches it, continuation of training by the same method will accomplish nothing.

Curiously, if a man's work has not yet reached statistical control, further training will help him.

In a state of chaos (poor supervision, bad management, nothing in statistical control), it is impossible for anyone in the organization to develop his potential ability and capacity for uniformity or for quality.

How many production workers ever saw the next operation, their customer? How many ever saw the finished product in the box, ready for purchase? After some study in a plant, I wrote to the management the following:

> Everyone in your company knows that the aim is perfection, that you can not tolerate defectives and mistakes. You make every worker responsible for the defectives that he has produced. Yet from the records that you have showed to me, it is obvious that you are tolerating a high proportion of defectives, and have been doing so for years. In fact, the levels of various kinds of mistake have not decreased; they have been pretty constant and predictable over a number of years.
>
> Have you any reason to think that the level of mistakes will decrease in the future? Have you ever thought that the problem could be in the system?

We shall learn from the theory in Chapter 11 that to hold a worker on the job without pay till he has cleaned up the defectives that were detected by inspection of his product, if he is in statistical control, is to charge him with faults of the system.

Another example of bad administration is the management's policy to penalize employees for coming in late in weather that has crippled the transportation system.

It is obviously equally stupid for a customer in a restaurant to blame the waitress for the food, or for delays in the kitchen.

A better way. The correct procedures are contrary to practice and advice in books on administration and management. There are two circumstances to consider.

1. The worker has achieved statistical control of his work.

or

2. The worker has not yet achieved statistical control of his work.

We first talk about the worker that has achieved statistical control of his work. Under statistical control, the answer to the question posed near the outset of this chapter is no, do not show to a production worker a defective item nor tell him about it, unless his chart detected the existence of a special cause, in which case he should have already noted it from his control chart and sought the cause and removed it.

A basic principle presumed here is that no one should be blamed or penalized for performance that he can not govern. Violation of this principle can only lead to frustration and dissatisfaction with the job, and lower production.

There is a better way: discover which people if any are out of control with respect to the group. If anyone is out of control on the side of poor performance, investigate the circumstances—his eyesight, tools, training—and take any remedial action indicated. Or is he simply in the wrong job? Perhaps the training that you gave him was inept and incomplete. Anyone out of control on the good side is there for reasons that need study. He may use methods or motions that other people could learn and thereby improve their performance.

If a company has a policy to fire people that do not come up to a certain standard level of production, and to retain those that meet it, there is a best way to do it. The standard can be fixed by statistical theory for maximum profit in consideration of:

The distribution of abilities in the reservoir of people not yet tried out

The cost of training a man to the point where you decide whether to retain him or let him go

The discounted profit in retention of a man that meets the goal

Example of use of $\bar{x}$- and R-charts in training. Fig. 17 shows average scores ($\bar{x}$) in golf for a beginner. His scores, before the lessons, were obviously not in a state of control: There are points outside the control limits. Then came lessons. His scores there-

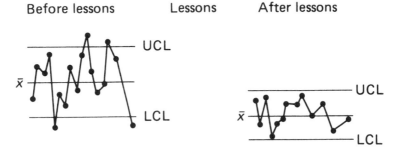

Fig. 17. Average weekly scores in golf for a beginner who took lessons before he reached a state of statistical control. Scores for four successive games constituted a sample of $n = 4$ for computation of $\bar{x}$ and R. The upper and lower control limits for $\bar{x}$ are calculated from the chart for ranges, not shown. From W. Edwards Deming, *Elementary Principles of the Statistical Control of Quality* (Union of Japanese Science and Engineering, Tokyo, 1950), p. 22. UCL and LCL mean upper control limit and lower control limit for $\bar{x}$.

upon showed a state of statistical control with the desired results, namely, an average score considerably below what his average was before the lessons. Here, lessons changed the system.

Application to administration in a hospital (from Japan[1]). A patient, after an operation, had to learn again to walk. Lessons are provided in a special training unit in the hospital in Osaka. Fig. 18 exhibits a record of improvement for a particular patient. The time for the left foot to move from floor to floor at each step was recorded by electric impulse. Ten successive steps (21st to 30th in 50 steps) furnish an average time $\bar{x}$ and a range (not

1 Shunji Hirokawa and Hiroshi Sugiyama, "Quantitative gain analysis," *Technology Reports of Osaka University, Faculty of Engineering* 30, no. 1520 (1980).

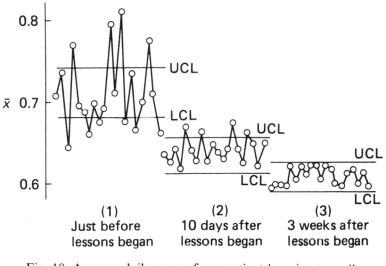

Fig. 18. Average daily scores for a patient learning to walk after an operation. The control limits came from the whole group of patients. From Hirokawa and Sugiyama (see footnote 1).

shown). Twenty such series of observations on the patient's performance conducted over a period of 5 to 10 days furnish 20 values of $\bar{x}$ and 20 ranges. The points for $\bar{x}$ are shown in Fig. 18. The ranges are not shown. The control limits for $\bar{x}$ are derived in the usual way from the average range.

The patient, as the reader will observe, was wildly out of control before lessons commenced; in better control after lessons through 10 days; still better, and ready for discharge after lessons through about another 10 more days.

The control chart so used is an important tool for administration in a hospital. The therapist provides lessons to the patient so long as lessons help him, but halts the lessons when continuation would not help him. In other words, the control chart protects the patient and makes the best use of the time of the therapist. A good physical therapist is scarce in anybody's country.

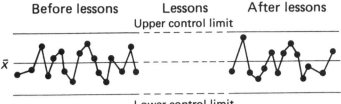

Fig. 19. Average scores in golf for an experienced golfer, before and after lessons. Here the player had already achieved statistical control before he took lessons. The lessons were accordingly ineffective. Scores for four successive games constituted a sample of size $n = 4$ for computation of $\bar{x}$ and R. From W. Edwards Deming, *Elementary Principles of the Statistical Control of Quality* (Union of Japanese Science and Engineering, Tokyo, 1950), p. 22.

Statistical control achieved, but output unsatisfactory. The first step here, as well as everywhere else, is to take a hard look at the figures from inspection.

A worker who is in a state of control but whose work is unsatisfactory presents a problem. It is usually uneconomical to try to retrain him on the same job. It is more economical to put him into a new job, with good training in the new job.

Fig. 19 provides an illustration. An experienced golfer hoped to improve his score by taking lessons. The chart shows that the lessons accomplished nothing. His techniques were already engrained: his teacher was unsuccessful in dislodging them and replacing them with better ones.

Another familiar example is someone who came to the United States years ago from a foreign country and learned English by forced draft after arrival. His vocabulary and grammar may be superb, but his accent is beyond repair. Or perhaps he learned to speak English in his own country, as a faithful, devoted, and admiring pupil of a teacher that himself had been a devoted pupil of a teacher that could not speak good English. The speech therapists that I have consulted tell me that a few rough edges can be smoothed out, but that the benefit is hardly worth the effort of either pupil or teacher. In other words, the man developed long ago a system of speech, and it is too late now to change it.

Another familiar example is the woman that taught herself to sing, without benefit of a teacher, or with benefit of an incompetent teacher, and has been singing for years, in her own way, pleasing some people and possibly herself; reducing others to shudders.

The following letter from one of my students at the Graduate School of Business Administration of New York University illustrates the above principles:

> I am a supervisor of a corporate accounting department. Many were the times I would look out on the office and wish that we could get rid of one or two mediocre employees and hire two top notch people to replace them. In one of your lectures, you showed us that the chance of drawing a better replacement out of the labor pool is slim. Firing someone, and taking a chance out of the labor pool, was not worth the risk of demoralizing the whole department.
>
> When I first started your course, I had a problem in the office. One of our graduate accountants was doing consistently poor work on a clerical-type assignment, which he had been on for some time. It was a rule that an employee could not be promoted until he put in good performance on his present job.
>
> After hearing your lecture on new principles in administration, I realized that this employee was probably in a state of statistical control, even though it was impractical for me to try to prove it with statistical methods. I then decided that the right approach would be to give to this employee training in another job. I am happy to report that this idea has worked out beautifully. The employee has mastered the new job and I feel as if I now have an extra member of the staff.

Warnings and exceptions. No problem in administration is simple. We must be on guard for apparent exceptions and changes that surprise the worker:

1. Even after someone has achieved statistical control of his work, he may lose it. A point may go out of control, indicating the existence of a special cause not heretofore encountered. The production worker must run down and eliminate from future work this special cause. He has lost statistical control till he does this.

2. Unfortunately, also, people may become careless, relying on momentum of past performance. It is for this reason that the control chart or other statistical tests should be reinstituted now and then for short periods of time to learn whether the work is still under statistical control.

3. New product, or new specifications, possibly on a new contract, may lead to a new kind of defect to be reckoned with. The production worker may have to put himself into statistical control with a new set of operations.

4. The inspection department may introduce a new kind of measure for some important quality-characteristic (e.g., viscosity). In effect, this could mean, to the worker, a new product.

Example in leadership: where are the defects coming from? There are 11 welders on a job. Faults per 5000 welds were counted for each welder (see Table 1 and Fig. 20). They all required about the same amount of time to perform 5000 welds.

$$\text{Average} = \frac{105}{11}$$

$$= 9.55 \text{ faults in 5000 welds}$$

$$\left.\begin{array}{l} \text{UCL} \\ \text{LCL} \end{array}\right\} = 9.55 \pm 3\sqrt{9.55}$$

$$= \begin{cases} 19.0 \\ 0 \end{cases}$$

Table 1

Welder	Number of faults
1	8
2	15
3	10
4	4
5	7
6	24
7	8
8	8
9	10
10	3
11	8
Total	105

Welder No. 6 lies outside the system. He is in need of individual attention. What kind of attention? Any observation and action that might help him.

1. Examine the streams of work that come in. Welder No. 6 may receive a stream that is comparatively difficult to work on. If this be the explanation, then Welder No. 6 needs no further attention at this time.

2. Examine his equipment, test his eyes, and look for other possible handicaps (health, trouble at home).

Then there is ever-present need to improve the work of all the welders. We could send them all to the oculist, not just No. 6. Effort might well be directed toward the previous state, to achieve better uniformity in the streams of incoming materials,

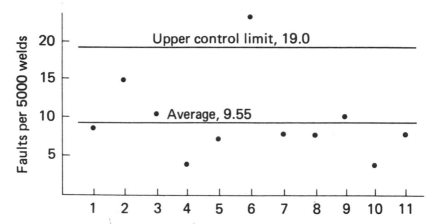

Fig. 20. Eleven welders, faults per 5000 welds. The welders are numbered 1 to 11 in order of duration of tenure on this job. The average is 9.55 faults per 5000 welds. Upper control limit, 19. Lower control limit, 0. Welder No. 6 is outside the upper control limit.

and to investigate the possibility to get materials that are easier to weld.

Overall improvement (reduction of the average number of faults per 5000 welds for everybody) will depend entirely on changes in the system, such as equipment, materials, training.

A forklift driver continually backed into obstructions. Reason: he had a bad neck, could not bend around to see where he was going. Solution: another job.

Example of aid to leadership.[2] The job is to put a page into the right pigeonhole. There are 80 pigeonholes, each representing specific characteristics of a page, which can supposedly be identified by reading the page. There are 240 women on the job. The

2 I thank Dr. Gipsie B. Ranney for the pleasure to work with her on this project.

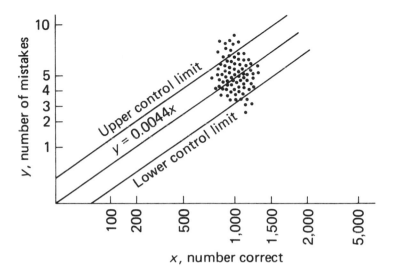

Fig. 21. Plot of number of mistakes on the vertical against number correct on the horizontal. Each point represents inspection of the output of one worker over the course of a month. There were 240 women on the job. Ten points lay beyond the upper control limit. Four lay below the lower control limit; 226 points between limits. No attempt is made here to show all the points. The ten points beyond the upper limit show the supervisor where to bend his efforts for help to individual people. He should also try to learn why the four people below the lower control limit show such excellent performance.

work is inspected 100 per cent at this writing. The overall proportion of mistakes of a critical category detected over the course of a month was 44 in 10,000. It is convenient to plot the work of each worker on the double square-root paper designed by Mosteller and Tukey (Codex Book Company, Norwood, Mass. 02062). We plot y on the vertical for the number of mistakes, x on the horizontal for the number of nonmistakes, as is done in Fig. 21. Then the overall average proportion of mistakes is represented by the line $y = 0.0044x$.

Construction of 3-sigma upper limits is remarkably simple: merely draw two lines parallel and at distances three standard deviations above and below the line $y = 0.0044x$. (A scale on the Mosteller–Tukey paper shows 1, 2, 3, and 4 standard deviations; 1 standard deviation = 5 mm. Suitable modification is required for compression of one of the scales, an example being Fig. 21.) The control limits divide the 240 women into three groups:

    A.   Performance above the upper control limit
    B.   Performance between the control limits
    C.   Performance below the lower control limit

The women in Group A are in need of individual help. No attempt can be made here to state what help this might be. This responsibility belongs to the supervisor and to the management of the company, but some suggestions might be illustrative.

    1. Some people can not grasp immediately the meaning of printed words (dyslexia to some degree). People with this imperfection should be transferred to other work. (Dyslexia is not indication of diminished intelligence or scholastic achievement.) A psychologist should be employed to design an appropriate test of ability to comprehend the meaning on a printed page.
    2. Some of the women may need spectacles (as on p. 384).

The women in Group B represent the system and are not subjects for individual help. It would be wrong procedure to inform them about mistakes that they made. They are not to be ranked No. 1, No. 2, and onward to No. last. Instead, the management must work on the system. No attempt can be made here to take over the job of the management of this operation, but it may be remarked here that a visit by a statistician discovered that some of the pigeonholes were too high for the women to reach. (One may wonder why this fault had not been observed by the management and corrected months ago.) Another suggestion for

Group B is to give everybody therein the same test on reading that was suggested above for Group A. People that show difficulty on this test should be transferred to other work. Continual improvement of the system will decrease the slope of the line through the origin that represents overall performance.

People in Group C also deserve special attention. They deserve suitable reward. It would be important to learn how they do their work, and what special facilities they possess.

A good first step would be to study the inspection. How good is it? It is well known that inspectors can miss up to 40 per cent of errors, and do so with variable quality. They can also classify as a mistake a perfectly good match.

Administration of inspection for extra high quality. There are instances in manufacturing and in service where perfect work has not yet been accomplished, but where a mistake or defect would be serious. Spindles on a front axle of an automobile may undergo 100 per cent inspection for reasons of safety. A better plan would be to achieve statistical control of the production of the spindles, with variation far inside the requirements. There is need for extreme care for calculations in a bank, in filling prescriptions in a pharmacy, in the tariffs published in a Rate Bureau.

Computations of interest, penalty, and other transactions in a bank may require 100 per cent inspection (or review or verification, as one might prefer to call it), not only for safety and preservation of reputation for accuracy, but for minimum total cost as well (see Ch. 15).

It is necessary that both people start off with a clean copy of the original document. The computations made by the two people should be punched separately by two punchers. Comparison by machine will discover a difference between the two computations, or a mistake in punching, but will not discover a computation that is wrong but in agreement.

Extreme care must be exercised in 100 per cent inspection (or review) to eliminate a common cause or interaction between the original work and the inspection. Supervision must make it clear to everybody concerned that absolutely no work is to be done on any document that presents a special problem or on a figure that is not clear. There must be no possibility of reading 8 as 5, for example. If a figure is not totally clear to one of the people on the job (a matter of individual judgment), then he must lay the document aside for attention of the supervisor. The supervisor may have to search backup papers, at times with letters, telegrams, or telephone calls, to clear the problem.

If interaction between the original work and the review be totally eliminated, and if both the original work and the review work were subject to a process average of 1 mistake in 1000 documents, then the two together would accomplish a process average of far better than $1/1000^2$ or $1/1,000,000$.

Example of faulty inspection. Faulty inspection brings three types of problems: (1) frustration of production workers; (2) wrong interpretation of points on a control chart; (3) faulty product going out to the consumer.

The following example illustrates a typical condition of faulty inspection, and a frustration to the production workers. There are 17 operators, 4 inspectors. The work of the 17 operators is allotted to the 4 inspectors by use of random numbers.

Table 2 shows the results of inspection over a period of three weeks, and Fig. 22 shows in graphic form the results by inspector. There is clearly something wrong: The pattern of differences between inspectors is disturbing. Inspectors 1 and 4 agree well. So do Inspectors 2 and 3, but the two pairs lie far apart.

What was needed here is operational definitions of what is acceptable and what is not. We met this problem in Chapter 1. An operational definition consists of a test method, a test, and a criterion by which to judge whether a piece of work may be classified as defective or acceptable (see Ch. 9). An operational defi-

Table 2. *Record of the number of defective pieces found on inspection over a period of three weeks, by operator by inspector*

Operator	Inspector				
	1	2	3	4	All
1	1	0	0	3	4
2	2	0	0	3	5
3	0	1	1	4	6
4	3	2	2	2	9
5	7	0	0	0	7
6	0	0	0	1	1
7	1	1	1	4	7
8	3	2	3	6	14
9	2	1	0	0	3
10	1	1	1	0	3
11	9	3	5	10	27
12	3	1	0	1	5
13	4	1	1	2	8
14	4	1	1	2	8
15	0	0	1	3	4
16	1	0	0	4	5
17	11	4	6	15	36
All	52	18	22	60	152
Total pieces examined, n	400	410	390	390	1590
Proportion defective, $\bar{p}$	0.130	0.044	0.056	0.154	0.096

Note: Cases of finished product (five pieces to a case) are allocated by random numbers to the inspectors. The number of pieces produced is about the same for all operators.

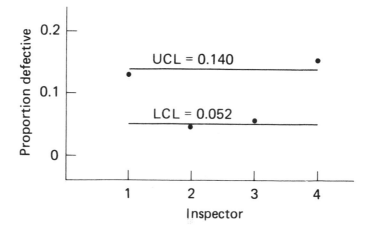

Fig. 22. Summaries in chart form for the four inspectors disclose problems with the inspection. Calculation of the control limits:

$$\bar{p} = 0.096, \qquad n = \frac{1590}{4} \cong 400$$

$$\left.\begin{array}{l}\text{UCL}\\\text{LCL}\end{array}\right\} = \bar{p} \pm 3\sqrt{\bar{p}(1-\bar{p})/n}$$

$$= \begin{cases}0.140\\0.052\end{cases}$$

nition is communicable: it is a language in which people may understand each other.

I am indebted to David S. Chambers for the privilege to work with him on this example.

Faulty inspection caused by fear. The control chart in Fig. 23 shows the daily record for two months of the proportion defective found on final audit of a product ready to ship out. The average proportion defective over the two months was 8.8 per cent. The control limits are:

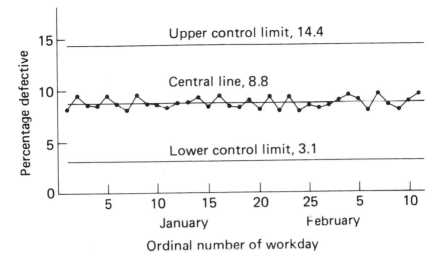

Fig. 23. Daily record of percentage of defective items; 225 items inspected per day.

$$n = 225, \qquad \bar{p} = 0.088 \text{ or } 8.8\%$$

$$\left.\begin{array}{l} \text{UCL} \\ \text{LCL} \end{array}\right\} = \bar{p} \pm 3\sqrt{\bar{p}(1-\bar{p})/n}$$

$$= 0.088 \pm 3 \times 0.0189$$

$$= \begin{cases} 0.144 & \text{or} \quad 14.4\% \\ 0.031 & \text{or} \quad 3.1\% \end{cases}$$

Fig. 23 indicates a curious condition. The up and down movements of the points are too narrow, in view of the control limits. Two possible explanations come to mind:

1. Uniformity of proportion defective is built in. This is not at all rare. An example is 12 pallets that do their stamping in rotation. One of the pallets has gone bad. The other 11 continue to do good work. The out-

going product has one defective stamping in 12; 1/12 is 8.3 per cent, perilously close to the average 8.8 per cent shown on the chart.

2. The figures on the chart are meaningless.

The first explanation we dismissed (David S. Chambers and I) through intimate knowledge of the process and the circumstances. The second explanation seemed to us plausible. The inspector was insecure, in fear. Rumor had it throughout the plant that the manager would close the plant down and sweep it out if the proportion defective on the final audit ever reached 10 per cent on any day. The inspector was protecting the jobs of 300 people.

Again, where there is fear, there will be wrong figures. An organization runs along the perception that its people hold in their heads. It matters not at all whether the manager would actually close the place down at 10 per cent defective.

We reported to the top management our explanation—fear. The problem disappeared when this plant manager migrated to another job, and a new manager came in.

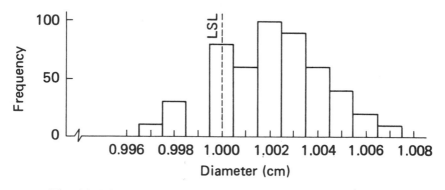

Fig. 24. Distribution of measurement on the diameters of 500 steel rods. The inspection was obviously faulty. (LSL means lower specification limit.)

More on fear. The histogram in Fig. 24 shouts a message. It tells us that the inspector distorted the data. One may encounter this histogram almost any day anywhere. Measurements pile up just inside the specification, followed by a gap. Possible reasons for the distortion are obvious:

1. The inspector is trying to protect the people that make the part.
2. He is afraid of his instrument—afraid that it may reject a part unjustly; that if it were in good order it might accept the part.
3. He is afraid of his own use of the instrument, which is of course confounded with No. 2.

Another example of faulty inspection from fear. Fig. 25 shows a distribution of measured values during production. The lower specification limit was 6.2 mils; no upper limit. No part was

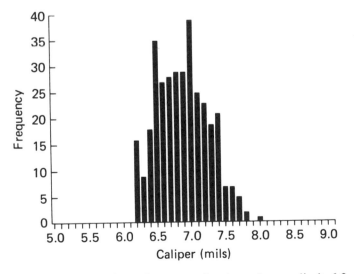

Fig. 25. Distribution of measured values. Lower limit 6.2 mils, no upper limit.

recorded a failure. Note the peak at 6.3 mils. Were there any failures? No one will ever know.

No one wishes to be a bearer of bad news.

The peaks at 6.5 and 7.0 may arise from rounding.

Another example. As I understand it, the Air Quality Index is reported daily at noon for 13 regions of the U.S. The upper limit is 150 (mg of contaminant per cubic metre). Beyond that figure, some government agency must take steps to discover the source of contamination. It may be nature itself; it may be smokestacks. The figure 150 is hardly ever reported, and a figure above 150 is rare indeed. There is concentration at 149, 148, 147, 146. People are afraid to report their results. No wonder: the precision of measurement is 20.

Still another example of loss from fear. This actual dialogue was reported to me by Kate McKeown.

Millwright (to his foreman): That bearing [in a blast machine] is about to go out, and it will ruin the shaft along with it when it goes if we don't take care of it now.

Foreman: This load of castings must be on its way today.

He is thinking of his production record, and says to the man: "We can't take care of it now." The foreman, for fear of his job, could not protect the best interests of the company. He is judged by numbers only, not for avoiding shutdowns. Can anyone blame him for doing his job?

Before they get the load out, the bearing freezes, as the mill-wright predicted. In the repair job, the millwright finds, sure enough, that the shaft is badly grooved: four days lost to get a new shaft from Baltimore and replace it.

Requirement of statistical control of a test method. A recorded measurement, whether visual, manual, or taken and recorded by instruments, is the end product of a long series of operations on the thing measured, and on the use of the instrument. Repeated measurements of the same item over a period of time must show statistical control in order for the instrument and operator thereof to qualify as a method of measurement. This characteristic alone is of course not sufficient. The level of the R-chart for repeated measurements for any operator must not be too big, else the precision of the method will not suffice for use. The method must be reproducible within specified limits with different operators (or with other observers, in the case of visual inspection).

No precision, good or bad, can be ascribed to a test method unless instrument and observer as a combination show statistical control.[3] This is so regardless of the cost of testing equipment.

Alleged shortages of material from vendors can arise from differences between vendor and purchaser in methods of measurement. What is the area of a hide, for example? What about ragged edges: How would they affect the measurement of the area of the hide, if you were selling the hide? What if you were buying it?

Differences between test instruments. Statistical investigation usually discovers within a few weeks that:

3 Stated by Walter A. Shewhart, *Economic Control of Quality of Manufactured Product* (Van Nostrand, 1931; American Society for Quality Control, 1980; reprinted by Ceepress, The George Washington University, 1986), Ch. 23; idem, *Statistical Method from the Viewpoint of Quality Control* (Graduate School, Department of Agriculture, Washington, 1939; Dover, 1986), Ch. 4. An excellent reference is Joseph M. Cameron, *Measurement Assurance*, NBSIR 77-1240 (National Bureau of Standards, Washington), April 1977. See also Charles A. Bicking, "Precision in the routine performance of standard tests," *Standardization*, January 1979, p. 13. The interested reader may well turn at this point to the masterful work by Churchill Eisenhart, "Realistic evaluation of the precision and accuracy of instrument calibration systems," being a chapter in the book edited by Harry H. Ku, *Precision Measurement and Calibration*, National Bureau of Standards Special Publication 300, Vol. 1 (Superintendent of Documents, Washington, 1969).

1. Few workers know what the job is.
2. Few inspectors know, either. Production worker and inspector do not agree on what is right and what is wrong. Right yesterday; wrong today.
3. The electronic testing equipment is not doing the job. It passes an item one minute, rejects it the next, and the converse.
4. Electronic testing machines do not agree with each other.
5. Vendor and purchaser do not agree: no wonder, the testing equipment used by the purchaser does not agree with itself. The vendor has the same problem. Neither one knows it.

Few people in supervisory positions and in management are aware how important reliable inspection is for morale of production workers.

Example. There are eight testing machines at the end of the line to separate good product from bad in order to protect customers. Around 3000 items run through this inspection every day. The compilation and chart (plotted by machine) shown in Fig. 26 show the results for a week. The rule was to rotate the test machine with the product as the pieces come off the line.

The eight testing machines obviously fall into two groups. The difference between their means is around 11 per cent. A serious problem exists. What the customer gets depends on what machine does the testing—an alarming condition. It is vital to find out the reason for the existence of two groups and for the difference between them.

One can imagine the frustration of the production workers, seeing apparent and unexplainable variation from day to day, unaware that much of the trouble lies in the testing equipment.

One might look first, in such a problem, for confounding of the operator with the machine. A machine

Testing machine	Yield	40%	50%	60%
0	66.2			×
7	66.3			×
8	54.1		×	
9	56.0		×	
10	56.9		×	
11	54.1		×	
12	66.5			×
13	57.3		×	
All	59.7			

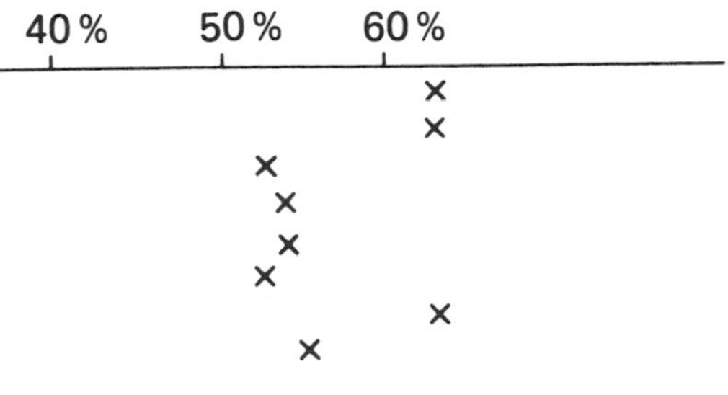

Fig. 26. Results of eight testing machines over the course of a week.

does not work by itself. It has no characteristic of its own. The machine and the operator form a team. Change of operator may give different results. In this case, the machines worked three shifts. It would be well to enquire whether the same operators worked all week on any one machine.

Comparison of two operators on the same machine. The above example is one in which test instruments (confounded with the operators) disagreed with each other. One may also expect to find that an instrument disagrees with itself, and that operators disagree with each other. Good supervision requires achievement of statistical control of the measurement system.

A convenient form of summary of the two sets of results is a 2 × 2 table. An example of a 2 × 2 table appears on p. 435 (Fig. 48). This table can be readily adapted to many kinds of comparisons. For this example, we could show Operator No. 1 on the horizontal axis and Operator No. 2 on the vertical. Or for testing the same operator on two instruments, the horizontal label could be one instrument, the vertical label could be the other instrument. Points on the diagonal indicate agreement. Points off the diagonal indicate disagreement. The scientist in charge of testing should lay down in advance criteria for satisfactory reproducibility of the test, then decide from the table whether the test is satisfactory.

Incidentally, chi-square and tests of significance, taught in some statistical courses, have no application here or anywhere.

If the inspection is in terms of a scale of centimetres, grams, seconds, millivolts, or other unit, one could plot first test on one axis, and second test on the other axis. Good agreement would appear as points on or close to the 45° line in Fig. 50 (p. 441).

Comparison of interviewers to improve performance. As was remarked in Chapter 2, page 94, nearly every activity is one of a kind. Once carried off, it is too late to amend it. Again, how do you test a battleship? A demographic survey is an example. It goes off reasonably well, or it is a flop. A survey in consumer research is another example. A study of the physical condition of the equipment owned by a telephone company, or by a railway, furnishes other examples.

There will be, during the training period, repeated tests of inspectors and of interviewers. There will be a dress rehearsal. In spite of care, one must be prepared for surprises, in the form of unforeseen problems and inconsistencies.

Results of the fieldwork can be analyzed two days at a batch, to compare the variance between investigators with the variance within investigators, thus to detect before it is too late a need to retrain investigators. Sometimes one investigator will go out on a limb. It is necessary to determine the reason why. It may be that his work is superior, and that all the other investigators need retraining. The first two days are crucial.

Fig. 27 provides an example. Each point shows the results of an interviewer at the end of the first two days. There were eight interviewers, hence eight points. As the legend explains, the dis-

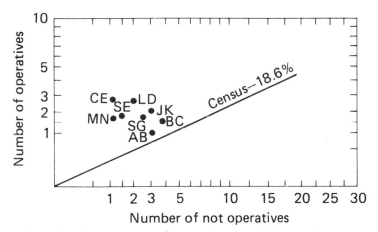

Fig. 27. The number of operatives and the number not operatives in the occupations recorded by interviewers during the first two weeks of a survey in Wilmington, Delaware, in 1952, compared with the Census of 1950. The points all fall above the Census line. This is a strong signal of a common lack of understanding amongst the interviewers concerning the definition of operatives. Further training was needed.

agreement between the present study and the recent Census was a common cause, with weakness in the instructions and in the training, especially for the definition of operatives (bus drivers, trainmen, lift operators, etc.). Retraining brought the interviewers into satisfactory agreement with the Census.[4]

Remark. A requirement of good practice is that allocation of interviewers and inspectors to sampling units be designated by use of random numbers, so that every interviewer or inspector investigates a random sample of all the sampling units drawn for the study. Otherwise, the results will be difficult to interpret.

4 These examples and the charts are taken from the author's *Sample Design in Business Research* (Wiley, 1960), Ch. 13.

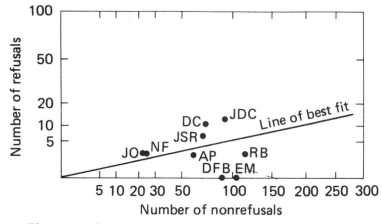

Fig. 28. Refusals and nonrefusals for nine interviewers at the end of four weeks. Interviewers DFB and EM are superior, or else there is something wrong with the records.

Fig. 28 shows the results from another survey at the end of three weeks, too late for a fresh start. The vertical scale is the number of refusals, and the horizontal scale is the number of nonrefusals (successes). Interviewers EM and DFB showed no refusals. The question was whether this exhibit of excellent performance is believable, or if there be a flaw in reporting. The next step was to have a talk with the two interviewers, EM and DFB. These talks required only a few minutes. Both women were in earlier careers visiting nurses. A friend in Hamburg told me years ago that any woman that had been a visiting nurse will be a good interviewer. She loves people, and people will talk to her. This is all that I needed to know.

The paper used here is Mosteller–Tukey double square-root paper (p. 259). The same conclusions would be drawn by use of any other graph paper.

Fallacies of reward for winning in a lottery. A man in the personnel department of a large company came forth with an idea, held as brilliant by all people there, namely, to reward the top man of the month on a certain production line (the man that made the lowest proportion defective over the month) with a citation. There would be a small party on the job in his honor, and he would get half a day off. This might be a great idea if he were indeed an unusual performer for the month. There were 50 men on the production line.

Do the results of inspection of their work form a statistical system like the work of the 20 operators in Fig. 41 (p. 364)? If the work of the group forms a statistical system, then the prize would be merely a lottery. On the other hand, if the top man is a special cause on the side of low proportion defective, then he is indeed outstanding. He would deserve recognition, and he could be a focal point for teaching men how to do the job.

There is no harm in a lottery, so far as I know, provided it is called a lottery. To call it an award of merit when the selection is merely a lottery, however, is to demoralize the whole force, prize winners included. Everybody will suppose that there are good reasons for the selection and will be trying to explain and reduce differences between men. This would be a futile exercise when the only differences are random deviations, as is the case when the performance of the 50 men form a statistical system.

9

Operational Definitions, Conformance, Performance

> I may express the opinion that some of the published explanations are more remarkable than the phenomenon itself.—Hugh M. Smith, "On the synchronous flashing of fireflies," *Science*, August 1935.

Aim of this chapter. In the opinion of many people in industry, there is nothing more important for transaction of business than use of operational definitions. It could also be said that no requirement of industry is so much neglected. One learns about operational definitions in colleges of liberal arts, in courses in philosophy and theory of knowledge, but hardly ever in schools of business or engineering in the United States. It could even be said that learning in physics, chemistry, and some natural sciences does not teach the philosophy of science. The aim of this chapter is to try to introduce the reader to the need for operational definitions and to lead him to inspiration to further study.

Meaning starts with the concept, which is in somebody's mind, and only there: it is ineffable. The only communicable meaning of any word, prescription, instruction, specification, measure, attribute, regulation, law, system, edict is the record of what happens on application of a specified operation or test.

What is an operational definition? An operational definition puts communicable meaning into a concept. Adjectives like good, reliable, uniform, round, tired, safe, unsafe, unemployed have no communicable meaning until they are expressed in operational terms of sampling, test, and criterion. The concept of a definition is ineffable: It cannot be communicated to someone else. An operational definition is one that reasonable men can agree on.[1]

An operational definition is one that people can do business with. An operational definition of safe, round, reliable, or any other quality must be communicable, with the same meaning to vendor as to purchaser, same meaning yesterday and today to the production worker. Example:

1. A specific test of a piece of material or an assembly
2. A criterion (or criteria) for judgment
3. Decision: yes or no, the object or the material did or did not meet the criterion (or criteria)

A specification of an article may refer to measurements of length, diameter, weight, hardness, concentration, flocculence, color, appearance, pressure, parallelism, leak, unemployed, or some other characteristic. A specification may refer to performance. For example, the average time between failures of a machine must not be less than eight hours. Or 95 per cent of the machines bought must run one hour or more without failure.

We have seen in many places how important it is that buyer and seller understand each other. They must both use the same kind of centimetre. Use of their instruments must agree well enough with each other. This requirement has meaning only if instruments are in statistical control. Without operational definition, a specification is meaningless.

Misunderstandings between companies and between departments within a company about alleged defective materials, or alleged malfunctioning of apparatus, often have their roots in failure on both sides to state in advance in meaningful terms the

1 Walter A. Shewhart, *Statistical Method from the Viewpoint of Quality Control* (Graduate School, Department of Agriculture, Washington, 1939; Dover, 1986), pp. 130–137; C. I. Lewis, *Mind and the World-Order* (Scribner's, 1929; Dover, 1956), Chs. 6–9.

specifications of an item, or the specifications for performance, and failure to understand the problems of measurement.

Operational definitions are vital to lawyers, vital to government regulations, vital to (voluntary) industrial standards. For example, what is care? What is due care? (See Principle 4 in Ch. 17.)

Practice is more exacting than pure science; more exacting than teaching. As Shewhart said, the standards of knowledge and workmanship required in industry and public service are more severe than the requirements in pure science.

> Both pure and applied science have gradually pushed further and further the requirements for accuracy and precision.
>
> However, applied science, particularly in the mass production of interchangeable parts, is even more exacting than pure science in certain matters of accuracy and precision. For example, a pure scientist makes a series of measurements and upon the basis of these makes what he considers to be the best estimates of accuracy and precision, regardless of how few measurements he may have. He will readily admit that future studies may prove such estimates to be in error. Perhaps all he will claim for them is that they are as good as any reasonable scientist could make upon the basis of the data available at the time the estimates were made. But now let us look at the applied scientist. He knows that if he were to act upon the meagre evidence sometimes available to the pure scientist, he would make the same mistakes as the pure scientist makes in estimates of accuracy and precision. He also knows that through his mistakes someone may lose a lot of money or suffer physical injury, or both.

The man in industry has yet another worry. He knows that specifications of quality involving requirements of fixed degrees of accuracy and precision may become the basis of contractual agreement, and he knows that any indefiniteness in the meaning of any of the terms used in such a specification, including those of accuracy and precision, may lead to misunderstandings and even to legal action. Hence the applied scientist finds it desirable to go as far as one can reasonably go toward establishing definite and operationally verifiable meanings for such terms.[2]

No exact value; no true value. The problem in commerce is never whether anything is exactly round, but how far in what way it departs from roundness. The pistons in your automobile are not exactly round. They could not be, because there is no way to define operationally exactly round.

Why not get help from the dictionary? The dictionary says that a figure is round if it is everywhere in Euclidian two-dimensional space equidistant from a point called the center. A very useful definition that is, for use in formal logic, such as for a theorem in Euclid. But if we try to use it in practice, we find that the dictionary provides a concept, not a definition for use in industry—that is, not an operational definition of what is round enough for a given purpose.

The train was not exactly on time.

To understand these truths, one need only to try to explain what measurements to make, and what criterion to adopt, to decide whether something is exactly round, or whether the train was exactly on time. He will soon discover that he has driven himself into an Irish bog.

---

2 Walter A. Shewhart, *Statistical Method from the Viewpoint of Quality Control* (Graduate School, Department of Agriculture, Washington, 1939; Dover, 1986), pp. 120–121.

Any physical measurement is the result of applying a given procedure. Likewise with the count of people in an area. It is to be expected that two procedures for measurement or for count (call them A and B) will give different results. Neither of two figures is right and the other wrong. The experts in the subject matter may have a preference, however, for Method A over Method B. As P. W. Bridgman put it, "The concept is synonymous with the corresponding set of operations."[3] Or perhaps easier to understand:

> A preferred procedure is distinguished by the fact that it supposedly gives or would give results nearest to what are needed for a particular end; and also by the fact that it is more expensive or more time consuming, or even impossible to carry out. . . . As a preferred procedure is always subject to modification or obsolescence, we are forced to conclude that neither the accuracy nor the bias of any procedure can ever be known in a logical sense.[4]

We have already seen that the process average will depend on the method of sampling lots, as well as of the method of test and the criteria imposed. Change the method of sampling or the method of test and you will get a new count of defectives in a lot, and a new process average. There is thus no true value for the number of defective items in a given lot, and no true value for the process average.

It comes as astonishment to most people that there is no true value for the speed of light. The result obtained for the speed of light depends on the method used by the experimenter (microwave, interferometer, geodimeter, molecular spectra). Moreover (as has been stressed before), a method of measurement does not exist unless the results show statistical control. The only test of

3 P. W. Bridgman, *The Logic of Modern Physics* (Macmillan, 1928), p. 5.
4 W. Edwards Deming, *Sample Design in Business Research* (Wiley, 1960), Ch. 4.

statistical control on record for results on the speed of light turned out to be negative.[5]

If two methods of measuring the speed of light, or for measuring anything, were in statistical control, there might well be differences of scientific importance. On the other hand, if the methods agreed reasonably well, their agreement could be accepted as a master standard for today.

This master standard would not be a true value, because some other method, yet to be agreed upon, might well give a value substantially different from today's master standard. It is better to regard an unresolvable difference, not as a bias, but as the natural result of a different method.

The speed 3×10^{10} cm/sec, as we learned it in school, is still good enough for most purposes for the speed of light, but today's requirements of science and industry need the results of other methods, sometimes to seven or eight decimal places. Shewhart on p. 82 of his book of 1939, already cited, showed a graphical record of all the published determinations of the speed of light, to date (Fig. 29). Every determination shows a lower figure than was ever before obtained. There have been a number of more recent determinations, every one, with one exception, still being lower than any ever obtained before.[6] The exception came from the USSR.

No true number of inhabitants in a Census count. Some fundamental principle of science seems to have escaped even officials of the Census. I heard one official say that the Census of 1980 was the most accurate ever taken, leading himself and other people, I fear, to suppose that an accurate figure exists and could be

5 Walter A. Shewhart, *Statistical Method from the Viewpoint of Quality Control* (Graduate School, Department of Agriculture, Washington, 1939; Dover, 1986), pp. 68, 69; C. K. Ogden and I. A. Richards, *The Meaning of Meaning* (Harcourt, Brace, 1956).
6 David Halliday and Robert Resnick, *Fundamentals of Physics* (Wiley, 1974), p. 655.

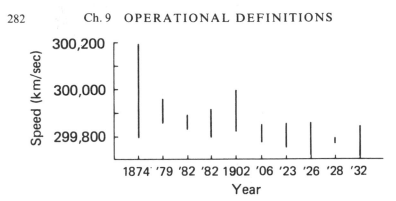

Fig. 29. Graphical record of published determinations of the speed of light, down to 1932. The vertical ranges are the physicist's so-called probable errors, calculation for which is usually not clear.

obtained if only everybody in the Census would work hard enough.

Claims put forth in 1980 by the mayors of various cities in America that the Census of April 1980 failed to count all their people showed dismal failure on the part of the mayors to understand what a count is. Threats by the courts to award to cities adjustments of recorded counts display equal failure. Why not give every area an additional $2\frac{1}{2}$ per cent?

There is no true value for the number of people in Detroit, but there is (was) a figure delivered by the procedures that the Census followed. If the procedures had been different in any way, a different figure would have been obtained.

I submit the thought that a sensible way for a mayor to satisfy himself about the count of people in his city would be to work in advance with the Bureau of the Census. He would:

1. Study and become familiar with the methods that our Census and other censuses have used to find people in an area, including the definitions of whom to count and whom to omit, plus the rules for allocating people from one area to another.

A count of vacant dwelling units in an area presents problems of classification as well as problems of total count. First, what is a dwelling unit? Second, what is a vacant dwelling unit? It seems simple till one enquires into the various kinds of vacant dwelling units. It might seem that a dwelling unit that is not occupied is vacant. But what if the dwelling unit is uninhabitable? Is it vacant? There are dwelling units vacant and for sale; vacant for rent; seasonally vacant (occupied only part of the year); vacant but neither for sale nor for rent; vacant held for occupancy.

Number of vacant dwelling units by type of vacancy is an important economic indicator, and useful for business purposes. Obviously, the Census must put interviewers through a course of training before they can be sent into the field to collect data on vacancies.

2. The best way to learn these procedures would be to apply to the Census for the four-day course of study, and take the examinations.

Anyone familiar with Census methods knows about the well-organized attempt on the night of 8 April of the Census year to find and count all the people in every mission, flophouse, or shelter, with no usual place of residence. Many of these people have no information about themselves; some are not sure of their names, still fewer of their ages. An army of enumerators and other Census employees take part in this dragnet, under close supervision and dress rehearsal.

It is notable that further efforts and expense beyond a reasonable level to find more people are singularly unsuccessful, especially for black males 18 to 24 years of age. Intensity of search may easily cost $100 for every addition to the count. Further effort raises the cost to $200 for each addition. Where should effort cease?

Again, what do you mean by the number of people in an area?

There would obviously have to be agreement in advance on just what effort is to be expended and who will pay the cost beyond regular authorized Census methods.

3. Learn the various techniques by which our Census and other censuses have estimated (a) the number of dwelling units and the number of people missed, (b) the number counted twice, and (c) the number counted in error.

Incidentally, a roster of people that claim that they were not enumerated in the Census is not worth the paper that it is written on. You do not have to be home to be counted. Only a search of the Census records can answer the question whether some particular person was enumerated, and allocated to his home address.

4. Make suggestions on the procedures until satisfied with them.

5a. Monitor the Census in action, to provide statistical evidence of exactly what happened, in a sample of small areas, appropriately selected.

An area in the sample could be a segment that (according to maps) contains housing units, anywhere from 10 to 50 (not rigid). The overriding requirement of an area is that it must have definite, unmistakable boundaries.

b. Accept the results of the Census unless the monitoring shows failure in execution. Failure in execution must be defined in advance.

Without this participation, the mayor must accept what the Census gives him. To complain afterward is to play heads I win, tails new flip. It is hard for me to find partners for a game governed by such a rule, yet this is precisely how the mayors are asking other people to play.

A judge and his staff, to qualify to hear with intelligence a claim for a shortage, would (like the mayor) require a short course in Census methods, and a briefing on the difference between a concept and an operational definition (the contents of this chapter, which ought to be included in education in law, engineering, business, and statistics).

More on operational definitions. Everyone supposes that he knows what pollution means until he begins to try to explain it to somebody. One requires an operational definition of pollution of rivers, pollution of land, pollution of streets. These words have no meaning until defined statistically. For example, it will not suffice to say that air with 100 parts per million of carbon monoxide is a hazard. One must specify (a) that this amount or more is a hazard if it exists at any instant, or (b) that this amount or more is a hazard if it exists throughout working hours. And how is the concentration to be measured?

Does pollution mean (e.g.) carbon monoxide in sufficient concentration to cause sickness in three breaths, or does one mean carbon monoxide in sufficient concentration to produce sickness when breathed continuously over a period of five days? In either case, how is the effect going to be recognized? By what procedure is the presence of carbon monoxide to be detected? What is the diagnosis or criterion for poisoning? Men? Animals? If men, how will they be selected? How many? How many in the sample must satisfy the criteria for poisoning from carbon monoxide in order that we may declare the air to be unsafe for a few breaths, or for a steady diet? Same questions if animals are used.

Even the adjective *red* has no meaning for business purposes unless it is defined operationally in terms of test and criterion. *Clean* is one thing for dishes and for knives and forks in a restaurant; something else in the manufacture of hard discs for a computer, or in the manufacture of transistors.

The man in business or in government can not afford to be superficial in his understanding of specifications for performance of product, or medicines, or human efforts. Principles of the theory of knowledge, often regarded as inconsequential or as pastime in pure science, as well as in textbooks on administration and management, become lively and gravely serious to the man that is faced with the problems of industry.

What is the meaning of the law that butter for sale must be 80 per cent butterfat? Does it mean 80 per cent butterfat, or more, in every pound that you buy? Or does it mean 80 per cent on the average? What would you mean by 80 per cent butterfat on the average? The average over your purchases of butter during a year? Or would you mean the average production of all butter for a year, yours and other people's purchases of butter from a particular source? How many pounds would you test, for calculation of the average? How would you select butter for test? Would you be concerned with the variation in butterfat from pound to pound?

Obviously, any attempt to define operationally 80 per cent butterfat runs headlong into the need for statistical techniques and criteria. Again, the words *80 per cent butterfat*, by themselves have no meaning.

Operational definitions are necessary for economy and reliability. Without operational definitions of (e.g.) unemployment, pollution, safety of goods and of apparatus, effectiveness (as of a drug), side effects, duration of dosage before side effects become apparent, such concepts have no meaning unless defined in statistical terms. Without an operational definition, investigations of a problem will be costly and ineffective, almost certain to lead to endless bickering and controversy.

An operational definition of pollution in terms of offensiveness to the nose would be an example. It is not an impossible definition (being close kin to statistical methods for maintaining constant quality and taste in foods and beverages), but unless it be statistically defined, it would be meaningless.

The number of samples for test, how to select them, how to calculate estimates, how to calculate and interpret their margin of uncertainty, tests of variance between instruments, between operators, between days, between laboratories, the detection and evaluation of the effect of nonsampling errors are statistical problems of high order. The difference between two methods of investigation (questionnaire, test) can be measured reliably and economically only by statistical design and calculation.

Laws passed by Congress and rulings by federal regulatory agencies are notorious for lack of clarity in definitions and costly confusion. The following excerpts from the *New York Times*, 9 April 1980, pp. D-1 and D-3, indicate that the Federal Communications Commission finally gave up on the distinction between data processing and the transmission and manipulation of data.

> The distinction between data processing (manipulation of data in the form of words and numbers) and telecommunications (the transmission of voices, the traditional domain of phone companies) will disappear.
>
> It is this last point that ultimately, in the eyes of many observers, forced the commission's hand in undertaking what has come to be known to the industry as Computer Inquiry II.
>
> For more than a decade the F.C.C. has been trying to resolve the basic question of what constitutes data processing and telecommunications. For just as long, the two technologies have outraced the regulatory environment. . . .
>
> "Every time the commission tried to separate the two fields, they got closer together," said one telecommunications industry observer. "Now the commission in effect is forcing the issue itself by opening up the data processing business to communications carriers."

What means a label " 50 per cent wool "? The label on a blanket reads " 50 per cent wool." What does it mean? You probably

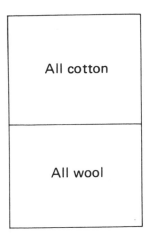

Fig. 30. This blanket is 50 per cent wool—by area.

don't care much what it means. You are more interested in color, texture, and price than in the content. However, some people do care what the label means. The Federal Trade Commission does, but with what operational meaning?

Suppose that you tell me that you wish to purchase a blanket that is 50 per cent wool, and that I sell to you the blanket shown in Fig. 30, one half by area being all wool and the other half all cotton. This blanket is 50 per cent wool, by one definition. But you may, for your purpose, prefer another definition: you may say that 50 per cent wool means something different to you. If so, then what? You may say that you meant for the wool to be dispersed throughout the blanket. You could come through with an operational definition like this:

Cut 10 holes in the blanket, 1 or $1\frac{1}{2}$ cm in diameter, centred by random numbers. Number the holes 1 to 10. Hand these 10 pieces to your chemist for a test. He will follow prescribed rules. Ask him to record x_i, the proportion wool by weight for hole i. Compute $\bar{x}$, the average of 10 proportions.

Criteria:

$$\bar{x} \geqslant 0.50$$
$$x_{max} - x_{min} \leqslant 0.02$$

If the sample fails on either criterion, the blanket fails to meet your specification.

There is nothing right or wrong about either of the above two definitions of 50 per cent wool. You have a right and a duty to specify a definition that suits your purpose. Later on, you may have another purpose, and a new definition.

There is no true value for the proportion of wool in a blanket. There is, however, a number that you can get by carrying out a prescribed test.

So far, we have been talking about a single blanket. Now comes the problem of a run of blankets. You may be buying blankets for a hospital or for the army. We face here the same fundamental difference that we faced in Chapter 2: a single-time purchase compared with continuing purchases. You could specify that for every 10 kg of clean wool, the manufacturer will use 10 kg of cotton. This would be a possible definition of 50 per cent wool, neither right nor wrong, but satisfying your purpose, if you say so.

Application. The following item appeared in the *U.S. News and World Report*, 23 November 1981, p. 82:

NEWS-LINES

What You Can and Can Not Do If You Run a Business as a Result of Recent Court and Government Decisions

An importer who relies on labels provided by foreign manufacturers is

acting illegally if the labels are not correct, says a consent decree filed in a
U.S. district court. A New York-based
importer of wool-blend fabrics has
agreed to pay a $25,000 fine to settle
charges that it sold fabrics with less
wool than labels claimed even after
being notified by the Federal Trade
Commission that to do so was illegal.
Under the agreement, the firm will
have fabrics tested by an independent
laboratory to determine the accuracy
of labels.

It would be interesting to learn what operational definition of
25 per cent wool plaintiff and defendant agreed to.

What is a wrinkle?

The product is instrument panels for automobiles.[7]
One style of panel was a special source of trouble. The
plant manager informed me that the proportion defective was anywhere from 35 to 50 per cent day after
day.

Examination of data showed that the inspectors differed markedly. It turned out that each inspector has
his own visual perception for the day of what constituted a wrinkle. The manager agreed to devote time to
operational definitions. Six men in top management
attended the session. The inspectors provided 20
panels for exhibits, some with wrinkles, so they said,
some without.

7 This section was contributed by Byron Doss, Consultant, Nashville.

As a first step, I asked everybody present—anyone willing to try—to define a wrinkle. Give us a definition of a wrinkle that everybody can understand. The challenge went unanswered. Let's try again: Can any inspector tell me what a wrinkle is? No answer. The manager of quality control then pointed to what he called an actual wrinkle. One of the inspectors agreed that that was indeed a wrinkle. Two of the other four inspectors came forth with the question, "What is it that you are looking at?" They could find no trace of a wrinkle.

The solution was to establish operational definitions of what a wrinkle is and what it is not. Definitions of other types of defects followed.

Result: The level of defectives dropped to 10 per cent in the space of one week. Employees on rework had time to do their job. The operational definition provided a basis of communication between the inspectors and operators. They trained themselves and each other. Production went up 50 per cent.

Cost: nothing. Same people, same materials, same machinery; nothing new except definitions that people on the job, and inspectors too, understood on a common basis.

Random selection of units. A random procedure for selection of a sample of units from a frame of N units could be defined in this way:

1. Number the units in the frame 1, 2, 3, and onward to N.
2. Read out by an acceptable procedure, to be written out in advance, n unduplicated random numbers between 1 and N. The numbers read out designate by serial number the selection of the sample.

This would be an operational definition of a random procedure. A sample is neither random nor not random. It is the procedure of selection that we must focus on. The procedure that selected the sample satisfies the prescribed definition of a random procedure, or it does not. A random variable is the product of a random operation.[8]

> It is presumed that one uses a standard table of random numbers, or generates random numbers under the guidance of a mathematician who knows the possible fallacies of generation of random numbers. (Continued on p. 353.)

EXERCISES

1. Why is it that there can be no operational definition of the true value of anything? (*Answer*: An observed numerical value of anything depends on the definitions and operations used. The definitions and operations will be constructed differently by different experts in the subject matter.)

2a. Explain why a system of measurement must show statistical control in order to qualify as a system of measurement. Go into some detail about repeated nondestructive measurement of the same item, interchange of operators, repeatability next month.

b. Explain why the accuracy of any system of measurement can be defined only as departure from the mean result of an accepted master standard of measurement.

c. The accuracy of a system of measurement will change if the master standard is changed. However, the precision of the system of measurement is unaffected by a change in the master standard.

d. What engineering and economic considerations would be

8 W. Edwards Deming, *Sample Design in Business Research* (Wiley, 1960), p. 54.

important to consider in your decision on whether to adjust your system of measurement to the master standard?

3. Explain why the accuracy of any measurement can be defined only as departure from the result of an accepted master standard of measurement. (*Answer*: Accuracy varies as the standard is altered.)

4. How would you answer the question that a manufacturer of bicycles brought up in Kaoschung?

> Your government [U.S.] has a regulation that states that a bicycle must be safe if assembled by a man of average intelligence.

His question was: What means this regulation? How would you explain to him its meaning? What is safe? What is unsafe? What is a man of average intelligence? What kind of intelligence? Could someone of lesser intelligence do better? How would you define lesser intelligence? One could only conclude that the regulation had no meaning.

Comment: A voluntary standard (see Ch. 10) developed by the industry could have forestalled this meaningless and burdensome regulation.

5a. Explain why it is that a system of measurement has no verifiable precision and no verifiable accuracy (comparison with a standard) unless the system of measurement and use of the standard are both in statistical control.

b. An assay of a compound for bromoform was shown as 86.5 ± 1.4 nanograms per microlitre. The interval ± 1.4 is described by the National Bureau of Standards as the 95 per cent confidence interval. Explain what operational meaning this interval (± 1.4) might have. Under what conditions could it predict the range of results six months hence in the same laboratory?

c. Could you lay out a plan that would provide evidence of statistical control of the measurement system?

d. Would the system of measurement include the sampling of

the material for assay? Would it include the variance between samples?

6. Why is survey experience desirable in order to understand and use economic and demographic data in business (including marketing research, of course)?

7. Explain why it is that the precision of a result, if valid at the time when an experiment is carried out, or a survey conducted, will always be valid, whereas the accuracy of this result will change from time to time with new definitions and with new preferred procedures.

8. A specification for castings contained this clause:

The castings shall be delivered to us reasonably clean.

What is "reasonably clean"? Was the specification referring to the flash, or to plain dirt? Obviously, the specification to have meaning requires operational meaning of "reasonably clean."

9. Show that there is no meaning in the content of the following paragraph:

Congress has passed legislation mandating the reconstruction of the north-east corridor, and has gone so far as to specify train speeds of 120 miles an hour, 99 per cent on-time performance, and running times of two hours and forty minutes between New York and Washington, three hours and forty minutes on the New York–Boston leg. (Tracy Kidder, *Atlantic*, July 1976, p. 36.)

Remarks: Obviously the definition of on-time performance must have an operational definition, to have meaning (Ch. 17).

Adjectives like *good service, bad service, deplorable service* have no communicable meaning, unless they are defined in statistical terms such as properties of a run chart of arrivals, or properties of a distribution of arrivals.

It is easy to see that this hope of Congress, 99 per cent on-time performance, without an operational definition of on-time performance, has no meaning. Anyone could guarantee to put a train into Penn Station day after day, 99 days out of 100, if on-time be defined as arrival any time within four hours of the printed timetable.

This illustration, referring to the performance of a train, is easily adapted to schedules of production.

10. Show that the following examples, taken from specifications used in industry and in government, have no meaning that can be communicated (i.e., no operational definition):

a. *Representative sample*—"A sample which has the same composition as the material sampled when this is considered as a homogeneous whole." (From British Standard 69/61888, "Methods of sampling chemical products.")

> How would you determine whether the sample had the same composition as the material sampled? Explain why the words "same composition as the material sampled" have no meaning.

b. *Spot sample*—"A sample of specified size or number taken from a specified place in the material or at a specified place and time in a stream and representative of its immediate or local environment."

> What is the meaning of the adjective *representative*? *Answer*: The word has no meaning. Statisticians do not use the word. Why not use sampling procedures that are dictated by statistical theory, with the advantage of less cost, and with meaningful, calculable tolerances?

11. *Best efforts*: "The contractor shall exert his best efforts."

(From a contract between the Tax Division of the Department of Justice and a statistician.)

> Who knows his best efforts? How would you decide whether he had exerted his best efforts? Can he deliver his best efforts on every engagement? Will any effort fall below his average?

12. Show that the following quotation from a famous textbook in experimental design is misleading, because the words *exact value* have no meaning:

> Obviously, it cannot be expected that the solution will provide the exact value of the unknown differences. (William G. Cochran and Gertrude M. Cox, *Experimental Designs*, Wiley, 1950, p. 3.)

13. What might be the meaning of "equal education for everybody"?

10

Standards and Regulations

Some man holdeth his tongue because he hath not to
answer; and some keepeth silence knowing his time.
A wise man will hold his tongue till he see oppor-
tunity; but a babbler and a fool will regard no time.
He that useth many words shall be abhorred.
—Ecclesiasticus 20:6–8.

Aim of this chapter. The aim of this chapter will be to show
that a government regulation, and likewise an industrial standard,[1] to be enforced, must have operational meaning. Conformance can be judged only in terms of a test and a criterion
(sometimes many tests and many criteria). The criteria and tests
must be in statistical terms to have a meaning. A regulation or
standard that is not so expressed will be devoid of meaning. A
regulation without meaning can have no legal force.

Regulations and standards. There are regulations made by
government, and there are voluntary standards made by committees, also unguided choices made by enterprises, and individuals.[2] The distinction between a regulation and a voluntary
standard lies essentially in the penalties attached to failure to
meet it.

1 The word *standard* in this book means a voluntary standard. The voluntary
   standards program in the United States was launched by Secretary of
   Commerce Herbert Hoover on 29 October 1921.
2 This section adapted from Pierre Ailleret, "The importance and probable
   evolution of standardization," *Standardization News* 5 (1977): 8–11. Mr.
   Ailleret is honorary president of the Union Technique d'Electricité in Paris.

A regulation is justifiable if it offers more advantage than the economic waste that it entails. For example, the obligation of a driver to stop at a red traffic light even when it is obvious that there is no vehicle in sight involves a waste of time and fuel, but if no such strict rule were imposed, the number of accidents at crossroads would be considerably higher.

One can not permit breaches of regulations to take place over any length of time without creating an increasing state of disorder, thereby destroying the public conscience. For this reason it is in the nature of regulations to be strict. In a permanent and well-organized system, checks and penalties are such that in the long run it is in no one's interest to break a regulation. Simultaneously, public authorities must not impose obligations that they are incapable of enforcing.

Ministers are responsible before Parliament and public opinion for regulation-making and it is for these government officials to decide which activities can be regulated without causing excessive waste, or barriers to progress. In particular, the suppression of fraud and protection of citizens against the rashness of others undeniably comes within the province of regulations. On the other hand, public authorities may or may not consider themselves obliged to protect individuals against the results of their own imprudence (whether in connexion with safety belts in cars, intoxication, or excessive smoking). They may consider it necessary to make rigid provisions for the packaging of agricultural produce, or unilaterally to select and mandate the technical characteristics of television systems.

Industrial standards. Aside from regulations, there remains a very wide area in which it is desirable for industry to make recommendations (voluntary standards) applicable in the majority of cases, and where enterprises or individuals are perfectly at liberty to disregard such recommendations. In this way, economic waste and hindrances to technical advancement are avoided.

As it does not involve any mandatory prohibitions, a voluntary standard does not require the signature of a minister before it can be put into effect. Instead of passing through the rather rigid filters preliminary to ministerial decisions, it can be prepared by the mutual agreement of all those who have contributed to it by their voluntary work, and who have decided that complete unanimity is not necessary since such a recommendation is not so severely restrictive as a regulation.

The framework of standardization provides greater clarity of expression between all the parties concerned and is much more flexible than the "consultation" process of regulation-making, where the number of people that take part is strictly limited. As a general rule, the interested parties are far more at ease in the technical committees of standards organizations than when sitting on the consultative boards of government ministries. For this reason it is often stated when defining standardization that it is based on agreement, although agreements are by no means excluded from the preparation of regulations.

Voluntary standards, if they exist, may avoid government regulation. One of the first advantages of standardization is that it enables public authorities to limit regulations to cases where compulsion is essential. Standardization thus economizes on the making of regulations. Government departments are thereby relieved of a mass of detailed work based on thousands of minor decisions.

For their part, enterprises and individuals benefit from being subjected to fewer restrictive rules and from enjoying greater freedom than if standardization did not exist. This is an important reason why they should contribute time and money to standardization, thus to avoid the useless proliferation of mandatory regulations to fill the gap left by a lack of voluntary standards. Many branches of industry have already realized this, but in agriculture, for example, numerous regulations have had to be imposed due to insufficient development of voluntary standards.

Further advantages of voluntary standards.[3]

Trains move across the country from one railway to another, with no unloading and reloading because of different gauge or different air pressure for brakes. A car may in fact move from Halifax through Montreal, Toronto, Buffalo, Philadelphia, Mexico, and up to Vancouver, over a number of routes, along with other cars, some owned by railways, some owned by private investment, as a routine matter. Refrigerator cars, when halted, tap into regular city current, anywhere.

Standardization is something that all of us take for granted. We ship an electric washer across the country with our household goods with never a conscious thought but that it is sure to meet the same voltage and current wherever it is plugged in. Our incandescent lamp finds the same socket in Springfield, Vermont, and Springfield, Illinois. The 15/34 shirt we send as a present from Iowa will fit the neck and arms that grew up to size in Virginia. We drive an automobile from coast to coast under uniform traffic signals. In Chicago we buy a tire that was made in Akron, and it will fit the wheel (made in Pittsburgh) of the car (built in Detroit) that we bought in New York.

The ratio of focal length to diameter of a lens (e.g., 2.8) is understood everywhere. We may buy an AA battery anywhere in the world to replace the one that just became too weak for service (though the quality of battery may differ markedly from brand to brand). The convenience of 110 volts and uniform outlets everywhere in the northern hemisphere would be difficult to express in words.

Competition for price and quality is not stifled by standardization.

On the contrary, as Shewhart often remarked, building-codes that differ ever so little from one country to another in Europe, or even from city to city anywhere, by obstructing mass produc-

3 Ralph E. Flanders, "How big is an inch?" *Atlantic*, January 1951.

tion, are more effective than tariff walls at throttling mass production and raising costs.

Senator Flanders continues:

The fact that we have a high degree of standardization has made life simpler for us in ways so basic and so obvious that we do not even realize they exist. It has given us the free national market which we take so casually. To the American consumer, it has given lower prices and better quality, more safety, greater availability, prompter exchange and repair service, and all the other material advantages of mass production. Is this something to be taken for granted?

American mass production, made possible by standardization, was our number-one weapon in World War II. And yet we cannot possibly estimate the loss we suffered in men and money, in time and resources, because of lack of certain proper standards. Our losses really began in the spring of 1940, when four hundred thousand Belgian troops might have fought better and longer if British ammunition had fitted their empty rifles. The losses continued at the first battle of El Alamein, where a contributing cause of the British defeat and retreat was the lack of standard interchangeable parts in the radio and other auxiliary equipment of the British tanks. At home we lost the services of thousands of small companies which could have participated in war production if there had been a comprehensive system of national defense standards that they were accustomed to. The complicated relationship of prime contractor to subcontractor would have been simplified.

At one moment early in the war, lack of a standard almost caused disaster on the grand scale. A part broke in one of the radar units protecting the length of the Panama Canal. Those in command were dismayed to discover that no replacement part was in stock. They put through a rush call to Washington to have the part flown from the factory to the canal. Long before it arrived, however, the officer in charge of stores made a foot-by-foot search of his warehouse. He found eight full bins of the needed part, each marked with a different stock number.

The problem has not been with us for long, for in our industrial beginnings our standards were written by only two men. The maker and the user alone were concerned, and perhaps their only exchange was the oldest of specifications, "Like the last one." Government obviously has the right to set standards for the goods it buys. It is an interested party, and should be an active and watchful one.

There are trends, plans, and proposals currently under way, however, that would make standardization wholly or mainly a function of government, and I am opposed to them. I do not want my talented, capable, and sincere friends in the federal agencies in Washington to write the industrial standards of this country. Too much is at stake.

If you control an industry's standards, you control that industry lock, stock, and ledger. On the day that standards become a governmental function and responsibility, as is now being threatened, the government will take a very long step toward the control of American industry.

In such a setup, government personnel will decide when and what standards should be developed and what the provisions of the standards should be. That method is inflexible. It does not permit the single manufacturer to depart from a standard in order to develop a specialized and useful business.

Standards made under such conditions tend to become limitations, controls, and restrictive procedures. They reduce consumer choice.

No government planner knows enough to write the standards for the rest of American industry and all other American people.

Nazi Germany practiced standards by decree and paid the price for it, notably when it standardized its military airplanes too much and too soon. Our own experience in World War II demonstrates that we worked best when industry was not only consulted in the development of the standards of the goods it was to manufacture, but also participated in decisions as to what the contents of the standards should be.

If an illustration is needed for an obvious truth, the case of the portable projector for training films may be briefly cited. One branch of the armed forces handed down specifications to the manufacturers that were quite out of line with the rigorous use for which the machine was intended, with the result that it frequently broke down after two or three uses. After the war a number of companies in the photographic equipment industry, working with a technical standards association, drew up specifications that harmonized the requirements of the machine and the ability of the industry to produce it. It is now in full military use.

We must work to achieve a higher degree of harmony and order in our world; to relieve the strain of modern living by simplification; to increase the standard of living through more efficient production of interchangeable parts in a free market. We must use standards as "the liberator that relegates the problems that have already been solved to the field of routine, and leaves the creative faculties free for the problems that are still unsolved." (Quoted from Senator Flanders, loc. cit.)

About four thousand executives and technical experts are now serving on committees that are developing and constantly revising American standards.

Those standards range from traffic signals to electric wiring, from specifications for fire hose to recent safety specifications for circus tents. They include standards for gear sizes; for the carat content of articles made of gold; for electric ranges, water heaters, and gas-burning appliances; for refrigeration equipment; and for eliminating variation in the shades of gray on industrial machines. There is an American standard that fixes the musical note A in the treble clef at 440 cycles per second, and one that accomplishes uniformity in kitchen measuring cups, pans, and spoons. A committee is now seeking to complete an American Standard which will set minimum standard and informative labeling for rayon fabrics.

In none of these cases did the American Standards Association (now the American National Standards Institute) initiate a standard or hand it down to others as a finished job. It simply provided the machinery by which those who are concerned developed the standard. In drawing up the proposed 160-page rayon fabrics standard, over 30 national organizations participated. Producers, distributors, consumers, service industries, and federal agencies helped in its development.

Links between regulations and standards. Reference in a regulation to an industrial standard provides a link that makes the regulation effective and meaningful. For example, a regulation specifies the maximum content of sulfur in the smoke given off by heating installations. It is left to industrial standards to define how this sulfur content is to be measured in practice by a convenient and effective method not involving excessive costs. Public authorities are always free to withdraw from a regulation, by amendment, a reference to a standard that no longer answers the purpose intended.

Development of techniques and methods—safety. In the early days of standardization, the main objective was to permit quantity production with the aim of reducing costs.

Today, however, the importance of the product itself fades into insignificance beside that of the service that it renders. The consumer's choice is nowadays based not only on the quality–purchase price relationship but also on working life, reliability, repairability, ease of replacement, and so forth. Producers have taken stock of this and are concerned not only with after-sales service, but with the subsequent fate of their product and how components can be replaced (such as fittings, leads and connexions). This is why problems of interchangeability and compatibility are most important in standardization.

Safety remains, of course, an essential preoccupation, but its field is limited by the fact that only a small proportion of products (and the characteristics of each product) are concerned with safety. Here again, changes are taking place. Safety is no longer considered absolute, and the concept of probability is unavoidably introduced because increasing awareness is attached to the uniformity necessary between the degrees of safety in agriculture, mining, manufacturing, and services.

The updating of international standards is a long process that can sometimes constitute a brake on innovation.

The international mail, as we know it today, came step by step from efforts of many people. Without much exaggeration, there was a day when the sender of a letter from one country to another had to negotiate a deal with a carrier, whose rates often differed by many fold.[4]

> A letter overland from Germany to Rome, for example, would be charged any one of three different transit rates: (1) by way of Switzerland, 68 pfennig; by way of Austria, 48 pfennig; and by way of France, 85 pfennig. A letter from the United States to Australia could be charged 5, 33, 45, 60 cents, or one dollar and 2 cents per ½ ounce, depending upon which one of the six available routes was used.
>
> The difficulties involved for the sender of a letter and for the various postal administrations were enormous. The sender did not know how much postage would be required for his letter until he went to a post office which had an up-to-date register of postal rates,

---

4 George A. Codding, *The Universal Postal Union* (New York University Press, 1964).

where the path the letter was to take was determined, the weight of the letter was transposed into the weight units of the countries through which it would pass, and all of the charges were added up.

Industry lags on standardization. Industry in the United States, unfortunately, possibly for lack of sufficient input of funds, possibly also being unwilling to run the risk of collusion, has not come forth with suitable industrial standards that would reduce pollution and improve the safety of a host of mechanical and electrical devices. Industry and the public have for this reason had to cope with government regulations, sometimes put together in haste, and sometimes by people that lack the necessary industrial and statistical experience for the job. The mechanism exists for the creation of standards through the American Society for Testing and Materials, the American National Standards Institute, and many other organizations.

The difficulties of definition and conflicting results of tests, so often mentioned in previous pages, come to the fore when some government agency must hastily construct a standard. The following headline in the *Wall Street Journal* for 4 March 1980 is illustrative:

Auto Crash Tests Yield
Bumper Crop of Confusing Data

U.S. Agency Admits Mix-up
in Tests But Uses Them
to Back Its Bumper Rules

Had the automotive industry gone to work years ago on standards for bumpers, solving in deliberate stride the problems that are now being patched up on a crash basis, the industry would not have to swallow and gag on hastily contrived untested regulations. Likewise, with respect to fuel economy, pollution, safety.

Contribution from William G. Ouchi. He was the guest speaker at the annual meeting of a U.S. trade association. The place was Florida, the audience of 300 or so leaders of companies in the industry. The audience adjourned at noon for golf. Next noon the audience adjourned for fishing. Dr. Ouchi's speech the third day commenced as follows.[5]

> While you are out on the golf course this afternoon, waiting for your partner to tee up, I want you to think about something. Last month I was in Tokyo, where I visited your trade association counterpart. It represents the roughly two hundred Japanese companies who are your direct competitors. They are now holding meetings from eight each morning until nine each night, five days a week, for three months straight, so that one company's oscilloscope will connect to another company's analyzer, so that they can agree on product safety standards to recommend to the government (to speed up getting to the market place), so that they can agree on their needs for changes in regulation, export policy, and financing and then approach their government with one voice to ask for cooperation. Tell me who you think is going to be in better shape five years from now.

Automotive companies work separately on safety, on catalytic converters, on fuel economy, and on other characteristics, all in a determined effort to serve their customers. No one company has garnered enough knowledge to give the consumer the best possible deal in consideration of performance and economy.

5 Taken from William G. Ouchi, *The M-form Society* (Addison-Wesley, 1984), p. 32.

The loss from separate efforts is incalculable. Who pays? The American consumer. Meanwhile, Japanese products come in with ever-increasing volume, giving to the American consumer the advantage of quality and economy from cooperative efforts between industry, government, and the consumer.

Lack of standards in the computer industry in America is choking the industry and robbing the consumer of more useful products.

11

Common Causes and Special Causes of Improvement. Stable System.

For indeed, he that preaches to those that have ears but hear not makes of himself a nuisance.—Chaucer, *The Tale of Melibeus*.

My two ears ache from all your worthless speech.—Chaucer, Prologue to *The Tale of Melibeus*.

Purpose of this chapter. The central problem in management and in leadership, in the words of my colleague Lloyd S. Nelson, is failure to understand the information in variation. He that possesses even a fuzzy understanding of the contents of this chapter would understand the futility of the annual rating of performance of people as a basis for raises or for promotion. He would understand that the type of action required to reduce special causes of variation is totally different from the action required to reduce variation and faults from the system itself; would understand the meaning of the capability of a process and of a system of measurement; would appreciate the necessity for statistical control of use of instruments and gauges; would understand that adjustment of an instrument to a standard should be carried out only on statistical evidence of stability of both instruments; would understand that leadership that takes aim at people that are below average in production, or above average in mistakes, is wrong, ineffective, costly to the company; that the same holds for a leader that supposes that everyone could be an achiever. He would understand why it is that costs decrease as quality improves. It is essential, however, in industry and in science to understand the distinction between a stable system and an unstable system, and how to plot points and conclude by rational methods whether they indicate a stable system. The points might show (e.g.) weekly figures on sales, quality incoming and outgoing, complaints of customers, inventory, absenteeism, accidents, fires, accounts receivable, beneficial days. (See Figs. 33 and 34, pp. 323 and 324.)

This is not a book on techniques. The reader that wishes to pursue study of techniques is advised to place himself under the guidance of a competent teacher, with help from some of the pamphlets and books listed at the end of this chapter.

Special Causes; Common Causes; Improvement of the System

Another run chart. We saw a run chart on page 7. It indicated that any substantial improvement must come from a change in the system, the responsibility of management. We take a look now at a portion of another run chart, Fig. 31, a simple exhibit of the number of miles per gallon from one filling to another of the tank on a vehicle. The points vary from one filling to another, sometimes close to the average, sometimes well above the average, sometimes below. The average of 25 miles per gallon had already been established for warm weather. Suddenly, the mileage dropped below average on nine successive fillings. Nine points fell below the average. What was the cause? Two or three successive points below the average, or above, we might expect, but nine points indicate a special cause of variation.[1]

The explanation of the special cause could be any or a combi-

---

1 Shewhart used the term *assignable cause* of variation where I use the term *special cause.* I prefer the adjective *special* for a cause that is specific to some group of workers, or to a particular production worker, or to a specific machine, or to a specific local condition. The word to use is not important; the concept is, and this is one of the great contributions that Dr. Shewhart gave to the world.

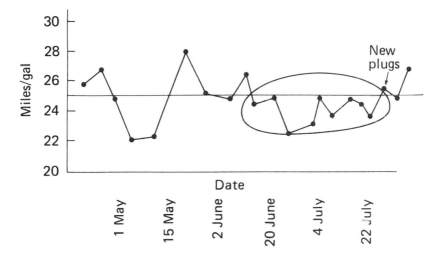

Fig. 31. Portion of a run chart for miles per gallon between fillings of the tank. The run of nine points below the average reflects a change. The cause was attributed to bad spark plugs. (This example was furnished by Messrs. Frank Belchamber and Robert B. M. Jameson of the Nashua Corporation.)

nation of a list of possibilities—cold weather (perhaps on the mountains), different gasoline, short runs, different driver, service in heavier loading, bad spark plugs. All these possible causes and others flash into mind. All were dismissed, leaving spark plugs as about the only explanation. New spark plugs brought the mileage back to its historic level.

Does this restoration of mileage indicate that spark plugs were the problem? Not with certainty. We simply establish in our minds a degree of belief that if the same sequence of events occurs again with any vehicle, we shall include spark plugs in the list of possible causes.

Many companies that own automobiles and trucks (2 million in the United States?) keep an accurate record of miles traveled and of gallons of fuel purchased. They could make good use of the data. A simple run chart could be kept up to date on each vehicle by the driver for indication of trouble. A chart might enchant the driver and open up a new world to him and to the owner.

A statistical chart detects the existence of a cause of variation that lies outside the system. It does not find the cause.

A run chart is not an instant indicator. A trend of six consecutive points, or a run of seven or eight points below or above the average, will usually indicate a special cause (see the references on p. 321).

A first lesson in application of statistical theory. Courses in statistics often commence with study of distributions and comparison of distributions. Students are not warned in classes nor in the books that for analytic purposes (such as to improve a process), distributions and calculations of mean, mode, standard deviation, chi-square, *t*-test, etc. serve no useful purpose for improvement of a process unless the data were produced in a state of statistical control. The first step in the examination of data is accordingly to question the state of statistical control that produced the data. The easiest way to examine data is to plot points in order of production to learn whether any use can be made of the distribution formed by the data.[2]

As an example, we turn attention to a distribution that appears to have all the good qualities that one could ask for, but which was misleading, not just useless. Fig. 32 shows the distribution of measurements made on 50 springs used in a camera of a certain type. Each measurement is the elongation of the spring under a pull of 20 g. The distribution is fairly symmetrical, and

2 See John W. Tukey, *Exploratory Data Analysis* (Addison–Wesley, 1977); Frederick Mosteller and John W. Tukey, *Data Analysis and Regression* (Addison–Wesley, 1977); Paul F. Velleman and David C. Hoaglin, *Applications, Basics, and Computing of Exploratory Data Analysis* (Duxbury Press, 1981); David C. Hoaglin, Frederick Mosteller, and John W. Tukey, *Understanding Robust and Exploratory Data Analysis* (Wiley, 1983); idem, *Exploring Tables, Trends, and Shapes* (Wiley, 1984).

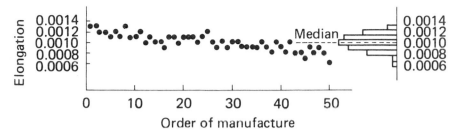

Fig. 32. Run chart for 50 springs tested in order of manufacture. The data form a symmetrical distribution, but when plotted in order of manufacture they show that the distribution is useless. The distribution would not, for example, tell us what specifications might be met. The reason is that there is no identifiable process.

both tails fall well within the specifications. One might therefore be tempted to conclude that the process is satisfactory.

However, the elongations plotted one by one in the order of manufacture show a downward trend. Something is wrong with the process of manufacture, or with the measuring instrument.

Any attempt to use the distribution in Fig. 32 would be futile. The standard deviation of the distribution, for example, would have no predictive value. It would tell nothing about the process, because this is not a stable process.[3]

We have thus learned a very important lesson in analysis of data—look at the data. Plot the points in order of production, or in some other rational order. A simple scatter diagram is helpful in some problems.

What if somebody would use this distribution to compute the capability of the process (p. 339)? He would walk into a bear trap. The process is not stable. No capability can be ascribed to it. We learned the same lesson in our study of Fig. 2 (p. 7).

3 Walter A. Shewhart, *Statistical Method from the Viewpoint of Quality Control* (Graduate School, Department of Agriculture, Washington, 1939; Dover, 1986), pp. 86–92.

A distribution (histogram) only presents accumulated history of performance of a process, nothing about its capability. As we shall learn, a process has a capability only if it is stable. The capability of a process can be achieved and confirmed by use of a control chart, not by a distribution, though (as we have seen) a simple run chart gives a lot of insight into the capability of a process.

What characteristic or characteristics are important? What figures are important? What figures should one study by use of a control chart or by any other method? The answer lies in the subject matter (engineering, chemistry, psychology, knowledge of the process, knowledge of materials, etc.), assisted by statistical theory.

Special causes and common causes. A fault in the interpretation of observations, seen everywhere, is to suppose that every event (defect, mistake, accident) is attributable to someone (usually the one nearest at hand), or is related to some special event. The fact is that most troubles with service and production lie in the system. Sometimes the fault is indeed local, attributable to someone on the job or not on the job when he should be. We shall speak of faults of the system as common causes of trouble, and faults from fleeting events as special causes.

> The term *common causes* for faults of the system was used first, so far as I know, in a conversation held about 1947 with Dr. Harry Alpert (deceased) on the subject of riots in prisons. The term first appeared in print in 1956.[4]

A riot occurs in a certain prison. Officials and sociologists turn out a detailed report about this prison, with a full explanation of

4 W. Edwards Deming, "On the use of theory," *Industrial Quality Control* 8, no. 1 (July 1956): 12–14.

why and how it happened here, ignoring the fact that the causes were common to a majority of prisons, and that the riot could have happened anywhere.

Costly confusion. Confusion between common causes and special causes leads to frustration of everyone, and leads to greater variability and to higher costs, exactly contrary to what is needed. I should estimate that in my experience most troubles and most possibilities for improvement add up to proportions something like this:

94% belong to the system (responsibility of management)
6% special

"Bill," I asked of the manager of a company engaged in motor freight, "how much of this trouble [shortage and damage] is the fault of the drivers?" His reply, "All of it," was a guarantee that this level of loss will continue until he learns that the main causes of trouble belong to the system, which is for Bill to work on.

The usual explanation offered by the man on the street for recall of automobiles is careless workmanship. This is entirely wrong. The fault, where there is any, lies with management. The fault may be in the design of some part, or in failure of management to listen to the results of tests, being too eager to put a new product on to the market before the competition beats him to it. Management may disregard early warning from tests conducted by the company's own engineers, and reports of trouble from customers. No amount of care or skill in workmanship can overcome fundamental faults in the system.

The boost in morale of the production worker, if he were to perceive a genuine attempt on the part of management to work on the 14 points of Chapter 2 and to hold the production worker responsible only for what he can govern, and not for handicaps placed on him by the system, would be hard to overestimate.

Good management and good supervision require knowledge of the calculations that will separate the two kinds of cause.

Ups and downs often lead management into costly mistakes. For example, at the headquarters of a railway, high-priced officials were concerned about the performance of the company's agent in Minneapolis. He sold last week only three carloads to a certain shipper (meaning that three loaded cars would move over the tracks of this railway). The year before during this same week he had sold four carloads to this shipper. What has happened? The men were ready to send off to the agent a telegram to ask for an explanation, but were halted by a brief exposition on the nature of variation. Agents of railways all over the country spend time explaining small variations in sales like this. They would make more sales if they would spend their time calling on shippers instead of trying to explain to headquarters nonsensical reasons for small variation. The fact is that constant sales week to week would indicate that the man had juggled his report to smooth out the variation and to avoid setting new standards.

The sign YOUR SAFETY IS UP TO YOU was prominently displayed. When I ascended steps to go another level, I nearly toppled off, the steps were so rickety. (Contributed by Heero Hacquebord, Pretoria.)

The manager of the bus company in Pretoria in November 1983 pledged to every driver a bonus of 600 rand ($540) if he had no accident up to New Year's Day. The supposition of the management was, of course, that drivers cause accidents, and that drivers can avoid accidents. Certainly, a driver has been known to cause an accident, but one also sees drivers avoid accidents several times every day. The management forgot that most accidents are not governed by the driver. What if the driver had a clean record nearly to the end of the allotted period, and then got side-swiped by a vehicle? He would lose his bonus through somebody else's action. (Contributed by Heero Hacquebord, Pretoria.)

"We rely on our experience." This is the answer that came from the manager of quality in a large company recently, when I enquired how he distinguishes between the two kinds of trouble, and on what principles. The answer is self-incriminating: it is a guarantee that this company will continue to pile up about the same amount of trouble as in the past. Why should it change?

Experience without theory teaches nothing. In fact, experience can not even be recorded unless there is some theory, however crude, that leads to a hypothesis and a system by which to catalog observations.[5] Sometimes only a hunch, right or wrong, is sufficient theory to lead to useful observation.

What is the system? To people in management, the system consists of

Management, style of
Employees—management and everybody
The people in the country
    Their work experience
    Their education
    The unemployed
Government
    Taxes
    Reports
    Tariffs
    Impediments to trade and industry
    Requirements to fill positions by quota, not by competence
    Quotas for import and export

5 C. I. Lewis. *Mind and the World-Order* (Scribner's, 1929; Dover, 1956), p. 195.

Foreign governments
   Quotas for import and export
   Manipulation of currency
Customers
Shareholders
Bank
Environmental constraints

Management has much power and discretion, but can not move all the earth. To the production worker, the system is all but him. (Contributed by someone unidentified in my seminar in Cape Town, November 1983.)

Two kinds of mistake. We may now formulate two sources of loss from confusion of special causes with common causes of variation.

> 1. Ascribe a variation or a mistake to a special cause when in fact the cause belongs to the system (common causes).
> 2. Ascribe a variation or a mistake to the system (common causes) when in fact the cause was special.

> Overadjustment is a common example of mistake No. 1. Never doing anything to try to find a special cause is a common example of mistake No. 2.

Supervisors commonly make the mistake of overadjustment when they direct to the attention of one of their people any mistake or defect, without first ascertaining that the worker was actually responsible for the mistake. Did the worker make the mistake, or was the system responsible for it? Examples abound in the pages of this book.

It is easy to establish a clean record on either mistake: never make mistake No. 1, or never make mistake No. 2. But in avoiding one mistake, one commits the other mistake as often as possible. There is no hope to avoid both mistakes all the time.

The action required to find and eliminate a special cause is totally different from the action required to improve the process. One should search at once for a special cause, once it is detected, before the trail grows cold (Robert Cowley, then manager of AT&T Network, Andover).

Need for rules. Shewhart (about 1925) recognized the fact that good management consists of making one mistake now and then, and the other one now and then. What was needed, he saw, is rules that can be put into practice by which to try to achieve minimum net economic loss from both mistakes. To this end, he contrived the 3-sigma control limits. They provide, under a wide range of unknowable circumstances, future and past, a rational and economic guide to minimum economic loss from both mistakes.

The control chart sends statistical signals, which detect existence of a special cause (usually specific to some worker or group or to some special fleeting circumstance), or tell us that the observed variation should be ascribed to common causes, chance variation attributable to the system.

There are several kinds of control charts, as the reader will already have observed. We have applied in each case the rules for calculation of the control limits, which the reader will find in any book on quality control.

Note in respect to any rule. Dr. George Gallup remarked in a speech one time (after a fiasco) that he made his prediction in advance of the election. Other people, smarter, made their predictions after the election, explaining how it all happened.

Rules have to be made in advance, for use in the future. Any rule, as a practical matter, must be constructed in the absence of full information about the future. (It is a fact, too, that we almost never have full information about what has happened to a process, even in the past.) One can always contrive, when more information is at hand, some rule that would have been better than the rule prescribed in advance with (of course) less information in hand.

These remarks apply to the Shewhart control limits. They serve the purpose well in the circumstances met in practice.

It is a hazard to use judgment to distinguish between special causes and common causes. Judgment has been wrong every time so far; see Examples 1 and 2 on pages 356 and 357. The naked eye looking at figures is not a safe guide, though I am certainly guilty of using the eyeball method in extreme circumstances.

Discovery of a special cause of variation, and its removal, are usually the responsibility of someone who is connected directly with some operation that yields data for the control chart.

Some special causes can be removed only by management. For example, production workers sometimes need engineering assistance to remove problems connected with malfunction of machinery in use. It is the responsibility of management to provide assistance when needed. Another instance of management's responsibility for special causes occurs in the current state of chaos in dealing with vendors. Production workers are sometimes forced to use unacceptable or inconsistent raw materials or parts. It is management's job to take corrective action to work with vendors to improve the quality of incoming materials, and to halt the practice of switching from one source to another. (This paragraph contributed by Gipsie B. Ranney, University of Tennessee.)

Patterns. A designated pattern of points may also indicate a special cause. We have in fact already used patterns in run charts. We were alerted to trouble by a pattern in the control chart in Fig. 23, page 265. One pattern to watch for is a trend of seven or more consecutive points up or down, or seven or more consecutive points above or below the average.

Search for a pattern can be overdone. It is necessary to state in advance what the rules are for indication of a special cause. One can always concoct a pattern that will indicate anything desired, once the chart is in hand.

The Western Electric book listed at the end of this chapter is excellent on patterns, as well as on most everything else. A convenient summary of useful patterns based on the Western Electric book has been compiled by my friend Lloyd S. Nelson.[6]

Statistical control. A stable process, one with no indication of a special cause of variation, is said to be, following Shewhart, *in statistical control*, or stable. It is a random process. Its behavior in the near future is predictable. Of course, some unforeseen jolt may come along and knock the process out of statistical control. A system that is in statistical control has a definable identity and a definable capability (see the section "Capability of the process," *infra*).

In the state of statistical control, all special causes so far detected have been removed. The remaining variation must be left to chance—that is, to common causes—unless a new special cause turns up and is removed. This does not mean to do nothing in the state of statistical control; it means do not take action on the remaining ups and downs, as to do so would create additional variation and more trouble (see the section on overadjustment, below). The next step is to improve the process, with never-ending effort (Point 5 of the 14 points). Improvement of the process can be pushed effectively, once statistical control is achieved and maintained (so stated by Joseph M. Juran many years ago).

Removal of common causes of trouble and of variation, of

6 Lloyd S. Nelson, "Technical aids," *Journal of Quality Technology* 16, no. 4 (October 1984).

errors, of mistakes, of low production, of low sales, of most accidents is the responsibility of management. A list of common causes appears further on. Poor sales may stem from a faulty product, or from high price. The worker at the machine can do nothing about causes common to everybody on the job. He is responsible only for the special causes chargeable to him. He can not do anything about the light; he does not purchase the raw materials nor the tools. His job is to try to use them. The training, supervision, and the company's policies are not his.

Sound understanding of statistical control is essential to management, engineering, manufacturing, purchase of materials, and service. Stability, or the existence of a system, is seldom a natural state. It is an achievement, the result of eliminating special causes one by one on statistical signal, leaving only the random variation of a stable process.

> One sees in practice countless control charts, most of which are unfortunately used incorrectly. It is to be feared that many of them do more harm than good. A necessary requirement for successful use of a control chart is a smattering of knowledge of the theory behind it. Some modicum of understanding of the preceding paragraphs in this book would help.
>
> Another point is that most control charts, even if used correctly, are used too late—too far downstream to be of any substantial benefit.
>
> Moreover, many people that use control charts suppose that statistical control is the end success of all effort. I have seen, for example, statistical control of contamination, where the big problem is to get rid of contamination.

A typical path of frustration (Fig. 33). A program of improvement sets off with enthusiasm, exhortations, revival meetings,

Fig. 33. Typical path of frustration. Quality improves dramatically at first; then levels off, becomes stable. The responsibility for improvement of quality shifts more and more to the management, and finally almost totally to the management, as obvious special causes are one by one detected and removed, and quality becomes stabilized, unfortunately at an unacceptable level.

posters, pledges. Quality becomes a religion. Quality as measured by results of inspection at final audit shows at first dramatic improvement, better and better by the month. Everyone expects the path of improvement to continue along the dotted line.

Instead, success grinds to a halt. At best, the curve levels off. It may even turn upward. Despondence sets in. The management naturally become worried. They plead, beg, beseech, implore, pray, entreat, supplicate heads of the organizations involved in production and assembly, with taunts, harassment, threats, based on the awful truth that if there be not substantial improvement, and soon, we shall be out of business.

What has happened? The rapid and encouraging improvement seen at first came from removal of special causes, detected

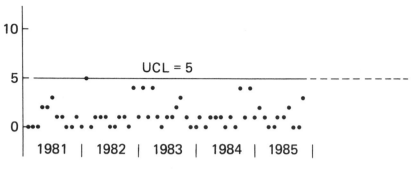

Fig. 34. Plot of the number of fires per month in a business establishment.

by horse sense. All this was fairly simple. But as obvious sources of improvement dried up, the curve of improvement leveled off and became stable at an unacceptable level.

It is interesting to note that when an attempt at improvement commences with a program of action on the 14 points and removal of deadly diseases and obstacles, led by management, the curve of improvement follows for the first few months or even as long as two years about the same curve as the one shown. The difference is that with a sound program, the curve for improvement of quality and productivity does not level off. Improvement continues so long as the management leads the program.

It takes about two years for people to discover that their program that started off with exhortations, posters, pledges, and revival meetings has come to a dead end. Then they wake up; we've been rooked.

Too many fires? A company received notice from their insurance company that unless there were a drastic reduction in the frequency of fires in the company's premises, the insurance company would cancel the insurance. A chart of the number of fires per month provided a good illustration of a stable system of fires, with an average of 1.2 fires per month, with a calculated upper limit of five fires per month (Fig. 34). The company has several products. One of them is fires, and their production of fires is stable. There will be no fires some months, one fire some months, two fires some months, with an upper limit of five fires per month.

The president of the company, naturally ill at ease, sent a letter to every one of the 10,500 employees of the company to plead with them to set fewer fires.

Had someone in the insurance company plotted Fig. 34 or something equivalent, he would have observed that the system of fires is stable and that this is one instance in which the insurance company has a good basis for the rate to set to make a little profit.

The system of fires will continue under the same system of fires until the management takes action to reduce their frequency. The insurance company was of course able to give expert advice on this matter.

For the calculation of the upper limit in Fig. 34, I used the moving range: total of all ranges, 77; 57 ranges. $\bar{R} = 77/57 = 1.35$. $\bar{R}/d_2 = 1.35/1.128 = 1.20$. Mean, $m = 67/58 = 1.16$. $m + 3\bar{R}/d_2 = 4.75$; round this to 5.

Does absenteeism exhibit the characteristics of a stable process? If so, only action by management can reduce it. Is any division or group of the company outside the system of absenteeism, a special cause, requiring separate study? (Ch. 11.)

Time of transit for deliveries to you, or to your customers: is it stable, or still afflicted with special causes of delays? If stable, how can the time of transit be reduced? (Continued on p. 211.)

How about accidents? How about beneficial days?

Does any division or group in the company stand out beyond the control limits calculated for the whole company?

Troubles in a spinning mill. A spindle halts in a spinning mill. The cause could be mechanical trouble in the spindle, or it could be a fault in the yarn. The manager had been keeping track of breakage, and had directed the efforts of the mechanic toward spindles that broke down most during the preceding week. This is a common error, encountered here and there in previous pages. It dissipates skill and effort of the mechanic.

Useful upper and lower limits for detection of spindles that are outside limits could be taken as

$$\bar{r} \pm 3\sqrt{\bar{r}}$$

where $\bar{r}$ is the average number of halts per spindle during a month. The supposition in this formula is that halts are independent: that one halt does not induce another halt in the same spindle nor in any other spindle, nor does it lessen the probability of another occurrence anywhere.

A spindle that falls beyond the upper limit raises a question. It may have had special usage or it may be in immediate need of adjustment. A spindle below the lower limit is an extra good spindle, or had special usage. Spindles that do not fall outside the above limits are simple spindles, to take their turn at regular maintenance.

Does the reader see the same error in the following rules for maintenance prescribed for aircraft?

1. The alert levels are set using the methods that apply to the industry generally. For reference purposes, refer to Civil Aviation Publication CAP 418 and the FAA Maintenance Review Board Circular 1971.

2. The method necessitates calculating the mean of the actual removal rates per 1000 landings over the last 12 periods and adding two standard deviations.

3. The standard deviation is a statistical parameter that senses the variability about its average value.

4. The 3-period alert rate is calculated using the previous 4 quarterly removal rates per 1000 landings.

A good first step, before one makes calculations, would be to plot the data in some form, such as a run chart by the week. Even a crude tool like a distribution of time to failure might disclose patterns and useful information about the failure of components.

Monte Carlo experiments with the funnel.

Monte Carlo experiments with the funnel.[7] If anyone adjusts a stable process to try to compensate for a result that is undesirable, or for a result that is extra good, the output that follows will be worse than if he had left the process alone (attributable to William J. Latzko).

A common example is to take action on the basis of a defective item, or on complaint of a customer. The result of his efforts to improve future output (only doing his best) will be to double the variance of the output, or even to cause the system to explode. What is required for improvement is a fundamental change in the system, not tampering.

The purpose of the experiment with the funnel is to demonstrate the unbelievable losses from overadjustment. The experiment requires only materials that are on hand in almost any household kitchen. Needed: (1) a funnel; (2) a marble that will fall through the funnel; (3) a table; (4) a holder for the funnel. A glance at Fig. 35 may help. Steps:

1. Designate a point on the table as the target.
2. Drop the marble through the funnel.
3. Mark the spot where the marble comes to rest.
4. Drop it again through the funnel. Mark the spot where it comes to rest.
5. Continue through 50 drops.

---

7 I am indebted to my friend Dr. Lloyd S. Nelson for this experiment. Discussions with Dr. Gipsie B. Ranney and Dr. Benjamin J. Tepping have helped to clarify the four rules. I am indebted to Dr. Tepping for many simulations of the four rules.

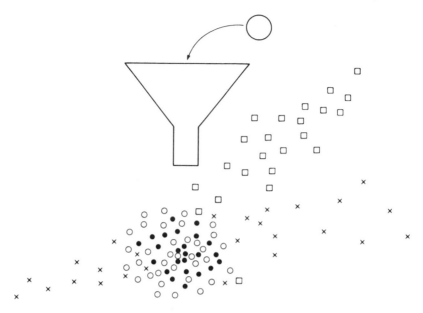

Fig. 35. Record of drops of the marble through the funnel under the four rules described in the text. • Rule 1, ○ Rule 2, × Rule 3, □ Rule 4. Only far-off points are shown, to avoid congestion.

As a preamble to Step 4 and subsequent drops of the marble, you must decide on a rule for adjustment of the funnel. The human mind can contrive four rules:

Rule 1. Leave the funnel fixed, aimed at the target, no adjustment.

Rule 2. At drop k ($k = 1, 2, 3, \ldots$) the marble will come to rest at point z_k, measured from the target. (In other words, z_k is the error at drop k.) Move the funnel the distance $-z_k$ from its last position. Memory 1.

Rule 3. Set the funnel over point $-z_k$, measured from the target. No memory.

Rule 4. Set the funnel at each drop right over the spot (z_k) where it last came to rest. No memory.

In Rules 2 and 3, the operator does his best, adjusting his machine to compensate for the last failure.

Results:[8]

Rule 1. This is by far the best choice. Rule 1 will produce a stable distribution of points. It produces minimum variance on any diameter drawn through the target.

Rule 2. Rule 2 produces a stable output, but the expected variance of the distribution of points along any diameter through the target will under Rule 2 be double the expected variance under Rule 1.

Rule 3. The system will explode. The marble will eventually move away further and further in opposite direction from the target, in some symmetrical pattern.

Rule 4. The system will explode. The marble will eventually move away further and further from the target in one direction.

The results of Rules 3 and 4 are unstable; the system will explode.

Rule 4 will yield a random walk. The successive drops of the marble resemble a drunk man, trying to reach home, who falls after each step and has no idea which way is north. He steps in any direction, with no memory. His efforts eventually send him by faltering steps further and further from the target.

Rule 4 corresponds to the operator that tries to achieve uniformity by attempting to make every piece like the last one. The system explodes.

Another example of Rule 4 is a man that matches color from batch to batch for acceptance of material, without reference to the original swatch. (Contributed by Ivor S. Francis.)

8 Mathematical solutions are shown in the author's book *Some Theory of Sampling* (Wiley, 1950; Dover, 1984), pp. 454–466. Reference is made there to Lord Rayleigh's solution in a paper entitled "On the resultant of a large number of vibrations," *Phil. Mag.*, vol. xlvii, 1899: pp. 246–251; also in his *Theory of Sound*, 2d ed. only (1894), Sec. 42a; and in his *Scientific Papers*, vol. iv, p. 370. The problem of optimum convergence to the target was treated by Frank S. Grubbs, "An optimum procedure for setting machines," *Journal of Quality Technology*, vol. 15, no. 4, October 1983: pp. 155–208. (The problem solved by Dr. Grubbs is not a solution for the funnel.)

A frightening example of Rule 4 occurs where the people on a job train a new worker. This new worker is then ready in a few days to help to train a new worker. The methods taught deteriorate without limit. Who would know?

Examples of application of Rules 2 and 3 have already appeared in the text. More will follow.

A good exercise for the reader would be to make a list of examples of losses in his own organization from application of Rules 2, 3, and 4, with an attempt to estimate the losses.

> The above experiment was described in two dimensions. It is simple to carry it out in one dimension. Simply construct a horizontal track for the marble to roll in, bounded by walls to hold the marble in the track.

Theory, demonstration, and application drawn from this experiment and from the experiment with the red beads (*infra*) would make an exciting beginning to a course in statistics.

Remark 1. We have already noted on page 141 that mechanical or electronic feedback to hold dimensions and other quality-characteristics within specifications actually by overadjustment causes loss in all the following stages. They thus increase costs. They do not help to improve the process.

Remark 2. Remark from a man in my seminar: "My son is on a submarine. It is the practice there to take a shot at a target first thing in the morning, then adjust the sights to compensate for the error. This adjustment, I now understand, is almost a sure guarantee of worse performance for the rest of the day than if they had left the sights alone." He is correct—a clever observation.

Remark 3. Adjustment of an instrument to a master standard (calibration) whenever the difference seems worrisome is almost always overadjustment, robbing the instrument of its built-in accuracy. A rule is needed on when to adjust. It is necessary that both measurement systems (master standard and test) be in statistical control. One may then decide on the basis of engineering and economics whether any adjustment at all is desirable.

Example 1. A manufacturer of carburetors for automobiles was using two tests. Test A: a cheap test with nonflammable gas, applied to every carburetor. Test B: an expensive test, with flammable gas, applied to a sample of 10 carburetors drawn from a lot. (No instruction about how to draw the sample of 10.)

Each carburetor in the sample of 10 was then tested by both methods. Rule: Compute the averages $\bar{A}$ and $\bar{B}$ for the two tests of the 10 carburetors in each lot. If $\bar{A}$ is below $\bar{B}$ in three successive lots, adjust Test A to conformity with Test B, and proceed. Likewise if $\bar{A}$ is above $\bar{B}$ in three successive lots.

What is wrong with this rule? Suppose that Test A gives results at random above and below the corresponding results of Test B. Then one-fourth of a long series of tests of three successive lots would show $\bar{A} < \bar{B}$, and one-fourth would show $\bar{A} > \bar{B}$. The rule stated thus leads to woeful overadjustment, the penalty being excessive costs through artificial increase in the magnitude of disagreement between the two tests. Worse, the rule does not bring either test into statistical control, nor the difference between the two tests.

A far better way to compare the two tests, if they provide actual measurements (in centimetres, milligrams, etc.) would be to plot the results of the two tests according to the suggestion in Fig. 50 (p. 441).

Example 2. The job in a certain staff area in a company that manufactures automobiles is to make monthly forecasts of sales. The men take into account many kinds of information. The forecast falls short or long, month by month, when compared with actual sales. The procedure for the next month had been to adjust the method up or down on the basis of this comparison. The reader may perceive that what the men were doing was guaranteeing that their method could never improve.

Statistical control of instruments and gauges. As we learned on page 268, a recorded measurement is the end product of a long series of operations from raw material on forward, plus the operation of measurement at some stage of the product, and the record thereof. As is emphasized in numerous places in this book, statistical control of the process of measurement is vital; otherwise there is no meaningful measurement.

Will this instrument give about the same results next week on 100 items as it gave today? What if we change operators? This subject appears in Chapter 8 on supervision and reappears in Chapter 15 in connexion with costs of inspection. The reader may wish to consult the book by Harry Ku and Part B of the excellent book by the Western Electric Company (pp. 84ff.), both listed at the end of this chapter. A.S.T.M. Standard 177 on precision and bias will be helpful to the reader. (American Society for Testing and Materials, 1916 Race Street, Philadelphia 19103.)

Another point about use of instruments is the importance to give an instrument a good chance to do its work. An example (furnished by my friend Dr. Lloyd S. Nelson) is a sample of fluid conveyed to the laboratory for measurement of viscosity. It ages on the way. If the measuring instrument could be placed at the source of the sample of fluid, the results would be different and more indicative of the material being sampled.

False signals from measuring instruments. An instrument that is out of control may give a false signal of a special cause when none exists, or the opposite, it may fail to detect a special cause when one does exist. An instrument, whether in statistical control or not, that is not of sufficient precision to do the job will give false signals. One may thus see the importance of paying attention to the precision and statistical control of instruments.

(Contributed by William W. Scherkenbach, Ford Motor Company.)

(From Jeffrey T. Luftig.) The man was making only one measurement of the distance between two flares. I asked him to make eight. He did. The range between the eight was four times the allowance in the specification.

Before I could accept the conclusions (about which parts were causing the trouble), I wished to know more about the system of measurement. The manager assured me that there could be nothing wrong with the measurements: he made them all himself.

Control limits are not specification limits. Control limits, once we have achieved a fair state of statistical control, tell us what the process is, and what it will do tomorrow. The control chart is the process talking to us.[9]

The distribution of a quality-characteristic that is in statistical control is stable and predictable, day after day, week after week. Output and costs are also predictable. One may now start to think about Kanban or just-in-time delivery.

Moreover, as Mr. William E. Conway pointed out, engineers and chemists become innovative, creative, toward improvement of the process, once they see it in statistical control. They sense the fact that further improvement is up to them (see Ch. 1).

Without statistical methods, attempts to improve a process are hit or miss, with results that usually make matters worse.

Question in a seminar. Please elaborate on the difference between conformance to specifications and statistical process control. My management feels that conformance to specifications is enough.

9 Eloquently stated thus by Irving Burr in *Engineering Statistics and Quality Control* (McGraw-Hill, 1953).

Answer. The aim in production should be not just to get statistical control, but to shrink variation. Costs go down as variation is reduced. It is not enough to meet specifications.

Moreover, there is no way to know that one will continue to meet specifications unless the process is in statistical control. Until special causes have been identified and eliminated (at least all that have appeared so far), one dare not predict what the process will produce the next hour. Dependence on inspection (the only alternative) is hazardous and costly. Your process may be doing well now, yet turn out items beyond the specifications this afternoon.

Where are your figures for the losses caused by the supposition made by your management? How could they know?

Specification limits are not action limits. In fact, severe losses occur when a process is continually adjusted one way and then the other to meet specifications. (See the sections "The supposition that it is only necessary to meet specifications" and "The fallacy of zero defects," pp. 139, 141.)

Curiously, a process may be in statistical control producing 10 per cent defective items, or even 100 per cent.

Control limits do not set probabilities. The calculations that show where to place the control limits on a chart have their basis in the theory of probability. It would nevertheless be wrong to attach any particular figure to the probability that a statistical signal for detection of a special cause could be wrong, or that the chart could fail to send a signal when a special cause exists. The reason is that no process, except in artificial demonstrations by use of random numbers, is steady, unwavering.

It is true that some books on the statistical control of quality and many training manuals for teaching control charts show a graph of the normal curve and proportions of area thereunder. Such tables and charts are misleading and derail effective study and use of control charts.

Rules for detection of special causes and for action on them are not tests of a hypothesis that the system is in a stable state.

More on specifications.[10] Maximum and minimum limits for the specification of a product are by themselves a costly and unsatisfactory guide to the production worker. Thus, specification limits for an outside diameter to lie between 1.001 and 1.002 cm tell the production worker that a diameter of 1.0012 cm meets the specification, but it is no help to him in an attempt to produce fewer defectives and to increase his production, both of which he can accomplish with less effort with the aid of statistical methods.

The production worker's job description should therefore, for best economy, help him to achieve statistical control of his work. His job, furthermore, is to reach an economic level of the distribution of his quality-characteristic, and to continually reduce its variation. Under this system, his output will meet the specifications and in fact leave them beyond the horizon, reducing costs in subsequent operations, and elevating the quality of the final product. Workers that are in statistical control but whose output is unsatisfactory can be transferred and trained in other work (see Ch. 8).

10 This section was the theme of a talk given by Dr. Joseph M. Juran years ago at a meeting of the Metropolitan Chapter of the American Society for Quality Control (New York). For a published reference, I cite Irving Burr, "Specifying the desired distribution rather than maximum and minimum limits," *Industrial Quality Control* 24, no. 2 (1967): 94–101.

Partial list of common causes of variation and of wrong spread, wrong level: the responsibility of management.

(The reader may supply other examples, appropriate to his own plant and conditions.)

Poor design of product or of service

Failure to remove the barriers that rob the hourly worker of the right to do a good job and to take pride in his work

Poor instruction and poor supervision (almost synonymous with unfortunate working relationships between foremen and production workers)

Failure to measure the effects of common causes, and to reduce them

Failure to provide production workers with information in statistical form that shows them where they could improve their performance and the uniformity of the product

Incoming materials not suited to the requirements

In a recent experience, leather would in one trial in three fail to stick to plastic as intended by the design of the product. The trouble, as it turned out, was too much grease in the leather. A change in the specifications for leather removed the trouble. This was a simple change in the system. (Incidentally, the manager declared that turnover dropped dramatically when he made this change.)

Procedures not suited to the requirements

Machines out of order

Machines not suited to the requirements

Settings of the machines chronically inaccurate (fault of the crew responsible for settings)

Poor light

Vibration

Humidity not suited to the process

Mixing product from streams of production, each having small variability, but different levels

Uncomfortable working conditions: noise, confusion, unnecessary dirt, awkward handling of materials, unnecessary extremes of heat or cold, poor ventilation, poor food in the cafeteria, etc.

Shift of management's emphasis from quantity to quality, back and forth, without understanding how to achieve quality

Another common cause is management's failure to face the problem of inherited defective material. Defective items or subassemblies fed into one operation from a previous operation in the same company, or from the outside, are demoralizing. No matter how well the operator performs his own work, the product will in the end still be defective. The multiplicative effect of intermediate defectives is disheartening. (More on this point in Ch. 8.)

Two Basic Uses of Control Charts

1. **As a judgment.** Was (past tense) the process in statistical control?[11] Here, we look at a control chart to observe whether the process that made a particular batch of product was in statistical control. If yes, then we know, for the quality-characteristic that was plotted on the chart, the distribution of this quality-characteristic for individual items. An example appears on page 372.

2. **As an operation (ongoing).** A control chart can also be used to attain and maintain statistical control during production. Here the process has already been brought into statistical control

---

11 The terms heading this section and the next, "As a judgment" and "As an operation," are Shewhart's.

(or nearly so, with only rare evidence of a special cause). We extend into the future the control limits on (e.g.) an $\bar{x}$-chart, and plot points one by one, perhaps every half-hour or every hour. The up and down movements of the points are to be disregarded by the production worker unless they show a run (as for wear of tool), or unless a point falls outside the control limits.

Removal of a special cause of variation, to move toward statistical control, important though it be, is not improvement of the process. Removal of a special cause only brings the system back to where it should have been in the first place (quoting a lecture by Dr. Juran). In repetition, as Dr. Juran also said, the important problems of improvement commence once you achieve statistical control.

Continual improvement of the system by the engineers may then take place. Improvement may be simple, some adjustment that will raise or lower the level of the control chart, to lessen the risk of production of defective items. On the other hand, improvement may be difficult and complex, the possible aim being to decrease use of certain materials (see Ch. 1) and to shrink the spread between the control limits.

Some advice about control charts as an ongoing operation. The production worker requires only a knowledge of simple arithmetic to plot a chart. But he can not by himself decide that he will use a chart on the job, and still less can he start a movement for use of charts.

It is the responsibility of management to teach use of control charts on the job (ongoing) where they can be effective. As we learned in Chapter 2, a control chart in the hands of an hourly worker can be effective only if he is not afflicted with barriers that rob him of pride in his work.

A chart for each member of the group is sometimes helpful. The production worker, seeing a point outside control limits, can almost always identify at once the special cause and eliminate it.

Only the production worker and the foreman see the chart, unless the worker elects to make his chart public.

A chart for fraction defective for a group, prominently displayed to indicate a special cause shortly after it occurs, is usually helpful to everybody.

Proliferation of charts without purpose is to be avoided. One plant that I visited near Nagoya had on that day 241 $\bar{x}$- and R-charts. All charts are reviewed every two months; charts added, charts discontinued when they have achieved their purpose, reinstituted later if needed.

Capability of the process. Once a process has been brought into a state of statistical control, it has a definable capability. It will show sustained satisfactory performance on the $\bar{x}$- and R-charts. The specifications that it can meet are predictable.

A simple way to describe the specifications that it can meet is to measure up and down from the mean $\bar{x}$ on the $\bar{x}$-chart $\sqrt{n}$ times the spread between the control limits for $\bar{x}$, where n is the size of the sample. An illustration appears on p. 342. The spread between individual parts is also equal to $6\bar{R}/d_2$.

The symbol d_2 is a number that depends on n, to be found in any book on the statistical control of quality. It is derived from the distribution of the range.[12] As an approximation,[13] d_2 is very nearly equal to $\sqrt{n}$ up to $n = 10$.

It is thus true that the R-chart, if in control, tells us the capability of the process.

12 The distribution of the range was published by L. H. C. Tippett, "On the extreme individuals and the range of samples taken from a normal population," *Biometrika* 17 (1925). An excellent book on the capability of the process is Masao Kogure, *Theory of Process Capability and Its Applications* (JUSE Press, Tokyo, 1975; rev. ed., 1981)—alas, in Japanese.

13 Nathan Mantel, "On a rapid estimation of standard errors for the means of small samples," *American Statistician* 5 (October 1951): 26–27; M. H. Quenouille, *Rapid Statistical Calculations* (Hafner, 1959), pp. 5–7.

A common fault in use of $\bar{x}$- and R-charts, and for calculation of the capability of the process, is failure to understand that the range must exhibit randomness, and that the range at a point must be the range of the observations that are plotted for $\bar{x}$, not from some other source.

One sees much wrong practice in connexion with capability of the process. It is totally wrong to take any number of pieces such as 8, 20, 50, or 100, measure them with calipers or other instruments, and take 6 standard deviations of these measurements as the capability of the process. The first step is to examine the data, as by a run chart (Ch. 1), or by $\bar{x}$- and R-charts, to decide whether the process of manufacture and the system of measurement show statistical control. If they do, then the capability of the process will be obvious from the $\bar{x}$- and R-charts. If they do not, then there is no capability.

Advantages of stability or statistical control. A process that is stable, in statistical control, presents a number of advantages over instability. In statistical control:

1. The process has an identity; its performance is predictable. It has a measurable, communicable capability, as we saw in the last section. Production and dimensions and other quality-characteristics, including the number of defects, if any, remain nearly constant hour after hour, day after day.
2. Costs are predictable.
3. Regularity of output is an important by-product of statistical control. The Kanban system of delivery of parts follows naturally when a whole system is in statistical control (William W. Scherkenbach).
4. Productivity is at a maximum (costs at a minimum) under the present system.

Ch. 11 COMMON CAUSES AND SPECIAL CAUSES 341

5. Relationships with the vendor who delivers material that is in statistical control are greatly simplified. Costs diminish as quality improves.
6. The effects of changes in the system (management's responsibility) can be measured with greater speed and reliability. Without statistical control it is difficult to measure the effect of a change in the system. More accurately, only catastrophic effects are identifiable.
7. The all-or-none rules of Chapter 14 apply for minimum total cost of incoming items that come from a process that is in statistical control.

Interlaboratory testing (closely allied with the statistical control of instruments and gauges). This activity is important for both buyer and seller, else the buyer may pay too much for his material purchased, or the seller may receive too little. Both are entitled to a square deal. This activity is also important in a company that has several plants that make the same or nearly the same products.

Another example of uses of a control chart as a judgment. Examples appeared in Chapter 1. We now turn to another. An executive of a large mail order company came with the problem of high costs. He also came with data which showed the number of orders filled every half-hour. Four half-hours provided data for $\bar{x}$- and R-charts (Fig. 36) with $n = 4$. Once he saw how wide the control limits were for the output of orders, he made the remark that the control limits were too wide: he preferred less variation. But how would you achieve it? I asked. He surmised that you just draw new lines closer together. It was my obligation to point out to him that the control limits were only telling him what the process is, not what he wished it to be; that any reduction in variation in the future was entirely up to him. He must

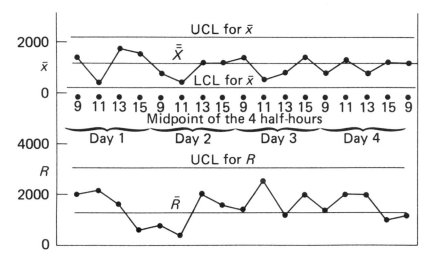

Fig. 36. The number of orders filled is recorded for each half-hour. Each point in the chart comes from four consecutive half-hours; $\bar{x}$ is the average number of orders filled in four consecutive half-hours; R is the range between these four numbers. The calculation of control limits follows the usual formulas:

$$\bar{x} = 1200, \qquad \bar{R} = 1372$$

For $\bar{x}$:
$$\left.\begin{array}{c} \text{UCL} \\ \text{LCL} \end{array}\right\} = \bar{x} \pm A_2\bar{R}$$

$$= 1200 \pm 0.729 \times 1372$$

$$= \begin{cases} 2200 \\ 200 \end{cases}$$

For R:
$$\text{UCL} = D_4\bar{R} = 2.282 \times 1372 = 3131$$
$$\text{LCL} = D_3\bar{R} = 0$$

where the numerical values of the constants $A_2 = 0.729$, $D_3 = 0$, and $D_4 = 2.282$ come from tables to be found in standard books on the statistical control of quality.

investigate possible common causes of variation and remove them. Any success in this endeavor would raise productivity and show narrower spread between control limits, which is what he wished to see.

The cause of the wide variation, it turned out, was simple—variable backlog of orders: nothing to do for a while, then slavery for a while. The management smoothed out the backlog, production increased, mistakes decreased—everybody, including customers, happier.

> One big payoff came in the dramatic reduction in complaints from customers about delays and mistakes. Five women had been on the payroll to try to explain delays and mistakes. One woman now takes care of the calls and has half her time left over for other work. Increase of customer satisfaction was automatic. A concomitant payoff was an equally dramatic increase in production from the same equipment. Nobody worked harder, only smarter.

Decrease inventory through improvement of quality. Fig. 37 shows inventory in process month by month by month, including incoming parts ready for use. The vertical scale is millions of dollars. The inventory was $30 million at the start of the program of improvement of quality, $15 million seven months later—a decrease of $15 million. At current rates of interest, this would mean a saving of something like $6000 per day every day, including Saturdays, Sundays, and holidays.

What brought the decrease? Better quality of incoming materials, through cooperation with vendors; reduction in number of vendors. It is no longer necessary to have on hand crippling allowances for defective incoming materials. A more important factor is fewer parts waiting for rework. It is well known that rework piles up: no one wishes to tackle it.

Kanban or just in time follows as a natural result of statistical

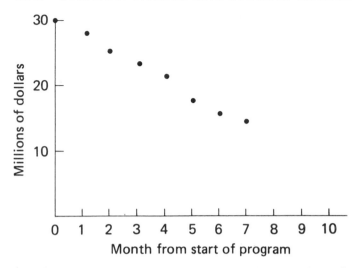

Fig. 37. Inventory in process, month by month, through seven months following the start of a program of improvement of quality, through better incoming quality and less rework throughout. (This chart came from my friend Ernest D. Schaefer of General Motors, 1982.)

control of quality, which in turn means statistical control of speed of production.

The most important figures are not on the chart. The chart in Fig. 37 is important, but figures even more important than the figures on the chart are unknown or unknowable (to quote Dr. Lloyd S. Nelson). For example, production workers in the entire plant now see improvement all along the line. They waste less time trying to hide impaired spots. Productivity goes up. Another unseen gain is that the ultimate customer receives better quality, and may bring in more customers. The gains in productivity and competitive position brought about by improvement of quality would be difficult to measure in dollars. Still another gain not mentioned is that here and there throughout the plant space that has been needed for lodgement of pieces waiting for rework, and space for the rework itself, is now vacated, ready for installation of useful pursuit.

Application to sales. A company receives reports from salesmen. Each salesman covers a territory in the Philadelphia area. What are the problems? Statistical thinking has something to offer on the problems of the system. It is possible that some salesmen are out of limits.

Now of course the company would wish to have a bigger slice of the pie for all its products. This would require action on the part of management in ways that are beyond the scope of this book, though three possibilities might be mentioned here, such as improvement in the efficiency of manufacture to permit lower prices, speedier and perhaps better and more dependable delivery, and perhaps better and more dependable quality. Would a wave of advertising help?

Salesmen No. 1 and No. 2 are having problems. No. 1 is outside the control limits compared with the group on both Product A and B; No. 2 is low only on Product B. It would be unwise to jump to the conclusion that replacements would do better in the areas served by No. 1 and No. 2. A first step for management would be to examine both the salesmen's territories and their competition. Brand loyalty to another company's product is sometimes a cause of low sales.

It is possible that the right kind of help to the low-volume salesmen could push them upward in both products. The result could be a large and immediate gain in profit in these areas, well worth much thought and effort on the part of management on how to help the low-volume salesmen in particular.

A second step would be to have a talk with them and with the district manager to try to find out what the specific causes are. The conclusion might be, of course, that the low-volume salesmen should be put into other jobs and replaced.

The company had a quota (a work standard) of $7200 per day.

Does anyone suppose that a salesman would ever report more than $7200 of business on one day?

Experiment with Red Beads to Show Total Fault in the System

In lectures, I have often made use of a simple experiment to demonstrate that it is all too easy to blame workers for faults that belong to the system.[14] Other lessons appear as well.

Apparatus: Red and white wooden beads, in box.

Total:	3750
White:	3000
Red:	750

Paddle: 50 beveled depressions, 10×5. One scoop with the paddle pulls up 50 beads. The paddle is depicted in Fig. 56 on page 459.

Advertisement on blackboard or on overhead projector, to draw volunteers from the audience:

Vacancies, 10. Applicants must be willing to work.
Educational requirements minimal.

Ten volunteers come forward. Six of them will go into apprenticeship for production. Two others are appointed as inspectors, another as chief inspector, the tenth as recorder. (Greatly overstaffed.) Names go on payroll (Fig. 38).

The foreman explains that our customer will accept only white beads; no red ones; that we do everything wrong here. We have work standards, 50 items per day, good and bad combined, for each worker. We have two inspectors, where one would be

14 I learned this demonstration from Mr. William A. Boller of the Hewlett-Packard Company, who kindly introduced it in a seminar there.

Interpretation of chart

$$\bar{\bar{x}} = \frac{238}{6\times4} = 9.92$$

$$\bar{p} = \frac{238}{6\times4\times50} = .198$$

$$\left.\begin{array}{l} \text{UCL} \\ \text{LCL} \end{array}\right| = \bar{\bar{x}} \pm 3\sqrt{\bar{\bar{x}}(1-\bar{p})}$$

$$= 9.9 \pm 3\sqrt{9.9 \times .802}$$

$$= \begin{array}{l} 18 \\ 1 \end{array}$$

5 mm wooden beads

Total 3750
Red 750
White 3000

Paddle No. 2

Record of number of defective items by operator, by day

Lot size 50, each operator per day

Name	Day				All 4
	1	2	3	4	
Neil	3	13	8	9	33
Jace	6	9	8	10	33
Tim	13	12	7	10	42
Mike	11	8	10	15	44
Tony	9	13	8	11	41
Richard	12	11	7	15	45
All 6	54	66	48	70	238
Cum $\bar{x}$	9.0	10.0	9.3	9.92	9.92

Inspectors: **Ben & Joe**

Chief inspector: **Robert** Recorder: **Wendy**

The process exhibits statistical control, with no evidence of difference in performance between operators nor between days.

The operators have put into the job all that they have to offer.

The only way to eliminate defective items in the product is to eliminate the red beads from the material used (management's responsibility).

The control limits are extended into the future as prediction of the limit of variation to expect in the near future from the same process.

Points added from San Diego to compare with prediction: same beads, same paddle, different people, same foreman.

For San Diego, $\bar{x} = 9.9$, UCL = 18, LCL = 1

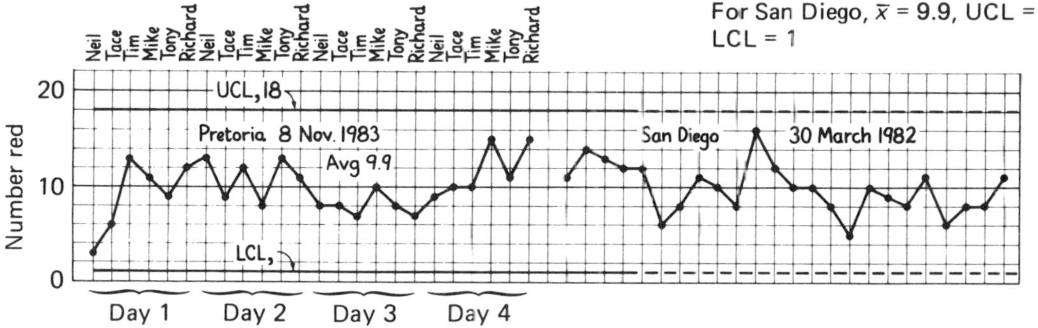

Fig. 38. Data produced by the experiment, the control chart to exhibit the results, with control limits; interpretation of the chart; and comparison with a previous experiment in San Diego 30 March 1982.

sufficient. Goal: no more than one red bead per day for anyone on the job.

There will be an apprenticeship of three days (compressed to 10 minutes) during which the foreman will explain the job. A Willing Worker will first stir the raw materials (the mixture of red and white beads). To stir the beads, pour them from one vessel to the other, at a height of 10 cm; then back again. Then scoop up a paddleful, the day's production. Carry your work to Inspector No. 1, then to Inspector No. 2. The two inspectors write down on paper, in silence, no comments, their counts of the number of red beads in the paddle. The chief inspector compares the counts of the two inspectors. When satisfied, he announces to everybody the count. The Recorder records the counts, work load by work load, in the table in Fig. 38.

> The foreman explains to everybody that the jobs of these six Willing Workers are totally dependent on their performance. The place will stay open if their performance is satisfactory.
>
> Independence of the two inspectors, the foreman explains, is the only thing that we do right here. He notes that inspection by consensus annihilates the possibility to compare inspectors, and thus destroys the possibility to discover whether a system of inspection actually exists.

All the people on the job agree that they understand what to do. All are ready.

The foreman is aghast at the number of red beads produced the first day, and pleads with the workers to study every red bead, and try not to produce any the next day. At the beginning of the second day, he can not understand why everyone did not do as well as Neil did on the first day—only 3 red beads. "If Neil can do it, anybody can do it."

Obviously, Neil at the end of the first day is man of the day, in line for a raise. Tim, on the other hand, is obviously the cause of all our problems. We all like him, but we may have to replace him.

At the end of the second day, he expresses disappointment. Even Neil let him down—3 red beads the first day, 13 the second. "What happened?" he asks. He can not understand such incredible variation lot to lot. There should be no variation, he argues. The procedures are fixed—the same for every lot. Why should one lot be different from another? He is also aghast at the low yield. No worker has met the goal of one red bead.

At the end of the third day, the management threatens to cease operations unless the fourth day brings substantial improvement. The workers are meeting their quotas of 50 per day, but the yield is too low. Their jobs are on the line.

The fourth day is no better, and the foreman tells the workers that though they have done their best, their best is not good enough. The management have decided to close the place. He is sorry, and tells them to collect their pay as they depart.

Everyone in the audience is asked to plot the chart for the number of red beads, lot by lot (Fig. 38).

Interpretation of the chart. The chart is shown in Fig. 38. One might conclude, for purposes of managing the business, that it would be wise to proceed as if the process were in statistical control, stable. Basis for this conclusion might be (a) knowledge of the intent, the instructions given by the foreman to the Willing Workers and to the inspectors, (b) confidence in the workers, (c) the table of results and the chart in Fig. 38. If the process is stable, then it would be futile to try to discover why Neil made only 3 beads the first day, and why he made 13 the second day, and why Richard made 15 the fourth day. These and all the other variations in the table arise wholly from the system, not from the people themselves.

What did we learn here?

1. The cause of the low yield was red beads in the incoming material. Get the red beads out of the system. The willing workers are totally helpless to improve quality. They will continue to make red beads so long as there are red beads in the raw material.

The experiment is stupidly simple, but it makes the point. Once people have seen it, they find red beads (sources of trouble) all over their organizations.

2. The variation between lots and between workers arose from the system itself, not from the workers.

3. The performance of anybody on any one day is useless as a basis for prediction of his performance on any other day.

4. We also perceive that mechanical sampling is not the same and that the results may be very different from sampling by use of random numbers (*vide infra*).

Prediction of variation. If we agree that the process showed statistical control good enough for use, we may extend the control limits into the future as prediction of the limits of variation of continued production. We have not in hand an additional four days, but we have data from the past to put on to the chart— same beads, same paddle, same foreman, different workers.

We repeat here an important lesson about statistical control. A process that is in statistical control, stable, furnishes a rational basis for prediction for the results of tomorrow's run.

What are the data of the experiment? Use of an experiment in industry and in science is for prediction of the results of future experiments. The data of an experiment, emphasized by Shewhart, comprise information that could assist prediction. What records need to be made about this experiment to assist prediction of future experiments?

Unfortunately, future experiments (future trials, tomorrow's production) will be affected by environmental conditions (temperature, materials, people) different from those that affect this experiment. It is only by knowledge of the subject matter, possibly aided by further experiments to cover a wider range of conditions, that one may decide, with a risk of being wrong, whether the environmental conditions of the future will be near enough the same as those of today to permit use of results in hand.

> Incidentally, the risk of being wrong in a prediction can not be stated in terms of probability, contrary to some textbooks and teaching. Empirical evidence is never complete.[15]

We recorded here the date and time, the names of the willing workers, the name of the chief inspector, a description of the beads, identification of the paddle (No. 2). What else might be important?

As the six hourly workers appear to form a statistical system (none beyond the control limits), we could perhaps hereafter, in another experiment, omit from the record their names. The paddle, however, is important (next section).

Other data of the experiment would be the foreman and his zeal to enforce the rule of thorough mixing of the raw materials (beads).

Cumulated average. Question: As 20 per cent of the beads in the box are red, what do you think would be the cumulated average, the statistical limit, as we continue to produce lots by the same process over many days?

The answer that comes forth spontaneously from the audience is that it must be 10 because 10 is 20 per cent of 50, the size of a lot. Wrong.

We have no basis for such a statement. As a matter of fact, the cumulated average for paddle No. 2 over many experiments in

15 C. I. Lewis, *Mind and the World-Order* (Scribner's, 1929; Dover, 1956), p. 283.

the past has settled down to 9.4 red beads per lot of 50. Paddle No. 1, used for 30 years, shows an average of 11.3.

The paddle is an important piece of information about the process. Would the reader have thought so prior to these figures?

The same question can be stated in a different way: Tell me some reasons why we could not expect the cumulated average to be 10. Answers: (1) Red pigment is different to the eye from white pigment. It feels different to the fingers, and obviously to the paddle. (2) The sizes of red and white beads may be different. Their weights may be different. Red beads are made by dipping white ones into red pigment, or is it the other way around?

The difference between the accumulated $\bar{r}$ and 10 is often alluded to by people in the audience as bias. No, this difference is not bias. It is the difference between two methods of selection: (1) mechanical sampling, used here; (2) selection by random numbers.[16] (See the paragraph on the next page about mechanical sampling.)

Exercise 1. Show that the spread of the control limits for the number of white beads, lot by lot, would be identical with the spread of the control limits for the red beads, already calculated. Show further that we have already plotted a control chart for the white beads. We only need to reverse the vertical scale; replace 0 by 50, 10 by 40, 20 by 30, 30 by 20, 40 by 10, 50 by 0. The control limits for the white beads will then stay right in place, 49 for the upper limit and 33 for the lower limit.

Exercise 2. Before any data were collected, it was a 50:50 bet that Richard would make more defective items in the four days than Tim would make. Afterward, there was no doubt about it. Suppose that the experiment is to be continued through another four days. Assume that the differences between the six operators

16 W. Edwards Deming, *Sample Design in Business Research* (Wiley, 1960), Ch. 5.

continue to show good statistical control. There is a 50:50 chance that the two workers will reverse themselves on the second four days. Show that the chance is 50:50 that the cumulated number of defective items for Richard will again exceed those made by Tim over all eight days.

Sampling by use of random numbers. If we were to form lots by use of random numbers, then the cumulated average, the statistical limit of $\bar{x}$, would be 10. The reason is that the random numbers pay no attention to color, nor to size, nor to any other physical characteristic of beads, paddle, or employee. Statistical theory (theory of probability) as taught in the books for the theory of sampling and theory of distributions applies in the use of random numbers, but not in experiences of life. Once statistical control is established, then a distribution exists, and is predictable.

Mechanical sampling will distort the process average. It is a fact that the cumulated average of proportion defective calculated from inspection of samples drawn by inspectors, however conscientious they be, may not be a good approximation to the process average. Samples of items for inspection may be selected by a conscientious inspector from top, bottom, and middle of the lot in an attempt to get a good cross-section of the lot, but there can be no assurance that his selection will approximate use of random numbers. The only safe plan is use of random numbers for selection of items from a lot, but it must be admitted that use of random numbers will in many cases not be practicable. The only way to eliminate possible distortion created by mechanical sampling is to carry out 100 per cent inspection of a random selection of lots, which may of course be all lots. (Contributed by Mr. Dave West in a seminar held in Pretoria in June 1982.)

A change in the method of selection of samples, when mechanical selection or judgment selection is used, could well throw a point out of control. This is an artifact that one should keep in mind in the interpretation of a chart. (Contributed also by Mr. Dave West.)

Further Remarks on Statistical Control

Statistical control does not imply absence of defective items. Statistical control is a state of random variation, stable in the sense that the limits of variation are predictable. A process may be in statistical control, yet produce defective items. In fact, it could produce a high proportion of defective items. We saw this in the experiment with the red and white beads.

Statistical control of a process is not an end in itself. Once statistical control is established, serious work to improve quality and economy of production can commence.

Intervention to change the system (to get rid of the red beads in the system) may be simple, or it may be complex and lengthy. A change in the average may be simple. It may require long experimentation (recall the example with the coated paper in Ch. 1). Reduction in spread is usually more difficult than change in level. Every problem is different from every other, and no general rule should be attempted. This is the task for the engineers on the job to work on.

Study of a mixture may obscure chance to improve. Let us think of three production lines, feeding their output into one channel. I like to think of three streams feeding into a river, the mixture (Fig. 39). The mixture is the final product. If the three production lines are in statistical control, the mixture in the channel will also be in statistical control, even though the means of the three separate production lines be wide apart.

In fact, if the material from the three production lines is thoroughly mixed, the variance of the mixture

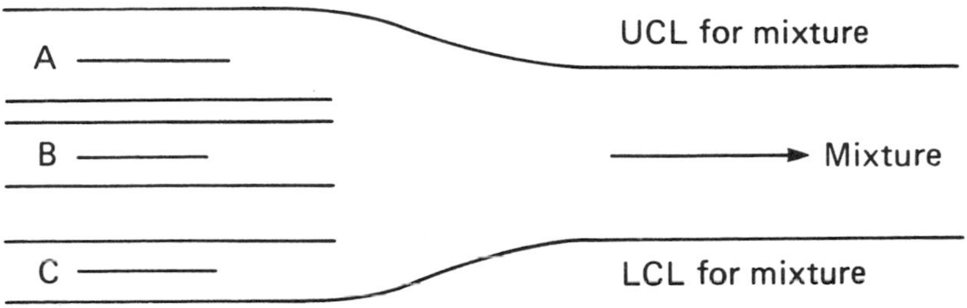

Fig. 39. Product comes in from three sources, all three in statistical control. The mixture from the three sources shows statistical control, but with wide spread.

will be the total variance between items in all three production lines. Students of statistics will recognize the formula

$$\sigma^2 = \sigma_b{}^2 + \sigma_w{}^2$$

where σ^2 is the variance between items in the mixture, $\sigma_b{}^2$ is the variance between the means of the three production lines, and $\sigma_w{}^2$ is the average variance between items within the separate three production lines.

The first step would be to decrease the variance of source A. Independently, try to bring the three streams to the same level.

In fact, whether the mixture gives a problem or not, it is good advice to study the sources. Bring them to the same level; reduce the variation of every one, especially those that show wide variation. Start this study by bringing every source into statistical control.

Search upstream provides powerful leverage toward improvement of a mixture. (William W. Scherkenbach.)

Even though the combined work of a group may be in pretty good statistical control, control charts for individuals may discover that one or two or more people are in need of more training or transfer. (See the example on p. 384.)

Nine grinding machines put the finishing touches on front

axles. The mixture from the nine machines contained 3 per cent defectives on the average. Data from the individual machines showed that Machines Nos. 2 and 3 were making the defectives, being in need of fine-tuning. When these two machines had the benefit of meticulous care, defective output of the battery of nine machines dropped to zero. Without data on the individual machines, all nine, improvement of the process would not have been accomplished.

In Fig. 20 on p. 258 the mixture is all 11 welders. Study of the 11 welders separately showed that No. 6 was producing more than his share of faults.

In an example of looping, furnished to me by Professor David S. Chambers, the combined output of 47 loopers was in reasonably good statistical control at 4.8 per cent downgraded and scrapped. Individual charts for everybody disclosed the fact that some of the women were making far more than their share of the faults. (Details in the next chapter, p. 380.)

Examples of Costly Misunderstanding[17]

Example 1. Action line placed on chart by judgment, not calculated. As we have learned, the control limits on a control chart tell what to expect from the process as it is, not what we wish it to be. Suppose that a worker draws a line on a chart that shows day by day the fraction defective. He draws a line at (e.g.) 4 per cent, which seems to him to be a reasonable goal. He showed me a point well above the line. Here, he said, was a point out of control.

"Where are your calculations for the control limit?" I asked. "We don't make calculations; we just place the line where we think it ought to be."

Some textbooks woefully mislead the reader by setting control

---

7 I thank Barbara Kimball of Cutter Laboratories, Los Angeles, for pointing out to me this error in a number of books. I have omitted these books from the titles shown at the end of this chapter.

limits based on specifications or on other requirements. One book sets control limits based on an OC-curve (not treated here). All these misunderstandings about control limits increase costs and fail to achieve quality.

Such placement of a line, as substitute for a control limit, leads to overadjustment or to underadjustment, and perpetuates whatever troubles exist. As a sad comment, people discard the chart, misused in this manner, with the comment that "quality control does not work here."

No wonder. They never tried it.

Specification limits should never be shown on a control chart.

A recent book on the statistical control of quality makes a similar mistake, stating that the customer's requirements form a basis for calculation of control limits. Such advice devastates the beginner, misleads him forever.

> Again, teaching of beginners should be done by a master, not by a hack.

Example 2. Same fault: action limit set by manufacturer's rating. It is easier than one might suppose to fall into the trap of using judgment for an action limit. I quote here a letter received from the vice-president of a company, pleased with the results of his efforts, but unaware that his methods are robbing him of quality and productivity that might be achieved with the same equipment and same people, given a better chance to exhibit their abilities. The manufacturer of the equipment might also be pleased to learn that his equipment might beat his claims, if given a chance. Here is the letter:

> In the last quarter of 1980, we reorganized and hired a consultant to teach and train through formal instruction and floor application the principles of effective supervision. We combined numerous jobs in both our salaried and hourly ranks. All standards were eliminated from our production people and we

set floor standards based on the maximum speed of the equipment as specified by the manufacturer. When 100 per cent is not achieved, the floor supervisor has to identify reasons for performance less than maximum. Our maintenance, technical, and service personnel work on correcting the identified problems.

Wrong way. His experts, using the manufacturer's claim for a control limit (action limit), were confusing special causes with common causes, guaranteeing trouble forever.

A wiser procedure would be to get statistical control of the machine, under the circumstances in place. Its performance might turn out to be 90 per cent of the maximum speed as specified by the manufacturer, or 100 per cent, or 110 per cent. The next step would be continual improvement of the machine and use thereof.

Example 3. So obvious, so fruitless. The vice-president of a huge concern told me that he has a strict schedule of inspection of final product. To my question about how they use the data came the answer: "The data are in the computer. The computer provides a record and description of every defect found. *Our engineers never stop* till they find the cause of every defect."

Why was it that the level of defective tubes had stayed relatively stable, around $4\frac{1}{2}$ to $5\frac{1}{2}$ per cent, for two years? The engineers were confusing common causes with special causes. Every fault was to them a special cause, to track down, discover, and eliminate. They were trying to find the causes of ups and downs in a stable system, making things worse, defeating their purpose. (See the pronouncements of Lloyd S. Nelson, p. 20.)

To the customer, the manufacturer's efforts were appealing. It appears to the customer that the manufacturer was conscientious, making every effort to reduce defective tubes in the future. This is so: he was. Unfortunately, these efforts were misdirected, and were obviously not effective. How would either one of them know?

Apparent exceptions arise from the circumstances wherein defective items occur with regularity. Regularity of appearance of a defective item should be regarded as a pattern, which signifies lack of statistical control. The same advice holds where there is only a single possible sporadic important cause of defective items. Study of defective items in such cases may indicate the cause of trouble.

Example 4. I saw in a factory that makes tires the defective tires of the day, lined up for the engineers to investigate. More of the same thing that we saw in Example 3: same guaranteed continuation of trouble.

Example 5. Wrong use of distribution: more on the unmanned computer. Ingots of copper are extruded, red hot and sputtering. A machine cuts off ingots, the desired weight being 326 kg. Every ingot is weighed automatically, and the data go into the computer.

The next step is electrolytic deposition of copper, the ingots forming the anode. An ingot that is light wastes space in the electrolytic bath while the heavy ones finish.

The operator's job, seeing that the weight of an ingot is low, is to adjust his cutoff to increase the weight of the next ingot, and to take the reverse action for an ingot that is overweight. The contrivance for automatic weighing plots at the end of the day a distribution of the weights of the ingots produced. The operator has in front of him every morning the distribution of weights produced the day before (Fig. 40)—an example of the unmanned computer.

What is the purpose of the histogram? I asked.

This is our system of quality control. It shows the operator how he is doing so that he can improve, was the answer.

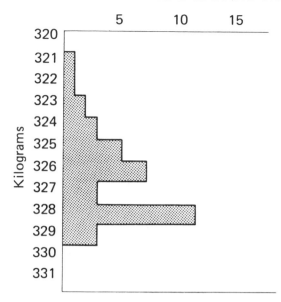

Fig. 40. Histogram of yesterday's production, constructed by automatic weighing and recording of every bar. The histogram shows the operator how he performed yesterday, but is no help to him toward achieving a narrower distribution about the desired average weight. The computer also printed the mean of the distribution, its standard deviation, skewness, and fourth moment coefficient, all of which were totally useless to the operator.

How long have you had the problem of nonuniform weights? I asked.

Ever since we started.

The fact is that the operator, by adjusting the machine up or down at every bar, was working against himself, widening the variance of weights. He was following Rule 2 or Rule 3 or Rule 4 (p. 329), making things worse, only doing his best. How could he know? The distribution in Fig. 40 is totally useless, a source of frustration.

What is wrong with the use of the distribution in Fig. 40? This distribution makes no distinction between (a) causes that arise from the system and (b) causes that the operator could correct. It thus helps the operator not at all. It only frustrates him. A control chart would make the necessary distinction, and thus help the operator.

The engineer in charge explained to me that he does not need the statistical control of quality here, because he has 100 per cent inspection and a record of the weight of every ingot. The operator only needs to adjust the machine after every ingot is weighed. The engineer knew all about the job except what was important. How could he know?

An additional interesting statistical problem arises in consideration of the best (most profitable) weight above the mean beyond which to cut off the excess weight from an ingot. This problem is fairly straightforward, but we do not pursue it here. It would involve the distribution of weights, the cost of cutting copper off an ingot of excess weight, and the cost of extending the electrolytic process a sufficient number of minutes to finish up the heavy ingots in the electrolytic bath.

I have seen pie diagrams on the floor of a laboratory that show everybody the number of mistakes by type that they made last week—same fault, for the same reasons. The supposition of the management was that the people that work there can correct all the mistakes—that is, do perfect work, if they only knew that they were making mistakes and would only try hard enough to do better.

Example 6. *Loss from index of performance.* Engineers in a company engaged in hauling general freight had developed so-called standards by which to measure the performance of the managers of their 70 terminals. Any manager that falls below 100 per cent must be delinquent in some way. Anyone above 100 per cent is doing his job.

This is the same mistake as the manager that examines only defective product in an effort to improve future product. What the management needs to investigate is the distribution of the

indexes. Does the distribution form a system, or are there outliers? Study of correlation of performance with type of business
handled might disclose reasons for what appears to be extra
good performance or extra poor performance. For example,
high ratio of inbound freight to outbound freight might explain
why some terminals show poor performance on profit. Thus,
much more freight moves into most points in Florida than moves
out: railway cars and trucks come north empty. The terminal
manager is helpless against this ratio.

What the management was doing was to perpetuate their
problems.

Example 7. Wrong procedure in early stage of production. This
example repeats a lesson already learned, but no harm will be
done if we go through it again.

Measurements on 10, 30, 40, or 100 pieces are examined to
learn whether the process will do the job. The next step (wrong)
is to examine the parts that fail, to try to discover the source of
the trouble.

This is an example of failure of analysis of failure. A better
procedure is to use statistical methods for a statistical problem,
as follows:

1. Use the measurements to plot a run chart or other statistical chart (such as $\bar{x}$- or R-chart if there are enough data) in order
of production to discover whether the process is in statistical
control.

2. If the chart indicates reasonably good statistical control,
one may conclude that the defective parts were made by the same
system that made the good ones. Only a change in the system can
reduce the number of defective parts in the future. This might be
a change in design of the part, or it might be a change in the
method of manufacture. One of the first steps would be to
examine the system of measurement to see whether it is sufficiently standardized and in statistical control.

A rational procedure with fewer than 15 or 20 pieces may well lead to difficulty in a logical answer to the question about the capability of the process. A smaller number sometimes nevertheless leads to a firm conclusion. Thus, if the entire initial run of 6 or 7 pieces all fail, one could conclude that the process is incapable of meeting the specifications, or that the system of measurement is out of order, or that the specifications should be relaxed.

Seven or eight pieces, all showing a trend upward or downward, no reversal, would indicate pretty definitely that something is wrong with the process, or with the system of measurement.

There is information in variation. If you stop at five or six measurements, you shut off most of the possibility to learn from the variation that more measurements would provide. (This paragraph comes from a conversation with Lloyd S. Nelson, 7 June 1984.)

3. If the chart shows lack of statistical control, then a search for special causes is the next step. Again, it would be wise to examine also the system of measurement. First, look for errors in the data.

Example 8. I complained to the postmaster in Washington about mistakes in mail that came to my address. Everyone in the neighborhood, including me, it seemed, received envelopes addressed to other people. As I redelivered an envelope to an address not far away, I was met at the door by a woman just on her way out with an envelope in her hand addressed to me. An even trade. My complaint to the postmaster brought the following reply:

Mistakes like the ones you point out are a source of irritation to us in the postal system, as they must be to you. This problem has been going on for years. We assure you that every mistake like the one that you mentioned is brought to the attention of the carrier at fault.

"Going on for years," is a confession that the fault lay in the system. The trouble was apparently not localized by neighborhood, nor in time, nor was it specific to any one carrier. It will continue till the system undergoes fundamental revision to reduce the possibility of mistakes like those of my complaint. Meanwhile, the management blames the carrier. My complaint only caused hardship on the carrier.

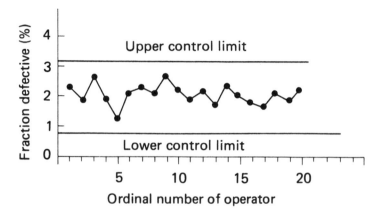

Fig. 41. Fraction defective produced by each of 20 operators. The points are in order of position. (All produced about the same number of items.)

Computation of control limits:

$n = 1225$, average production per man per month

$$\left.\begin{array}{c} \text{UCL} \\ \text{LCL} \end{array}\right\} = 0.02 \pm 3\sqrt{\bar{p}\bar{q}/n} \quad (\text{where } \bar{q} = 1 - \bar{p})$$

$$= 0.02 \pm 3\sqrt{0.02 \times 0.98/1225}$$
$$= 0.02 \pm 0.012$$
$$= \begin{cases} 0.032 \\ 0.008 \end{cases}$$

Further Applications

Use of chart to measure combined faults of the system. Fig. 41 shows the fraction defective made by 20 production workers that performed essentially the same operation last month. It shows clearly that:

1. The output of the 20 production workers constitutes a stable, definable process, with a process capability.
2. The capability of the process is 2 per cent defective.

The production workers have put into their jobs all that they have to offer. Improvement can come only from management, whose duty is now clear: find and remove (or reduce so far as practicable) some of the common or environmental causes of trouble, or accept the inevitable continuation of 2 per cent defective.

An example of benefit from studying the system and changing it.

From the *Daily News*, Budapest, 29 May 1980.

Revolution in Management

LONDON (AP)—London's famous red buses scored a big productivity increase in the last six months and officials say that a "revolution in management" is the main reason.

London Transport, which runs the publicly owned system, attributes the improvement to the end of central control. The 5500 buses on 300 routes were split into eight districts, each responsible for finances, repairs and complaints.

Scheduled mileage—the number of

miles covered by buses on the road—
increased by 10 per cent.

Waiting time at bus stops has been
slashed and the number of buses off
the road and waiting for repairs was
cut from more than 500 to 150.

The buses now carry labels naming
a district official to whom passengers
can complain.

Next day in the same newspaper appeared an account of a
speech by the First Secretary of Hungary, the Honorable János
Kádár, with the heading:

Living Standards Dependent on Work-Performance
Requirements of quality have to be
raised. Proper work-performance
must be demanded from everyone.

The Honorable The First Secretary of Hungary had the right
idea—better living depends on greater production. Top management in Hungary attended my lectures and learned about their
responsibilities. They also learned not to expect much improvement in production from efforts of the work force, unaided by
management.

People are part of the system; they need help. In spite of the fact
that management is responsible for the system, or for lack of the
system, I find in my experience that few people in industry know
what constitutes a system. Many people think of machinery and
data processing when I mention system. Few of them know that
recruitment, training, supervision, and aids to production
workers are part of the system. Who else could be responsible for
these activities?

A man came from London. He was having problems, mainly in his billing department. His cash was low for two reasons: (1) He was behind in sending out monthly bills, mainly to big customers. His billing department had made so many mistakes in the past, especially to big customers, that he was afraid to send bills to them without many verifications. (2) Customers, especially big ones, were refusing to pay their bills for the last two or three months until errors in previous bills were cleared up.

He declared that the cause of these problems was careless work in his billing department—many mistakes between shipment of goods and the invoice:

1. Wrong item shipped: he must pay the transportation both ways. Customer impatient.
2. Item shipped to wrong address: transportation to pay both ways. Customer impatient.
3. Invoice incorrect, such as no allowance for discount for cumulated number of items purchased.

These errors created a multitude of debits and credits with mistakes. Bills for transportation mounted. He did not mention getting sued for loss of profit for sending the wrong goods to a store for the Christmas season, but he had every other kind of problem. He claimed that the people that worked for him were the worst that anyone could pull together in London.

He could borrow money from the bank: he was a good risk, in spite of his problems. But to pay interest (18 per cent at that time) on what people owe you is not the way to get ahead.

All these problems would disappear, he said, when his new data-processing machinery goes into operation, two years from now. Meanwhile, what can be done?

I assured him that he would encounter a whole new set of problems when his new data-processing machinery starts up, unless he would take steps:

1. To simplify the system of charges for his product. It

is too complicated. For example, he should eliminate rebate for cumulated purchases of a large
quantity over a stated period (six months).

2. To provide better training and continual retraining. What do you know about the frequency of certain important errors? Where do they occur? What
is the cause? Which workers are not part of the system? He had no answers to any of these questions.
He was a manager.

It had never occurred to him that his people are part of the system, and that he is responsible for them and for answers to all
these questions. System, to him, meant hardware, locations of
warehouses, finance, etc. He went away an enlightened man,
with a promise to engage a statistician in London to help him.

Five months later he returned, delighted. The most important
mistake had tumbled from 39 to 6 per cent, the second from 27 to
4 per cent. He was on the way to further reduction.

Limited Selection of Text Material

The serious reader will take steps to improve his knowledge
about variation and its meaning. Nothing takes the place of a
good teacher.

RECOMMENDED

American National Standards Institute, *Guides for Quality Control.*
(Identified as A.S.Q.C. B1 and B2, published by the American
National Standards Institute, 1430 Broadway, New York 10018.)

Kaoru Ishikawa, *Guide to Quality Control,* Asian Productivity Organization, 1976. Available from Unipub, P.O. Box 433, Murray Hill
Station, New York 10157.

What Is Total Quality Control? Prentice-Hall, 1985.

Nancy R. Mann, *The Keys to Excellence: The Story of the Deming Philosophy,* Prestwick Books, Los Angeles, 1985.

William W. Scherkenbach, *The Deming Route to Quality and Productivity,* CEEP Press, The George Washington University, Washington 20052, 1986.

Walter A. Shewhart, *Economic Control of Quality of Manufactured Product*, Van Nostrand, 1931; repr. ed., American Society for Quality Control, 1980.

Statistical Method from the Viewpoint of Quality Control, Graduate School, Department of Agriculture, Washington, 1939; repr. ed., Dover, 1986.

Western Electric Company, Bonnie B. Small, Chairman of the Writing Committee, *Statistical Quality Control Handbook*, Indianapolis, 1956. Available from AT&T Customer Information Center (specify Code 700-444), P.O. Box 19901, Indianapolis 46219.

There are many other books on so-called quality control. Each book has something good in it, and nearly every author is a friend and colleague of mine. Most of the books nevertheless contain bear traps, such as reject limits, modified control limits, areas under the normal curve, acceptance sampling. One book sets control limits based on an OC-curve (not treated here). Another sets control limits to match specifications. Some books teach that use of a control chart is test of hypothesis: the process is in control, or it is not. Such errors may derail self-study.

The student should also avoid passages in books that treat confidence intervals and tests of significance, as such calculations have no application in analytic problems in science and industry. (See the section "Poor teaching of statistical methods in industry," p. 131.)

FOR STUDY IN BASIC STATISTICS AND METHODS

A. Hald, *Statistical Theory with Engineering Applications*, Wiley, 1952.

Harry H. Ku et al., *The Measurement Process*, National Bureau of Standards, Special Publication No. 300, U.S. Government Printing Office, Washington 20402, 1969.

Ernest J. Kurnow, Gerald J. Glasser, and Fred R. Ottman, *Statistics for Business Decisions*, Irwin, 1959.

Eugene H. Mac Niece, *Industrial Specifications*, Wiley, 1953.

Alexander M. Mood, *Introduction to the Theory of Statistics*, McGraw-Hill, 1950.

Frederick Mosteller and John W. Tukey, *Data Analysis and Regression*, Addison-Wesley, 1977.

Ellis R. Ott, *Process Quality Control*, McGraw-Hill, 1975.

L. H. C. Tippett, *The Methods of Statistics*, Wiley, 1952.
Statistics, Oxford University Press, 1944.

John W. Tukey, *Exploratory Data Analysis*, Addison-Wesley, 1977.

W. Allen Wallis and Harry V. Roberts, *Statistics: A New Approach*, Free Press, 1956.

W. J. Youden, *Experimentation and Measurement*, National Science Teachers Association, Washington, 1962. Also, *Statistical Methods for Chemists*, Wiley, 1951.

12

More Examples of
Improvement Downstream

> For in much wisdom is great grief; and he that increaseth knowledge increaseth sorrow.—Ecclesiastes 1:18.

Aim of this chapter. We have already seen a number of examples of improvement of the system downstream. These examples were all unbelievably simple. Many more examples will appear in later chapters. The aim of this chapter is to reemphasize that improvement of the system, downstream or upstream, is the responsibility of management to perceive and to act on.

> *Remark.* It would be incorrect to suppose that improvement of a system is always so stupidly simple as the illustrations shown in this chapter and in other parts of this book. Improvement may require simultaneous tests of two or more factors, by appropriate statistical design. Tests one at a time run the risk of failure to observe interaction between the two factors. A common example is alcohol and an antidepressant taken simultaneously. The effect may be dangerous expansion of the effect of both the alcohol and the antidepressant. Another common example is soap and detergent used together: they may nearly annihilate each other.

Example 1. This example illustrates how simple changes in the system could virtually eliminate the possibility of defective items.

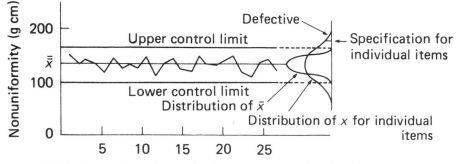

Fig. 42. Chart for $\bar{x}$ for test of uniformity of wheels turned out by a production worker. The distribution of the non-uniformity test for the individual wheels will be centered at $\bar{\bar{x}}$. Its range will be $\sqrt{3} = 1.73$ times the distance between the control limits for $\bar{x}$.

The ordinates in Fig. 42 are the means ($\bar{x}$) of samples of $n = 3$ for tests of uniformity of finished wheels. The test is the running balance of the wheel. Observations based on study of the chart:[1]

1. The production worker is in a state of control with respect to his own work (which is the only work that he is responsible for). No point falls outside the control limits.

2. He is under the handicap of the system. He can not beat the system and the capability of his process: he will once in a while produce a defective wheel, even though he is a good worker and in a state of control.

3. He is meeting the requirements of his job. He can do no more. He has nothing further to offer.

4. The main trouble lies in the system.

Action by the supervisor (incoming materials better adapted to the job; better maintenance and more careful setting) of this production line lowered the entire chart and distribution so far

1 From my paper "On some statistical aids to economic production," *Interfaces* 5 (August 1975): 1–15.

that no wheels thereafter fell above the upper specification: no more defective wheels.

Example 2. The second example deals with a service industry, motor freight. Drivers of trucks pick up shipments and bring them into a terminal for reload and onward movement. Other drivers deliver. A large company in motor freight may have anywhere from 10 to 40 terminals in or near large cities. There is a long chain of operations between the request of a shipper to the carrier (usually by telephone) to come and pick up a shipment, and placement of the shipment on the platform of the carrier, ready for reload and line haul to the terminal that serves the destination of the shipment. Every operation offers a chance for the driver to make a mistake. The accompanying table shows six types of mistakes, plus all others. Although the frequency of mistakes is low, the total loss is substantial.

In mistake No. 1, the driver signs the shipping order for (e.g.) 10 cartons, but someone else finds, later on in the chain of operations, that there are only 9 cartons—one carton missing. Where is it? There may have been only 9 cartons in the first place; the shipping order was written incorrectly; or, more usual, the driver left one carton on the shipper's premises. Let us list some of the sources of loss from mistake No. 1:

1. It costs about $25 to search the platform for the missing carton, or to find the truck (by now out on the road) and to search it.
2. It costs $15 on the average to send a driver back to the shipper to pick up the missing carton.
3. It costs $10 to segregate and hold the 9 cartons for the duration of the search.
4. If the carrier does not find the carton, then the shipper may legitimately put in a claim for it. The carrier is responsible for the 10th carton. Its value may be anywhere from $10 to $1000 or more.

It is obvious that mistake No. 1 may be costly. Any one of the 7 mistakes will on the average lead to a loss of $50. There were a total of 617 mistakes on the record, and they caused a loss of $31,000 for claims alone. Multiplied by 20, for 20 terminals, the total loss from the 7 mistakes was $620,000. (This amount is a minimum. It does not include the expenses of searches nor administration.)

Type of mistake	Description
1	Short on pickup
2	Over on pickup
3	Failure to call in (by telephone) on over, short, and damaged cartons on delivery
4	Incomplete bill of lading
5	Improperly marked cartons
6	Incomplete signature on delivery receipt
7	Other

There were 150 drivers that worked all year long. Fig. 43 shows the distribution of the 150 drivers by number of mistakes, all 7 mistakes combined.

We postulate the following mechanism, which will distribute errors at random to drivers. We imagine a huge bowl of black and white beads, thoroughly mixed. Each driver scoops up a sample of 1000 or more (the number of trips that an average driver makes in a year) and returns the beads to the bowl for more mixing. The total number of mistakes in Fig. 43 is 617, and there were 150 drivers. An estimate of the mean number of mistakes per driver would be

$$\bar{x} = \frac{617}{150} = 4.1$$

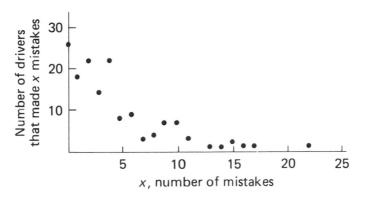

Fig. 43. The distribution of drivers by number of mistakes, all 7 errors combined.

Upper and lower limits may be calculated as

$$4.1 + 3\sqrt{4.1} = 11 \quad \text{(upper limit)}$$

and

$$4.1 - 3\sqrt{4.1} \text{ gives } 0 \quad \text{(lower limit)}$$

We interpret the upper limit to mean that a driver that made more than 11 mistakes in the year is not part of the system. He contributes more than his share. He is a special cause of loss.

There are two groups of drivers:

A. Drivers that made more than 11 mistakes
B. Drivers that made 11 mistakes or fewer

What have we learned from this simple statistical model?

1. The seven drivers with more than 11 mistakes accounted for 112/617 or 18 per cent of the mistakes.
2. Drivers that made fewer than 11 mistakes measure the losses that arise from the system itself. They make the system what it is. They account for $100 - 18 = 82$ per cent of the mistakes.

No problem with people is simple. It would be wise for the management to defer criticism of Group A, to determine first whether these drivers worked unusually difficult routes or extra-long routes. As it turned out, they had.

Here we encounter an important lesson in administration. This company had been sending a letter to a driver at every mistake. It made no difference whether this was the one mistake of the year for this driver, or the 15th: the letter was exactly the same. A letter sent to a driver in Group B is demoralizing: the driver's interpretation thereof is that he is blamed for faults of the system.

One might pause here in passing to ask a question: what does the driver who has already received 15 warnings, all alike, think of the management?

And what about a driver that made only one or two mistakes during the period of study, and who may have made none or only one during the preceding six months? He receives the same letter as the man that has already made 15 mistakes during the period of study. What does he think of the management?

> A man in one of my seminars related the fact that any policeman in his home city receives for every complaint against him the same letter, no matter whether this was the first complaint in years or the 10th within a few weeks. Good management?

Customers of the carrier would, I think, be eager to work with the carrier to reduce mistakes if they had any idea of what to do. A mistake costs the customer more than it costs the carrier. Here was my suggestion.

> Bill, you have two snoopers driving around to follow your drivers and to make notes. They record the routes that your drivers take, how much time they spend trying to find a space to park a truck in, time

spent for coffee. What you could do is to give these two snoopers another job, one that would be useful. Some docks are open, not covered. A driver must try to read shipping orders in the wind and rain and snow and under poor light. Let these two men call on customers to persuade them to cover their docks, to put lights on the dock. Customers would, I think, on suggestion, separate one shipment from another, either by tape or space or by a chalk line on the floor, so that drivers could pick up a whole shipment and not leave part of it behind, and not haul away part of another shipment. Customers would, I think, take more care on legibility of shipping orders.

Example 3. A small manufacturer of shoes was having trouble with his sewing machines, rent of which was costly. The operators were spending a lot of their time rethreading the machines, a serious loss.

The key observation was that the trouble was common to all machines and to all operators. The obvious conclusion was that the trouble, whatever it was, was common, environmental, affecting all machines and all operators. A few tests showed that it was the thread that caused the trouble. The owner of the shop had been purchasing poor thread at bargain prices. The loss of machine-time had cost him hundreds of times the difference between good thread and what he had been buying. Bargain prices for thread turned out to be a costly snare.

This was an example of getting rooked by the lowest bidder and being taken in by price alone without regard to quality or performance.

Better thread eliminated the problem. Only management could make the change. The operators could not go out and buy better thread, even if they had known where the trouble lay. They work in the system. The thread was part of the system.

Prior to the simple investigation that found the cause,

pedestrian but effective, the owner had supposed that his troubles all came from inexperience and carelessness of the operators.

Example 4. *Number of mechanics needed in the tool room.* The job of the tool room is to make machines (especially prototypes), to modify existing equipment, and to take care of emergencies from breakdown of equipment in use anywhere in the whole plant. The foreman was sometimes caught short with not enough mechanics to take care of emergencies. On other days, there were few emergencies, and his people could devote a lot of effort to development.

About how many emergencies occur per day, on the average?

He had no figures, but a possible number could be 36, perhaps 40.

On the supposition that breakdowns are independent, not chain reactions, the number of breakdowns day by day will form a Poisson distribution. If the average number is 36, the standard deviation of this distribution will be $\sqrt{36} = 6$.

$$36 + 3\sqrt{36} = 54$$

It might thus be reasonable to prepare for a maximum of 54 emergencies. Plots to accumulate further experience will confirm or modify this expectation.

If the average number of breakdowns per day were 40, he would need to prepare for 58 emergencies, not 54. The upper limit is sensitive to the average and to cycles.

If he is willing to get caught short only now and then, possibly once in two months, he could use the upper 2-sigma limit, which would be

$$36 + 2\sqrt{36} = 48$$

This limit is also sensitive to the average and to trends and should be increased by 4 if the average were 40, not 36.

The next step would be to compile figures day by day for a few

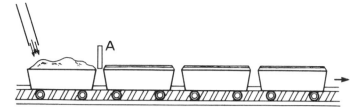

Fig. 44. Railway cars, as they pass by, are loaded with hot iron ore pellets. The plate at A smooths out the mountains and valleys in the top surface of the pellets as the loaded cars move by it. The result is improved uniformity and greater tonnage per car. Heavy loads are desirable; also uniformity in weight. These requirements were difficult to achieve prior to installation of the strong steel plate at A.

weeks, and plot a run chart to examine the distribution for randomness.

Example 5. Pellets of iron ore are loaded into railway cars. The cars move past the loader at about 4 mph.

Desired: more uniform loads (net tons per car).

A loader manipulates the mechanism for loading the cars, trying to achieve uniformity of weight. Uniformity is desirable for several reasons. It is feasible, for a customer that orders some large numbers of cars such as 100 or more in a week, to compute the total weight of the order, and the cost of transportation, by use of a sample of 10 or 15 cars. Use of the sample decreases the cost of weighing the cars, and it also speeds up the movement of cars in the yards. The capacity of every car should be utilized, but not overdone. Pellets piled too high in a car may fall off and be lost as the train goes around a curve. Loss of half a metric ton of pellets in this way from a car was not unusual.

Then a solution was found (Fig. 44). A heavy horizontal steel beam (A in Fig. 44) smoothed off the loads at the right level. Why had not the engineers thought of this before? They had supposed that the loader, if she tried hard enough, could shrink the variation. Their thoughts had not before turned to the possibility that the system could be changed.

Example 6. Improved production of stockings. Here, the management looked ahead and foresaw that costs would overtake revenue in the near future and the company would move into the nonprofit category unless something were done soon.[2] Any plan that would increase the proportion of first grade of stocking would increase net revenue and put the company into better competitive position, even at current volume. There were other reasons to improve production: Workers were paid by the piece, with a penalty of two pieces for every bad piece made, and the company had to pay the difference between a worker's pay for the week and the minimum wage, if she fell below it. Any increase in productivity would help the worker as well as the company. Initial steps:

1. The big step was that the manager saw trouble ahead, and sought help from a statistician (David S. Chambers).
2. The second step was indoctrination of the management.
3. Then, on advice of Professor Chambers, the company sent 20 supervisors to a 10-week course at the University of Tennessee, $2\frac{1}{2}$ hours per week.

   Incidentally, this course gave 20 supervisors their first chance to get acquainted and to talk about their problems.

4. After the training sessions were finished, the supervisors were asked by the management to try to

---

2 I have borrowed this example from an unpublished paper written by my friend David S. Chambers.

make some applications of the principles learned and to prepare a report on the results achieved.

The report was presented at one of the weekly supervisors' meetings which had been initiated during the training period. Management wished these meetings to be a forum for exchange of ideas between the operating personnel, and they were successful. It was the first indication to supervisors that their work was important to the management and to the plant. They developed teamwork and interest that had been totally lacking heretofore. This group was, in effect, a QC-Circle composed of supervisors, a hitherto untapped resource.

5. After several meetings of supervisors had been held, the consultant recommended, as a start, a study of the problems of the looping department. The main reason for choice of this department was that (1) there appeared to be problems there; (2) the supervisor had learned the philosophy of supervision; and (3) the supervisor had the ability to work well with the machine operators and with the other supervisors.

First step. Stockings, at the end of the production line, were graded into piles—firsts, irregulars, seconds, thirds, and rags. An enterprising man bought the rags and found that some of the rags turned out to be, on scrutiny, saleable as third grade or even irregular. He hired menders and raised most of the remaining rags to first grade.

It is important to note that the cost of production is the same for rags as it is for first grade. The profit, however, lies in the first grade. The irregulars, seconds, and thirds sell at or below cost; the rags fetch nearly zero.

One of the first steps was to institute inspection of the looping, to learn whether the system of looping was under statistical control or if there was evidence of wild variation from special causes. There were two shifts, day and evening. Inspection of 16 stockings per day from each looper commenced the first working day of June. The two months June and July were used as the test period. Forty-seven loopers worked nearly every day through the test period. The overall percentage defective, day by day, for these 47 loopers, is shown in Fig. 45. The overall average turned out to be 4.8 per cent defective, with control limits computed as follows:

$$\bar{p} = 0.048, \quad \bar{q} = 1 - \bar{p}, \quad n = 47 \times 16 = 752$$

$$\left.\begin{array}{c} \text{UCL} \\ \text{LCL} \end{array}\right\} = \bar{p} \pm 3 \sqrt{\bar{p}\bar{q}/n}$$

$$= 0.048 \pm 3 \sqrt{0.048 \times 0.952/752}$$

$$= \begin{cases} 0.071 \\ 0.025 \end{cases}$$

Two points (days) of the test period were out of control. The explanation of the first point was that there had never before been an inspector in the department, and his presence upset the operators. The reason for the second point out of control was that it was Monday after the week that contained the Fourth of July, during which week the plant was shut down—an exaggerated case of problems on a Monday morning.

Shock to management. Incidentally, the vice-president of operations almost went into a panic when he saw the figure 4.8 per cent below first grade. He had never before known what he was producing. He declared that the company could not have been in business making a product that is 4.8 per cent below first grade. The business would have closed down long ago. He forgot that the plant had been operating for 65 years.

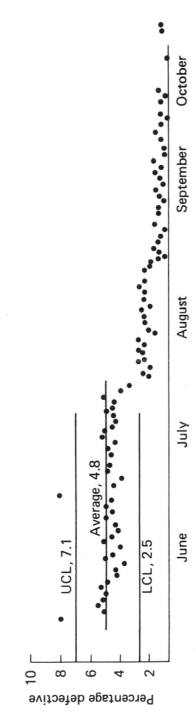

Fig. 45. Chart for percentage of stockings downgraded. June and July constituted the test period. Action commenced near the end of July. Improvement commenced at once, as shown by chart for August and September, and continued beyond the range of the chart (see the text for figures on improvement).

The only record that had been kept was the number of downgraded stockings at the pairing and boxing operation. Causes of trouble could not be traced backward from that point. In other words, the management had no idea where they were.

Charts for each looper (Fig. 46). The next step was to provide every looper with her own control chart so that she could perceive week by week how well she was doing. The following remarks about some of the individual charts may be of interest to the reader:

> *Operator* 75. An excellent looper. The supervisor was able to incorporate much of her techniques into general departmental routine to the benefit of all.
>
> *Operator* 22. This looper did much worse in July than in June. The supervisor, after he studied her work habits in August, referred her to the personnel department, with the suggestion that she have her eyes examined. Her previous examination, it turned out, was about eight years earlier. The physician found her to be blind in the left eye and with vision 6/20 in the right eye. He was able to correct her right eye to 20/20. Her work improved at once. Her earnings increased 19¢ per hour.

This incident with Operator 22 caused management to think about its policy with respect to examination of eyes. They faced the fact that they had no policy, except for new employees, learners in the school for looping, run by the company, a course of six weeks. But if a person with previous experience in looping applied for employment, the procedure was to try her out and let the supervisor decide whether she could do the job. For regular employees, there had been no examination given or required.

The new policy was to examine all loopers for eyesight, and to establish a regular pattern of reexamination.

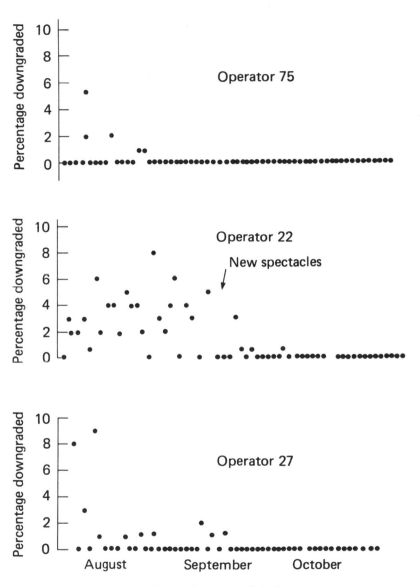

Fig. 46. Charts for three of the loopers.

The initial examination discovered a dozen operators that had difficulty to see what they were doing.

> *Operator* 27. This operator was perhaps the poorest one of all during the test period. All that the supervisor did was to show the chart to her. Her response was, "I have been here for five years, and this is the first time that anybody ever told me that care mattered. I could do a much better job, if it makes any difference." Her record in August and thereafter showed great improvement.

Another looper (chart not shown) with many errors beyond the control limits for the group explained that she had been on the job five years and that no one yet had ever explained to her what looping meant. She had observed other workers, and they had tried to help her, but she had learned a lot of bad habits, still not understanding what the job should have been.

Summary of accomplishments. The record was one of continued improvement. Beginning in August, the first month of genuine effort to improve, the level of defectives dropped to 2.4 per cent, then to 1.4, 1.3, 1.2, 1.1, and, finally, by February to 0.8 per cent, a dramatic change in only seven months. Instead of making every week 11,500 stockings to be downgraded, the department was by February making less than 2000. Results:

> Increase in production of first-grade stockings
> Lower costs; greater profit
> Increased earnings of employees through increased productivity (incidentally, at less effort)
> Evidence of maintenance of quality to show customers, an aid to sales
> Dramatic reduction in complaints from customers

The net cost of the program was close to zero. Some inspectors were added, but some 100 per cent inspection was abandoned, not being needed. One secretary did all the plotting of charts. No positions were added.

I remind the reader that the improvements took place with the same people and with no new equipment.

13

Some Disappointments in Great Ideas

The aim is admirable, but the method is madness.—Attributed to the (Republican) minority report of the Joint Economic Committee, *Wall Street Journal*, 15 March 1977.

For every problem there is a solution: simple, neat, and wrong.—Advertisement of the Mobil Oil Company, 1972. (Perhaps borrowed from H. L. Mencken, who said, "For every complex question there is a simple answer, and it is wrong.")—cited in *Business Week*, 21 April 1980.

Basic principles to be used here. The examples to be discussed here arise from failure to understand four basic axioms:

Some points of a group must lie above the average of the group.

Not all points will lie on the average (except by rare coincidence).

There is in the ideal state of statistical control variation of quality and quantity, but the ups and downs satisfy criteria of randomness. In other words, the variation is stable. The quality-characteristic under control is stable, constant; it reproduces itself hour after hour (Ch. 11). Responsibility for shrinkage of variation and for more suitable level rests almost solely on the management.

There are not only special causes of variation and loss,

but also common causes of loss arising from the system itself, if there be a system (Ch. 11).

The first two axioms may lead the reader to suppose that I am trying to write a comic strip. Not so. The sad truth is that much practice in administration and management in America ignores all four axioms.

Example 1. Some people are above average. On a professional engagement, the president of the company wished to show me his data-processing machinery. In one part of his establishment were about 60 women punching cards. I asked him what was the error rate in punching cards, and to my pleasant surprise, he knew. He was one step ahead of most people. Most people say that they have no error, or that this is not the place for error. The average error rate was 3 errors per 100 cards, he told me. He receives every Wednesday a report compiled from the records of verification of punching to show how many errors each woman made during the preceding week.

And here came forth his great idea for supervision: he has a talk with every woman that made more than the average number of errors during the preceding week.

"Well, that means that you talk to about thirty women every week, week after week?" I asked.

"Yes," he said, "that is about the number. How did you know?"

I thereupon told him about a recent letter to the editor of *The Times* of London. The writer had been studying a report from the Ministry of Health, whence it was obvious that half the children in the United Kingdom were below average weight. A disgrace on the nation. We must do something about the nourishment of our children.

My listener laughed at this joke, but his understanding thereof was not deep enough to see that his style of supervision fell into the same trap, causing more errors, not fewer.

Without knowing it, he was in danger of simply selecting week by week a random selection of women from the 60. Some simple statistical techniques would have told him which women need help, if any (e.g., better training, transfer to other work).

"How effective have your efforts been?" I asked him. The answer was predictable: he was disappointed—no improvement. Worse, whether he knew it or not; his efforts were creating frustration and difficulties.

Example 2. The end product is refined sugar. The raw materials are mostly raw sugar and seawater. The cost of water is a factor of importance, because the factory is located on a bay with no supply of fresh water suitable for use in refining sugar. It is necessary to make fresh water by removing the salt and other chemicals from seawater.

Objective: Reduce the consumption of seawater to 3.5 tons per ton of end product.

Method (wrong): Investigate conditions on any day for which the ratio falls above 3.5.

Where did the figure 3.5 come from? I asked.

We held a meeting and decided that we could meet it.

What I saw, when I visited the factory at the invitation of the management, was a bulletin board with a row of slats, some green, some red, one for each day of the month. The purpose of a green slat was to indicate that the ratio of seawater to refined sugar was below 3.5. A red slat indicated the opposite. The production workers were informed day by day about the ratio for the day before. A red slat sent them into a huddle to try to discover what they did the day before that was wrong. Naturally, they came up with all sorts of explanations and with attempts to take corrective action, all wrong. If the next day went green, they were jubilant over the thought that they had discovered a cause of waste, only to see a red slat turn up in a day or two, or perhaps two or three red slats in a row.

The goal of 3.5 tons of water per ton of sugar was a numerical goal, which, although agreed upon by all the people involved in the activity, was still only a numerical goal with no plan except to try to discover what went wrong when on any day the goal was not achieved. The plan adopted exposed the same fault as we saw in Example 1 on page 356. It led to unnecessarily heavy losses from overadjustment (mistake No. 1 on page 318) or from underadjustment (mistake No. 2), a thorny, treacherous, doubtful road to any improvement whatever, and certainly not to optimum operating conditions.

A better plan would be to study the process by group therapy and by trying changes suggested with the aid of knowledge of chemistry, following the Shewhart cycle (p. 88), with care to use good experimental design.

A chart to make from the daily consumption of water per ton of sugar would indicate a special cause if one turned up, and would display the record of improvement.

It should be noted that it is not always necessary to perform experimentation to accumulate data for understanding and improving the process. Temperature will vary, naturally: nothing is constant. There may be a continuing record of the temperatures of a number of solutions and processes and mixing. There may be a continuing record of pressure. There may be a continuing record of speed. Intermittent records will serve the purpose. Engineering judgment to observe the effect of high temperature, low temperature, high pressure, low pressure, etc. on production and on measured values of product may lead to clues to improvement of the process. This is a cheaper and better way than to start out with the express purpose of conducting experiments that will require a plan for varying the temperature, pressure, and speed. My friend Dr. E. E. Nishibori of Tokyo first mentioned to me the economy and efficiency of making observations on natural variation, leaving experimentation for problems not solved by simple observation. The same theme has long been voiced by my friend Dr. Hugh Hamaker, for years with the Philips Corporation in Eindhoven.

In other words, as this book pleads in so many places, make use of existing information.

Example 3. Out by automobile near Lancaster, to attend a convention of a client, need arose for a new fan belt. During the repair, I observed a placard on the wall:

TOP TECHNICIAN OF THE MONTH

FOR GREATEST CUSTOMER SATISFACTION

Tom Jones

"What is 'greatest customer satisfaction'?" I asked the foreman.

"Fewest complaints by customers. Fewest comebacks for the month."

Then followed this exchange of question and answer:

Q. Is the number ever zero for some mechanic?

A. Frequently.

Q. What is the average per month per man? Do you keep any records?

A. No, but I have a pretty good idea about the average. I have to use a little discretion now and then. For example, those new carburetors. They are difficult to adjust. I don't count a complaint on those new carburetors.

Q. Do the mechanics all have about the same average, month after month?

A. Yes, they do. It varies, of course, but they all come out about the same.

(I ought to have asked him: how do you know?)

Q. Does any one mechanic ride along month after month without ever getting his name on the wall?

A. Not forever; they take turns pretty well.

Q. What do you do if two men tie over the month?

A. We put them both on the wall.

Q. How do you know whether they tie, unless you keep records?

A. I know pretty well how the men do.

Q. Does a man ever get his name on the wall an excessive number of times in the span of a year or two?

A. No, they take turns, naturally.

Q. Does a man ever achieve zero complaints two months in a row?

A. Yes, it has happened.

Q. Is this merit system effective, do you think?

A. Well, it was at first, for a few years. Now it is not exciting.

I thought that the foreman would ask me why I was so interested, but he did not. I would conclude, from his answers, that this honor system is a lottery. His answers fitted neatly a random pattern. Figures would have made possible tests for randomness. Let us look at some of the implications of randomness (state of statistical control).

With an overall average of two complaints per month per man, a man would have a chance of $e^{-2} = 1/7.4$ to have no complaints during any month. (This calculation is based on the assumption that complaints are independent.) With an overall average of three complaints per month per man, on the average, a man would have a chance of $e^{-3} = 1/20$ in one month. These probabilities show that if a man has reached statistical control of his work, with an average of one or two complaints per month, he need only be patient to make the honor roll. He might in fact find himself man of the month two successive months. If he makes it one month, he has a good chance to make it the next month. On the other hand, he may also have to wait for a long time, purely by chance.

In summary, here we have a system that supposedly improves the quality of service. Actually (on the supposition that the men don't care about it any more), it accomplishes nothing. Or (on the supposition that the men care and try to get on to the honor roll), it actually depresses the morale and quality of service.

Restatement of the moral. A student at New York University, after hearing a lecture on the subject of this chapter, sent to me the following quotation with the resolution "From now on, I will view differently awards to great generals":

> As to the influence and genius of great generals—there is a story that Enrico Fermi once asked Gen. Leslie Groves how many generals might be called "great." Groves said about three out of every 100. Fermi asked how a general qualified for the adjective, and Groves replied that any general who had won five major battles in a row might safely be called great. This was in the middle of World War II. Well, then, said Fermi, considering that the opposing forces in most theaters of operation are roughly equal, the odds are one of two that a general will win a battle, one of four that he will win two battles in a row, one of eight for three, one of sixteen for four, one of thirty-two for five. "So you are right, General, about three out of every 100. Mathematical probability, not genius."
> (John Keegan, *The Face of Battle*, Viking, 1977.)

Example 4. One may read now and then in a journal of business about a manufacturing concern that has adopted a plan by which, if sales of some product or line of products drop two years in a row, the company will threaten to go to another advertising agency.

Now anyone that has tried by inappropriate statistical techniques to measure the effect of advertising is painfully aware of the multitude of forces that can cause a decrease in sales, or a decrease in the share of the market. Advertising, or the failure of advertising, could be one of the forces, but to ascribe hard luck to the advertising agency, in an ocean of possible other causes, is sheer guesswork. Such a system could best be described as a lottery, in which the advertising agency takes a chance: it may win, it may lose.

And somebody gets a promotion for thinking up such a great idea. The man's colleagues may be fooled into thinking that his promotion was based on merit. The man himself (the one that gets promoted) can hardly be persuaded otherwise.

Example 5. Fallacies in cost/benefit analysis. Cost/benefit analysis requires $\Delta C/\Delta B$, where ΔC is the additional cost of a plan, in use or proposed, and ΔB is the added benefit. The idea sounds good; catches on. But there are ofttimes serious difficulties.

1. Costs are sometimes elusive; difficult to estimate. For example, no one knows the cost of a defective item (e.g., TV tube) that reaches a customer. A customer dissatisfied with an item of small cost (a toaster, for example) may be influential in the decision on a huge contract and see to it that some other manufacturer gets it.

2. Same for benefits. Benefits are even more difficult to evaluate in dollars. However, by use of the idea of a trade-off, one benefit against another, a scale of ranks for benefits can sometimes be achieved.[1]

---

1 Jerome E. Rotherberg, "Cost/benefit analysis," being Ch. 4 in Vol. 2 of *Handbook on Evaluation*, edited by Elmer L. Struening and Marcia Guttentag (Sage Publications, Beverly Hills, Calif., 1975), pp. 53–68.

If you can not estimate satisfactorily the numerator or the denominator of a fraction, it is impossible to calculate the value of a fraction. This is where cost/benefit analysis often leaves us.

I would not participate in any attempt to use cost/benefit analysis for design of product where possible injury or loss of life is at risk.

14

Two Reports to Management

> As Goethe observed, where an idea is wanting, a word can always be found to take its place.—Quoted from a review by Ashley Montagu in *The Sciences*, September 1977.

Purpose of this chapter. The two reports to management reproduced in this chapter describe actual problems encountered, along with suggestions for solution. They were not selected for presentation for being unusual or out of line. In fact, quite the opposite: they were selected because they describe typical circumstances and problems.

Recommendations for Changes in Policy at a Factory

This memorandum was written by the author and David S. Chambers after study of the problems at a factory owned by a large corporation. The statisticians completed this work and wrote this report in a space of about three weeks. The management had known for years that the factory was teetering on the edge between profit and nonprofit and had supposed that new machinery was the only answer.

The records of the quality-audit (showing $7\frac{1}{2}$ per cent major defects) had been generated day after day, but they had heretofore served no purpose.

1a. Your factory at Nightingale [name fictitious] is running along day after day sending out items, 7½ per cent of which on the average have one or more major defects. There are, of course, daily variations above and below the average. On some days, the average must run up to 11 per cent or even 12 per cent. These figures are for major defects only: not minor defects.

b. These major defects are going out to customers.

c. This proportion is well documented by your own records that you collect through your quality-audit.

d. This proportion of major defects in your product may well explain some of your problems with sales and profits.

2a. Your factory at Nightingale is a good example of an attempt to build quality by inspection. The idea never works. The result is always poor quality and high costs.

b. There are cheaper ways to produce 7½ per cent defective product, if that were your aim.

3. The amount of rework along the production line is stifling your profits, and is obviously ineffective.

4a. The problems start this way. If an inspector at a certain point declares a defect to be minor, she repairs it herself—i.e., if she sees it and has time to repair it. The rule is that a major defect should go back to the operator, provided that the supervisor of production does not intercept it to avoid getting caught short of material to work on.

b. Major defects, and minor ones too, once sent into the production line, cause trouble at nearly every stage of production from that point onward. Once defective, always defective. Defects beget defects.

c. An operator turns out work. She looks it over. She may rework a major defect herself. By a major defect she means one that runs a chance of coming back to her. The inspector may see it and rework it herself, and not send it back to the operator.

Also, the inspector may not see it. Even if the inspector sees it, the supervisor may send it on through production. Why not take a chance? She can't lose, and she may gain a link in her production record.

d. As for a minor defect, why bother? The inspector will take care of it. So on she goes to the next piece.

e. Supervision that overrides inspection is frustrating to operators and inspectors.

5a. In effect, your inspectors are not inspectors at all. Their job is rework, as part of the production line. They are unable to keep up with the rework.

b. In other words, the operator's job is to produce defects. She gets paid for them. This is the system. The operator is not responsible for the system.

6. Your quality-audit takes place after every finished item is put through 200 per cent final inspection. This final inspection is obviously a joke. Your quality-audit must convince you, we should suppose, that quality by inspection is not working. As we said, it never does. It is in fact working against you.

7. There are three possible paths for you to consider, as we see it:

i. Continue with no change.

ii. Continue to produce items that show $7\frac{1}{2}$ per cent major defects at reduced cost and with greater profit.

iii. Reduce the proportion of defects, reduce costs, and increase profits. We are only interested in pursuing this course.

8. A complete overhaul is necessary. Here are some suggestions that we believe would increase production, greatly improve quality, with consequent inescapable greater profit, and more satisfied work force.

9a. Your factory runs on piece work. There is no better assurance of defective workmanship.

b. Piece work is a sure road to dissatisfaction of employees. Piece work robs the employee of his right to do work that he can be proud of.

c. Our suggestion is to get off piece work. This act will require better training and a new mode of supervision.

10a. Abolish the distinction between major and minor defects. A defect will be a defect, except possibly in the quality-audit.

b. Construct operational definitions so that the operators may understand what is right and what is wrong. This task was set in the meeting on 8 August. As we tried to make clear, this is the responsibility of your company. It is not a statistical problem, though it is only by statistical methods that you can learn whether a proposed definition is working to your satisfaction.

c. It is of course our job as statisticians to lay out tests to learn whether and how well a proposed definition works in practice.

11a. Meanwhile, cut out rework at inspection. Pieces that need rework should go (i) back to the operator if she has not yet achieved statistical control, or (ii) to a special group if her work is in statistical control.

b. Abolish pressure on foremen for production. Make them responsible to assist their people to produce quality. A control chart for a group may be helpful, and in some stations individual charts.

12a. There will be, in the end, fewer inspectors, better inspection, useful information from inspection by which to improve quality, greater satisfaction of customers, greater profit.

b. The work load of an inspector would be geared to inspection, not to production. Her job would be to inspect.

13a. Randomization of cases of items to inspectors, and random selection of items from cases, would be the rule. (By random, we mean use of random numbers.)

b. The system of inspection when revised will give to us a picture of each operator's work, percentage defective by type of defect, by style of item. It will tell which inspectors are out of line with the others, and which operators are out of line, perhaps some extra good, some extra poor.

14a. Our job as statisticians is to provide methods by which you may discover sources of trouble and reasons for high costs.

b. We do not attempt to tell you whether nor how to go about making the changes that are necessary.

15. You must remove barriers that rob your hourly workers of pride of workmanship.

16. We doubt that new machinery would bring any improvement. In fact, we fear that new machinery would bring on a whole new set of problems until management understand what is wrong under present circumstances and what their responsibilities are for improvement.

Extracts from Another Report to Management

1. This report is written at your request after study of some of the problems that you are having with low production, high costs, and variable quality, which altogether, as I understood you, have been the cause of considerable worry to you about your competitive position.

2. My opening point is that no permanent impact has ever been accomplished in improvement of quality unless the top management carry out their responsibilities. These responsibilities never cease: they continue forever. No short-cut has been discovered. Failure of your own management to accept and act on their responsibilities for quality is, in my opinion, the prime cause of your trouble, as further paragraphs will indicate in more detail.

3. You assured me, when I began this engagement, that you have quality control in your company. I have had a chance to see some of it. What you have in your company, as I see it, is not quality control, but guerrilla sniping—no organized system, no provision nor appreciation for control of quality as a system. You have been running along with a fire department that hopes to arrive in time to keep fires from spreading. Your quality control department has done their duty, as I understand it, if they

discover that a carload of finished product might cause trouble (even legal action) if it went out. This is important, but my advice is to build a system of quality control that will reduce the number of fires in the first place. You spend money on quality control, but ineffectively.

4a. You have a slogan, posted everywhere, urging everyone to do perfect work, nothing else. I wonder how anyone could live up to it. By every man doing his job better? How can he, when he has no way to know what his job is, nor how to do it better? How can he, when he is handicapped by defective materials, change of supply, machines out of order? Exhortations and platitudes are not very effective instruments of improvement in today's fierce competition, where a company must compete across national boundaries.

b. Something more is required. You must provide methods to help the hourly worker to improve his work, and to accomplish your exhortation toward perfect work. Meanwhile, the hourly worker sees your exhortations as cruel jokes, management unwilling to take on their responsibilities for quality.

5. A usual stumbling block in most places is management's supposition that quality is something that you install, like a new Dean or a new carpet. Install it, and you have it. In your case, you handed to someone the job of manager of quality, and paid no further attention to the matter.

6. Another roadblock is management's supposition that the production workers are responsible for all trouble: that there would be no problems in production if only the production workers would do their jobs in the way that they know to be right. Man's natural reaction to trouble of any kind in the production line is to blame the operators. Instead, in my experience, most problems in production have their origin in common causes, which only management can reduce or remove.

7a. Fortunately, confusion between the two sources of trouble (common or environmental causes, and special causes) can be eliminated with almost unerring accuracy. Simple statistical charts distinguish between the two types of cause, and thus point the finger at the source and at the level of responsibility for action. These charts tell the operator when to take action to improve the uniformity of his work, and when to leave it alone. Moreover, the same simple statistical tools can be used to tell management how much of the proportion of defective material is chargeable to common (environmental) causes, correctable only by management.

> Be it noted, though, that statistical techniques for detection of special causes alone will be ineffective and will fizzle out unless management has taken steps to improve the system. You must remove the common (environmental) causes of trouble that make it impossible for the production worker to turn out good work. You must remove the obstacles that separate the production worker from the possibility to take pride in his work. Failure of management to take this initial step, before teaching the production worker how to detect his own special causes, accounts, in my belief, for some of your troubles.

> The benefit of this communication with the worker, if he perceives a genuine attempt on the part of management to show him what his job is, and to hold him responsible for what he himself can govern, and not for the sins of management, is hard to overestimate.

b. Thus, with simple data, it is possible and usually not difficult to measure the combined effect of common causes on any operation.

8a. "We rely on our experience," is the answer that came from the manager of quality in a large company recently when I enquired how they distinguish between the two kinds of trouble (special and environmental) and on what principles. Your own people gave me the same answer.

b. This answer is self-incriminating—a guarantee that your company will continue to have about the same amount of trouble. There is a better way, now. Experience can be cataloged and put to use rationally only by application of statistical theory. One function of statistical methods is to design experiments and to make use of relevant experience in a way that is effective. Any claim to make use of relevant experience without a plan based on theory is a disguise for rationalization of a decision that has already been made.

9. In connexion with special causes, I find in your company no provision to feed back to the production worker information in a form that would indicate when action on his part would be effective in helping to improve his work. Special causes can be detected only with the aid of proper statistical techniques.

10a. Statistical aids to the production worker will require a lot of training. You must train hundreds of hourly workers in use of simple control charts.

b. Who will do the training? My advice is to start with competent advice and assistance for training. For expansion, search in your own ranks for people with a considerable amount of statistical knowledge and talent. Such people, taught and nurtured under competent guidance, may be able to take on training of other people. Leave that to your advisor.

11. There is no excuse today to hand a worker specifications that he can not meet economically, nor to put him in a position where he can not tell whether he has met them. Your company fails miserably here.

12a. When a process has been brought into a state of statistical control (special causes weeded out), it has a definite capability, expressible as the economic level of quality for that process.

b. There is no process, no capability, and no meaningful specifications, except in statistical control.

c. Tighter specifications can be realized economically only by reduction or removal of some of the common causes of trouble, which means action on the part of management. A production worker, when he has reached statistical control, has put into the process all that he has to offer. It is up to management to provide better uniformity in incoming materials, better uniformity in previous operations, better setting of the machine, better maintenance, change in the process, change in sequencing, or to make some other fundamental change.

13. In connexion with the above paragraph, I find that in spite of the profusion of figures that you collect in your company, you are not discovering the main causes of poor quality. Costly computers turning out volumes of records will not improve quality.

14. An important step, as I see it, would be for you to take a hard look at your production of figures—your so-called information-system. Fewer figures and better information about your processes and their capabilities would lead to improved uniformity and greater output, all at reduced cost per unit.

15. I should mention also the costly fallacy held by many people in management that a consultant must know all about a process in order to work on it. All evidence is exactly the contrary. Competent men in every position, from top management to the humblest worker, know all that there is to know about their work except how to improve it. Help toward improvement can come only from outside knowledge.

16. Management too often suppose that they have solved their problems of quality (by which I mean economic manufacture of product that meets the demands of the market) by establishing a Quality Control Department, and forgetting about it.

17. Management too often turn over to a plant manager the problems of organization for quality. Your company provides a good example. This man, dedicated to the company, wonders day to day what his job is. Is it production or quality? He gets blamed for both. This is so because he does not understand what quality is nor how to achieve it. He is harassed day by day by problems of sanitation, pollution, health, turnover, grievances. He is suspicious of someone from the outside, especially of a

statistician, talking a new language, someone not raised in the manufacturing business. He has no time for foolishness. He expects authoritative pronouncements and quick results. He finds it difficult to accustom himself to the unassuming, deliberate, scholarly approach of the statistician. The thought is horrifying to him, that he, the plant manager, is responsible for a certain amount of the trouble that plagues the plant, and that only he or someone higher up can make the necessary changes in the environment. He should, of course, undergo first of all a course of indoctrination at headquarters, with a chance to understand what quality control is and what his part in it will be.

18. Proper organization and competence do not necessarily increase the budget for improvement of quality and productivity. Management is already, in most instances, paying out enough money or more for proper organization and competence, but getting tons of machine-sheets full of meaningless figures—getting rooked, I'd say, and blissfully at that. Your company is no exception.

19a. Your next step will be for your top management, and all other people in management, engineering, chemistry, accounting, payroll, legal department, consumer research, to attend a four-day seminar for indoctrination in their responsibilities.

b. You will engage on a long-term basis a competent consultant. He will attend the seminar and guide your work on the 14 points and removal of the deadly diseases.

20. You should then establish appropriate organization for improvement of quality. (Here is appended Ch. 16.)

15

Plan for Minimum Average Total Cost for Test of Incoming Materials and Final Product

> I stick fast in the deep mire where no ground is. I am
> come into deep waters; floods run over me.—Psalms 69:2.

Introduction

Content of this chapter.[1] Even though vendor and purchaser work together to reduce the proportion of defective parts, it is nevertheless necessary for best economy to have theory for guidance in the use of incoming items. Should we try to screen out some or all of the defective items in a lot that comes in? Or should we send every lot straight into the production line, defective parts and good ones, just as they come in?

We shall develop principles that will, in a wide variety of circumstances met in practice, tell us what to do to minimize the average total cost of inspection of incoming materials plus the cost to repair and retest product downstream that fails because of a defective item that went into production.

This chapter consists of a number of sections. The following section describes conditions for the all-or-none rules for inspection of incoming items, to achieve minimum average total cost. The section "Other conditions met in practice" extends the all-or-none rules to items that come from a production process that is not in good control, but not wild enough to be classed as chaotic. Next comes treatment of the state of chaos—incoming

---

1 It is a pleasure to acknowledge deep gratitude to Dr. Louis K. Kates, statistician and consultant in software, Toronto, who has helped me on this chapter with fraternal devotion.

quality totally unpredictable. Then follow three examples of application of the all-or-none rules. The text then moves into the circumstance where the final product can not be repaired, but only downgraded or scrapped. Then comes a section that treats multiple parts, followed by a section that disposes of standard acceptance plans; they are not adaptable to the aim of minimum average total cost. The section "Additional problems with measurement and with materials" treats additional problems and circumstances, such as use of a test method that is less costly than the master method, but which lets some defective items get into the production line and scraps some items that would cause no trouble in production. Next come some hints on examination and comparison of methods of measurement. In particular, consensus, however important for a committee or for management, is fatal for visual inspection. Agreement may only indicate that one inspector goes along with the other out of fear or from a feeling of inadequacy. Next comes a section of exercises that develop the fundamental theory of the all-or-none rules and stress the fact that in good statistical control there is no correlation between sample and remainder. Rounding out the chapter are a section that further explores the implications of the earlier paddle-and-beads experiment and a bibliography of sources for advanced study.

Some Simple Rules of Wide Application

Suppositions.

> We deal at first only with a single part. We later introduce the problem of multiple parts (p. 425 and Exercise 4, p. 449).

> We shall test the final product before it leaves the plant.

> If an incoming part is defective and goes into an assembly, the assembly will fail its test. If the incoming part is not defective, the assembly will not fail.

Our vendor furnishes to us a supply of parts (call it S), for replacement of any defective part found.

Of course, he adds that cost of these parts to his bill. This cost is an overhead cost. We deal here only with variable costs. There is no point in bringing into the theory overhead costs that would be there anyway, no matter what be our plan of inspection.

A defective part is one that by definition will cause the assembly to fail. If a part declared defective at the start will not cause trouble further down the line, or with the customer, then you have not yet defined what you mean by a defective part. The next step in this circumstance would be to examine the test method that declares a part to be defective or not defective.

There are, of course, examples where a defect in an incoming part can be discovered in the factory only at great expense, and must be left for the customer to discover, often after some months or years. These are commonly called latent defects. Chromium plate is one example. The best solution to this problem is to avoid it by improving the process. This is also the solution to the problem of a destructive test, a test that destroys the item.

Let

p = average fraction defective in incoming lots of parts (which could be a day's receipt of material)

$q = 1 - p$

k_1 = cost to inspect one part

k_2 = cost to dismantle, repair, reassemble, and test an assembly that fails because a defective part was put into the production line

k = average cost to test sequentially enough parts to find a good one in the supply S (k is evaluated as k_1/q in Exercise 7 in a later section)

k_1/k_2 = break-even quality, or break-even point (k_2 will always be bigger than k_1; hence k_1/k_2 will lie between 0 and 1)

The reader may appreciate the suggestion to move at this point to the three examples that begin on page 418, and then to return to this point.

All or none. The rules for minimum average total cost turn out to be extremely simple under certain conditions, labeled Case 1 and Case 2 in what follows.

Case 1: The worst lot to come in will have fraction defective less than k_1/k_2. In this case,

No inspection

Case 2: The best lot to come in will have fraction defective greater than k_1/k_2. In this case,

100 per cent inspection

The proof of the rules for Case 1 and Case 2 is exceedingly simple: See Exercise 4 in a later section.

To treat as Case 2 a clean example of Case 1 will maximize the total cost, and the converse is true.

No inspection is not a directive to proceed in ignorance. One must be sure, for Case 1, on the basis of past performance that the worst lot (or week's receipts) to come in will lie to the left of the break-even point k_1/k_2 or, for Case 2, that the best lot to come in will lie to the right of this point. Control charts that vendors and purchaser keep, preferably as a joint venture, will place the incoming product in Case 1 or in Case 2 or in some kind of straddle, for the near future. A state of chaos, if it exists, will be no secret; it will be well known. The purchaser will always examine incoming materials to identify them with invoices, and to be sure that this is what he ordered. See the section entitled "Never be without information" (p. 417).

Cases 1 and 2 achieve minimum average total cost for many problems met in practice. Examples appear further on.

Binomial straddle. Suppose that the process is in statistical control delivering lots in which the defective items are binomially distributed around the mean p. Then the rules for average minimum total cost will be equally simple:

Case 1:   If $p < k_1/k_2$, no inspection

Case 2:   If $p > k_1/k_2$, 100 per cent inspection

even though the distribution of fraction defective in lots straddles the break-even point k_1/k_2.

The state of statistical control thus has distinct advantages worth striving for. To learn whether the stream of incoming lots lie in Case 1 or in Case 2, or are in a state bordering on chaos, it is only necessary to keep an eye on the state of statistical control and on the average fraction defective, which will be obvious from charts plotted on the basis of routine testing of small samples (as we should do anyway), preferably in cooperation with the supplier, on his premises.

It is important to note that in a state of statistical control samples from lots and remainders are uncorrelated. That is, in the state of statistical control, samples furnish no information about remainders (unbelievable; but see Exercise 1, p. 446, and Figs. 57–60, pp. 461–462).

Other Conditions Met in Practice

Other straddles in moderate departure from statistical control. We explore now two other simple straddles of the distributions of the proportion defective in incoming lots. We may be willing to predict, on the basis of control charts kept by the vendor or by us, or as a cooperative effort, that only a small portion of the distribution will fall to the right of the break-even point. We may for this condition adopt the rule of no inspection. This rule will come close to minimum average total cost, provided the portion of the distribution that lies to the right of the break-even point is not large, and is not detached, far out, to form a worrisome tail.

Second, the converse: only a small portion of the distribution of the fraction defectives in lots to come in lies to the left of the break-even point. With this knowledge in hand, one may well adopt the rule of 100 per cent inspection of the incoming lots.

Fig. 47 portrays the circumstances encountered, including the state of chaos, soon to appear.

Trend in the fraction defective in the incoming lots. Let us suppose that the trend is upward. Today, we are in Case 1, no inspection, but p is time-dependent, increasing, perhaps with a steady trend, perhaps with irregularities. Two days from now, we shall be in Case 2: We are forewarned. Control charts furnished by the vendor, or which you yourself keep, will indicate a trend, if there be one. This problem is simple enough.

Problems caused by switching sources of incoming material. We learned in Chapter 2 about the problems created in any operation by change of source of incoming material. Let us be content to deal with two sources. If the two sources are in good or moderate statistical control, and can be kept separate for a few days at a time, it would in principle be possible to treat each source as Case 1 or Case 2, depending on whether the average of that source falls to the left or to the right of the break-even point

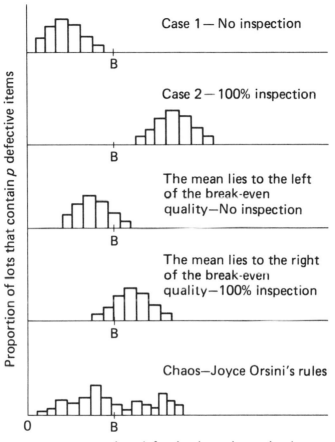

Fig. 47. Possible circumstances encountered with lots of incoming items. Point B is at the break-even quality, where $p = k_1/k_2$.

Such an idea is easy to talk about, but might in some plants be difficult to accomplish.

If the materials from the two sources be mixed intimately and in constant proportion, and if the two sources show fair statistical control, then lots from the mixture may well be treated, for use, as a binomial, for which new minimum average cost may be achieved by the all-or-none rules. Materials from two sources cause grief in production, as we have already learned (Ch. 2). An intimate mixture of materials from two sources would create the worst possible world for the plant manager.

A good first step would be to reduce the source to one supplier. (We saw in Ch. 2 advantages of having only one supplier for any one item.)

If there be only a single supplier, sending to us variable quality, then he and his customers need to go into a joint venture of improvement toward Case 1, and ultimately into zero defects. Meanwhile, we face the state of chaos, now to be considered.

State of chaos. Narrow swings back and forth across the break-even point are easy to dispose of. It makes little difference near the break-even point whether we do no inspection or 100 per cent inspection. My choice would be 100 per cent inspection, to accumulate information as rapidly as possible. If we dare not predict that the quality of incoming material stays predominantly to one side or the other of the break-even point, and that it will take wide swings back and forth across the break-even quality, we are in a state of chaos. This intolerable circumstance could arise from a single source that sends to us material of highly variable and unpredictable quality, or it could exist when material comes in from two or more sources of widely different quality, straddling the break-even quality, one source used for a while, then the other a while, devoid of rhyme or reason. One should, of course, as soon as possible, work himself out of this state and into Case 1. Meanwhile, lots keep coming in, and we must dispose of them. What shall we do with them?

Now if every lot came in with a tag on it to tell us the fraction defective in the lot, there would be no problem: We could achieve minimum average total cost by placing each lot, one by one, to the right or to the left of the break-even point and applying lot by lot the all-or-none rules. The lots do not come in tagged. But in a state of chaos there is some correlation between the qualities of samples and the corresponding remainders. One might accordingly be tempted in a state of chaos to try to test samples and decide by some rule whether to send a remainder into production as it is or to screen it. Samples and any rule for use of samples will place some lots on the wrong side of the break-even point, the unfortunate result of which is to maximize the total cost for a lot misplaced.

One might adopt, in a state of chaos, the rule of 100 per cent inspection. Actually, this decision deserves consideration, but an alternative procedure is provided by Joyce Orsini's rules, now to appear.

Joyce Orsini's rules. A simple alternative to 100 per cent inspection in the state of chaos is Joyce Orsini's rules.[2] They are easy to administer. They reduce the average total cost considerably below the cost of 100 per cent inspection. Comparison with 100 per cent inspection is meaningful because we know the average cost thereof: it is $k_1 + kp$ per item. Her rules are these:

For $k_2 \geq 1000k_1$: Inspect 100% the incoming lots.
For $1000k_1 > k_2 \geq 10k_1$: Test a sample of $n = 200$.
 Accept the remainder if you find no defective in the sample. Screen the remainder if you encounter a defective item in the sample.
For $k_2 < 10k_1$: No inspection.

2 Joyce Orsini, "Simple rule to reduce total cost of inspection and correction of product in state of chaos," Ph.D. dissertation, Graduate School of Business Administration, New York University, 1982. Obtainable from University Microfilms, Ann Arbor, 48106.

The samples of $n = 200$ will provide a running record of the quality of the incoming product. A good form of running record would be a chart for the number of defective items encountered, sample by sample. It might be advisable, for this chart, to combine several samples in order to have on the average something like three to four defective items to the point. The running record will tell you about the swings in quality day by day. Information like this will be helpful to you and to your vendor to identify the kind of problem that he is having. They will also tell you whether the incoming quality is actually in chaos, or, contrary to expectations, may be treated, with little loss, as Case 1 or Case 2.

It would of course be possible next week—even easy—to beat Joyce Orsini's rules used last week. We could look back and learn what the distribution of fraction defective was (past tense) in incoming lots. This statement is unfortunately of little interest, the reason being that in the state of chaos, no particular distribution is predictable. If we knew the distribution of lots to come in, we should not be in the state of chaos.

A procedure that is easy to describe and which achieves nearly minimum average total cost under any circumstance is Anscombe's sequential plan.[3] Anscombe suggests that if the preceding assumptions all fail, we should sequentially sample the lot where the first sample is of size

$$n = 0.375 \sqrt{N(k_2/k_1)}$$

where N is the size of the lot, then take subsequent samples of size $n = k_2/k_1$. Continue sampling "until either the total number of defectives found is one less than the number of samples inspected, or the whole lot has been inspected."

Unfortunately, Anscombe's rule is a bit difficult to administer.

The above theory and the rules arrived at would apply to repairs and replacement of parts on a customer's premises (or in a

---

3 Francis J. Anscombe, "Rectifying inspection of lots," *Journal of the American Statistical Association* 56 (1961): 807–823.

repair shop), if we knew the costs. The only hitch is that the out-of-pocket cost of repairs and replacement, once your product reaches a customer, is only a small part of the cost of a defective. Loss of future business from a dissatisfied customer, and from potential customers that learned about his experience, may be enormous, and is unfortunately impossible to estimate.

Necessity for simplicity in administration. Any rule, if it is to be practicable, must be simple in administration. Total cost must take into account difficulties of administration and losses from falls into the bear traps that lie in wait around any plan that requires even intermittent attention of a statistician. Joyce Orsini's rules have the advantage of simplicity.

Grief from variable work load. All rules by which inspection of the remainder depends on a sample share a common disadvantage, whatever be the purpose of application of the rule. They all beget grief from a variable work load for inspection. Moreover, the already beleaguered manager of production must now cope with additional woes from an uncertain on and off supply of incoming parts. He may need parts, and he may demand them and get them, inspection or no inspection, defective or not, and thus shatter well-laid plans for inspection. A possible exception occurs when the number of items that come in is so enormous, and the level of quality so bad, that the crew of inspectors is kept busy most of the time inspecting samples and remainders.

Never be without information. The rule for no inspection does not mean to drive in the dark with no lights. One should take a look at all incoming material, possibly on a skip-lot basis, for information and for comparison with your vendor's bill of lading and with his tests and charts.

If there are two suppliers, keep separate records for each one.

A further point of advice (already offered in Point 4 of Ch. 2) is to move toward a single vendor on a long-term relationship, for any one item, and to work with him to improve incoming quality.

Mistakes and corrections in a service organization. The above theory applies to mistakes in processing, in a bank, in a department store, payroll of any company, and in a host of other situations (see Example 3, p. 421). Work moves along in various stages and finally comes out on a customer's bill, or as figures on a cheque, or on a statement. Work may proceed through several stages before the mistake is discovered. By the time it has proceeded through several stages, the cost of correction may be 20, 50, or 100 times the cost to catch it and correct it in the first place. In Example 3 ahead, furnished by Mr. William J. Latzko of the Irving Trust Company, k_2 is 2000 times k_1.

Destructive testing. The foregoing theory is based on nondestructive testing: a part is not destroyed by the test. Some tests are destructive; they destroy the sample that is tested. An example is the length of life of a lamp, or the number of Btus per cubic foot of gas, or the time to action of a fuse, or test for the wool content of a sample of fabric. Screening a rejected lot would have no meaning, as nothing would be left to put into the production line.

Obviously, the only solution in destructive testing is to achieve statistical control in the manufacture of the part, to make it right in the first place. This solution is the best solution, destructive or nondestructive.

Examples of Application of the All-or-None Rules

Example 1. A manufacturer of TV sets was inspecting every incoming integrated circuit.

> *Question:*   How many defective integrated circuits do you find?

Answer: "Only very few." He looked at figures for the past few weeks and announced, "On the average, one or two defective circuits out of ten thousand tested."

Thus, we take

$$p = \frac{1}{2}\left(\frac{1}{10,000} + \frac{2}{10,000}\right) = 0.00015$$

Further questions gave forth the information that the cost of the initial test is $k_1 = 30\cancel{c}$, and that every subassembly with integrated circuits is tested down the line, after a considerable amount of value has been added to them. At this point, replacement of a defective integrated circuit incurs costs

$$k_2 = 100\, k_1$$

Thus

$$p = 0.00015 < \frac{k_1}{k_2} = \frac{1}{100}$$

He should accordingly do no inspection of the integrated circuits. He was in Case 1, but he was following the procedure of Case 2. In other words, he was maximizing his total cost. His total cost per integrated circuit was on the average, with his plan,

$$k_1 + kp$$

whereas with no inspection of the incoming integrated circuits, his average cost would be

$$p(k_2 + k)$$

The difference is

$$\begin{aligned}\text{Loss} &= [k_1 + kp] - [p(k_2 + k)] = k_1 - pk_2 \\ &= 29.6\cancel{c}\end{aligned}$$

on each integrated circuit. There are from 60 to 80 integrated circuits in one TV set. At 60, the loss from the wrong choice of plan would be $60 \times 29.6¢ = 1776¢$, nearly 10 per cent of the manufacturer's cost—an example of waste built into the product.

The engineer in charge explained to me at the start that he did not need the statistical control of quality because his inspections are all 100 per cent. He had been carrying out 100 per cent inspection of integrated circuits, he said, because his supplier had not facilities requisite for conducting the tests under the severity required. The manufacturer of the integrated circuits was nevertheless doing a pretty good job, it seemed to me—so good that $p = 0.00015$.

As so often happens in the absence of theory, this man was maximizing his cost. He was only doing his best. The calculations that we have just made, when he saw them, marked a turning point in his career.

Incidentally, the engineer had placed in front of every group of production workers on a TV screen a display of the number of faults of each type that this group had introduced into their work the day before. This display was not only totally useless; it was frustrating and counterproductive. It helped nobody to do a better job.

Example 2. A manufacturer of automobiles tests motors before they go into the power train. Call this point A. Further on, the motor is part of the power train, ready to propel an automobile. Call this point B. The cost of the test at A is $k_1 = \$20$. The cost to repair a motor that fails the test is $k = \$40$. The cost to repair a motor that fails at B is \$1000. We divide this cost into $k_2 = \$960$ and $k = \$40$. One motor in 1000 that passes all the tests at A fails at B. The question is whether to test at A. We may make up a table of costs to answer the question.

Table 1

Inspect at A?	Average total cost per motor
Yes	$k_1 + pk + (1/1000)\ \$1000$
No	$0 + p(k_2 + k) + (1/1000)\ \$1000$

The break-even quality falls at

$$p = \frac{k_1}{k_2} = \frac{\$20}{\$960} = \frac{1}{48}$$

Thus, if 2 per cent of the motors will fail at A, it would be wise to continue 100 per cent inspection at A, and try to improve quality to the point where inspection at A should, for minimum total cost, be omitted.

If k_2 were $500, the break-even quality would be at $p = 20/500 = 1/25$. Thus, if p will be (e.g.) 1 in 50, the difference between 100 per cent inspection at A and none would be $k_1 - pk_2 = \$20 - (1/50)\ \$500 = \$10$. It would obviously be wise, under such conditions, to discontinue the test at A.

Example 3. (Contributed by William J. Latzko, at that time with the Irving Trust Company, New York.) Work moves from one section to another in a bank or in a department store, or payroll department. The cost of review (inspection) in a particular section is 25¢ per transaction processed, and the average cost to correct further downline a mistake made here is $500 = 50,000¢. One error in 1000 transactions is about the limit of accuracy in the section under consideration, so we take

$$p \geqslant 1/1000$$

$$k_1/k_2 = 25/50,000 = 1/2000$$

As $p > k_1/k_2$, this is Case 2, and the plan for minimum average total cost is to do 100 per cent verification at the outset.

It is difficult to find errors in transactions processed in a service industry, perhaps even more difficult than in manufacturing. A verifier might find only half the errors made, or at best two out of three. It is obviously important to improve the system, which might be to improve legibility of figures, light, hiring, placement, training, and to provide statistical aids to supervision.

The procedure to recommend here, as advised in Chapter 3, is parallel computations by two people, both working on legible clean copies, not to betray methods or results of a calculation. Punch both sets of computations into a machine, and let the machine detect differences.

Parallel work with comparison by machine is in my experience the only satisfactory way to verify critical work.

The resulting quality will be far better than p_1p_2, where p_1 is the predictable quality-level for one worker and p_2 is the predictable quality-level for the other. If $p_1 = p_2 = 1/1000$, then the resulting quality will be far better than $1/1000^2 = 1/10^6$. This is so because the probability is very low that both people could make the same error in choice of procedure and come to the same result. But Murphy's law is also dependable—anything that can happen will happen.

> Both people should be encouraged to halt work on any figure that could possibly be misread, no matter how much time be lost to trace the figure to its source for verification. Production of an illegible figure anywhere along the line is as bad as starting off with defective material in manufacturing.

Modification of the rules for value added to substrate. Work is done on incoming material, the substrate.[4] The finished product

4 I am indebted to my friends William J. Latzko and Jerome Greene for conversations that led to these rules.

will be inspected and will be classed as first grade or second or third grade or scrap. Let k_2 be the net average loss from downgrading the final product or for scrapping finished items. The average cost to inspect one incoming item in the substrate will be

$$k_1 + kp$$

and the average cost to downgrade an assembly will be pk_2 if we do not inspect the substrate in advance. The break-even quality is now the value of p that satisfies

$$k_1 + kp = pk_2$$

With $k = k_1/q$ (Exercise 5, p. 452), this gives

$$k_1 + pk_1/q = pk_2$$

The left-hand side is merely k_1/q, so the equation is satisfied if

$$p = k_1/k_2 q$$

The rules now become

Case 1: $p < k_1/k_2 q$ no inspection
Case 2: $p > k_1/k_2 q$ 100 per cent inspection

where k_2 is now the average loss from downgrading or scrapping finished product that fails.

Note that the value of q will nearly always be near 1, so the rules for all-or-none are for practical purposes the same as before.

Example 4. This example takes the form of a memorandum that I am sending to a company at this date of writing. The memorandum follows.

As I understood it in our meeting yesterday, the coated rods, Part No. 42, are to you an important product, production at present being 20,000 per week, soon to be increased to 40,000.

Table 2. *Costs under the two possible procedures*

Inspection of incoming rods	Total cost per item
None	$pk_2 = 0.01 \times 1500¢ = 15¢$
100%	$k_1/q = 7.07¢$

Note: Costs are in cents per piece; $k_1 = 7¢$, $k_2 = 1500¢$, $p = 0.01$.

The size of incoming lots of unfinished rods is 2800, though the size of the lot is irrelevant.

The costs that you gave to me, supposedly fully allocated for labor, material, testing, and other burden, are as follows:

$$k_1 = 7¢, \quad k_2 = 1500¢$$

The average fraction defective, according to your figures, is about 1 per cent. Your break-even point is accordingly

$$p = k_1/k_2 q = 7/1500 \times 0.99 = 0.00471$$

or just below 1/200.

I show here Table 2, which I put on the blackboard yesterday. It is obvious that for minimum average total cost you ought to carry out 100 per cent inspection of the incoming rods. You are in Case 2.

If your incoming average fraction defective were (e.g.) 1/300 or 1/500 on the average, you should do no incoming inspection at all, but rely on inspection at the point where your final product undergoes test.

You raised the question about need for keeping track of the incoming quality. Certainly you must do this. For this purpose I recommend that you plot a *p*-chart for all types of defects combined, and one also for the predominant type of defect. You could plot a point for each lot, or possibly, later on, a point every day. As I understood you, your vendor wishes to study with you your methods and your results of inspection. Copies of your *p*-charts on a current basis, possibly monthly, would be helpful to him. Why are you not receiving charts from him?

Multiple Parts

Probability of defective assembly in the case of multiple parts. The foregoing sections apply to any one part. We turn to Exercise 4 on page 449 for helpful theory. Some parts may, for minimum total cost, require 100 per cent inspection. Once inspected, they will cause no failure of the assembly. The remaining parts will not be inspected, but a defective part, if it goes into production, will cause failure. Suppose that we have two parts not to be inspected.

We start with two parts with fraction defective p_1 and p_2, not to be inspected. Then the probability that the assembly will fail will be

$$(1) \qquad \begin{aligned} \Pr(\text{fail}) &= 1 - \Pr(\text{not fail}) \\ &= 1 - (1-p_1)(1-p_2) \\ &= p_1 + p_2 - p_1 p_2 \end{aligned}$$

If p_1 and p_2 are both small, this probability will be very near to $p_1 + p_2$. For example, if $p_1 = p_2 = 1/20$, the probability that an assembly would fail is $1/20 + 1/20 - 1/20^2 = 1/10 - 1/400$. Clearly, we may neglect the cross-product $p_1 p_2$.

An easy way to write down the probability of failure for any number of parts is by use of a Venn diagram (for which, see any book on probability). Thus, for three parts,

$$(2) \quad \begin{aligned} \Pr(\text{fail}) &= p_1 + p_2 + p_3 - (p_1 p_2 + p_1 p_3 + p_2 p_3) + p_1 p_2 p_3 \\ &\doteq p_1 + p_2 + p_3 \end{aligned}$$

provided that every p_i is small. Extension to m parts gives

$$(3) \qquad \Pr(\text{fail}) \doteq p_1 + p_2 + \cdots + p_m$$

provided again that every p_i is small.

The probability of failure thus increases as the number of parts increases. A radio may have 300 parts, though the number will depend on how you count them. An automobile may have 10,000 parts, again depending on how you count them. Is the radio in the automobile 1 part or 300? Is a fuel pump 1 part or 7? However you count parts, the number of parts can be enormous in one assembly.

Another problem arises: k_2 (the cost to correct a faulty assembly) increases as the number of parts increases. When an assembly fails, which part is at fault? It is all too easy to make a wrong diagnosis. Moreover, two parts may both be faulty.

> The more complicated products become, the more reliable components must be if costs are to be held down. Poor work affects expenses all along the line— in scrappage, repairs, larger inventories to provide a cushion against defective parts, higher warranty costs, and eventually lost reputation and sales.[5]

We thus face the fact that for multiple parts:

1. We can tolerate only a few parts in Case 2 (100 per cent inspection); otherwise costs of inspection for these parts will be excessive.
2. We can tolerate for the remaining parts only quality at or close to zero defective.

Tests of complex apparatus may require time and careful planning, as the various components in the apparatus may be subject to different stresses and have different times to failure.[6]

The problems are not simple. A company may pur-

5 Jeremy Main, "The battle for quality begins," *Fortune*, 29 December 1980, pp. 28–33.
6 J. D. Esary and A. W. Marshall, "Families of components and systems," being a chapter in the book *Reliability and Biometry*, edited by Frank Proschan and R. J. Serfling (Society for Industrial Applied Mathematics, Philadelphia, 1974).

chase many types of supplies and have many types of problems with them. One problem that appears frequently is where quality and uniformity of some incoming material are vital to the purchaser. Wide swings in quality are a constant problem to him. The material purchased, however, may be a by-product of the supplier, and less than 1 per cent of his business, and he offers little hope for improvement. You can hardly expect the supplier to go to the expense and risk of installing equipment for refinement.

A possible recommendation is to treat such material like iron ore or other raw materials that come in, variable and impure. Install your own refinery for the material, or send it out for refinement. This plan has turned out, in actual instances, to be a good solution.

Multiple exposure to the same defect has the same effect as multiple parts. A simple example was pointed out to me by Dr. Myron Tribus of MIT. Suppose that small motors (in the vacuum cleaner, blender, household space heater) now fail in the hands of a customer only 1/10th as often as they did 15 years ago. The fact is, however, that a household may now have, on the average, 10 times as many motors as it had 15 years ago. Today's household will thus see as many failures of motors as it had before. Other examples come to mind.

The design of a ceiling light fixture calls for three bulbs of some specified candlepower. A bulb might have an average life of three months under usage of the household, but with three bulbs in the fixture, the master of the household has to keep a stepladder handy, as he will now need it, on the average, once a month.

Take spot welding of seams in the trunk of an automobile. Anyone that has ever tried to spot-weld would agree that 1 fault in 2000 is marvelous performance. Automatic machinery is not much better. Yet such splendid performance leads to expensive testing and rework of trunks in the factory.

Thus, suppose that there are 70 seams in the trunk of your automobile, and that the welder, whether by hand or by machine, makes 1 fault in 2100. Then the chance that a trunk will be found leaky on test will be $70/2100 = 1/30$. In other words, about 3 per cent of the trunks would leak and require rework. (Fortunately, very few of these leaks get out of the factory.)

To reduce the frequency of leaks to 1 trunk in 100, performance of welding would need improvement to roughly 1 fault in 7000 welds.

Conclusion: defective material and workmanship not permissible anywhere on the line. The foregoing theory teaches us how important it is not to tolerate defective material at any stage of production. The product of one operation is incoming material for the next one. A defective, once produced, stays until and unless it is discovered on a later test, to be corrected and replaced at what is usually great cost.

The costs k_1 and k_2 in the foregoing theory are not the only costs to consider. Defects beget defects. A production worker suffers a powerful demoralizing effect to receive a partially finished item or assembly that is already defective. How can she put forth her best efforts when no matter how carefully she works, the item will still be defective? If no one cares, why should she? In contrast, when defects are rare or nonexistent or well explained, she understands that the management are accepting their proper responsibility, and she feels an obligation to put forth her best efforts: they are now effective.

Unfortunately, defects are sometimes created along the line, as by faulty installation of a perfectly good part, by crisscrossing a pair of wires, or by handling damage—that is, damage suffered by finished or partly finished product as it moves from one location to another. Handling damage may arise from carelessness or from sheer ignorance. It also happens in packing and shipping, as everyone knows. Simon Collier, when he was with the Johns-Manville Company, showed moving pictures of damage that men do by inadvertent acts, as by bumping a load of finished shingles on a forklift into a steel pillar, ruining the work that men had put forth on the shingles; or by tossing into the gypsum instead of into the waste barrel the string that had closed the sack. No one had explained to the men how much damage these little acts create. I saw a woman handle a hard disc with forceps, as carefully as a nurse handles surgical instruments in the operating room, then ruin the disc by putting her thumb on it. Had anyone explained to her that she could so easily spoil the work of all the effort put in on that disc up to that point? I saw a black streak on a white shoe, otherwise perfect, ready to go into the box. Somebody's carelessness caused expensive rework or scrap.

Exception. Many incoming materials are not amenable to the theory in this chapter. An example could be a tank car of methanol after agitation with an air hose. A ladle of methanol drawn from almost anywhere in the tank will be nearly the same as a ladle of methanol drawn from any other part of the tank. In practice, however, chemical companies draw off ladles of methanol from several levels. A more familiar example might be a jigger of gin or whiskey. We accept the fact that it matters little whether we draw off a jigger from the top of the bottle or from the middle or from the bottom.

A heat from a blast furnace gives problems and is another example that the theory of this chapter does not apply to. The contents of the heat are not homogeneous. Some companies pour a small sample along with every casting. These samples, if analyzed, would provide data for a run chart that would show variation of quality from the first casting to the last one, and provide clues to improvement.

Disposal of Standard Acceptance Plans

Standard sampling plans. There are so-called standard acceptance plans for acceptance, lot by lot, of incoming material, or for release of outgoing product. In brief, they require test of a sample and application of a decision rule, screening the remainder, or putting it straight into production, depending on the number of defective items found in the sample.

The theory behind the Dodge–Romig tables is to minimize the cost of inspection, to achieve the level of quality prescribed. In contrast, it is difficult to understand what the aim of Military Standard 105D is, except to hit the vendor in the pocketbook if his quality takes a bad turn.[7]

Hald, in his book listed in the bibliography at the end of this chapter, regards Military Standard 105D as a method of indexing a sampling plan by its AQL (average quality limit). Give me the AQL and the lot size N, and I will find in Military Standard 105D a plan to give this AQL. Military Standard 105D forces you to state the AQL desired. It uses no figures on costs. It should thus be no astonishment to anyone to learn that it can lead to a plan whose total cost is double the cost of 100 per cent inspection.

Any sampling plan whatever introduced initially with the aim to decrease the average incoming quality denoted by p in this chapter will only increase above minimum the average total cost per item. (See Exercise 5 at the end of this chapter.)

A company that purchases items on an AOQL (average

---

7 For a discussion of the economic incentive in sampling plans and its relationship to Military Standard tables, see I. D. Hill, "The economic incentive provided by sampling inspection," *Applied Statistics* 9 (1960): 69–81.

outgoing quality limit) of 3 per cent is making it known to the vendor that the purchaser is in the market for 97 good items and 3 bad ones out of 100. The vendor will be pleased to meet these requirements.

One manufacturer told me recently, for example, that he aims to send out to his customers not more than 3 per cent defective items. Some customers will get far more than their share of them. Is this good business practice? Would you wish to be a customer, to receive not more than 3 per cent defective items?

Unfortunately, standard acceptance plans occupy a prominent place in textbooks on statistical methods of quality control, my own books on sampling being no exception. It is time, as Anscombe says, that "we realize what the problem really is, and solve that problem as well as we can instead of inventing a substitute problem that can be solved exactly but is irrelevant."[8]

It is time to throw out such plans, and the teaching thereof, and to talk about total cost and the problems of practice.

Pro forma application of standard plans. Most applications of the Dodge–Romig plans of acceptance and of Military Standard 105D are, I fear, pro forma, merely conforming to the requirements of a contract, drawn up by people without qualifications for drawing up a plan, and carried out by another group of people equally qualified. Everybody does it, so we do too. The result is increase in cost. As Feigenbaum says:

> A major problem . . . is unwise use of these [acceptance] plans in situations for which they have no application.[9]

8 Francis J. Anscombe, "Rectifying inspection of a continuous output," *Journal of the American Statistical Association* 53 (1958): 702–719.

9 A. V. Feigenbaum, *Quality Control Principles, Practice, and Administration* (McGraw-Hill, 1951). See also p. 530 in his book *Total Quality Control* (McGraw-Hill, 1983).

Example: how to increase costs with Military Standard 105D.
A subassembly comes from a manufacturer in lots of 1500
assemblies.[10] It takes approximately two hours to test the assembly at an average cost (including burden) of \$24 per as-
sembly. The process average of the manufacture is 2 per cent,
and recent quality information confirmed this experience with
lots received. The cost to replace defective parts in final inspection is \$780, fully distributed. What sampling plan should be
used? Here,

$$p = 0.02 < k_1/k_2 = 24/780 = 0.031$$

This is clearly Case 1. Hence, for minimum total cost, no inspection. Use of Military Standard 105D as recommended
would run up the total cost to double the minimum total cost.
This is easy to see from the results in Exercise 5, page 452.

What could be even worse is that if the process were in good
statistical control, tests of samples would provide no more information about lots than tossing coins (Exercise 1).

Additional Problems with Measurement and with Materials

Possible economy in intermediate construction of subassemblies.
The cost k_2 in the preceding theory usually increases rapidly
(perhaps 10-fold) with each stage of work along the production
line, and may reach a very high number at the final assembly. It
is sometimes possible to avoid extreme cost through construction
of subassemblies that flow together to form the final assembly.

---

10 This example is adapted from William J. Latzko, "Minimizing the cost of in-
    spection," *Transactions of the American Society for Quality Control, Detroit,*
    May 1982, pp. 485–490. See also the chart on p. 234 of David Durand,
    Stable Chaos (General Learning Press, Morristown, N.J., 1971). See also let-
    ters to the editor of the *Journal of Industrial Quality Assurance* (London),
    (April, May 1985).

The several subassemblies, once they pass through inspection and receive attention with whatever replacements and adjustments are found necessary, form a new starting point. The cost k_2 in the foregoing theory will then be the cost to inspect and adjust a subassembly. The theory, along with meaningful records of experience, may show that some subassemblies need not be inspected at all, while others should be subjected to rugged 100 per cent inspection to avoid higher costs further along the line. The theory of this chapter provides guidance.

Our aim in the foregoing paragraphs is merely to show that there are ways to come close to minimum costs and maximum profit if one uses the right theory as a guide.

Meanwhile, we make every effort to eliminate defective items entirely. This we do on a systematic basis, comparing our tests with the vendor's, and by use of appropriate statistical methods, such as $\bar{x}$- and R-charts.

Successful cooperation with suppliers of parts, especially of critical parts, and success in tests and adjustments of subassemblies, reduce to a rarity any major trouble in tests of the final assembly.

Difficulties of finding extremely rare defects. Rare defects are difficult to find. As the fraction defective decreases, there is ever-increasing difficulty to find out just how small it is. Inspection simply does not find all the defectives, especially when they are rare, and this is so whether the inspection be visual or by machine. There would be little reason to put more faith in one manufacturer for his claim that only 1 piece in 10,000 is defective, against another one that claims that only 1 piece in 5000 is defective. The proportion in either circumstance is difficult to estimate.

Thus, if p were 1/5000, and if the process were in statistical control, one would have to inspect 80,000 parts to find 16 defectives. This number would provide the estimate $\hat{p} = 1/5000$ for the production process, with standard error $\sqrt{16} = 4$ or 25 per cent. The estimate of the fraction defective is thus not highly precise, in spite of the load of inspection of 80,000 parts. And one may ask whether the production process stayed stable during the production of the 80,000 parts. Was it the same process at the end of the 80,000 as it was at the beginning? If not, what would be the meaning of 16 defectives? A difficult question.

There are instances of no failure in millions of parts—even of few failures or none in 10^9. No amount of inspection of finished product can provide the required information when the fraction defective is so low. The only possible way to know what is happening under extreme requirements is by use of control charts with actual measurements on the parts in process. One hundred observations, such as on 4 consecutive items 25 times per day, would provide 25 points of samples of 4 for $\bar{x}$- and R-charts. The charts would show that the process is continuing unchanged, or that something had gone wrong, and that a run of product must be held up until the cause of the trouble is found. Once the cause of trouble is found, a rational decision can be made on whether to condemn the whole run, or to release some of it. The multiplying power of $\bar{x}$- and R-charts may be seen at once.

Use of redundancy. It may be possible and wise in the design of complex apparatus to put two or more parts in parallel, so that if one fails, another one will jump in automatically to take its place. Two parts in parallel, each with average fraction defective p_i, are equivalent to one part of average fraction defective equal to p_i^2. If, for example, p_i were $1/1000$, p_i^2 would be $1/1,000,000$. Restrictions on weight and size may of course not permit redundancy. There are other problems: will the redundant part step in when needed? The best solution may be high reliability of a single part.

The mathematical theory of failure and the theory of redundancy are extremely interesting and are important statistical

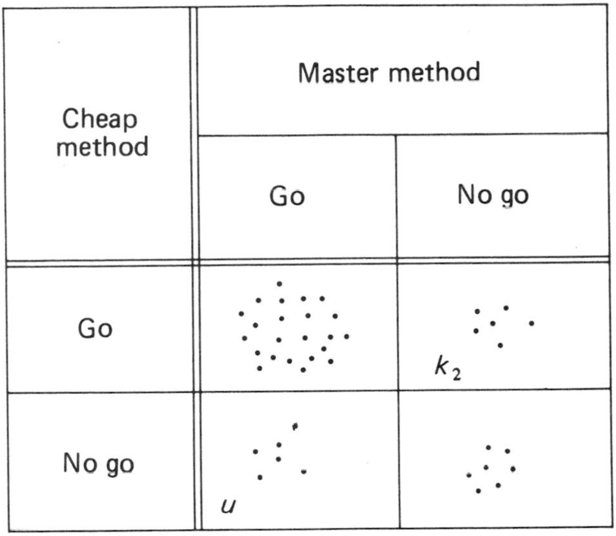

Cheap method	Master method	
	Go	No go
Go	 	k_2
No go	u	

Fig. 48. A 2 × 2 table of costs for tests of a number of pieces by the two methods of test. The two tests produce a point in one of the four cells.

techniques, but we must drop the subject here with only this glimpse into its importance.

Would a cheaper method of inspection really be cheaper? A perennial question is how to cut the cost of inspection, if inspection there must be (as in Case 2). Let us suppose that there is a master method of inspection, and a method that costs less per unit (smaller k_1) than the master method. Is the cheaper method really cheaper when we consider total cost? What one can do on a nondestructive test is to subject 200 items to the two test methods, and make a 2 × 2 table with the results, illustrated in Fig. 48. Each point is the result of the two tests on one part. A point on the diagonal represents agreement of the two tests. A point off the diagonal represents disagreement. A part that would be rejected by the master method of test but passed by the cheap method (a false positive) would cause failure of the assembly at cost k_2. On the other hand, a part that would be passed by the master method and rejected by the cheap method (a false negative) would incur cost u, where u is the cost of one part.

It is easy to quantify the results of the 2×2 table. Take the layout

$$n_{11} \qquad n_{12}$$
$$n_{21} \qquad n_{22}$$

for the numbers in the four cells. Let M be the cost to measure the 200 items by the master method, and C be the cost by the cheap method. Then the saving effected by use of the cheap method will be

$$S = M - C(n_{12}k_2 + n_{21}u)$$

The numbers off the diagonal will usually be small and hence subject to wide statistical fluctuation. The standard error of a number in a cell off the diagonal would with good approximation be the square root of the number itself. Thus, if a number were 16, this figure would be subject to a standard error of 4. If the number were 9, the standard error would be 3. (These statements are based on a Poisson distribution of differences.)

If it appears to be doubtful that the cheap method is really cheaper than the master method, one could test another 200 parts for more precision, or even another 400. If there still be doubt, my advice would be to stay with the master method of test.

Multiple parts. The advice and calculation just prescribed apply to a single part. Suppose that there are two or more parts that go into the assembly, and that we wish to consider a cheap method for each part. We may in fact apply the above calculation to any part, and come to a decision on it, no matter how many.

Let us be careful. Tests by the cheap method of any one part will make a selection of assemblies to test. The selection arises from the false positives in the upper right-hand corner in Fig. 48. Some of the selections for any part may overlap the selections made by some other part, but as the number of parts increases, the proportion of assemblies tested increases. Thus, with 20 parts, each tested by a cheap method that gives (e.g.) one false positive in 20, the proportion of assemblies tested because of false positives will be $1 - (1 - 0.05)^{20} = 1 - 0.36 = 0.64$.

If the assembly is made up of parts in series, it may be necessary to test all the parts on one failure of the assembly.

The moral is that testing may cause more trouble than the product itself. Much product is condemned falsely in industry only because of measurement processes that give answers that do not agree with other answers.

> Use of the master method and of the cheap method must both be in statistical control, stable, else the comparison may be misleading.

Improved 2×2 table to retain information—comparison of two certifiers. Fifty items are presented one after another to two certifiers, Certifier No. 1 and Certifier No. 2, to determine whether the two certifiers give substantially the same results. Certification is protection to the customer and to the manufacturer as well. Each certifier classifies an item as top grade or not top. The 50 tests are recorded in two columns on 50 lines, in order of test, one column for Certifier No. 1 and one column for Certifier No. 2.

Instead of showing a dot for each pair of tests as in Fig. 48, one may retain more information about the test by showing, not a dot, but in the proper cell the item number in order of test. An example appears in Fig. 49.

It will be observed that the upper-right-hand cell shows a run of four successive numbers (35, 36, 37, 38). The probability of this occurrence is very small, and may indicate a special cause of disagreement. Thus, if (e.g.) 1 test in 10 falls in this cell, the probability of a run of four successive lines would be only $(1/10)^3$.

Certifier No. 2	Certifier No. 1	
	Top grade	Not top grade
Top grade	5 15 17 18 19 20 21 22 25 26 27 29 30 32 33 34 39 43 44 45 48	1 14 35 36 37 38 41 42
Not top grade	4 49 50	2 3 6 7 8 9 10 11 12 13 16 23 24 28 31 40 46 47

Fig. 49. A 2 × 2 table for tests by two certifiers of 50 items. The item numbers are shown. The difference between this figure and the preceding one is that this one shows the item numbers.

Possible use of cheap method for screening. A plan that is well known in surveys of morbidity may be useful at times in testing.[11] Suppose that calculations show that $pk_2 > k_1$; that is, 100 per cent testing of a part will deliver minimum total cost. A

---

11 Aaron Tenenbein, "A double sampling scheme for estimating from binomial data with misclassifications," *Journal of the American Statistical Association* (1970): 1350–1361; idem, "A double sample scheme for estimating from misclassified multinominal data with applications to sampling inspection," *Technometrics* (1972): 187–202; W. Edwards Deming, "An essay on screening, or on two-phase sampling, applied to surveys of a community," *International Statistic Review* 45 (1977): 29–37; Martin Roth and Valerie Cowie, *Psychiatry, Genetics and Pathology: A Tribute to Eliot Slater* (Gaskell Press, London, 1979), pp. 178–187. See also Peter Giza and Emmanuel P. Papadakis, "Eddy current tests for hardness certification of gray iron castings," *Materials Evaluation* (37). I am indebted to the New York State Psychiatric Institute for the privilege to work there on projects that made use of theory presented here; also to Dr. Papadakis and Dr. Tenenbein for stimulating observations on application.

cheap test is at hand, and can be adjusted so that it will accept no part that the master test would reject. We first screen the n parts by the cheap test, and thus divide the batch into two classes, acceptable and not acceptable, the numbers being n_1 and n_2, as shown in Table 3.

Table 3. *Cheap test*

Total:	n
Acceptable:	n_1
Not acceptable:	n_2

We may safely put into production the n_1 parts that the cheap test classed as accepted. (We have by supposition adjusted the cheap test to make this so.) Next, subject to the master test the n_2 parts not accepted by the cheap test. The results are in Table 4.

Table 4. *Master test*

Total:	n_2
Acceptable:	n_{21}
Not acceptable:	n_{22}

If the cost of testing the n_2 parts by the master method is not too great, this plan may accomplish savings worth consideration. The calculations are simple. Let

k_1 = cost to test a part by the master method

k_1' = cost to test a part by the cheap method

Use of screening would thus save

$$D = nk_1 - nk_1' - n_2 k_1$$
$$= n(k_1 - k_1' - k_1 n_2/n)$$

the quantity in parenthesis being the difference per unit. For illustrative figures, take

$$k_1 = \$1.20$$
$$k_1' = \$0.10$$
$$n_2/n = 0.4$$

Then the difference would be

$$D = n(1.20 - 0.10 - 0.4 \times 1.20)$$
$$= 62\cent$$

which represents a saving of about 50 per cent.

Advantages in use of a scale for comparison. A more efficient method of comparison should be used if the measurements are in units of some sort, such as centimetres, grams, seconds, amperes, pounds per square inch (psi), or other measure. One may then plot the results of the n measurements on the x, y plane. Fig. 50 contains four displays of possible comparisons of the cheap and master methods of tests. A much smaller value of n than for the 2×2 table in Fig. 48 will here suffice for decision. Points on the 45 diagonal line indicate agreement between the two methods. Points off this line indicate disagreement. Study of the chart will quickly indicate where the two methods differ, and how much. Adjustment of the cheap method to bring it into better line with the master method might be obvious to someone with knowledge and skill in use of the two methods.[12]

12 John Mandel and T. W. Lashof, "The interlaboratory evaluation of testing methods," a chapter in the book *Precision Measurement and Calibration*, edited by Harry H. Ku, National Bureau of Standards Special Publication 300 (U.S. Government Printing Office, Washington, 1969), pp. 170–178. See also in the same book P. E. Pontius and Joseph M. Cameron, "Realistic uncertainties and the mass measurement process," pp. 1–20; and Churchill Eisenhart, "Realistic evaluation of the precision and accuracy of instrument calibration systems," pp. 21–47.

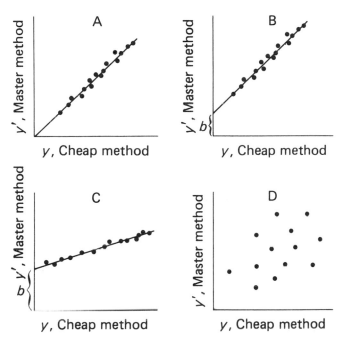

Fig. 50. Comparisons between the master method and the cheap method. Measurement of an item by both methods yields a point on a chart. A point on the 45° line indicates perfect agreement. (A) The points lie on or close to a 45° line. Here the two methods agree well. (B) The slope of the line is close to 45°, but there is an intercept. Some simple adjustment will usually bring the two methods into good agreement. (C) The slope of the line departs far from 45°, and has an intercept. Some simple adjustment might bring the two methods into good agreement. Or one could use a simple formula for correction of the cheap method. (D) The points are scattered over the chart, indicating serious problems.

Another possibility, under the simplicity of part B of Fig. 50, is to leave the cheap method unadjusted and to convert its readings to the master method. Thus, let

$y' =$ a measurement produced by the master method

$y =$ a measurement produced by the cheap method on the same item

$m =$ slope of the line of best fit in the relationship (assumed to be linear) between the two methods

$b =$ intercept on the y' axis

Then a convenient conversion would be $y' = y + mb$ in part B of Fig. 50.

Incidentally, agreement between the two methods does not mean that they are both correct. Agreement merely means that a system of measurement exists. Part C of Fig. 50 is interesting. As drawn (slope less than 45°), the line would indicate that the cheap method is more sensitive than the master method. If it retains this superiority, we should discard the master method and put the cheap method into use, after adjustment. (Contributed by Peter Clarke of Hammersdale, Natal, in a seminar in Cape Town, November 1983.) Slope greater than 45° would indicate that the cheap method is less sensitive, as one usually finds. One could then adjust the cheap method to the master method, convert it by the equation $y' = my + b$, m being the slope of the line.

An excellent treatment of the precision of instruments and errors of measurement is Sec. B-3 of the *Statistical Quality Control Handbook* produced and published by the Western Electric Company in 1956. (See reference at the end of Ch. 11.)

Hazards of consensus in inspection. Consensus that comes forth after everyone has had a chance to present his views and to ask questions, all without fear, secure (p. 59), reaps the benefit of the entire team, plus the benefit of interaction from learning from one another.

Unfortunately, consensus in inspection or anywhere else may only mean that one head overpowered the other, and the consensus is only one man's opinion.

For example, two physicians may record a consensus in respect to a patient—improved, unimproved, or worse. This report

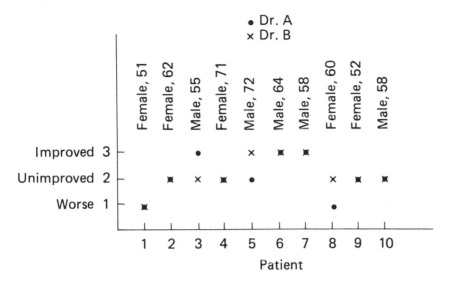

Fig. 51. Record of judgments of two physicians, patient by patient. Study of agreements and of disagreements, by type of patient, may assist both men to understand better what they are doing, and to bring them nearly into full and dependable agreement.

may only be the older physician's opinion, the younger one glad for the privilege to accompany the older man and to listen to whatever words of wisdom came forth. The cordial relationship between the two men might come to an end if the younger man has too many ideas. Perhaps the younger one is an intern. He dare not run the risk of losing out on reappointment next year, so he agrees to anything, and is careful about questions.

A better plan would be for each man to record on his own form his judgment concerning each patient—improved, unimproved, or worse. Then, when convenient, compare notes. The young man may then without confrontation ask questions concerning any patient on which there be disagreement or agreement. In other words, this suggested system removes the young man's fear to ask questions. A simple chart like Fig. 51 will display agreements and disagreements. (Suggested by this author, working as a consultant to Dr. Franz J. Kallmann, deceased, at the New York State Psychiatric Institute, about 1960, and accepted.)

> Simple notations on the chart, such as age and sex of patient, would indicate where the young man needs help.

Incidentally, good agreement between independent results of two men would only mean that they have a system. It would not mean that they are both right. There is no right answer except by methods agreed upon by experts.

Comparison of two inspectors. Two inspectors of leather had for years recorded the consensus of the two on each bundle of leather drawn as a sample for inspection from an incoming shipment of bundles. They readily understood, when we talked it over, the hazards of consensus and the need to have individual data so that they could compare results and learn from each other if their results diverged.

A bundle of leather is graded 1, 2, 3, 4, or 5, No. 1 being the best grade. The plan arrived at was this:

1. Each inspector shall select from each shipment one bundle of items. Take a bundle from the top, middle, bottom, scattering the selections. (This would be what we have already called mechanical sampling, not use of random numbers.)
2. Each inspector shall examine independently the bundle that he selected, and record the result.
3. Both inspectors will examine and record their results independently for every 20th bundle. They will take turns on the selection of the bundle.
4. Plot the results on a chart, a simplified section of which is shown in Fig. 52.

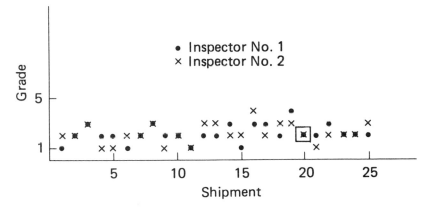

Fig. 52. Scheme for display of the results of two inspectors working independently. The chart shows no indication of divergence. The box around the 20th point signifies that, by design, both inspectors examined the same bundle of hides.

Differences between the two sets of results could arise from two sources: (a) differences between the two men; (b) differences between the samples. The results have shown so far (nearly a year) no appreciable difference. One inspector is not running away from the other one. Disagreement is rare on the 20th bundle that they both inspect. Other applications have shown need of better definitions.

Again, as has been emphasized elsewhere, their agreement does not mean that they are recording correct values but merely that their sampling and inspection constitute a system of grading.

Further note on graphical presentation. The plan on presentation in Figs. 51 and 52 can be adapted readily to four or five inspectors. (Six inspectors create a problem in multiplicity of symbols.) I have also used the same plan to indicate with three symbols ($\bullet$, $\bigcirc$, $\times$) the quality-characteristics obtained at a later stage from material drawn off at (1) the beginning of a heat, (2) the middle, (3) the end. In an actual case, the three symbols appeared in the same vertical relationship over 12 heats, except for a tie between ○ and ×. This repeated relationship indicated the possibility (a) of failure to mix sufficiently the components in the heat, or (b) that the mixture aged appreciably during production.

Exercises

Exercise 1. Given: a bowl of red and white beads, p the proportion red, q the proportion white (Fig. 53).

Step 1. Draw from the bowl by random numbers with replacement a lot of size N. Result:

$$N \quad \text{total}$$
$$X \quad \text{red}$$
$$N - X \quad \text{white}$$

Step 2. Draw from the lot by random numbers without replacement a sample of size n. Result:

In the sample	In the remainder
n total	$N - n$ total
s red	$r = X - s$ red
$n - s$ white	$N - n - r$ white

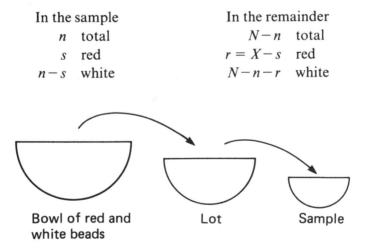

Bowl of red and   Lot   Sample
white beads

Fig. 53. Lots are drawn from a bowl of red and white beads. A sample is then drawn from the lot. Replacement of each bead drawn into the lot ensures constancy of the proportion p in the lot at every draw.

Step 3. Restore to the lot the beads in the sample.

Step 4. Repeat many times Steps 1, 2, 3, holding constant the size of the lot and the size of the sample drawn therefrom. Record the results for r and s.

Show that the theoretical distribution of r and s will be

$$(4) \qquad P(r, s) = \left[\binom{N-n}{r} q^{(N-n)-r} p^r\right]\left[\binom{n}{s} q^{n-s} p^s\right]$$

Conclusions: (a) The number of red beads in the samples of size n, and the number of red beads in the remainders, are both binomially distributed about the same proportion p; and (b) they are independent. That is, the number r of red beads in the remainders that correspond to samples with $s = 17$ defective items will be distributed exactly the same as the red beads in the remainders that correspond to samples with $s = 0$ defective items.

This theorem is frightening. It shows that if the individual defective items are independent, as will be nearly the case when the process is in fairly good statistical control, any attempt to construct an acceptance plan would accomplish no more than tossing coins for selection of remainders to screen.[13] (Tossing coins is a lot cheaper than testing samples of items.)

> Instead of drawing a sample from a lot, one could merely separate the lot by random numbers into two parts, sample and remainder.

Exercise 2. If the distribution of defectives in lots be tighter than binomial, and if the rule for acceptance of the remainder is based on test of a sample, then the rule should be to accept the remainder as it is when the sample shows many defective parts,

---

13 Alexander M. Mood, "On the dependence of sampling inspection plans upon population distributions," *Annals of Mathematical Statistics* 14 (1943): 415–425. The proof of Eq. 4 is also in W. Edwards Deming, *Some Theory of Sampling* (Wiley, 1950; Dover, 1984), p. 258.

and to reject and screen the remainder when the sample shows few defectives, or none, not the usual reverse rules.[14]

An easy way to understand the above results is to consider the circumstance wherein all lots come in with exactly the same number of defective items. Defectives not in the remainder will be in the sample, and the converse. Hence, a large number of defective items in the sample will indicate a small number in the remainder.

I. D. Hill (1960) pointed out a simple way to produce lots of uniform quality. Let there be 20 machines producing the same item, 19 producing no defective items, one of them producing nothing but defective items. Take one item from each of the 20 machines to build up a lot. Then any lot formed as a multiple of 20 items will contain exactly 5 per cent defective items.

Lots of nearly constant quality are not unusual. An example is a battery of pallets, possibly 12 in number. They rotate to stamp sheet metal that passes through the operation. One of the pallets is out of order. Nearly all items that it stamps turn out to be defective. The other 11 pallets are in good order. The total output of lots formed with 12 consecutive items is constantly close to 1/12 or 8.3 per cent defective.

Exercise 3. *Proof of all-or-none rules.* Draw at random (by random numbers) a part from the lot. Call it Part *i*. It will be defective or not defective. Should we inspect it, or put it straight into the production line without inspection, defective or not? We may put the average total cost into a convenient table (Table 5).

We observe that Yes and No are equal if $p = k_1/k_2$. This quality was named by Alexander Mood the *break-even quality*. At the break-even quality, the total cost is the same for No as it is for Yes. We observe further that if $p < k_1/k_2$, No will give the

14 I. D. Hill, "The economic incentive provided by sampling inspection," *Applied Statistics* 9 (1960): 69–81.

Table 5

Inspect the part?	Average total cost
Yes	$k_1 + kp + 0$
No	$0 + p(k_2 + k)$
Yes − No	$k_1 - pk_2$

lesser total cost, and if $p > k_1/k_2$, Yes will give the lesser cost. (See Fig. 54.)

It is obvious that if the worst lot to come in over (e.g.) the next week will lie to the left of the break-even point, then all other lots will be better, further to the left. Clearly, under this circumstance, no inspection will achieve minimum average total cost, Case 1.

If, on the other hand, the best lot to come in lies to the right of the break-even point, then all other lots will be worse, further to the right. This is Case 2. Inspection 100 per cent of all lots would then achieve minimum average total cost.

Minimum average total cost thus lies on the broken line OCD. For values of p close to the point B, the break-even point, the difference between no inspection and 100 per cent inspection will be trivial.

Exercise 4. *Minimum average total cost for multiple parts.*[15] Let there be a total of M parts. Let p_i be the average fraction defective of part i, and k_i the cost to inspect one part. The additional cost of failure of the assembly will be denoted by K, assumed to be the same for one part as for another. (Some switch in notation is necessary, as we now need the symbol k_2 for the cost to inspect part No. 2.) Shall we inspect all the parts, or only

---

15 This exercise was contributed by Dr. P. S. Dietz and Dr. E. L. Chase of AT&T Technologies, Merrimack Valley, Mass.

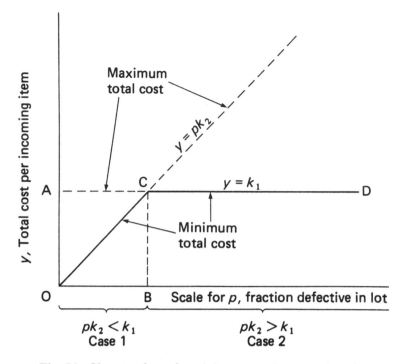

Fig. 54. Chart to show the minimum total cost per item in a lot of fraction defective as a function of the incoming quality p. Minimum fraction defective lies along the broken line OCD. The break C occurs at the break-even quality, Point B, where $p = k_1/k_2$. Total cost is maximized by using 100 per cent inspection where no inspection would give minimum total cost, and conversely.

some of them? If only some of them, which ones? Use the approximation in Eq. 3, page 425.

The difference between the two plans will be in favor of Plan 2 by the amount

$$\sum_{1}^{m-1} (k_i - Kp_2)$$

Which parts should we inspect, and which should we not inspect, to minimize total cost? In other words, how may we maximize the diff^rence between the two plans? The answer is obvious. Arrange the M terms of the series

$$k_i - Kp_i, \quad i = 1, 2, 3, \ldots, M$$

in descending order of magnitude. The terms will start off positive, decrease, cross over zero, and continue to decrease. For minimum average total cost, the summation written above must be as big as possible. The rule for minimum average total cost is accordingly:

1. No inspection for parts for which $k_i - Kp_i$ is positive.
2. Inspect all the others, those for which $k_i - Kp_i$ is negative.

Plan	Average total cost
1. Inspect all parts.	$\sum\limits_{1}^{M} k_i + 0$
2. Inspect only parts m, $m+1, m+2, \ldots, M$.	$\sum\limits_{m}^{M} k_i + K \sum\limits_{1}^{m-1} p_i$

Work with all the vendors to get statistical control of all parts and to reduce the p_i. Success in this endeavor will reduce the total cost, and may admit, from time to time, transfer of some part from inspection to no inspection.

Remark 1. Shift from barely negative to barely positive will only slightly reduce costs, but a big shift— large negative to large positive—will bring substantial reduction in cost.

Remark 2. We could say that each part has a break-even quality defined as $p_i = k_i/K$. Our result for multiple parts thus only repeats Plan 1 and Plan 2 for a single part.

Remark 3. A part whose distribution of fraction defective straddles its own break-even quality would be treated in the same way as a single part.

Remark 4. Use 100 per cent inspection for any part that is not in fairly good statistical control—and certainly if it is in a state of chaos.

Exercise 5. (*Aim: to show that when the incoming quality will dependably lie predominantly on one side of the break-even quality, adoption of any plan of inspection other than the all-or-none rules runs the risk of increase of overall cost.*) Suppose that we inspect the fraction f of lots of incoming items whose average defective is p. Selection of the items will be made at random (i.e., by random numbers). Then the average total cost on a per item basis for the inspection of the incoming material and the additional cost to repair and retest an assembly that failed because of a faulty item will be

(5) $y = fk_1 + (1-f)pk_2$ (the cost kp neglected)

The question is what should f be to minimize y? We note first that $y = k_1$ regardless of f at the point where $p = k_1/k_2$ (the break-even point).

On the left of the break-even point, $p < k_1/k_2$. It is convenient to rewrite Eq. 5 in the form

(6) $y = pk_2 + f(k_1 - pk_2)$

Obviously, if we let f vary from 0 to 1 to the left of the break-even quality, y will vary from its minimum pk_2 up to k_1. That is, any inspection whatever in the region to the left of the break-even point $(p < k_1/k_2)$ will increase total cost. One can easily see that an acceptance plan in this region could double or treble the minimum total cost.

To investigate the right side of the break-even point, where $p > k_1/k_2$, we rewrite Eq. 5 in the form

(7) $$y = k_1 + (1 - f)(pk_2 - k_1)$$

If we let f vary from 0 to 1 in this region, y will vary from pk_2 down to its minimum k_1. That is, 100 per cent inspection in the region to the right of the break-even quality gives minimum total cost. Inspection short of 100 per cent (i.e., $f < 1$) will increase the average total cost above the minimum.

Reference was made on page 432 to an example furnished by William J. Latzko. We now turn to another example.

Illustrative example. A company receives aluminium substrate in lots of 1000 pieces, for use in manufacture of hard discs. The first step on receipt of a lot had been to give a visual test to a sample of 65 pieces drawn by random numbers from the lot. Experience shows that an incoming piece that fails the visual test would, if put into production, cause failure of the finished disc. Any piece of substrate that fails the visual test was replaced by a good one.

The average proportion of pieces that failed the visual test had been running around 1 in 40, or 0.025. The rule was to reject a lot if 5 or more pieces in the sample failed (5 being the upper 3-sigma limit). The record showed that very few lots were ever rejected: a moderate state of statistical control may accordingly be assumed for the immediate future.

The average proportion of defective pieces in terms of visual defects put into production was therefore $0.025 - (65/1000) \times 0.025 = 0.023$.

The cost of the visual test is 7¢ per piece, fully allocated.

One per cent of the pieces of substrate is ruined by handling damage in preparation of the visual inspection, and in the inspection itself.

The test just described was for visual defects only. Other defects not caught in the visual test cause one finished disc in 100 to fail in the final test. This is an overhead cost, common and constant regardless of the proportion of incoming pieces that are subjected to the visual inspection; hence we omit it from the table of costs to follow.

The value added to make the finished disc is $11. The cost of the substrate is $2; $13 total. The substrate in a finished disc that fails can be reclaimed; hence the loss of a finished disc is $11, disregarding the cost of reclaim. Let

f = proportion inspected on the plan described
    $(= 65/1000 = 0.065)$
k_1 = cost for visual inspection of one piece $(= 7¢)$
B = cost of 1 piece of substrate $(= \$2)$
k_2 = value added $(= \$11)$ to make one piece
p = average incoming quality in terms of visual defects discoverable $(= 0.025)$
p' = average proportion of discs lost from nonvisual faults $(= 0.01)$
p'' = average proportion of pieces put into production on the plan described, but which would fail in the visual test if inspected $(0.025 [1 - 65/1000] = 0.023)$
F = proportion of pieces ruined by handling in preparation for the visual inspection, and in the visual inspection itself $(= 0.01)$

We may now prepare Table 6 for prediction of costs.

Conclusion. The margin of difference between 100 per cent inspection and the plan in use is so wide that one might well recommend immediate change. This recommendation would stand in

Table 6

Plan	Average cost per incoming piece			
	Visual inspection	Handling damage to substrate	Failure of finished disc	Total
As carried out	$fk_1 = 0.065 \times 7¢$ $= 0.46¢$	$0.01 \times 200¢$	$(p'' + 0.01)k_2$ $= (0.023 + 0.01)k_2$ $= 0.033 \times 1100¢$	39¢
100% visual inspection	$k_1 = 7¢$	$0.01 \times 200¢$	$(0 + 0.01)k_2$ $= 0.01 \times 1100¢$	20¢
No visual inspection	0	$0.01 \times 200¢$	$(0.025 + 0.01)k_2$ $= 0.035 \times 100¢$	40¢

the face of considerable departures from the proportions defective and the costs used in the above table.

Meanwhile, joint effort with the vendor to improve the quality of incoming pieces continues, in hope to cross over the break-even point to zero visual inspection, to save this operation and the handling of the pieces.

Note: The break-even quality is here not the simple fraction k_1/k_2 as it was heretofore, but we do not pause for the complication.

Exercise 6. Show the futility of the following rule put forth to vendors by a large concern:

Because of our reliance on sampling inspection to determine acceptability of material provided, one defective part will reject an entire lot.

Comments: (1) What actually happens is that most lots are put straight into production, with or without inspection. The customer can not afford delay for further inspection nor for return to the vendor. (2) If $k_1 > pk_2$, then sampling inspection would increase total cost over the minimum of no inspection. Why increase costs? (3) If $k_1 < pk_2$, then 100 per cent inspection, not sampling inspection, would minimize total cost. Again, why increase costs? (4) If the distribution of the quality of the incoming material is badly out of control and straddles the break-even point, the best solution would be 100 per cent inspection or use of Joyce Orsini's rules (p. 415). Then get out of this deplorable state. Work with the vendor to improve quality to get into Case 1 $(k_1 < pk_2)$, and keep on improving to zero defects if possible. (5) In short, the requirement quoted is outmoded and ineffective, and ensures poor quality at high cost.

Exercise 7. Evaluation of k. We make the supposition that the cost to inspect a part drawn from the supply S is the same as the regular cost to inspect a part drawn from the lot of size N. Let $x_i = 1$ if the part is defective; 0 if not. Suppose that $x_i = 1$; then Part i turns out to be defective. We must then draw one from the supply S and inspect it—cost k_1. This one may also be defective, in which case we draw and inspect another, and so on until we come to a good one. We may show these possibilities in the probability tree of Fig. 55. The average cost k will obviously be[16]

(8) $$k = k_1(q + 2pq + 3p^2q + \cdots) = \frac{k_1 q}{(1-p)^2} = \frac{k_1}{q}$$

where

$$q = 1 - p$$

---

16 I am indebted to Joyce Orsini for Eq. 8 and for much other technical help on this chapter and other parts of the book.

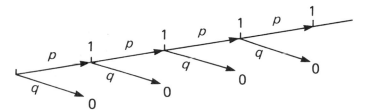

Fig. 55. Inspection of a part leads with probability p to $x_i = 1$, defective, and with probability q to $x_i = 0$, not defective.

The total average cost to inspect an item and to replace a defective item with a good one will therefore be

$$k_1 + pk = k_1/q$$

As p will be in most applications small, q will be close to 1, in which circumstance we may replace k_1/q by k_1.

Exercise 8.

Notation

$N =$ number of pieces in the lot

$n =$ number of pieces in the sample (supposedly selected by use of random numbers from the lot)—replace any defective item with a good one

$p =$ average incoming fraction defective; this value of p is a rough prediction of an average value over the next few weeks

$q = 1 - p$

$p' =$ average fraction defective in lots that are rejected and to be screened

$p'' =$ average fraction defective in lots that are accepted and put straight into the production line

$k_1 =$ cost to inspect one part

$k_2 =$ cost to dismantle, repair, reassemble, and test an assembly that fails because a defective part was put into the production line

P = average proportion of lots set off for screening at initial inspection (rejected)

$Q = 1 - P$ = proportion of lots accepted at initial inspection

Whatever be the plan of acceptance, we can be sure that

$$P = 0 \quad \text{and} \quad Q = 1 \quad \text{if} \quad n = 0$$
$$P = 1 \quad \text{and} \quad Q = 0 \quad \text{if} \quad n = N$$

Now let us see what will happen for the average lot when we put the plan into action.

n	parts will go into the production line with no defectives.
$(N-n)Q$	parts will go straight into the production line with no testing, average quality p.
$(N-n)P$	parts will be rejected and screened. They then all go into the production line with no defectives.

a. Show that the total average cost per part will be

$$C = k_1[1/q + Q(k_2/k_1)(p'' - k_1/k_2)(1 - n/N)]$$

b. If $p < k_1/k_2$, then $p'' - k_1/k_2$ will be negative, and we shall achieve minimum average total cost by setting $n = 0$ (Case 1).

c. If $p > k_1/k_2$, and if we are successful in finding a plan that will render $p'' - k_1/k_2$ negative, then the average total cost will be less than the cost of 100 per cent inspection.

d. But if in spite of our best efforts, our plan leaves us with $p'' - k_1/k_2$ positive, then the total cost will be greater than it would have been with 100 per cent inspection of all incoming parts. This is the same bear trap that Exercise 5 taught us to avoid.

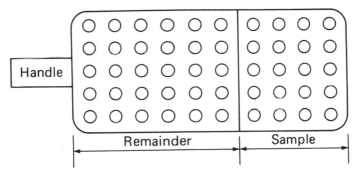

Fig. 56. A lot of 50 beads is drawn mechanically by a paddle with 50 holes in it from a large supply of red and white beads. We designate 20 beads as the sample, the remaining 30 as the remainder.

Appendix to Chapter 15
Empirical Demonstration of Zero Correlation between the Number of Defectives in the Sample and the Number of Defectives in the Remainder When the Process Is in the State of Statistical Control

The experiment with red and white beads described in Chapter 11 (p. 346) can easily be modified to demonstrate in a few minutes zero correlation between the number of defective items in samples from lots and the number of defective items in the remainders.

The mathematical proof is contained in Eq. 4 in Exercise 1 (p. 447). The same experiments demonstrate the existence of a slight correlation between samples and lots.

It is only necessary to divide into two parts the lot of 50 beads in the experiment, one part to be the sample, the other part the remainder (Fig. 56). At each lot, count and record the number of red beads in the sample and the number in the remainder; then restore to the supply the 50 beads in the lot. Stir the supply, and draw a new lot.

Some notation will be helpful. Lots of constant size N come in with defectives binomially distributed about the mean p. Draw without replacement from each lot a sample of constant size n. Count the defectives in each sample and in each remainder. Let s be the number of defectives in a sample, and r the number in the remainder (as above). Then s and r will be random variables, with the joint distribution shown in Eq. 4, p. 447. Let

$$\hat{p} = s/n, \text{ the proportion red in the sample}$$
$$\hat{p}' = r/(N-n), \text{ the proportion red in the re-}$$
$$\text{mainder}$$
$$E\hat{p} = p$$
$$\text{Var } \hat{p} = pq/n$$
$$E\hat{p}' = p$$
$$\text{Var } \hat{p}' = pq/(N-n)$$
$$\text{Cov } (\hat{p}, \hat{p}') = 0$$

Var $\hat{p}$ and Var $\hat{p}'$ decrease as N and n increase. Hence a large sample from a large lot provides information about the number of defectives in the population of remainders; hence also about defectives in lots.

Moreover, we may in an enumerative problem (wherein the aim is to learn from a sample characteristics of the lot) apply the theory of sampling for estimates of characteristics of the lot, and for the standard errors of these estimates.

We now take a look at some actual results with selected sizes of lot and sample. Figs. 57, 58, 59, and 60 show the proportion of red beads in binomial samples and remainders for selected values of N and n (kindly prepared by my friend Benjamin J. Tepping, on his computer). Sample and remainder are, in effect, both samples from the same lot. There are 100 samples in each plot. The plots clearly illustrate zero correlation between sample and remainder. Yet the larger the sample, the better the estimate of the proportion of red beads in samples and remainders. Thus, Fig. 60 for sample $n = 1000$ and remainder of size $N - n = 9000$ clearly indicates that a large sample provides a good estimate of

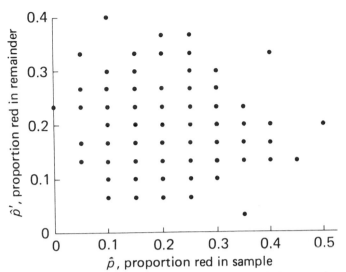

Fig. 57. $N = 50$, $n = 20$. Here the sample and the remainder are not far apart in size, being 20 and 30 respectively. The chart indicates no correlation between the proportion of red beads in the sample and the proportion of red beads in the remainder.

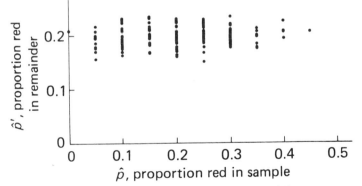

Fig. 58. $N = 600$, $n = 20$. Here the variation of the proportion red in the remainder is clearly much smaller than the variation in the sample. The reason is that the remainder is of size $N - n = 600 - 20 = 580$, many times the size of the sample. Here again, the correlation between the proportion of red beads in the sample and the proportion of red beads in the remainder appears to be zero.

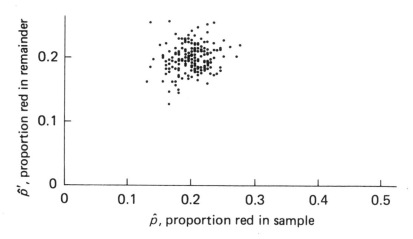

Fig. 59. $N = 600$, $n = 200$. Here we see what happens when we increase the size of the sample to 200 and decrease the remainder to 400. This chart, as before, illustrates zero correlation between the proportion of red beads in the sample and the proportion of red beads in the remainder.

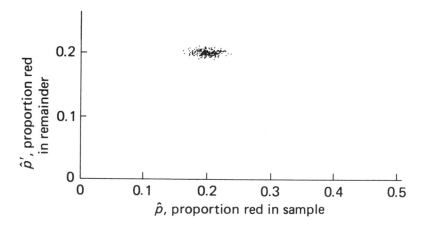

Fig. 60. $N = 10,000$, $n = 1000$. Again, no correlation.

the content both of the remainder and of the whole frame (sample plus remainder—in this case, bowl of red and white beads), even though sample and remainder be uncorrelated. A striking feature of statistical theory is that it enables us to calculate from a single sample, if it be large enough, the size of the football that emerges in Figs. 57–60 to contain (e.g.), on the average, 95 per cent of the points. The theory of sampling thus provides estimates of characteristics of the remainder and for the whole lot, and for standard errors of these estimates.[17]

Abbreviated List of References

George A. Barnard, "Sampling inspection and statistical decisions," *Journal of the Royal Statistical Society*, ser. B, vol. 16 (1954): 151–171. (Discussion of Mood's theorem.)

David Durand, *Stable Chaos*, General Learning Press, 1971. (See p. 234.)

A. Hald, "The compound hypergeometric distribution and a system of single sampling plans based on prior distributions and costs," *Technometrics* 2 (1960): 275–340. (Discussion of prior distributions.)

Statistical Theory of Sampling Inspection by Attributes, Academic Press, 1981.

H. C. Hamaker, "Economic principles in industrial planning problems: a general introduction," *Proceedings of the International Statistical Conference* (India, 1951) 33, pt. 5 (1951): 106–119.

"Some basic principles of sampling inspection by attributes," *Applied Statistics* (1958): 149–159. (Interesting discussion of various approaches.)

I. David Hill, "The economic incentive provided by sampling inspection," *Applied Statistics* 9 (1960): 69–81.

"Sampling inspection in defense specification DEF-131," *Journal of the Royal Statistical Society*, ser. A, vol. 125 (1962): 31–87.

Alexander M. Mood, "On the dependence of sampling inspection

---

17 I am indebted to my friend Dr. Morris H. Hansen for pointing out this feature of samples drawn from large lots for enumerative purposes. See W. Edwards Deming, "On probability as a basis for action," *American Statistician* 29, no. 4 (1975): 146–152.

plans upon population distributions," *Annals of Mathematical Statistics* 14 (1943): 415–425.

Joyce Orsini, "Simple rule to reduce cost of inspection and correction of product in state of chaos," Ph.D. dissertation, Graduate School of Business Administration, New York University, 1982.

J. Sittig, "The economic choice of sampling systems in acceptance sampling," *Proceedings of the International Statistical Conferences* (India, 1951), vol. 33, pt. 5 (1951): 51–84.

P. Thyregod, "Toward an algorithm for the minimax regret single sampling strategy," Institute of Mathematical Statistics, University of Copenhagen, 1969.

B. L. van der Waerden, "Sampling inspection as a minimum loss problem," *Annals of Mathematical Statistics* 31 (1960): 369–384.

G. B. Wetherill, *Sampling Inspection and Quality Control*, Methuen, London, 1969. (Gives a concise, excellent summary.)

S. Zacks, *The Theory of Statistical Inference*, Wiley, 1971. (Discusses in sec. 6.7 minimax under partial information.)

16

Organization for Improvement of Quality and Productivity

Research in statistical theory and technique is necessarily mathematical, scholarly, and abstract in character, requiring some degree of leisure and detachment, and access to a good mathematical and statistical library. The importance of continuing such research is very great, although it is not always obvious to those whose interest is entirely in practical applications of already existing theory. Excepting in the presence of active research in a pure science, the applications of the science tend to drop into a deadly rut of unthinking routine, incapable of progress beyond a limited range predetermined by the accomplishments of pure science, and are in constant danger of falling into the hands of people who do not really understand the tools that they are working with and who are out of touch with those that do. . . . It is in fact rather absurd, though quite in line with the precedents of earlier centuries, that scientific men of the highest talents can live only by doing work that could be done by others of lesser special ability, while the real worth of their most important work receives no official recognition.—Harold Hotelling, Memorandum to the Government of India, 24 February 1940.

Aim of this chapter. The central problem in management, leadership, and production, as my friend Lloyd S. Nelson put it, and as we have remarked in earlier chapters, is failure to understand the nature and interpretation of variation.

Efforts and methods for improvement of quality and productivity are in most companies and in most government agencies fragmented, with no overall competent guidance, no integrated system for continual improvement. Everyone, regardless of his job, needs a chance to learn and develop. In a climate of fragmentation, people go off in different directions, unaware of what other people are doing. They have no chance to work to the best advantage of the company nor with themselves, and little chance to develop. This chapter provides guidance for organization to make optimum use of knowledge, and for continual development of people and processes.

Knowledge is a scarce national resource. Knowledge in any country is a national resource. Unlike rare metals, which can not be replaced, the supply of knowledge in any field can be increased by education. Education may be formal, as in school. It may be informal, by study at home or on the job. It may be supplemented and rounded out by work and review under a master. A company must, for its very existence, make use of the store of knowledge that exists within the company, and learn how to make use of help from the outside when it can be effective.

Why waste knowledge? Waste of materials, waste of human effort, and waste of machine-time have been deplored in earlier chapters. Waste of knowledge, in the sense of failure of a company to use knowledge that is there and available for development, is even more deplorable.

Suggested plan. A schematic diagram of organization for quality and productivity appears in Fig. 61. It is possible here only to sketch principles of organization for quality. No attempt is made here to fit it to any particular company or industry.

There will be a leader of statistical methodology, responsible to top management. He must be a man of unquestioned ability. He will assume leadership in statistical methodology throughout the company. He will have authority from top management to be a participant in any activity that in his judgment is worth his pursuit. He will be a regular participant in any major meeting of the

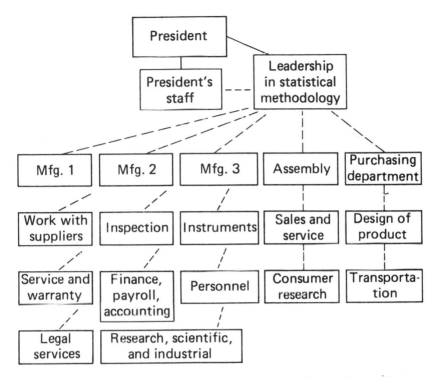

Fig. 61. Schematic plan for organization for quality and productivity. No attempt is made here to draw a diagram for any particular company. It applies to service and sales, as well as to manufacturing. This type of organization for quality and productivity originated with Dr. Morris H. Hansen in the Bureau of the Census, about 1940.

president and staff. He has the right and obligation to ask questions about any activity, and he is entitled to responsible answers. The choice of application for him to pursue must be left to his judgment, not to the judgment of others, though he will, of course, try to be helpful to anyone that asks for advice. The nonstatistician can not always recognize a statistical problem when he sees one.

What would be the minimum qualifications for this job? (1) equivalent of a master's degree in statistical theory; (2) experience in industry or in government; (3) authorship of published papers in theory and in practice of statistical methodology; (4) demonstrated ability to teach and to lead top management toward constant improvement of quality and productivity. He himself will constantly improve his education.

As stated on page 131, no one should be teaching statistical theory and application, especially to beginners, unless he possess knowledge of statistical theory through at least the master's level, supplemented by experience under a master. A hack of a statistician should be studying, not teaching.

Part of his job will be to work with universities in an attempt to help them to provide education in statistical theory and methods, and to provide examples of application.

Organization for statistical work in the Census was instituted in 1940 by Dr. Morris H. Hansen along the plan shown in Fig. 61. Preeminence for quality and productivity in the Census was recognized in census offices the world over by 1945. Incidentally, the Census is a service organization, and a governmental organization.

Where may you find the right man? The combination of knowledge and leadership is exceedingly rare, and will require patience and earnest prayer to find. Enquiry of competent consultants may bring forth candidates. You may have to interview many applicants to find the right one.

An incumbent as head of statistical methodology will command a high salary. The problem will be to find someone competent, not what his pay will be.

A man competent to hold the position as leader of statistical methodology should enquire diligently into the aims and constancy of purpose of the company. Are they serious about quality?

Mere hiring of a statistician is not conformance to the recommendations of this chapter. The incumbent must possess other qualifications, severe and essential, as noted above.

On the line. Every appalling example in this book turned up because I was there, on the line, on the job, trying to be helpful by looking for sources of improvement and wrong practices. If I had waited for them to come for help, I'd still be waiting. It is obviously essential to have on the line, where the action is, as depicted in Fig. 61, people with knowledge of statistical theory, to find sources of improvement, and wrong practices that other people can not see.

What would be the qualifications of these people? Preferably, the same as for the leader, but in practice something less.

It may be necessary, because of a shortage of statistical people, but subject to decision of the statistical leader, to place two or more activities under one statistician.

For men on the line, to work with the various divisions, examine your own resources. One may find right within the company people with master's degrees in statistical theory or mathematics or probability that are eager to advance their education and experience under competent leadership, and who enjoy teaching. Some people will be qualified by self-study.

It is clear that no plan will work—not even the one proposed here—without competence and confidence in the statistical leadership, and without people in the divisions that have a burning desire to improve their work.

The statistician on the line must be acceptable to the chief of the line, but the effectiveness of his work will be judged by the leader of statistical methodology. Under this plan, a man can not be promoted for justifying bad statistical practice proposed by the division. The leader of statistical methodology is on hand to assist the statistician in a division and the head of the division, concerning any problem that comes up, or on any difference of opinion. He operates by pedagogy and guidance.

It is true that the statistician in a division is responsible to two people—to the head of the division for day-by-day output of procedures and analysis, and to the statistical leader for his statistical work and continuing education. The plan nevertheless gives no problems.

The advantages of the plan recommended here can not be questioned. It works. Any other plan that I have seen has failed to serve the best interests of the company, and has brought disappointment.

Examples of other dotted-line relationships. In fact, a parallel dotted-line relationship exists in practically every corporation.[1] A vice-president and chief financial officer (VP/CFO), reporting to the president or the chief executive officer, is responsible for the financial condition of the corporation. At each manufacturing facility there is a local comptroller who is responsible for the financial condition (budget, operating expenses) related to that specific location. He reports jointly to the VP/CFO and to the manager of the facility. For example, the budgets are established by the plant, and the degree to which they are met is reported by the plant manager to the local comptroller. But because of the complex nature of the accounting procedures and taxes, the financial direction of the plant is provided by the VP/CFO. The technical aspects of the position are guided by the VP/CFO, and the administrative responsibilities are directed by the management of the facility. No one questions the value or necessity of this organization, and no problem arises from the fact that the local comptroller of the plant reports to two men. Other examples of positions requiring dual reporting structures are engineering, research and development, environmental, medical, legal, and safety officers.

1 I thank Dr. Harold S. Haller for contribution of this paragraph.

Achievements at the Bureau of the Census. Papers and books that came out of the U.S. Census have led the whole world of social and demographic studies into better methods of sampling, reduction of nonsampling errors, and better survey design, as well as the conduct of complete censuses, all with continual improvement in quality of data and with continual reduction in cost.

To appreciate the method of the Census, one needs only the reminder that the results of the *Current Population Survey*, which includes the *Monthly Report on the Labor Force*, are widely accepted and used. This is a miniature monthly census of about 55,000 households, carried out by the Bureau of the Census using the most advanced statistical procedures. The Census also carries out, monthly, quarterly, or annually, many other miniature censuses—for example, studies on health and use of medical facilities by people, housing, vacancies, housing starts, retail sales, manufacturing.

Additional remarks on educational needs of industry. Industry in America (as Shewhart said[2]) needs thousands of statistically minded engineers, chemists, physicists, doctors of medicine, purchasing agents, managers. Fortunately, anyone in these fields can learn to use in many problems simple but powerful methods of statistics, and can understand the statistical principles behind them, without becoming a statistician. Guidance from a theoretical statistician is necessary, however. Without such guidance, wrong and costly practices take root, and some problems of production and distribution may be overlooked entirely.

There is a parallel between statisticians and statistical work on the one hand, and medicine and public health on the other. Millions of people have learned useful rules and practices of public

2 Walter A. Shewhart, *Statistical Method from the Viewpoint of Quality Control* (Graduate School, Department of Agriculture, Washington, 1939; Dover, 1986), Ch. 7.

health, and understand the basic principles of infection, diet, and exercise. Thousands of people have learned how to render first aid without being doctors of medicine. Thousands of people carry out medical and psychological tests, and give inoculations, under the direction of doctors of medicine and psychologists. We all live better and longer because of the contributions that these people make.

Almost every large company already has on the payroll people here and there that are studying statistics at a nearby university and whose talents are not being used. I have found such people with master's degrees, wondering if they will ever have a chance to use their knowledge. Companies take inventory of physical property, but they fail in taking inventory of knowledge. Anyone who is getting a statistical education should have a chance to work under a statistician of competence, and to continue his education in statistics.

It is good advice to anyone that is interested in improving his ability to find problems and to help in their solution to take any course that he can get into in theoretical or applied statistics (including, of course, decision theory and theory of failure), provided the teacher is competent in theory. The mature student will recognize and improve inappropriate applications in the classroom and in the text.

Advice to consultants and to companies. The following rules have been helpful in the guidance of my own practice.

1. The invitation to work with a company must come from top management.

2. The management (all management, president, head of divisions, engineers, personnel, purchasing, marketing, service, sales, legal department, all people in staff positions, including people designated to work on quality, strategic planning, research, reliability, costs of warranty, public relations, etc.) will spend time with me, to study the responsibilities of management. They will put forth effort to create a critical mass of people to

study and act on the 14 points and on diseases and obstacles of management.

3. A necessary condition for my participation is that the company will build with prudent speed an organization consistent with Fig. 61. One of my chief responsibilities will be to help the company to build this organization. The aim of this organization is to make the best use of all knowledge and skill in the company to improve its quality, productivity, and competitive position. Without proper organization and without competent incumbents, my participation would have little chance to accomplish these aims.

4. Top management will understand that my work is companywide. It will be my responsibility to work with any activity in the company where in my judgment participation might be effective. I will visit plants, divisions, departments, on request, or at my discretion, with the aim to try to help on improvement of performance.

5. The arrangement will be long-term, though the company or I may break it off at any time. My annual fee will be stated at the outset.

6. I will put in enough time to satisfy myself.

7. I will continue beyond three years if in my judgment further participation would accelerate further advancement.

8. I may suggest to the company engagement of a specialist on a temporary basis for a specific problem, as for education in techniques, or for simple expansion of my efforts. The company will engage anyone for such purposes only on my recommendation, and I will be responsible for the joint effort and for continuation thereof.

9. I may accept engagements from competitive firms. My aim is not to concentrate on the welfare of any particular client, but to raise the level of service of my profession (see paragraphs 1 and 2).

Further obligations of statistician and client are set forth in my "Code of professional conduct," *Inter-*

national Statistical Review 40, no. 2 (1972): 215–219. See also a paper by the author, "Principles of professional statistical practice," *Annals of Mathematical Statistics* 36 (1965): 1883–1900.

17

Some Illustrations for Improvement of Living

I speak no more than everyone doth know.—Gardener, in Shakespeare's *Richard II*, III. iv.

Aim of this chapter. The aim here is to show how some simple applications of principles learned in this book could contribute to better living in America. Dependable performance of service would simplify life and would reduce the cost of living. But quality of performance and dependable performance must be defined, a task for the future.

The reader must have observed on page after page my plea for clarity in specifications and in instructions for jobs. The purpose of a sign along the road, for example, should be to help the stranger to find his way. Too often, however, signs are confusing. There is unfortunately not enough time for the driver to ponder over the various possible meanings that a sign might lead to. Statistics on accidents merely show figures, not root causes.

Principle 1. On-time performance of delivery or product exhibits early delivery some days and later delivery some days. There is no such thing as arrival exactly on time. In fact, exactly on time can not be defined.

This principle came to my mind one day in Japan as I stepped on to the railway platform and observed the time to be six seconds before the scheduled time of arrival. "Of course," I observed, "it has to be ahead

half the time, and behind half the time, if its performance is on time."

Principle 2. It is easy to observe and record whether a train will
come in late or will depart late on any one day. One need only
own or borrow a watch and set it carefully to the time signal. A
train due to arrive today at three o'clock may then be observed
to be early or late by so many seconds or minutes.

However, it is not so simple to describe the performance of
this train over a period of time. Performance can be judged only
by statistical study of historical record of arrivals. A run chart of
arrivals, day after day, would be simple and powerful in meaning.

A distribution of times of arrival or of delivery conveys information about the performance of a train. Fig. 62 shows a
number of possible distributions. Chart A shows on-time performance but with a spread that indicates uneconomical operation,
and uneconomical use of the time of patrons. This train is on
time, on the average, many minutes early some days, many
minutes late other days, sometimes very nearly on time. Chart B
shows on-time performance with better performance—that is,
less waste of the railway's resources. Patrons can depend on arrival within a few minutes or possibly within a few seconds, as in
Japan. The legend for Chart C is self-explanatory. The system is
working well, but the timetable needs to be rewritten. The train
simply can not make the trip in the time shown. This resembles
the circumstance where a production process is in control and is
economical, but can not meet the specifications. Chart D depicts
a state of chaos.

Principle 3. Tests of components in stages of development can
not provide (a) assurance that they will work together satisfactorily as a system in service; nor (b) the average run between
failures of the system; nor (c) the type and cost of maintenance
that will be required in service.

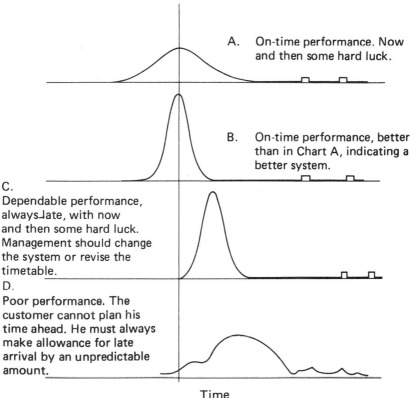

A.   On-time performance. Now and then some hard luck.

B.   On-time performance, better than in Chart A, indicating a better system.

C. Dependable performance, always late, with now and then some hard luck. Management should change the system or revise the timetable.

D. Poor performance. The customer cannot plan his time ahead. He must always make allowance for late arrival by an unpredictable amount.

Time

Fig. 62. Some possible distributions of time of arrival.

Tests in early stages can of course provide negative results— prediction that the system will be unsatisfactory.

Principle 4. Due care in manufacture can not be defined operationally, hence any requirement of due care in manufacture can have no legal force. Care in manufacture, however, can be defined and measured. Evidence of care in manufacture and test is provided by records, in the form of meaningful data (which might take the form of charts and statistical calculations), supplemented by records of corrective action on the process, or action on a particular machine once designated as a special cause of variation, and the result of this action. Instructions for use of the product, and warnings on misuse, are part of the record that measures the care taken on the part of the manufacturer.

Principle 5. No system, whatever be the effort put into it, be it manufacturing, maintenance, operation, or service, will be free of accidents.

Accidents are all around us, like bacteria. Most bacteria are harmless, some cause a lot of suffering. Most accidents are of little consequence. An assistant in a retail store that sells men's clothes put a suit on the rack only to observe that it had no buttons. This suit had slipped through two 100 per cent inspections. It was an accident, to come through without buttons, but it was a harmless accident. No one was hurt. In fact, some of us had a good laugh.

I received from the printer 500 copies of an article that I had published, only to discover, after I had distributed a few score of them, that pages 6 and 7 were blank in some of the copies. This was an accident: no harm done. In fact, some readers may have been grateful for the blanks. The supervisor at the printing company nevertheless, when I told him about it, went into a rage about his careless employees. Was it his fault, or theirs?

Figures on accidents do nothing to reduce the frequency of accidents. The first step in reduction of the frequency of accidents is to determine whether the cause of an accident belongs to the system or to some specific person or set of conditions. Statistical methods provide the only method of analysis to serve as a guide to the understanding of accidents and to their reduction.

People naturally suppose that if something happened here and now, there must be something special at the spot where it happened. The usual reaction of almost everyone, when an accident occurs, is to attribute it to somebody's carelessness or to something unusual about the equipment used. It is wise not to jump to this conclusion: it may lead to the wrong answer, wrong solution, continued trouble, more accidents. The system guarantees an average frequency of accidents to occur at unpredictable places and times. (See p. 323 in Ch. 11.)

Engineers often predict accidents. Their predictions are uncanny for correctness in detail. They fail in only one way—they can not predict exactly when the accident will happen. The well-publicized trouble at Three Mile Island provides a documented example.[1]

Accidents that arise from common causes will continue to happen with their expected frequency and variations until the system is corrected. The split is possibly 99 per cent from the system, 1 per cent from carelessness. I have no figures on the split, and there will not be any figures till people understand accidents with the aid of statistical thinking.

Unfortunately—incredible without statistical thinking—the proportion of failures of manufactured apparatus will not decrease as the precision of manufacture improves, nor will the number of medical disappointments decrease as medical practice improves. The reason is that as the requirements that define good quality and good results continually become more severe as precision and performance improve, the proportion of outliers, by any criterion, remains constant.

Accidents on the highway: faults of road signs in the United States. A high proportion of accidents on the highways in America may well come from signs that are confusing to drivers. If such a possibility exists, then it is imperative that there be instituted at once a massive, well-planned program of revision. What could be more important for the welfare of the American people?

What proportion of accidents on the highways is caused by failure of the driver (human error, a special cause), or by failure of equipment (another, possibly a special cause, possibly not),

---

1 "Three Mile Island," *The New Yorker*, 6 and 13 April 1981.

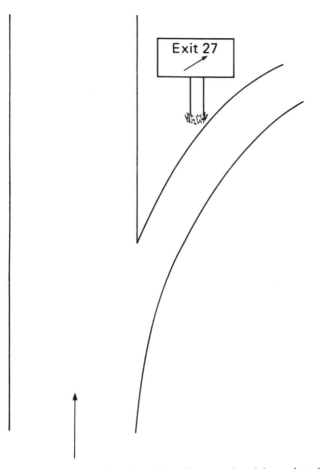

Fig. 63. This road sign is misleading to the driver that is looking for Exit 27. The first impulse that this sign conveys to the driver is that Exit 27 lies some distance ahead, and will lead off to the right. The fact is that the driver has already arrived at Exit 27. Second thoughts, a tenth of a second later, may be too late; he is on his way straight ahead, and must find a way out.

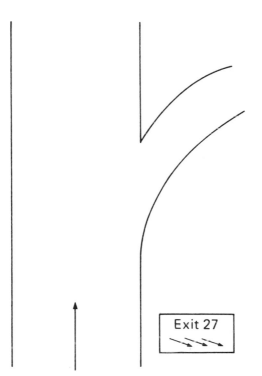

Fig. 64. Good. This sign conveys instantly to the driver the message that to take Exit 27 he must move into the right lane and exit.

and what proportion is built into and guaranteed by the system, for example, by road signs whose meaning is misleading or debatable? The answer may never be forthcoming because a controlled experiment can not be carried out. Moreover, it would be hard to find two systems of road signs that are sufficiently different, all else being equal, to provide numerical data for comparison.

The purpose of a road sign is to teach, to tell a driver what to do, and its message must do so in a flash. At 60 mph, a vehicle moves 88 feet in one second, 8.8 feet in a tenth of a second. An interval of indecision that extends over a tenth of a second may

Fig. 65. Overhead sign, very clear. It conveys instantly its message. It tells the driver to take the left fork to Louisville, or the right fork to Chattanooga.

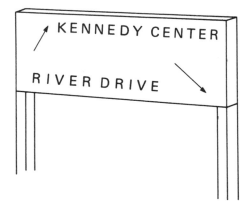

Fig. 66. Which way to Kennedy Center? Tossing a coin would be as helpful as this sign.

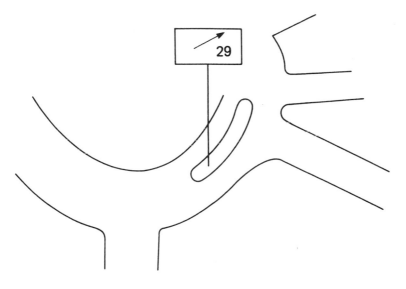

Fig. 67. Which way to Route 29? Taken from Washington Circle in the City of Washington.

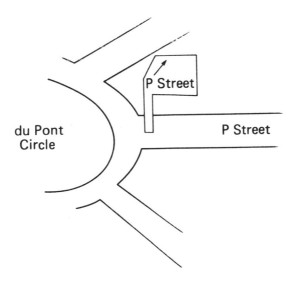

Fig. 68. Which way to P Street?

land a vehicle against a concrete abutment, or against a tree, or it may cause a collision from the rear. It is thus of utmost importance that a road sign convey instantly its message.

Road sign is in German *Wegweiser*, information or enlightenment concerning the way. In the United States, do road signs trigger confusion or enlightenment in the mind of the driver?

Fig. 63 shows a sign all too common in the United States for an exit. Its message is exactly opposite to the action needed to go out on Exit 27. It tells the driver that Exit 27 lies ahead, when actually, he is already at it, and may not have time to adjust himself to the fact. In contrast, the sign in Fig. 64 conveys instantly its message to the driver—namely, move into the right lane and go out on Exit 27. The sign in Fig. 65 is clear.

Most drivers require no direction, as they are merely moving toward home or toward work, and need no help. Unfortunately, however, 1 driver in perhaps 100 is new to the route, and requires help. No one will ever know the number of injuries to man and vehicle caused by signs that do not instantly convey their message, or which, unfortunately, convey instantly the wrong message to drivers that need guidance. No one will ever know the proportion of drivers that fail to make the exit, and the resulting inconvenience and loss of time as they find their way back to the route intended.

Figs. 66, 67, and 68 provide further illustrations of confusion.

Malpractice in medicine. This can only be understood with the help of statistical theory. The result of a medical intervention is interaction between physician, treatment, and patient. Two thousand million (2×10^9) medical interventions take place every year in the United States. A hundred thousand cases of unfavorable results seem like a large number, yet this number represents reliability of 1 part in 20,000. It would be difficult to find a mechanical or electrical system with greater reliability. Most of the 100,000 unfavorable results (if that be the number) belong to the system. Some small fraction of the 100,000 unfavorable results could possibly be caused by carelessness, including incompetence. One per cent of 100,000 is 1000, still a large number. Any number is too big. The problem is to discover whether the cause of an unfavorable outcome (a) lies in the system of medical care, including the patient; or (b) may be ascribed to some special cause such as carelessness on the part of the physician, or carelessness on the part of the patient, who may fail to follow instructions or to get in touch with his physician as directed. An important step would be for medical people to construct operational definitions of special causes of unfortunate results from medical interventions of various kinds. This is a huge task, and a never-ending one, but until it is brought to a usable stage, physicians in the United States, and their insurance companies, will continue to fight off unjustified accusations of carelessness and will live a life liable to legal tangles.

Appendix
Transformation in Japan

Do not confuse your wits with wisdom.—Tiresius to
Dionysus, in Euripedes' *The Bacchae*.

Wisdom sounds foolish to fools.—Dionysus to Cadmus,
in Euripedes' *The Bacchae*.

Motive for this appendix. The whole world is familiar with the
miracle of Japan, and knows that the miracle started off with a
concussion in 1950. Before that time, the quality of Japanese
consumer goods had earned around the world a reputation for
being shoddy and cheap. Yet anyone in our Navy will testify that
the Japanese knew what quality is. They simply had not yet bent
their efforts toward quality in international trade.

Suddenly, Japanese quality and dependability turned upward
in 1950 and by 1954 had captured markets the world over. The
new economic age had begun. What happened?

The answer is that top management became convinced that
quality was vital for export, and that they could accomplish the
switch. They learned, in conference after conference, something
about their responsibilities for the achievement of this aim, and
that they must take the lead in this aim. Management and factory workers put their forces together for quality and jobs.

JUSE. As I understand it, Japanese military authorities
formed for the War effort several groups of scientists. One group
was under the leadership of Kenichi Koyanagi. He held his

486

group together after the War with a new aim, the reconstruction of Japan. The name of the group became the Union of Japanese Science and Engineering, abbreviated JUSE. As recounted on p. 2ff. a number of Japanese engineers had acquired appreciation for the contribution to quality and productivity that the Shewhart methods might make to Japanese industry. The time was 1948 and 1949.

> Men from the Bell Laboratories explained to members of JUSE that statistical methods had improved accuracy of American weapons. My friend Dr. E. E. Nishibori, listening to them, came forth with the remark: "Yes, I know something about that. Six fire bombs fell on my house during the war, and they were all duds."

JUSE thereupon took up seriously education in methods for improvement of quality. The Japan Management Association did likewise. The men of JUSE decided that the next step was to bring in a foreign expert. The invitation came in 1949, and I was able to accept it in June 1950. (The purpose of two previous trips to Japan was to assist Japanese statisticians in studies of housing and nutrition, and for preparation of the census of 1951.)

Conferences with top management. Statistical methods had taken fire in America around 1942, following a series of 10-day intensive courses for engineers initiated by Stanford University on a suggestion from this author.[1] The War Department also gave courses at factories of suppliers. Brilliant applications attracted much attention, but the flare of statistical methods by themselves, in an atmosphere in which management did not know their responsibilities, burned, sputtered, fizzled, and died out. What the men did was to solve individual problems. Control

1 W. Allen Wallis, "The statistical research group," *Journal of the American Statistical Association* 75 (1980): 320–335, p. 321 in particular.

charts proliferated, the more the better. Quality control departments sprouted. They plotted charts, looked at them, and filed them. They took quality control away from everybody else, which was of course entirely wrong, as quality control is everybody's job. They put out fires, not perceiving the necessity to improve processes (Point 5, p. 49). There was no structure to teach management their responsibilities. Attempts by Dr. Holbrook Working, one of the instructors in the 10-day courses given in 1942–45, to reach management by inviting them to come to the course for half a day, were noble but ineffective.

Japan, 1950. It was vital not to repeat in Japan in 1950 the mistakes made in America. Management must understand their responsibilities. The problem was how to reach top management in Japan. This hurdle was accomplished through the offices of Mr. Ichiro Ishikawa, president of the great Kei-dan-ren (Federated Economic Societies) and president of JUSE, who in July 1950 brought together the 21 men in top management. Further conferences with top management were held that summer of 1950, and still more on two trips to Japan in 1951, again in 1952, more in subsequent years. The simplified flow diagram in Fig. 1 (p. 4) was helpful in the conferences with top management.

The consumer is the most important part of the production line—a new principle for Japanese management. It would be necessary for Japanese management to stand behind the performance of product. They must look ahead and design new products and services. They must work with the chosen vendor for any one item on a long-term relationship of trust and loyalty to improve the uniformity and dependability of incoming materials. Management must give rigid attention to maintenance of equipment and to instructions and gauges (Chs. 9 and 16).

It will not suffice to achieve brilliant successes here and there. Disjointed efforts will have no national impact. Quality in terms of present and future needs of the consumer became at once companywide and nationwide in every activity. Improvement of quality became in 1950, in Japan, total.

Expansion of education to management, engineers, foremen. JUSE, with confident support of Japanese industry, expanded on a vast scale education of management, engineers, and foremen in rudiments of statistical methods for improvement of quality, and advanced statistical theory to statisticians and engineers. The plague of barriers that rob the hourly worker of his pride of workmanship in American companies today was zero or at a low level in Japan. Hourly workers could thus learn to make, understand, and use control charts.

Over 400 engineers studied in eight-day courses in the summer of 1950 in Tokyo, Osaka, Nagoya, Hakata, given by this author, on the methods and philosophy of Shewhart.

Sessions with top management and the teaching of engineers continued in January 1951 and in subsequent visits.

The teaching of consumer research, with an introduction to modern methods of sampling, began in January 1951. The students divided themselves into teams for door-to-door enquiries into the needs of households for sewing machines, bicycles, and pharmaceuticals.

Dr. Joseph M. Juran made his first visit to Japan in 1954, at the request of JUSE. His masterful teaching gave to Japanese management new insight into management's responsibility for improvement of quality and productivity.

Between 1950 and 1970 JUSE taught statistical methods to 14,700 engineers and thousands of foremen. Courses for management are at this writing booked to capacity, in fact, with a waiting period of seven months. Courses in consumer research, taught by Japan's foremost statisticians, are in equal demand.

Further notes in respect to top management in Japan. The first hurdle to overcome with top management in Japan in 1950 was the general supposition that it would be impossible for them to compete with industry of America and Europe in view of the reputation for shoddy quality of consumer goods that Japan had earned. The year 1950 was the beginning of a new Japan in quality. I predicted in 1950 that Japanese products would within five years invade the markets of the world, and that the standard of living in Japan would in time rise to equality with the world's most prosperous countries.

The basis for my confidence in this prediction was (1) observations on the Japanese work force; (2) knowledge and devotion to their jobs of Japanese management, and their eagerness to learn; (3) faith that Japanese management would accept and carry out their responsibilities; (4) expansion of education by JUSE.

Encouragement from further results. Mr. Keizo Nishimura of the Furukawa Electric Company, working with the help of Dr. Nishibori, reported in January 1951 reduction to 10 per cent of its former level the amount of rework in insulated wire in Furakawa's cable plant at Nikko, and equal success in the manufacture of cable; also reduction in the frequency of accidents. Productivity soared; profits likewise.

Mr. Kenichi Koyanagi (deceased 1965), cofounder and managing director of JUSE, reported at the meeting of the American Society for Quality Control in Syracuse in 1952 great strides in quality and output that had been made by 13 Japanese companies. Every one of these 13 reports was written by top management.[2] These men were out in the plants at work.

Mr. Gohei Tanabe, president of Tanabe Pharmaceutical Company, reported that, through improvement of processes, his company was producing three times as much PAS (para-

---

2 Kenichi Koyanagi, "Statistical quality control in Japanese industry," report to the Congress of the American Society for Quality Control held in Syracuse, 1952.

aminosalicylic acid) as they had been getting earlier with the same people, same machines, same plant, same materials.

Fuji Steel Company reported reduction of 29 per cent in the fuel required to produce a ton of steel.

Examples like these spread the word throughout Japan that improvement of quality means improvement of the process, which in turn improves the product and productivity.

It has been said that all Japanese industry has achieved the best practice for quality. This is not so. Five of the horrible examples recorded in this book, of what not to do, came from Japan.

QC-Circles. The formalization of QC-Circles was accomplished by Dr. K. Ishikawa by 1960. A QC-Circle is the natural Japanese way of working together. Dr. Ishikawa brought to the attention of management the importance of making full use of the successes of small groups of workers in the elimination of special causes of variability of product, and in improvement of the system, through changes in tools, changes in design, and in scheduling and even in alterations of the production process. Accomplishments of a QC-Circle in one spot may well have wide application throughout the company and in other companies. It is the responsibility of management to carry the fire from one success to another.

The journal *Quality Control for the Foreman*, established in 1960 by JUSE and edited by Dr. K. Ishikawa, enables QC-Circles all over Japan to learn from each other. Exchange visits to other companies, and regional conventions of QC-Circles, stimulate interest of members. The national convention in Tokyo brings 1800 members together from all over Japan, from the total spectrum of products and services. Leaders of QC-Circles that have achieved extraordinary results are selected by their companies for group tours, arranged by JUSE, to plants in America and in Europe.

One of the hundred reports given at the national convention of the QC-Circles held in Tokyo in November 1980 was an explanation of how with rearrangement of work, five people now do the same work that previously required seven. Translated, 100 people can now do the work of 140. Forty people did not lose their jobs: they merely transferred to other work.

Contributions like this help to put the company in better competitive position, with the ultimate result that the company will need more employees, not fewer.

Index